REINFORCING RULE OF
IN THE EUROPEA

C000186586

This book provides the definitive reference point on all the issues pertaining to dealing with the 'crisis of the Rule of Law' in the European Union. Both Member State and EU levels are considered. Particular attention is paid to the analysis of the concrete legal bases and instruments that the EU may avail of enforcing Rule of Law, and the volume clearly demonstrates that a number of legally sound ways of Rule of Law oversight are available. Contributors are leading scholars who assess the potential role to be played by the various bodies in the context of dealing with the EU's Rule of Law imperfections.

CARLOS CLOSA is Professor of Political Science at Institute for Public Goods and Policies (IPP) at the Consejo Superior de Investigaciones Cientificas (CSIC), Madrid. He has been member of the Venice Commission for democracy through law and consultant for the Council of Europe, the European Commission and the European Parliament. He has researched and published widely, focusing on the areas of EU citizenship, the EU's constitutional structure, and relations between the EU and its member states.

DIMITRY KOCHENOV is Martin and Kathleen Crane Fellow in Law and Public Affairs at the Woodrow Wilson School, Princeton University (2015–2016); Professor of EU Constitutional Law in Groningen and Visiting Professor at the College of Europe, Natolin. He has advised international institutions and governments, including Dutch and Maltese. He has researched and published widely, focusing on EU constitutional law, EU citizenship, and EU overseas territories law.

REINFORCING RULE OF LAW OVERSIGHT IN THE EUROPEAN UNION

Edited by

CARLOS CLOSA

DIMITRY KOCHENOV

CAMBRIDGE
UNIVERSITY PRESS

CAMBRIDGE
UNIVERSITY PRESS

University Printing House, Cambridge CB2 8BS, United Kingdom

One Liberty Plaza, 20th Floor, New York, NY 10006, USA

477 Williamstown Road, Port Melbourne, VIC 3207, Australia

314-321, 3rd Floor, Plot 3, Splendor Forum, Jasola District Centre, New Delhi - 110025, India

79 Anson Road, #06-04/06, Singapore 079906

Cambridge University Press is part of the University of Cambridge.

It furthers the University's mission by disseminating knowledge in the pursuit of education, learning and research at the highest international levels of excellence.

www.cambridge.org
Information on this title: www.cambridge.org/9781107519800

© Carlos Closa and Dimitry Kochenov 2016

This publication is in copyright. Subject to statutory exception and to the provisions of relevant collective licensing agreements, no reproduction of any part may take place without the written permission of Cambridge University Press.

First published 2016
First paperback edition 2018

A catalogue record for this publication is available from the British Library

ISBN 978-1-107-10888-2 Hardback
ISBN 978-1-107-51980-0 Paperback

Cambridge University Press has no responsibility for the persistence or accuracy of URLs for external or third-party internet websites referred to in this publication, and does not guarantee that any content on such websites is, or will remain, accurate or appropriate.

CONTENTS

FIGURES

CONTRIBUTORS

Paul Blokker
Charles University, Prague; University of Trento, Department of Sociology

Bojan Bugarič
Center for European Studies, Harvard University; University of Ljubljana, Faculty of Law

Carlos Closa
Instituto de Políticas y Bienes Públicos (IPP); Consejo Superior de Investigaciones Científicas, CSIC

Jonas Grimheden
EU Fundamental Rights Agency, Vienna; Faculty of Law, Lund University

Christophe Hillion
Leiden University, Faculty of Law; University of Gothenburg, Department of Law; Swedish Institute for European Policy Studies, Stockholm; University of Oslo, Centre for European Law and Norwegian Institute of International Relations.

Ernst Hirsch Ballin
Amsterdam University, Faculty of Law; Tilburg University, Faculty of Law; Member of the Netherlands Advisory Council for International Affairs; Former Minister of Justice of the Netherlands

András Jakab
Hungarian Academy of Sciences, Budapest; Max Planck Institute for Comparative Public Law and International Law, Heidelberg

Dimitry Kochenov
LAPA Fellow, Woodrow Wilson School, Princeton University (2015–2016); University of Groningen, Faculty of Law; College of Europe, Natolin

Jan-Werner Müller
Princeton University, Department of Politics

Gianluigi Palombella
Scuola Superiore Sant'Anna, Pisa; Università di Parma

Martin Scheinin
European University Institute, Florence, Law Department

Kim Lane Scheppele
Princeton University, Department of Sociology and Woodrow Wilson School

Gabriel N. Toggenburg
EU Fundamental Rights Agency, Vienna;University of Graz, Faculty of Law

Kaarlo Tuori
University of Helsinki, Faculty of Law; Member of the Venice Commission for Democracy through Law of the Council of Europe

Milada Anna Vachudova
University of North Carolina at Chapel Hill, Department of Political Science

J. H. H. Weiler
President, European University Institute, Florence

PREFACE

What to do when the Rule of Law in the Union is apparently crumbling under pressure from Member States deviating from the foundational values on which the whole edifice of European integration rests? What kind of tools do we have at our disposal, able to go beyond the established Treaty mechanisms, which have seemingly been proved ineffective by the recent developments and ongoing persistence of fundamental deviations from EU norms? Should the EU be more proactive and why?

This book aims to discuss the normative issues related to the role of the EU in the Rule of Law enforcement field and to list and scrutinise innovative tools of potential use for the Union in asserting its own values. The key scholars behind virtually all the most important proposals have participated in this volume to outline their position firsthand. In addition, the book also considers and discusses the complexity of the broader landscape of European constitutionalism to warn against any course of action which would not be extremely carefully thought over, considering the key strengths and, crucially, also notable weaknesses of the EU's legal–political edifice.

This collection of essays aims at a broad, positive outline: *there are tools to solve the outstanding problems*, all the words of caution notwithstanding. The detailed presentation of these tools is the core mission of this book and its key added value as we designed it. Where there are many proposals, there are bound to be many disagreements – such is life. The editors fully realise this, and one of the key strengths of the book was allowing the participating scholars to engage with each other's methods for overcoming the common problem, the assumption being that such a dialogue, at times very polemical, will result in a more comprehensive description of the key avenues for *Reinforcing Rule of Law Oversight in the European Union.*

The project thus started with a vivid meeting of the majority of the contributing scholars at the European University Institute in Florence at a one-day seminar co-sponsored by the EUI and University of Groningen, which occurred in January 2014 and was opened by the EUI President, Professor J. H. H. Weiler. All the chapters have been profoundly updated and reworked since then, so this book should not be regarded in any sense as a set of conference proceedings.[1] We are overwhelmingly grateful to the Global Governance Program at the Robert Schuman Centre for Advanced Studies of the Institute as well as to the Groningen Centre for Law and Governance for co-sponsoring the event, and to all those colleagues who participated in the seminar without contributing a chapter, including but not limited to: Laszlo Bruszt, Clare Kirkpatrick, Brigid Laffan, and Bruno de Witte, as well as our assistants who worked with us on this project at different stages, in particular Elena Basheska, Martijn van den Brink, Ryan Chavez, Justin Lindeboom, Harry Panagopoulos, and Suryapratim Roy. Grisha Kochenov painted the blue-wheeled whale of the EU for the cover.

The book does not aim to be merely a piece of academic scholarship detached from the perils and problems of the 'real' world. Rather, concerns with events in some European states have prompted reflections on possible action with a clear guideline: the Rule of Law, democracy and human rights should not be taken as a foregone conclusion within the EU. A time during which thousands of people are fleeing conflict and die trying to reach European shores while some European states are busy dismantling their democracy and Rule of Law guarantees reminds us that engagement with values should not be a mere and empty exercise of academic rhetoric and eloquence but should be meaningful to the lives of the persons whose welfare depends precisely on the stringent enforcement of these values. We therefore make a case for Union action, list its tools, but voice a note of caution against overestimating the Union's abilities. As you will notice, it is up to the reader to choose the most convincing tool for herself: this collection is a cookbook without a suggested menu, which is, we believe, also one of its strengths.

C.C., D.K.
Florence and Princeton

---

[1] The main outcome of the seminar was an EUI working paper, which is a natural accompanying text to this volume: C. Closa, D. Kochenov and J. H. H. Weiler, 'Reinforcing Rule of Law Oversight in the European Union', EUI Working Paper No. 2014/25, RSCAS.

ABBREVIATIONS

CFR	Charter of Fundamental Rights of the EU
CJEL	*Columbia Journal of European Law*
CMLRev	*Common Market Law Review*
CRPD	UN Convention on the Rights of Persons with Disabilities
ECHR	European Convention on Human Rights
ECJ	Court of Justice of the European Union
EJIL	*European Journal of International Law*
ELJ	*European Law Journal*
ELRev	*European Law Review*
EUConst	*European Constitutional Law Review*
FRA	Fundamental Rights Agency of the European Union
HRQ	*Human Rights Quarterly*
I-CON	*International Journal of Constitutional Law*
ICLQ	*International and Comparative Law Quarterly*
JCMS	*Journal of Common Market Studies*
JEPP	*Journal of European Public Policy*
ODIHR	OSCE Office for Democratic Institutions and Human Rights
OJLS	*Oxford Journal of Legal Studies*
OSCE	Organisation for Security and Cooperation in Europe
TEU	Treaty of European Union
TFEU	Treaty on the Functioning of the European Union

TABLE OF CASES

European Union (Supranational Courts)

European Court and Commission of Human Rights

Other Courts and Tribunals

~

Introduction

How to Save the EU's Rule of Law and Should One Bother?

CARLOS CLOSA AND DIMITRY KOCHENOV

I Point of Agreement: There Is a Problem and Something Needs to be Done

This book is rooted in the shared sense of urgency among the editors and the contributors alike that the very core of the constitutional system of the European Union is being put to the test through some of the Member States' non-compliance with the basic principles and values of the Union.[1] The Union is learning the hard way that it is not at all as powerful and well equipped as one would like to deal with the most fundamental constitutional problems which ultimately affect all of its members: the failure of its Member States to adhere to the values of democracy, the Rule of Law and the protection of human rights on which the legal systems of the Union and its Member States alike are presumed to be founded.[2] There is a growing array of Member States providing abundant examples of such deviations[3] and the EU, faced with this new

---

[1] For a normative analysis of the context necessitating intervention, see, for example, A. von Bogdandy and M. Ioannidis, 'Systemic Deficiency in the Rule of Law: What It Is, What Has Been Done, What Can Be Done', 51 (2014) *CMLRev.* 59; C. Closa in this volume.

[2] Art. 2 TEU.

[3] J.-W. Müller, 'Safeguarding Democracy inside the EU: Brussels and the Future of Liberal Order', Working Paper No. 3 (Washington DC: Transatlantic Academy, 2013); V. Perju, 'The Romanian Double Executive and the 2012 Constitutional Crisis', 13 (2015) *International Journal of Constitutional Law* 246; L. Sólyom, 'The Rise and Decline of Constitutional Culture in Hungary', in A. von Bogdandy and P. Sonnevend (eds.), *Constitutional Crisis in the European Constitutional Area: Theory, Law and Politics in Hungary and Romania* (Oxford: Hart Publishing, 2015); M. Bánkuti, G. Halmai, and K. L. Scheppele, 'Hungary's Illiberal Turn: Disabling the Constitution', 23 (2012) *Journal of Democracy* 138. See also the chapter by Paul Blokker in this volume.

problem of fundamental importance in turbulent times,[4] has not been particularly successful in taming its deviant members.[5]

The problems stemming from this situation are far-reaching indeed. This crisis of constitutionality entirely derails the traditional picture of the Union as an entity based on the Rule of Law.[6] Consequently, mutual trust, on which the Union is constructed,[7] does not work as smoothly as it should[8]: being a Member State of the Union does not automatically imply living by the book of principles and values of which the Rule of Law is the key component. The presumptions made in the past[9] – and seemingly valid in the past[10] – must now be laid to rest: mutual trust

---

[4] On the crisis of values, see, for example, A. Williams, 'Taking Values Seriously: Towards a Philosophy of EU Law', 29 (2009) *OJLS*. See also J. H. H. Weiler's unpublished paper 'On the Distinction between Values and Virtues in the Process of European Integration' (2010). www.iilj.org/courses/documents/2010Colloquium.Weiler.pdf. On the crisis of justice: D. Kochenov, G. de Búrca, and A. Williams (eds.), *Europe's Justice Deficit?* (Oxford: Hart Publishing, 2015). On the economic side of the crisis: A. J. Menéndez, 'The Existential Crisis of the European Union', 14 (2013) *German Law Journal*; M. Adams, F. Fabbrini and P. Larouche (eds.), *The Constitutionalisation of European Budgetary Constraints* (Oxford: Hart Publishing, 2014).

[5] Cf. Bogdandy and Sonnevend, Constitutional Crisis in the European Constitutional Area; Müller, 'Safeguarding Democracy inside the EU'.

[6] M. L. Fernández Esteban, *The Rule of Law in the European Constitution* (The Hague: Kluwer Law International, 1999); L. Pech, 'The Rule of Law as a Constitutional Principle of the European Union' (2009) *Jean Monnet Working Paper* No. 04/09 (NYU Law School) and the literature cited therein. For the EU as a constitutional system, see J. Larik, 'From Speciality to Constitutional Sense of Purpose: On the Changing Role of the Objectives of the European Union', 63 (2014) *I-CON* 935.

[7] For the latest forceful restatement by the ECJ see Opinion 2/13 (*ECHR Accession II*) ECLI:EU:C:2014:2454, para. 192.

[8] D. Halberstam, '"It's the Autonomy, Stupid!" A Modest Defence of Opinion 2/13 on EU Accession to the ECHR, and the Way Forward', 16 (2015) *German Law Journal* 105; P. Eeckhout, 'Opinion 2/13 on EU Accession to the ECHR and Judicial Dialogue – Autonomy or Autarky?', 38 (2015) *Fordham International Law Journal* 955; M. Poiares Maduro, 'So Close yet so far: The Paradoxes of Mutual Recognition', 14 (2007) *Journal of European Public Policy* 814; K. Nicolaïdis, 'Trusting the Poles? Constructing Europe through Mutual Recognition', 14 (2007) *Journal of European Public Policy* 682; V. Mitsilegas, 'The Limits of Mutual Trust in Europe's Area of Freedom, Security and Justice: From Automatic Inter-State Cooperation to the Slow Emergence of the Individual', 31 (2012) *Yearbook of European Law* 319.

[9] Every Member State admitted was presumed to be compliant. Far-reaching pre-accession Rule of Law and democracy promotion engagement would thus stop on the day of accession: D. Kochenov, *EU Enlargement and the Failure of Conditionality* (Alphen aan den Rijn: Kluwer Law International, 2008), chapters 1 and 2.

[10] The only time the EU harboured some doubts and extended the validity of the pre-accession values-promotion machinery is the mechanism applicable to Bulgaria and Romania in force even after they became full members: M. A. Vachudova and A.

among the Member States in the checks and balances of each other's constitutional systems cannot simply be mandated, which has always been the traditional view: enforcing trust in each other without enforcing adherence by the Member States to the essential principles which would justify such trust in the first place cannot produce a lasting constitutional edifice.[11] The departures from what Article 2 TEU simultaneously proclaims and requires are too obvious[12] and the legal-political tools to deal with this situation[13] (no matter, however, much such tools have recently been upgraded)[14] are still left unused, even though we could argue that the current enforcement *acquis* potentially does offer important space for an effective Union response to at least some of the outstanding problems it is facing.[15] The adherence to the key values and principles needs to be enforced both in theory and practice. This book substantiates the theoretical arguments in favour of this and shows how such enforcement can come about in practice.

The acuteness of the problem this volume investigates is such that it occupies a host of the leading legal minds in the academia and in practice alike. The conclusion from the literature so far has been, with a handful of exceptions,[16] mostly pessimistic: little can be done. It almost seems as if the law is on the 'bad guys' side. If the Union is to have a bright future, this definitely should not be the case. The key ambition of this volume is thus to send a more optimistic signal: Reinforcing of the Rule of Law Oversight

---

Spendzharova, 'The EU's Cooperation and Verification Mechanism: Fighting Corruption in Bulgaria and Romania after EU Accession', 1 (2012) *SIEPS European Policy Analysis*.

[11] D. Kochenov, 'Self-Constitution through Unenforceable Promises', in J. Přibáň (ed.) *Self-Constitution of European Society* (Adingdon: Routlegde, 2016).

[12] See, Paul Blokker's chapter in this volume, taking Hungary as an example; Sólyom, 'The Rise and Decline of Constitutional Culture in Hungary'.

[13] See most notably Art. 7 TEU, analysed by B. Bugarič in this volume. Compare, most importantly, W. Sadurski, 'Adding Bite to a Bark: The Story of Article 7, EU Enlargement, and Jörg Haider', 16 (2010) *Columbia Journal of European Law* 385; L. F. M. Besselink, 'The Bite, the Bark and the Howl: Article 7 and the Rule of Law Initiatives', in A. Jakab and D. Kochenov (ed.), *The Enforcement of EU Law and Values: Methods against Defiance* (Oxford: Oxford University Press, 2017, forthcoming).

[14] Some of the recent upgrades are analysed, for example, in D. Kochenov and L. Pech, 'Monitoring and Enforcement of the Rule of Law in the EU: Rhetoric and Reality' 11 (2015) *EUConst* 512. See also the analysis in Carlos Closa's chapter in this collection.

[15] This is the focus of Christophe Hillion's contribution to this volume.

[16] For example, Bogdandy and Sonnevend, *Constitutional Crisis in the European Constitutional Area*; C. Closa, D. Kochenov and J. H. H. Weiler, 'Reinforcing Rule of Law Oversight in the European Union', EUI Working Paper No. 2014/25, RSCAS, 25. See also Jakab and Kochenov, *The Enforcement of EU Law and Values*.

in the EU *is* possible.[17] Moreover, it could also be achieved without Treaty change. To this end, the scholars invited to contribute chapters – each an unrivalled expert in a particular field – investigate new ways of thinking about the concrete tools to deal with the current situation. This tackles two fundamental issues. The first is repairing the damage already done to the Union by deviant Member States failing to heed the EU's ideal of the Rule of Law. The second is guaranteeing that deviations from the promise to uphold the Rule of Law of Article 2 TEU are not tolerated in the future either.

Innovative proposals aiming at solving the outstanding problems with respect to the Rule of Law lie at the core of this work and form a varied palette of possible scenarios to consider, embedded in the rich analysis of the legal–political context we are dealing with: the core focus of those contributions, which are not directly engaged with promoting clear-cut 'how to' packages, nevertheless contributing to the understanding of the current problems' causes, contexts and implications. To this end, while the core of the book concentrates on the issue of solutions, the story of solutions is not the only story this volume tells.

II   The Complexity of the Problem

Laying stress on the possible solutions and approaches which could bring an effective end to the current problems, the work does not stop there. Instead, it starts with a clear line-up of the normative foundations behind the swift deployment of the proposed ways to deal with the outstanding problems, that is, taking Rule of Law seriously.[18] Hesitant voices are equally invited and heard. Indeed, solving problems in the most pragmatic sense could raise even more far-reaching issues than the ones occupying the majority of our contributors. Delving deeper into the possible dangers in the context of the EU's democratic deficit[19] and its traditional understanding of the Rule of Law,[20] the volume broadens the picture beyond the problem of Rule of Law oversight and its numerous proposed solutions, charting a landscape more complex than the one which a proverbial action–reaction world-view would imply. Like a baby azure whale on a

---

[17] For a precursor of the volume coming to the same conclusion, see Closa et al., 'Reinforcing Rule of Law Oversight in the European Union'.

[18] Carlos Closa's contribution in this volume.

[19] See Joseph Weiler's 'Epilogue' in this volume.

[20] See the contributions by Gianluigi Palombella and Dimitry Kochenov in this volume.

bicycle wheel,[21] the fabric of European constitutionalism is much more complex at this stage than any two-dimensional representation of it would presuppose. To be absolutely clear: adding doubt is not done to undermine the potential workability of the proposals for dealing with the Rule of Law disease which ails the EU. Rather, the goal is to provide the tint of complexity which necessarily marks the background of the on-going Rule of Law debate.

While plenty of possible ways to enforce the Rule of Law have been proposed so far[22] – some more likely to be effective than others[23] – this volume aims at bringing the majority of the key proposals under one roof as it were, to empower the reader – either scholar or policymaker – to make her own choices from among the options the volume offers. The majority of the proposals formulated in the literature overwhelmingly focus on institutional action both within and outside the Union context. The former proposals include actions by the existing institutions – the Council,[24] the European Parliament,[25] the European Commission,[26] the Fundamental Rights Agency of the EU (FRA)[27] – and actions by institutions yet to be created, such as the Copenhagen Commission.[28] The latter, focusing on what can be done outside the EU context, include

---

[21] Similar to the one commissioned by the editors to represent the EU with its challenging Rule of Law dilemmas for the cover of this collection and painted by Grisha Kochenov.

[22] For a brief overview, see Closa et al., 'Reinforcing Rule of Law Oversight in the European Union'.

[23] For comparative analyses, see *Ibid*. See also D. Kochenov, 'On Policing Article 2 TEU Compliance – Reverse Solange and Systemic Infringements Analyzed', 33 (2014) *Polish Yearbook of International Law* 145.

[24] Council of the EU, press release no. 16936/14, 3362nd Council meeting, General Affairs, Brussels, 16 December 2014, pp. 20–21; See also E. Hirsch Ballin's contribution to this volume.

[25] A detailed analysis is offered in the special issue of the *Journal of Common Market Studies*, co-edited by D. Kochenov, A. Magen, and L. Pech, forthcoming in 2016.

[26] European Commission, 'A New EU Framework to Strengthen the Rule of Law', Strasbourg, 11 March 2014, COM(2014) 158 final. For an analysis, see Kochenov and Pech, 'Monitoring and Enforcement of the Rule of Law in the European Union'. See also, crucially, K. L. Scheppele's contribution to this volume (outlining the way to empower the Commission to intervene in the cases related to the breach of Art. 2 TEU based on a so-called 'systemic infringement procedure', allowing for a more effective deployment of Art. 258 TFEU).

[27] See, for example, the chapter by G. N. Toggenburg and J. Grimheden in this volume.

[28] See, J.-W. Müller's contribution to this volume. See also J.-W. Müller, 'Should the European Union Protect Democracy and the Rule of Law in Its Member States', 21 (2015) *ELJ* 141; J.-W. Müller, 'The EU as a Militant Democracy', 165 (2014) *Revista de Estudios Políticos* 141.

the involvement of the Venice Commission for instance,[29] or proposals to draw on the lessons stemming from the operation of universally respected international actors, including the UN.[30] Perusal of the literature reveals that reliance on Member State courts[31] and the potential fine-tuning of the powers of the EU through a broad interpretation by the Court of Justice of the European Union (ECJ) of the Charter of Fundamental Rights of the EU (CFR)[32] have also been advocated. Last but not least, Member State action either through 'soft law' via mutual monitoring[33] or through their direct involvement in infringement proceedings before the ECJ – while going against the Member States seen as the cause of the problem[34] – have also been defended as potentially viable approaches to solve the Article 2 TEU compliance problems the EU confronts. The majority of the proposals outlined are discussed by the scholars contributing to this volume. While dedicating a chapter to each would be impossible due to the obvious physical limitations of a book format, all the key ideas flowing from each and every leading proposal on the table appear recurrently in the

---

[29] Kaarlo Tuori's chapter in this volume; J. Nergelius, 'The Role of the Venice Commission in Maintaining the Rule of Law', in A. von Bogdandy and P. Sonnevend (eds.), *Constitutional Crisis in the European Constitutional Area: Theory, Law and Politics in Hungary and Romania* (Oxford: Hart Publishing, 2015).

[30] See, for example, the chapter by Martin Scheinin in this volume.

[31] A. von Bogdandy et al., 'Reverse Solange – Protecting the Essence of Fundamental Rigths against EU Member States' 49 (2012) *CMLRev.* 489. For analyses, see J. Croon-Gestefeld, 'Reverse Solange – Union Citizenship as a Detour on the Route to European Rights Protection against National Infringements', in D. Kochenov (ed.), *EU Citizenship and Federalism: The Role of Rights* (Cambridge: Cambridge University Press, 2016); Kochenov, 'On Policing Article 2 TEU Compliance'. See also the improved versions of the proposal: A. von Bogdandy et al., 'A European Response to Domestic Constitutional Crisis: Advancing the Reverse-Solange Doctrine', in A. von Bogdandy and P. Sonnevend (eds.), *Constitutional Crisis in the European Constitutional Area: Theory, Law and Politics in Hungary and Romania* (Oxford: Hart Publishing, 2015); A. von Bogdandy, C. Antpöller and M. Ioannidis, 'Enforcing European Values', in A. Jakab and D. Kochenov (eds.), *The Enforcement of EU Law and Values* (Oxford: Oxford University Press, 2017, forthcoming).

[32] András Jakab's chapter in this volume. The Charter's potential is as far-reaching as it is unused: F. Hoffmeiser, 'Enforcing the EU Charter of Fundamental Rigths in Member States: How Far Are Rome, Budapest and Bucharest from Brussels?', in A. von Bogdandy and P. Sonnevend (eds.), *Constitutional Crisis in the European Constitutional Area: Theory, Law and Politics in Hungary and Romania* (Oxford: Hart, 2015); A. Łazowski, 'Decoding a Legal Enigma: The Charter of Fundamental Rigths of the European Union and Infringement Proceedings', 14 (2013) *ERA Forum* 573. See also P. Eeckhout, 'The EU Charter of Fundamental Rights and the Federal Question', 39 (2002) *CMLRev.* 945.

[33] See also E. Hirsch Ballin's contribution to this volume.

[34] D. Kochenov, 'Biting Intergovernmentalism: The Case for the Reinvention of Article 259 TFEU to Make it a Viable Rule of Law Enforcement Tool' 7 (2015) *The Hague Journal of the Rule of Law* 153.

book and are discussed by the contributing scholars in abundant detail,[35] elaborating a complex web of strong and weak features for each proposed solution, helping move our thinking further.

This edited volume is directly rooted in the concerns about the quality of national-level compliance with the fundamental values of the Union as expressed in Article 2 TEU and in particular with the Rule of Law as one of the core values mentioned in that provision, which the constitutional and legal changes in a growing number of the Member States of the European Union (in particular in Hungary and, though less so, in Romania, Greece and others) have caused across the continent. These developments have engendered the perception that whilst the EU is well equipped with the means to shape the democratic systems of candidate countries,[36] aspires to do the same with the European Neighbourhood Policy partners,[37] and is even able to shape third states' legal systems via cooperation and other agreements, the EU is poorly equipped to deal with similar issues concerning actual Member States.[38] The key issue is that the promise contained in the values the EU embraces in public might not be enforceable in practice,[39] throwing a shadow on the self-constitution of the Union as a constitutional system.[40]

It is thus not surprising at all that these concerns – crucially important as they are – resulted in the plethora of (at times vocal) responses from governments, institutions and academics mentioned above. It is clear, however, that the whole debate – however rich some elements of it might seem to the participants at the moment – is, but at its starting point, amounting to little more than a tip of the iceberg on a long road of

---

[35] With the sole exception, probably of the Article 259 one, which is the newest addition to the toolkit menu, only published around the time when the manuscript of this book went to print.

[36] M. A. Vachudova, *Europe Undivided* (Oxford: Oxford University Press, 2004); but see Kochenov, *EU Enlargement and the Failure of Conditionality*.

[37] R. Petrov and P. Van Elsuwege (eds.), *Legislative Approximation and Application of EU Law in the Eastern Neighbourhood of the European Union* (London: Routledge, 2014); L. Pech, 'The EU as a Global Rule of Law Promoter: The Consistency and Effectiveness Challenges' 14 (2016) *Asia Europe Journal* 7; L. Pech, 'Promoting the Rule of Law Abroad', in D. Kochenov and F. Amtenbrink (eds.), *The European Union's Shaping of the International Legal Order* (Cambridge: Cambridge University Press, 2013), p. 108.

[38] While this problem has been known for decades as one of the curiosities of the legal context of EU enlargement regulation, the ongoing developments in Hungary, in particular, gave it a practical twist for the first time in its long career.

[39] It has been suggested that the new Member States were joining the Union partly attracted by the promise of the eventual enforcement of these key principles, should something go wrong in the national constitutional system: W. Sadurski, *Constitutionalism and the Enlargement of Europe* (Oxford: Oxford University Press, 2012).

[40] D. Kochenov, 'Self-Constitution through Unenforceable Promises'.

endowing the EU with adequate legal and political means to solve the outstanding issues caused by its inability to ensure that all of its Member States fully adhere to the basic principles – especially democracy and the Rule of Law – on which the Union is founded. A long process, which goes far beyond the rethinking of the actual modalities of operation of Article 7 TEU and the infringement procedures, possibly also confronting the atypical nature – if not deficiency – of the Rule of Law at the supranational as opposed to the Member State level,[41] if not the democratic deficit of the EU, as Joseph Weiler warns in the Epilogue.[42]

It thus becomes clear in this context that the focus on enforcement should not distract the vigilant observer of the Rule of Law from the problems of understanding and interpreting this very notion at the supranational level: while numerous necessary elements of EU Rule of Law have been outlined by academics and the institutions alike,[43] problems still abound, caused the mechanical and uncritical approach to the Rule of Law,[44] where tautologies in the vein of 'Rule of Law means being bound by the law' seem not infrequent guests.[45] This is precisely why a focus only on the modalities of the normative necessity for the enforcement of the Rule of Law or, which is the flipside of the same coin, on the practical tools of such enforcement, however innovative, is bound to be insufficient in the eyes of those theorists who are rightly sceptical, including Joseph Weiler, Gianluigi Palombella and Dimitry Kochenov in this volume. The differences in the vectors of such scepticism – whether they come from the quarters of democracy,[46] 'pure' Rule of Law[47] or even justice considerations[48] – are less important in the context of the discussion carried out in this collection than the conclusions reached: the substance is as important – if not more important – than the tools.

---

[41] See the contribution by Dimitry Kochenov in this volume.

[42] See Joseph Weiler's contribution to this volume.

[43] See, most importantly, Pech, 'The Rule of Law as a Constitutional Principle of the European Union'. The Commission, to look at the institutional side, supplied its vision of the Rule of Law in the Pre-Article 7 Mechanism: COM(2014) 158 final. See also D. Kochenov and L. Pech, 'Better Late than Never?' 54 (2016) *JCMS*.

[44] The crucial problems are brilliantly analysed by Gianluigi Palombella in his contribution to this volume.

[45] *Ibid.* See also Dimitry Kochenov's chapter in this collection.

[46] J. H. H. Weiler, 'Europa: "Nous coalisons des Etats nous n'unissons pas des homes"', in M. Cartabia and A. Simoncini (eds.), *La sostenibilità della democrazia nel XXI secolo* (Bologna: Il Mulino, 2009).

[47] G. Palombella, *È possibile la legalità globale?* (Bologna: Il Mulino, 2012); G. Palombella, 'The Rule of Law and Its Core', in G. Palombella and N. Walker (eds.), *Relocating the Rule of Law* (Oxford: Hart Publishing, 2009).

[48] Kochenov et al. (eds.), *Europe's Justice Deficit?*

III The Structure of the Collection

This collection constitutes a creative attempt to bring the discussion of precisely such tools forward, while keeping an eye on the bigger picture. This is done through a detailed analysis of the concrete ways of dealing with the current state of affairs, which the editors and all the authors alike consider as profoundly problematic. The project adopts a clear starting assumption, discussed and developed throughout all the contributions, that a strengthened role for the EU in dealing with the problems of democracy and the Rule of Law is both *possible* and *desirable*. This position flows from a combination of the factual environment, which encouraged these reflections, but also from a detailed examination of the legal structure of the EU with a special emphasis on the position occupied by the principle of the Rule of Law at its very core.[49]

The work splits into three parts. The first, *Establishing Normative Foundations* restates the normative foundations on which the volume builds (Closa), also looking at the legal–philosophical core of the Rule of Law, creating an innovative and for some uneasy picture (Palombella). Crucially, however, the first part makes clear that the EU is potentially empowered to intervene to defend the Rule of Law *already* under the Treaties in force (Hillion), particularly with the constructive potential of the much criticised Article 7 TEU in mind (Bugarič), thus setting the stage for the concrete proposals for how to do this.

The second part of this collection, entitled *Proposing New Approaches*, focuses on the most important among the proposals on the table, many of which were also discussed by the EU institutions and by the organs of other European international organisations, including in the context of the Council of Europe.[50] These include the Copenhagen Commission (Müller), systemic infringement action (Scheppele), EU's internal strategy for fundamental rights (Toggenburg and Grimheden) and the reliance on checklists as a prevention mechanism (Scheinin), as well as reassessing the scope of the EU Charter of Fundamental Rights (Jakab) and granting a larger role to the Venice Commission for Democracy through Law of the Council of Europe (Tuori). Peer review by the Member States is also discussed in detail (Hirsch Ballin).

The third part, *Identifying Deeper Problems*, provides a broader critical assessment of the issues we are dealing with, looking at the difficulties with probing deeply enough into the domestic constitutional context (Blokker), problematic post-accession legacies (Vachudova) and the

---

[49] Palombella in this volume.   [50] See Kaarlo Tuori's contribution to this collection.

possibly deficient framing of the Rule of Law at the supranational context – which is potentially concerned with two things. The first aspect outlined in this volume relates to the departure by the EU from what Gianluigi Palombella calls 'the Rule of Law as an Institutional Ideal',[51] thus establishing a direct connection with the first part of this book (Kochenov). The second aspect of the problem concerns the necessary interplay between the Rule of Law and democracy in the EU in a context where the unconventional character of the EU's democracy is something we can all agree upon. The Epilogue thus provides a cautionary tale of why, when going about with the starting assumptions on the Rule of Law adopted in the EU, one has to tread extremely carefully, as the EU itself is liable to criticism on many grounds when viewed through a lens of democracy and legitimacy. The implications of this legitimate criticism are far-reaching (Weiler).

IV Pending Decisions for the Future

This volume does not take a definitive stance on any of the possible courses of action it offers, rather inviting the reader to extract her own conclusions. The volume does nonetheless call for including a critical stance on the definition and elaboration of the ontological character of the notion of 'Rule of Law' as a preliminary step before deciding how the EU should deal with the potential breaches of this principle. In this sense, both the editors and the majority of the contributors concur in not assuming that these complex issues will be solved once the (institutional) alternatives are identified. Rather, academic debate should become the trigger of a richer institutional debate which bridges into the ontological dimension: what the Rule of Law is, especially for the EU. A permanent critical stance toward the constitutional structure of the Rule of Law in the EU will definitely not solve the challenges and issues raised here but it will no doubt help avoid outright bluffing and assumptions of empowerment based precisely on the situations where change is unquestionably required, such as in instances of institutional capture.[52]

This critically reflective stance not only refers to 'Rule of Law' but to the whole ensemble of values enshrined in Article 2 TEU. One of its key normative proposals is therefore a comprehensive reading of the set of values comprised therein. Human rights, democracy, dignity, equality

---

[51] Gianluigi Palombella's chapter in this volume, p. 36.
[52] As discussed *inter alia* by Jan-Werner Müller: Müller, 'The EU as a Militant Democracy'.

and freedom (next to pluralism, non-discrimination, tolerance, justice, solidarity and equality between women and men) as much as Rule of Law make up the axiological block on which the EU is founded. The different institutional configurations (in terms of the legal and political deployment, the instruments for application and the enforcement mechanisms) have elicited separate treatments and have also fuelled specialised academic inquiry and temptations of theoretical colonisation from mechanisms and normative foundations developed on a single value. Instead, our suggestion for future developments tends towards calling for a comprehensive treatment which will cause a holistic vision of EU value-based constitutionalism emerge.[53] This is the future. For now, however, whether the EU can legitimately take pride in the Rule of Law is a question more acute than ever, as this volume vividly demonstrates. Besides all the institutional and instrumental *richesse*, we can only observe one development: inaction.[54] The EU thus emerges as an antithesis of Roosevelt's famed policy advice: 'speak softly and carry a big stick'.

---

[53] C. Closa, 'Deliberative Constitutional Politics and the Turn towards a Norms-Based Legitimacy of the EU Constitution' 11 (2005) *ELJ* 411.

[54] The Commission's activation of the Pre-Article 7 Mechanism against Poland in early 2015 cannot possibly be effective in solving the outstanding problems with the adherence to the Rule of Law in that country: Kochenov and Pech, 'Better Late than Never?'

PART I

Establishing Normative Foundations

1

Reinforcing EU Monitoring of the Rule of Law

Normative Arguments, Institutional Proposals and the Procedural Limitations

CARLOS CLOSA*

I Introduction

Concern and anxiety about (perceived or real) systematic breaches of basic EU values in several member states has grown in the last years. In response, the Council has approved a new mechanism 'to promote and safeguard the Rule of Law in the framework of the Treaties'.[1] The mechanism's strong intergovernmental bias and its lack of binding and coercive power scale down the ambition inspiring previous proposals. This unsatisfactory outcome requires a critical review which, in this chapter, proceeds by presenting, first, three normative arguments in favour of a reinforced EU supervision of the respect for the Rule of Law in Member States. Then, it discusses the different institutional proposals which led to the final procedure to outline their relative strengths.

II Normative Arguments Supporting EU Monitoring of Member States Compliance with Rule of Law

Three normative arguments justify the involvement of the European Union in a reinforced monitoring of compliance of the Rule of Law requirement by its Member States. The first argument derives from the model of community that the EU stands for: the EU is a *community of*

---

* Instituto de Políticas y Bienes Públicos (IPP); Consejo Superior de Investigaciones Científicas (CSIC).
[1] Conclusions of the Council of the European Union and the member states meeting within the Council on ensuring respect for the rule of law. General Affairs Council meeting, Brussels, 16 December 2014 Doc. 16862/14 COR 1 www.consilium.europa.eu/uedocs/cms_Data/docs/pressdata/EN/genaff/146323.pdf.

law which depends on mutual recognition and mutual trust. Secondly, the breach of the principle of the Rule of Law affects all the members of this community. This principle can be labelled the *all affected principle*. The third argument refers to the consistency between the EU's own proclaimed values and policies. Consistency demands that the same requirements apply through time and across policies (unless there are overriding normative arguments which cancel this requirement).

(a) Mutual Recognition and Mutual Trust in a Community of Law

The EU has constructed a community based on the Rule of Law[2] and in fact the whole process has been characterised as 'integration through law'.[3] Essentially, this means that legal means enacted through legally valid and legitimate procedure regulates Community actions. The absence of specific EU implementation and judicial structures at the national level requires that member states' domestic administrative and judicial structures secure domestic implementation and compliance. This is only possible if each member state recognises those in other member states as equally valid to their own. Failure to accept other Member States' court decisions, European arrest warrants, newly issued nationalities or the quality of phytosanitary measures, etc. are generally *prohibited* by EU law.[4] States are bound to recognise each other legal structures or to presume that each of them is at least as good as any other in terms of the governance, democracy and the Rule of Law standards. Hence, this 'community of law' relies on the mutual recognition that Members owe to each other.

Behind mutual recognition stands mutual trust: recognition (of laws, regulations, etc.) is possible because members trust their fellow union members and their respective legal systems. This makes mutual trust the foundation of the Union and it is the view behind Commission's approach to Rule of Law:

> the way the rule of law is implemented at national level plays a key role in this respect. The confidence of all EU citizens and national authorities in

---

[2] Judgment of the Court of 23 April 1986: Case 294/83 *Parti écologiste "Les Verts"* v. *European Parliament* ECLI:EU:C:1986:166 [1986] ECR 1339.

[3] The key reference is, of course, M. Cappelletti, M. Seccombe, and J. Weiler (eds.) *Integration through Law: Europe and the American Federal Experience. Vol. 1: Methods, Tools and Institutions* (New York: Walter de Gruyter and Co., 1986).

[4] See C. Closa, D. Kochenov and J. H. H. Weiler (2014) 'Reinforcing Rule of Law Oversight in the European Union', EUI Working Papers No. 2014/25, RSCAS, 6.

the functioning of the rule of law ... will only be built and maintained if the rule of law is observed in all Member States.[5]

Mutual recognition and mutual trust in a community of law creates the basis for legitimate concerns at each other's Rule of Law systems. In principle, mutual trust and recognition assume that EU citizens within a given member state are protected from abuse. However, disrespect or erosion of this fundamental value can affect how the Union works in a given member state, and this also means that the EU and Member States can have an interest in protecting EU citizens within a given member state. Moreover, mutual trust and mutual recognition are deeply linked to the principle of 'sincere cooperation' (Article 4(3) TEU) in a dual way. On the one hand, a potential offending member state must refrain from adopting measures that may affect trust and recognition from other states. Whether a measure will have this potential effect may be assessed in a complementary way: any domestic measure reacting to a loss of trust or recognition with another Member State (for instance, measures expressing mistrust in the judicial system of that state) can be considered contravening the principle of sincere cooperation. Accordingly, the scrutiny of measures affecting mutual trust/recognition contributes to guaranteeing the principle of sincere cooperation.

This essence of the EU as a 'community of law' based on mutual recognition and mutual trust sets it apart from traditional international organisations but also from international society wright at large. While it can be argued that some element of mutual recognition can be found in specific functional arenas covered by bilateral or multilateral agreements, they are much weaker and not comparable to the EU holistic approach. Even accepting the emergence of a 'global constitutionalism' and taking for granted that it embodies the Rule of Law at a global level, only a huge imaginative effort would permit describing international society as one based on mutual recognition and trust. This difference serves to substantiate the normative claim for a reinforced scrutiny of Member State compliance with the Rule of Law: even though the Lisbon Treaty

---

[5] See European Commission, Communication from the Commission to the European Parliament and the Council, A new EU Framework to strengthen the Rule of Law, Brussels, 11 March 2014 COM (2014) 158 final. See also European Commission, 'Discussion Paper 4: Rule of Law', the Assises Working Paper, 2, which argued that: 'an efficient and independent justice system ensures predictable, timely and enforceable judicial decisions [which] can contribute to trust and stability [...] Properly functioning justice systems at national level play a key role in creating confidence ...', at http://ec.europa.eu/justice/events/assises-justice-2013/files/rule_of_law_en.pdf.

has renounced to the notion of a 'community of states and citizens' expressed in the 2004 EU constitution, EU constitutionalism is based on a thicker sense of community (implying trust) than the global one (although admittedly thinner than national ones).

(b)   The 'All Affected' Principle

Erosion of the Rule of Law extends its effects beyond the offending member state: a state which does not comply with the Rule of Law can affect its own citizens, other EU citizens and legal persons operating within it but it can also externalise its effects beyond its borders. On the one hand, it will affect the quality of EU decision-making in a normative sense: the state will participate in decision-making in EU institutions and, because of this, at least indirectly participate in governing the lives of *all* the citizens of Europe. On the other hand, it could project the effects of its decisions beyond its own borders. Thus, disrespect for the Rule of Law and democracy in a particular Member State can have negative externalities on other Member States and the effects (real or hypothetical) which a Rule of Law incompliant Member State extends into the whole of the Union to affect all citizens and states. The deep interpenetration and mutual interdependency between the Member States of the Union at the current stage of European integration means that all are affected. The externalisation effects appear constantly in discussions of the flaws of national democracies within the context of European integration.[6]

The 'all affected' principle has become common in debate on the question of the boundaries of the democratic demos.[7] In very simple terms,

---

[6] See *inter alia*, J. Neyer and C. Joerges, 'From Intergovernmental Bargaining to Deliberative Political Processes: The Constitutionalisation of Comitology', 3(3) (1997) *ELJ* 273 (who argue that national democracies are burdened with a grave deficiency which makes them systematically predisposed to disregard the interest of these who, in spite of being affected by their operation, remain in a disenfranchised state); M. Maduro, 'Reforming the Market or the State? Article 30 and the European Constitution: Economic Freedom and Political Rights', 3(1) (1997) *ELJ* 55; and A. Somek, 'The Argument from Transnational Effects I: Representing Outsiders through Freedom of Movement', 16(3) (2010) *ELJ* 315 (who makes the argument that supranational forms of integration are desirable on account of democracy itself: national democracies are forced to confront and to internalise the externalisation effects which they may cause for one another. The argument favours normative limitation of national political processes).

[7] T. Christiano, 'A Democratic Theory of Territory and Some Puzzles about Global Democracy', 37(1) (2006) *Journal of Social Philosophy* 81; R. Goodin, 'Enfranchising All Affected Interests, and Its Alternatives', 35(1) (2007) *Philosophy & Public Affairs* 40; S. Näsström, 'The Challenge of the All-Affected Principle', 59(1) (2011) *Political Studies* 116; D. Owen,

the all affected principle redefines a community in that all those affected by a decision should participate in decision-making. The application of this principle in the context of the EU and the debate on scrutinising national compliance with the Rule of Law has a different reach. It does not serve to delimitate the boundaries of the community, but rather all affected means that in a community of interdependence, all affected have an entitlement to propose to limit the externalities created by the functioning of national democratic policy making. The all affected principle signifies a community of *demoi*-cracy, to use the felicitous expression coined by Nicolaïdis[8] for setting limits to the externalisation of unwanted and potentially damaging national democratic decisions.

The translation of the principle into the terrain of the Rule of Law works almost mechanically: all citizens and states are affected when a Member State breaches the Rule of Law (in fact, the all affected principle also applies to the other values listed in Article 2 TEU). In a reverse sense, the erosion of these values and in particular the Rule of Law affects trust and recognition, spilling over into specific policy areas. In any case, the all affected principle cannot be interpreted as an authorisation to shape domestic law according to some supranational standard but rather to check its compatibility with some basic structural values. Responsibility ultimately lies with the national polity.

(c)   The Principle of Consistency

The *principle of consistency* or *congruence* provides a second normative argument. This principle projects its requirements both internally (and temporally) and externally.

Internally, the principle of consistency addresses a basic incongruence of the EU legal and political order: the assumption that EU member states do comply with EU values while those would-be members do not. Conditionality policies embody precisely this assumption. In fact, as

---

'Constituting the Polity, Constituting the Demos: On the Place of the All Affected Interests Principle in Democratic Theory and in Resolving the Democratic Boundary Problem', 5(3) (2012) *Ethics & Global Politics* 129; A. Ron 'Affected Interests and Their Institutions' 'The Institutions of the "All-Affected Interests"', Annual Meeting of the Association for Political Theory (University of South Carolina, 11–13 October 2012); R. Bauböck, 'The Rights and Duties of External Citizenship', 13(5) (2009) *Citizenship Studies* 475; R. Bauböck, 'Morphing the Demos into the Right Shape. Normative Principles for Enfranchising Resident Aliens and Expatriate Citizens', 22(5) (2015) *Democratization* 820.

[8] K. Nicolaïdis, 'The New Constitution as European Demoi-cracy?', 7(1) (2004) *Critical Review of International Social and Political Philosophy* 76.

Kochenov argues in relation to the ECtHR *MSS* case, instances can arise when a faithful application of EU law potentially violates the ECHR, and he concludes that the presumption of a full and automatic adherence to the values in Article 2 TEU by the supranational law-giver in the EU can be unfounded.[9]

The temporal dimension of consistency refers to the maintenance of the conditionality requirements after accession. This reflects the so-called Copenhagen dilemma: the EU requires strict compliance with the common values and standards on the part of candidate countries but lacks effective monitoring and sanctioning tools once they have joined the EU.[10] The dilemma is in reality a paradox: whilst scrutinising the fulfilment of normative standards (such as the Rule of Law) in would-be members effectively externalises its costs, scrutiny of current members might project costs in an unpredicted way on any of them (rather than exclusively externalising them to third parties). In fact, discussions during the creation of Article 7 TEU provisions at the 1996 IGC illustrate the reluctance of existing member states to submit themselves to a federal legal mechanism which could grow, at least partly, beyond their complete control.[11] Moreover, cost-bearers can be undefined, since no state can calculate *a priori* who will be affected by these mechanisms. In this respect, the case of Austria in 1999 is illustrative. Provisions in the current Article 7 TEU were drafted with Central and Eastern European applicants in mind,[12] and nevertheless they were invoked (although not effectively implemented) for the first time against a 'respectful member of the club'. These arguments provide states with powerful reasons to resist such clauses and may explain the inability of the EU convincingly to implement additional measures to Article 7 TEU.[13] Future unintended

---

[9] D. Kochenov, 'The Issue of Values', in R. Petrov and P. Van Elsuwege (eds.), *The Application of EU Law in the Eastern Neighbourhood of the European Union* (London: Routledge, 2013), p. 50. He refers to the ECtHR Case *M.S.S.* v. *Belgium and Greece* [2011] App. No. 30696/09.

[10] V. Reding first formulated the dilemma in an intervention at the EP European Parliament: Plenary debate on the political situation in Romania, statement by V. Reding, 12 September 2012. See, *inter alia*, D. Kochenov, *EU Enlargement and the Failure of Conditionality: Pre-accession Conditionality in the Fields of Democracy and the Rule of Law* (Alphen aan den Rijn: Kluwer Law International, 2008); and M. Maresceau, 'The EU Pre-Accession Strategies: A Political and Legal Analysis', in M. Maresceau and E. Lanon (eds.), *The EU's Enlargement and Mediterranean Strategies: A Comparative Analysis* (Basingstoke: Palgrave, 2001), p. 18.

[11] W. Sadurski, 'Adding Bite to a Bark? The Story of Article 7, E.U. Enlargement, and Jörg Haider', 16 (2010) *CJEL* 385, 394.

[12] *Ibid.*

[13] See B. Bugarič, 'Protecting Democracy inside the EU: On Article 7 TEU and the Hungarian Turn to Authoritarianism' in this volume.

effects, though, have to be balanced against the functional properties of such provisions. Consistency in demanding the maintenance of same accession conditions for current members serves to reduce uncertainty about their future behaviour by locking them into specific features consistent with the objectives of the organisation. Introducing scrutiny of compliance and, potentially, sanctions could raise the costs of defecting from the commitments accepted when entering the organisation.[14]

Beyond the functional dimension, the normative foundation for consistency derives from *equality* considerations (which EU institutions have repeated *ad nauseam*):[15] given that acceding states need to comply with the values in Article 2 TEU, the absence of similar monitoring mechanisms for current members treats the two state groups unequally, and this inequality is more clear if the existence of post-accession monitoring mechanisms (such as the ones created for Bulgaria and Romania)[16] is taken into account.

[14] T. Ginsburg, 'Locking in Democracy: Constitutions, Commitment and International Law', 38 (2006) *NYU Journal of International Law and Politics* 707; A. Moravcsik, 'The Origins of Human Rights Regimes: Democratic Delegation in Postwar Europe', 54 (2000) *International Organizations* 217.

[15] See, *inter alia*, European Parliament, Resolution of 3 July 2013 on the situation of fundamental rights: standards and practices in Hungary (pursuant to the European Parliament resolution of 16 February 2012) (2012/2130(INI)) P7_TA-PROV(2013)0315 www.europarl.europa.eu/sides/getDoc.do?type=TA&language=EN&reference=P7-TA-2013-315 (the EP 'attaches the utmost importance to respect of the principle of equality between all Member States and refuses the application of double standards in the treatment of Member States'); European Parliament, Resolution of 27 February 2014 on the situation of fundamental rights in the European Union (2013/2078(INI)) (asking 'every decision (to be) taken on the basis of objective criteria and an objective evaluation, in order to address criticisms of a lack of indicators and evaluation criteria, of differential treatment and of political bias'); Conclusions of the Council of the European Union, 16 December 2014, Doc. 16862/14 COR 1 (the Council Conclusions, point 2: 'underline that this dialogue will be based on the principles of objectivity, non-discrimination and equal treatment of all Member States'); European Commission, 'Respect for and Promotion of the Values on Which the Union Is Based', Brussels, 15 October 2003 COM(2003) 606 final (where the Commission requests that 'similar situations in Member States should be monitored in accordance with the same pattern, since otherwise the principle of equality of the Member States before the Treaties is not respected').

[16] European Commission, Commission Decision of 13 December 2006 establishing a mechanism for cooperation and verification of progress in Romania to address specific benchmarks in the areas of judicial reform and the fight against corruption, Brussels, 13 December 2006 C(2006) 6569 final and Commission Decision of 13 December 2006 establishing a mechanism for cooperation and verification of progress in Bulgaria to address specific benchmarks in the areas of judicial reform and the fight against corruption and organised crime, Brussels, 13 December 2006 C(2006) 6570 final. See M. A. Vachudova, 'EU Leverage and National Interests in the Balkans: The Puzzles of Enlargement Ten Years On', 52 (2014) *JCMS* 122.

The external dimension of the principle of consistency points to the kind of requirements that the Union usually puts for engaging in co-operation with third parties. The protection of fundamental rights, the Rule of Law and democracy all together or individually feature systematically in EU external actions and instruments. Moreover, the EU even attempts to shape international law to its liking, using its own fundamental values and principles as a basis for this.[17] It thus appears inconsistent to have a more lenient or soft set of domestic formal requirements than those applied externally, and on the other hand, a mechanism for scrutinising the internal compliance with these values would clearly also reinforce the EU's credibility in the wider world. This is crucial, in particular, given that the EU sets high standards for the candidate countries in the course of the pre-accession process,[18] which contrasts sharply with what is required of those Member States, which are already 'in'. Consistency is required for reasons of credibility and efficacy. On the one hand, the credibility of EU policy which requires reforms in the areas of the Rule of Law and fundamental rights for third countries must be consistent with internal requirements on these areas. On the other hand, efficacy considerations derive from the fact that internal compliance with the Rule of Law is also a prerequisite for upholding all rights and obligations deriving from the Treaties and from international law.

III. Institutional Proposals for Reinforcing EU Rule of Law Scrutiny of Member States

The design of EU mechanisms for scrutinising member states' compliance with the Rule of Law and other values listed in Article 2 TEU has followed the dynamics created by the breaches or, rather, fear of breaches by national governments. Accordingly, the EU's forthcoming eastward enlargement prompted the creation of a sanctioning mechanism,[19] and the experience of the EU sanctions against Austria triggered the addition of a preventive (alongside the existing sanctions) stage for Article 7 TEU.[20] Similarly, constitutional and legal changes in Hungary and, less so,

---

[17] D. Kochenov and F. Amtenbrink (eds.), *The European Union's Shaping of the International Legal Order* (Cambridge: Cambridge University Press, 2013).

[18] See Maresceau, 'The EU Pre-Accession Strategies'.

[19] For an assessment of *ex ante* conditionality, see Kochenov, *EU Enlargement and the Failure of Conditionality*.

[20] W. Sadurski, 'Adding Bite to a Bark?', 387.

in Romania[21] by ruling majorities have triggered concerns and activated the search for additional mechanisms.[22] EU institutions (EP, EU Commission and Council) shared this diagnosis and demanded action for an increased EU monitoring of the situation of Rule of Law and democracy in member states. Initially, institutional proposals echoed each other, but the European Council mechanism has totally sidelined the EP's and Commission's ones. The final (so far) mechanism seems rather irrelevant and inefficient.

(a) The European Parliament's Approach

The European Parliament (EP) entered the discussions on the need to reinforce the monitoring of Rule of Law compliance by Member States quite incidentally. In July 2013, it approved a Resolution[23] following the Tavares Report, which explicitly examined the case of Hungary (although it indicated that the Resolution was about the Union as a whole) and hence proposals related very closely to this case. The EP thus demanded an Article 2 TEU 'alarm' by which all dealings between the EU Commission and a given member state (i.e. Hungary) will be blocked until issues relating to Article 2 TEU are addressed satisfactorily. A three-way dialogue (Trilogue) in which the Commission, the European Council and the Parliament would delegate members to a new committee which would engage in a close review of all activities of the Hungarian government related to the Tavares Report. This committee would assess whether

---

[21] In Romania, concerns referred to the failure to respect constitutional court judgements in the summer of 2012. The Roma crisis in France (summer 2010), involving the attempt to deport secretly Romani citizens, affecting thus the right of free movement for Roma people, enters also in the set of cases triggering concerns. Lately, Viktor Orbán's advocacy of 'illiberal democracy' taking China and Russia as possible models runs deeply counter to the EU's values as enshrined in Article 2 TEU, despite their vagueness. See H. Mahony, 'Orbán Wants to Build "Illiberal State"' *EU Observer* (28 July 2014) https://euobserver .com/political/125128. See A. von Bogdandy and P. Sonnevend (eds.) *Constitutional Crisis in the European Constitutional Area: Theory, Law and Politics in Hungary and Romania* (Oxford: Hart Publishing, 2015).

[22] Both the Venice Commission and the EP Tavares Report comprehensively listed the defects of the new set of Hungarian laws and constitutional revisions enacted by the Orbán government. In Romania, the newly elected government sought to impeach President Traian Băsescu and called an impeachment referendum, but the Romanian Constitutional Court ruled that it failed to achieve the necessary quorum.

[23] European Parliament, Resolution of 3 July 2013 on the situation of fundamental rights: standards and practices in Hungary (pursuant to the European Parliament resolution of 16 February 2012) (2012/2130(INI)) P7_TAPROV(2014)0173 A70051/2014.

Hungary makes progress in complying with the objective that the Report identifies.

The Resolution also contained a set of recommendations to the EU institutions on setting up a new mechanism to enforce Article 2 TEU effectively. More precisely, the EP called for the different stages in the Article 2 procedure to be distinguished: an initial phase (aimed at assessing any risks of a serious breach of the values referred in Article 2 TEU) and a more efficient procedure at a subsequent phase, where action would need to be taken to address actual serious and persistent violation of those values. The EP also endorsed the creation the 'Copenhagen Commission' which Jan-Werner Müller had pioneered:[24] a high-level expert body of distinguished and independent experts with the power to review continued compliance with the Copenhagen criteria used for admission to the EU.

However, the EP Committee on Civil Liberties, Justice and Home Affairs (LIBE) changed tack later on. The LIBE Kinga Göncz Report[25] (not voted in plenary) repeated the request for an effective mechanism for a regular assessment of Member States' compliance with the fundamental values of the EU, as set out in Article 2 TEU, providing a basis for an early warning tool, and it added a demand for a mechanism for crisis situations with appropriate forms of intervention, more effective infringement proceedings and the possibility of sanctions should systematic breaches of the principles of democracy and the Rule of Law occur. The Report, however, departed from early EP lobbying in favour of a 'Copenhagen Commission' and stressed instead the reinforcement with the Council of Europe and its different bodies. The Report thus identified the European Court of Human Rights as the 'primary body at European level responsible for decisions on fundamental rights and the Rule of Law, including in the area of criminal justice'.[26]

In 2015, the EP kept monitoring the issue and held two plenary debates on the Rule of Law, democracy and fundamental rights and on the situation in Hungary. After the second debate, the EP adopted a Resolution[27] calling on the Commission to present a proposal for an EU mechanism on

---

[24] See J.-W. Müller, 'The EU as a Militant Democracy, or: Are there Limits to Constitutional Mutations within EU Member States?', (2014) *Revista de Estudios Políticos*, No. 165; as well as his contribution in this volume.

[25] K. Göncz, 'Report on evaluation of justice in relation to criminal justice and the rule of law' (2014/2006(INI)) European Parliament, Committee on Civil Liberties, Justice and Home Affairs A7-0122/2014 17 February 2014.

[26] *Ibid.*, 9, para. 5.

[27] European Parliament resolution of 10 June 2015 on the situation in Hungary 2015/2700(RSP) P8_TA-PROV(2015)0227.

democracy, the Rule of Law and fundamental rights as a tool of compliance with the EU Charter of Fundamental Rights and the Treaties, relying on uniform and objective indicators, and to carry out an impartial, yearly assessment of the situation in all the Member States. The Resolution also warned that the developments in Hungary could represent an emerging systemic threat to the Rule of Law in that state.

(b)   The Commission Framework

Despite the EP's activity, the Commission waited for a call to act to come from the national governments. In 2003, the Commission itself had reviewed Article 7 TEU, but its communication[28] was not continued. Driven by the urgency of the Hungarian case, national governments first constructed the case for increased EU involvement and then identified the Commission as the actor to propose new instruments. In September 2012, an intergovernmental group of Foreign Affairs ministers, the *Future of Europe Group*, called for the strengthening of the mechanisms for ensuring respect for the fundamental values under Article 2 TEU.[29] Later on, a different group of ministers (the Danish, Finnish, Dutch and German Foreign Affairs Ministers) issued a Joint Letter on March 2013 which called for a new mechanism to safeguard fundamental values of the EU and secure compliance and for the Commission to take an increased role in it.[30] The Council of Ministers took notice of the Joint Letter[31] and it later discussed the issue (June 2013) at the Justice and Home Affairs Council and called on the Commission to take forward the debate (in line with the treaties) on how to tackle the issue.[32]

---

[28] European Commission, Communication from the Commission to the Council and the European Parliament on Article 7 of the Treaty on European Union Respect for and Promotion of the Values on Which the Union Is Based, COM/2003/0606 final.

[29] '[A] new, light mechanism should be introduced enabling the Commission to draw up a report in the case of concrete evidence of violations of the values under Article 2 of the TEU and to make recommendations or refer the matter to the Council. It should only be triggered by an apparent breach in a member state of fundamental values or principles, like the rule of law'. Future of Europe Group (2012) Final report of the Future of Europe Group 17 September 2012, 1–8.

[30] Available at www.Ministerie van Buitlendlandse Zaken brief-aan-europese-commissie-over-opzetten-rechtsstatelijkheidsmechanisme%20(1).pdf.

[31] See Council of the European Union, Press Release 3235th Council meeting General Affairs Luxembourg, 22 April 2013 www.consilium.europa.eu/uedocs/cms_Data/docs/pressdata/EN/genaff/136915.pdf.

[32] Council conclusions on fundamental rights and rule of law and on the Commission 2012 Report on the Application of the Charter of Fundamental Rights of the European Union Justice and Home Affairs Council meeting Luxembourg, 6 and 7 June 2013

Encouraged by both Council and EP[33] demands for action, the Commission reacted. Barroso proposed the development of better instruments for securing respect for Union values in 2012[34] and later in 2013 for a robust European mechanism to be 'activated as in situations where there is a serious, systemic risk to the Rule of Law'.[35] Former Commission Vice-President Viviane Reding also noticed the shortcomings in the available instruments for addressing breaches in the Rule of Law and announced that the Commission would present a new policy communication, which could be politically endorsed by the European Council and the European Parliament.[36] The Commission included 'the Rule of Law' among its consultation process on justice (the *Assises de la Justice*). The discussion paper on the Rule of Law[37] argued that 'a better developed set of instruments is needed, going beyond the alternatives of "soft power" of political persuasion and the "nuclear option" of Article 7'. This perception, also expressed by Barroso and recurrent in Commission and other analysis, located the position of the new instrument: before the preventive stage of Article 7 TEU procedure.

In March 2014, the Commission delivered its Communication proposing a new framework to strengthen the Rule of Law.[38] The Commission justified its move since current EU mechanisms and procedures have not always been appropriate to ensuring an effective and timely response to

Doc.10168/13, Brussels, 29 May 2013. http://data.consilium.europa.eu/doc/document/ST-10168-2013-INIT/en/pdf.

[33] The Tavares Resolution had invited the Commission to implement and if necessary update its 2003 communication on Article 7 TEU and to draw up a detailed proposal for a swift and independent monitoring mechanism and an early-warning system.

[34] He argued for the need of a better developed set of instruments which would fit in the space that exists at present between the Commission infringement procedure as guardian of the Treaties, and the Article 7 TEU procedure. J. M. D. Barroso, 'State of the Union 2012 Address', Plenary session of the European Parliament (Strasbourg: 12 September, 2012) SPEECH/12/596. http://europa.eu/rapid/press-release_SPEECH-12-596_en.htm.

[35] J. M. D. Barroso, 'State of the Union address 2013', Plenary session of the European Parliament (Strasbourg: 1 September, 2013) SPEECH/13/684. http://europa.eu/rapid/press-release_SPEECH-13-684_en.htm.

[36] V. Reding, 'The EU and the Rule of Law – What Next?', Centre for European Policy Studies (Brussels: 4 September, 2013) SPEECH/13/677. http://europa.eu/rapid/press-release_SPEECH-13-677_es.htm. See the criticism of J. Cornides, 'The European Union: Rule of Law or Rule of Judges?', (2013) *EJIL Talk* 11, www.ejiltalk.org/the-european-union-rule-of-law-or-rule-of-judges/.

[37] European Commission, Assises de la Justice, 'Discussion Paper 4: Rule of Law', http://ec.europa.eu/justice/events/assises-justice-2013/files/rule_of_law_en.pdf.

[38] European Commission, Communication from the Commission to the European Parliament and the Council 'A new EU Framework to Strengthen the Rule of Law' COM(2014) 158 final/2 (Brussels, 19 March 2014).

threats to the Rule of Law, and this forced the Commission and the EU to find *ad hoc* solutions. This reasoning and the Commission proposals closely mirrored the suggestions of the four Ministers' letter.[39]

The Commission took the precaution of presenting this as a rather residual instrument: it would be activated only in cases of *systemic threat* to the Rule of Law in Member States, and it would operate only when national mechanisms cease to operate effectively, thus constructing it as a subsidiary mechanism. The *Framework* does not substitute any existing instruments, and it rather complements the existing Article 258 TFEU (infringement) and Article 7 TEU procedures.[40] The Framework contained three main elements: the definition of the situations which would activate the procedure, the identification of the principles grounding action and the procedure's stages. With respect to the situations to ground action, these responded to the idea of 'systemic threats' (for which the Commission referred to consolidated case-law definitions)[41] excluding individual breaches of fundamental rights or miscarriages of justice. However, the idea of 'systemic threat' remains undefined, and this has elicited calls for further clarification.[42] The Commission identified the following four principles: finding a solution through dialogue with the Member State concerned, ensuring an objective and thorough assessment of the situation, respecting the principle of equal treatment and indicating swift and concrete actions.

Finally, the Commission designed a three-stage process: assessment, recommendation and follow-up. The assessment is perhaps the more salient novelty: during this stage, the Commission would gather information and would initiate a political dialogue with the Member State concerned. Exchanges and dialogue would remain confidential with the expectation that the duty of sincere cooperation would prevent any further and/or irreversible measures by the member state and will secure cooperation. Kochenov and Pech have argued that this confidential nature avoids naming and shaming which would be a recipe for ineffective outcomes.[43]

---

[39] *Ibid.*

[40] For a more complete overview, see D. Kochenov, and L. Pech, 'Upholding the Rule of Law in the EU: On the Commission's "Pre-Article 7" Procedure as a Timid Step in the Right Direction', EUI Working Papers No. 2015/24, RSCAS. They conclude that the Commission's mechanism may be reasonably described as anything but revolutionary.

[41] The Commission referred to Joined cases C-411/10 and 493/10 *N.S.* ECLI:EU:C:2011:865, paras 94 and 106; and Case C-4/11 *Germany* v. *Kaveh Puid* ECLI:EU:C:2013:740, para. 36.

[42] See the Meijers Committee (quoted in Kochenov and Pech, 'Upholding the Rule of Law in the EU') which called for clearly defining this concept.

[43] Kochenov and Pech, 'Upholding the Rule of Law in the EU'.

If the first stage does not produce the results sought, the Commission would activate the second one: a 'Rule of Raw recommendation' which would identify the source of concerns and recommends that the Member State should address them. The Commission could also recommend specific measures. Commissioner Reding explicitly argued that Article 7 TEU could be interpreted on the model of the infringement procedure (Article 258 TFEU).[44] She advocated a proactive stance modelled on the existing infringement procedure: it chose to precede the reasoned opinion with a letter of formal notice, a kind of formalised first warning by which to present concerns to a Member State and give it the opportunity to submit its observations.[45] Finally, the follow-up stage leads to the possibility of activating one of the mechanisms of Article 7 TEU, although this did not result in any way automatically from previous stages. The Commission thus responded to the joint letter's concerns by locating the mechanism between lack of action and the Article 7 TEU nuclear option.

The Commission explicitly established its competence *ratione materiae*: 'there are situations of concern which fall outside the scope of EU law and therefore cannot be considered as a breach of obligations under the Treaties but still pose a systemic threat to the rule of law [. . .] Article 7, though, is not confined to areas covered by EU law, but empowers the EU to intervene with the purpose of protecting the rule of law also in areas where Member States act autonomously'.[46] Moreover, the Commission also appealed to its general power to issue recommendations.[47] However, the Commission remained cautious since the Communication (which contained the Framework) did not specify a particular legally binding character or legal value for the Framework and did not commit the Commission to specific future actions.

(c)   Governmental and Council Reactions

Being a Commission's response to a governmental demand, Member State support could have been expected. The Dutch government did endorse most of the recommendations of the Dutch Advisory Council for Foreign Affairs (AIV) Report recognising that the Commission initiatives

---

[44] Reding, 'The EU and the Rule of Law – What Next?'.   [45] *Ibid.*
[46] European Commission, 'A new EU Framework to Strengthen the Rule of Law'.
[47] V. Reding 'A New EU Framework to Safeguard the Rule of Law in the European Union', Presentation at the General Affairs Council (Brussels: 18 March, 2014) Speech 14/228.

and peer review could work together.[48] However, the UK government criticised the proposal arguing that a new Rule of Law mechanism was not needed as lobbying and dialogue served well to address the recent concerns on the issue. The British government raised two critical objections: the duplication of existing institutions and procedures to deal with the issue and the undermining of the role of Member States in the Council by the Commission's enhanced role.[49] The UK House of Commons endorsed and amplified the criticism of Commission's mechanism, adding a further point to these two concerning the uncertainty about what exactly would activate the Framework.[50]

British criticism anticipated the cool reception from the Council which came very indirectly: its Legal Service issued an Opinion which argued that the absence of solid and unambiguous Commission competence made the Commission-proposed procedure incompatible with the principle of conferral.[51] The Council Legal Service did not question the Commission's competence *ratione materiae* but denied that the legal basis for the procedures developed in the new Framework existed: according to the Council Legal Service, the use of recommendations as the basis for EU action does not permit disregarding the precise procedure and limits created by Article 7 TEU. In the absence of an explicit competence, the institutions cannot even act by means of a non-binding instrument (such as recommendations). The Council Legal Service ruled out the possible use of an alternative legal basis such as Articles 70, 241, 337 and

---

[48] See E. Hirsch Ballin, 'Mutual Trust: The Virtue of Reciprocity: Strengthening the Acceptance of the Rule of Law through Peer Review' in this volume.

[49] UK Government Review of the balance of Competences between the UK and the EU – EU enlargement (December 2014) para. 2.116: 'The Government does not accept the need for a new EU rule of law framework applying to all Member States. There are already mechanisms in place to protect EU common values and a further EU mechanism would risk undermining the clear roles for the Council and the European Council in the area'. Similarly, J.H.H. Weiler refers to the 'jurisdictional and competences appetite of the Union generally and the Commission in particular': see his chapter in this volume, p. 313.

[50] See UK House of Commons, European Scrutiny Committee Documents considered by the Committee on 7 May 2014 – Commission Communication, A new EU Framework to strengthen the Rule of Law. www.publications.parliament.uk/pa/cm201314/cmselect/cmeuleg/83-xliii/8304.htm.

[51] Council of the European Union, Opinion of the Legal Service, Commission's Communication on a new EU Framework to strengthen the Rule of Law: compatibility with the Treaties Doc 10296/14. http://data.consilium.europa.eu/doc/document/ST-10296-2014-INIT/en/pdf. Kochenov and Pech argue that the Council Legal Service's 'arguments are based on a superficial and selective reading of EU Treaties': Kochenov and Pech, 'Upholding the Rule of Law in the EU', 39.

352 TFEU. In particular, with reference to Article 241 TEFU (which empowers the Council to request the Commission to undertake studies and to submit proposals), the Council Legal Service concluded that the 'Council may wish to make use of this possibility in specific circumstances. But to build a permanent mechanism for a rule of law study and proposal facility operated by the Commission on the combined bases of Article 7 TEU and Article 241 TFEU would undermine the specific character of the procedure of Article 7(1) – particularly concerning the way it can be initiated'.[52]

In conclusion, for the Council Legal Service, 'there is no legal basis in the Treaties empowering the institutions to create a new supervision mechanism of the respect of the rule of law by the Member States, additional to what is laid down in Article 7 TEU, neither to amend, modify or supplement the procedure laid down in this Article. Were the Council to act along such lines, it would run the risk of being found to have abased its powers by deciding without a legal basis'.[53] Leaving aside the formal fact that Article 7 TEU does not explicitly require a recommendation, the Council Legal Service did not explicitly question the heart of the matter: the insertion of a political dialogue between the Commission and the affected state. The proof is that the Council Legal Service did not question the 'assessment stage' which involved precisely this kind of interaction. As for the argument that the Framework amends, supplements or modifies Article 7 TEU, it seems clear that the proposal can be regarded as a supplement but with little legal implication: it leads only to the first stage of Article 7 (i.e. Commission initiative). It therefore does not change the procedure. Moreover, in the absence of a recommendation, and as the French Roma case demonstrated, discrete Commission–Member State conversations may occur also in the absence of a clear and explicit procedure.

The opinion of the Council Legal Service seemed to close the Commission's path and question future developments. The Legal Service, however, offered an alternative solution: Member States (not the Council) could agree on a peer-review system of the functioning of the Rule of Law in member states which may also permit the participation of the Commission and other EU institutions if necessary. The basis for such a system should be an intergovernmental agreement to supplement the law of the

---

[52] Council of the European Union, Opinion of the Legal Service, Doc 10296/14.
[53] *Ibid.*

Union which should respect very clear limits: the possibility of the Union to use the powers provided in Article 7 TEU and Articles 258, 259 and 260 TFEU must be unaffected.

However, national governments opted for an even weaker option. The joint programme of the Italian, Latvian and Luxembourg Presidencies retained the issue as one of their priorities, and it declared that:

> the Council will closely accompany the future developments of a possible new framework to strengthen the Rule of Law which seeks to resolve future systemic threats to the Rule of Law in Member States before the conditions for activating the mechanism foreseen in Article 7 TEU would be met.[54]

The Italian Presidency committed itself to continue the 'work on the Commission proposal to establish a mechanism for monitoring respect for fundamental rights within the EU, in accordance with Article 7 of the Treaty on the European Union (TEU)'.[55] The Italian Presidency prepared a short paper[56] which outlined the clear limits to any eventual mechanism (respect for the principles of conferred competences and national identity and sincere cooperation) and outlined its two central elements: an exclusive role for the Council and the method of 'constructive dialogue' (which could allegedly have drawn inspiration from the human rights dialogues with third countries that the EU conducts, though with limited success).

The Council endorsed both the 'dialogue' and its own exclusive *role* under the new mechanism.[57] The Council advanced the principles for the later European Council decision: the dialogue must be constructive, non-discriminatory and should, in the first instance, focus on best practices. The Italian Presidency interpreted the conclusions more ambitiously: 'We would like to promote the debate on the issue on a regular basis, once or twice a year. We believe that this can ... prevent, rather than address,

---

[54] Council of the European Union Note, 'The future Italian, Latvian and Luxembourg Presidencies 18 month programme of the Council (1 July 2014–31 December 2015)' Brussels, 23 June 2014 11258/14. http://data.consilium.europa.eu/doc/document/ST-11258-2014-INIT/en/pdf.

[55] Italian Presidency of the Council of the European Union A Fresh Start Programme of the Italian Presidency 1 July to 31 December 2014. http://italia2014.eu/media/1349/programma_en1_def.pdf.

[56] Council of the European Union Note from Presidency to Council, 'Ensuring respect for the rule of law in the European Union', Brussels, 14 November 2014 15206/14. http://register.consilium.europa.eu/doc/srv?l=EN&f=ST%2015206%202014%20INIT.

[57] Council of the European Union, Press Release 3347th Council meeting General Affairs Brussels, 18 and 19 November 2014 15578/14, pp. 8–9. www.consilium.europa.eu/uedocs/cms_data/docs/pressdata/EN/genaff/145844.pdf.

the risks of threats to the rule of law', said State Secretary Gozi after the meeting.[58]

IV   The Council 'Dialogue' on the Rule of Law

The Council closed the institutional search for additional instruments for the present by agreeing on what allegedly is the weakest one among all previously discussed alternatives. In fact, the content of the Council agreement does not even reflect the institutional and governmental rhetoric since 2012 calling for a transformation of the institutional design for the scrutiny of the Rule of Law. In particular, the new mechanism is not explicitly (nor even implicitly!) related to Article 7 TEU provisions despite the original aim to create a short of preliminary warning mechanism for offending member states. This nuances (or even questions) the Italian Presidency's objective, as expressed in its work programme to explore a new EU Framework which 'seeks to resolve future systemic threats to the rule of law in Member States before the conditions for activating the mechanism foreseen in Article 7 TEU would be met'.[59]

The Council opted for the lowest possible level of formalisation. Firstly, the specific configuration chosen erodes institutional legitimacy, since the decision was adopted by the General Affairs Council *and the member states meeting in the framework of the Council.* This formulation underlines the intergovernmental nature of the decision and also of the procedure agree. Secondly, the Council (and Member States) have disregarded even the soft-law instruments available, such as Decisions or Declarations, and they have preferred to construct the new instrument as merely one of points in the 'conclusions'. Moreover, the level of obligation for Member States is minimal since they merely 'commit' to establishing the mechanism (but nothing on scrutiny, monitoring, exchange of information or even follow-up!). The new procedure marks a total shift towards an intergovernmental approach to the issue: the (General Affairs) Council of Ministers will gather once a year to discuss the issues, and preparation is entrusted to COREPER and the Presidency of the Council. No role is envisaged for the EP and/or the Commission, or any other EU body.

The conclusions outline, in six points, a mechanism, its principles, its limitations and some procedural aspects, all of them highly unspecific both in terms of their meaning and reach and their legal implications.

---

[58] *Ibid.*, 2.
[59] European Commission, 'A New EU Framework to Strengthen the Rule of Law'.

Specifically, the new mechanism is a 'dialogue among all Member States' whose purpose is to 'promote and safeguard the rule of law'.[60]

What a dialogue is remains very vague and imprecise. The Council can propose debating 'thematic subject matters'.[61] Ultimate consequences for the dialogue seem to be non-existent (although a pious interpretation could argue that the Council would take bold decisions); the new dialogue is deprived of any coercive power even in its softer form; and the procedure does not mention peer review or, indeed, any kind of review! Furthermore, there is no explicit obligation to make the dialogue itself or its conclusions public, thus avoiding public scrutiny and even the soft coercion mechanisms associated with naming and shaming. In an intriguing move, the European Council has entrusted the General Affairs Council with the dialogue while, traditionally, the Justice and Home Affairs Council has dealt with Rule of Law.

The Council sets three limitations for the dialogue. The first is the principle of conferred competences around whose interpretation differences exist between Commission and Council Legal Service. The second refers to the protective core of Article 4(2) TEU: the respect for the national identities of the Member States and their essential state functions. Finally, the third limit is the adherence to the principle of sincere cooperation which the European Council uses, surprisingly, in order to prevent rather than to incentivise scrutiny. In summary, the Council emphasises the guarantes for states and the best example of this excessive *guarantist* bias can be seen if we apply a literal interpretation to the first limit: respect of the principle of conferred competences could lead to the somehow ridiculous conclusion that Ministers' members cannot *dialogue* about competences which are not conferred to the EU!

The principles for debate are those distilled out of the institutional debate – objectivity, non-discrimination and equal treatment of all Member States – and the conclusions add some interesting operational principles: dialogue will proceed on a non-partisan and evidence-based approach. While the latter principle refers to some kind of fact finding to obtain evidence for the dialogue, the Council has avoided mentioning the different alternatives discussed (such as a Copenhagen commission, the Venice Commission, etc.). The Council preferred to refer to the principle of complementarity as an indirect mechanism for gathering facts: 'dialogue will be developed in a way which is complementary with other EU Institutions and International Organisations, avoiding

---

[60] See Council Conclusions, para. 1.   [61] *Ibid.*, para. 6.

duplication and taking into account existing instruments and expertise in this area'.[62]

The institutions have reacted differently to the Council mechanism. The EP held a debate on the issue on February 2015 in which almost all political groups criticised its lack of ambition and demanded further action from the Commission. The ALDE group proposed a new EU Democratic Governance Pact[63] modelled on the Stability and Growth Pact which included a European Semester for Democracy, Rule of Law and Fundamental Rights (DLR) and a DLR Scoreboard. The Commission, however, offered mixed reactions.[64] On the one hand, it stuck to the Council line and rejected the EP's demands for a new mechanism, arguing that already there are sufficient instruments. It also underlined the value of existing mechanisms such as infringement procedures. On the other hand, however, the Commission indicated its willingness to use the Framework notwithstanding the Council Legal Service's objections. Vice President Timmermans (who had signed the four Ministers' letter as Dutch Foreign Affairs minister (as he then was)) endorsed the Framework arguing that a more systematic approach was needed to avoid 'rule of law backsliding'.[65] In fact, a spokeswoman from the Commission confirmed that the Framework remained in place and could be activated if needed in November 2014.[66] At the February 2015 EP Plenary debate, the Commission added a proposal for an annual Colloquium on Fundamental Rights. In his intervention in the Plenary,[67] Timmermans outlined his approach albeit not very systematically. Firstly, he announced that he would not hesitate to use the Commission's Framework. Secondly, he also declared that Commission's approach to member states' infringements will pay special attention to rule of law-related cases. Finally, he stated

---

[62] Conclusions of the Council of the European Union, 16 December 2014, Doc. 16862/14 COR 1.

[63] The EU Democratic Governance Pact Upholding the Rule of law and Fundamental Rights ALDE initiative outline, https://d66.nl/content/uploads/sites/2/2015/01/ALDE-Democratic-Governance.pdf

[64] Commission Statement: EU Framework for Democracy, Rule of Law and Fundamental Rights, Speech of First Vice-President, Frans Timmermans, to the European Parliament, Strasbourg, 12 February 2015. http://europa.eu/rapid/press-release_SPEECH-15-4402_en.htm.

[65] Answers to the European Parliament, Questionnaire to the Commissioner-Designate Frans Timmermans, Question 6: http://ec.europa.eu/about/juncker-commission/docs/2014-ep-hearings-reply-timmermans_en.pdf.

[66] V. Pop, 'Hungary Triggers Rule of Law Debates in EU Council' *EU Observer* (20 November, 2014) https://euobserver.com/political/126592.

[67] Timmermans' speech to the European Parliament (Strasbourg: 12 February 2015).

that the Commission would act in an unbiased manner, will assess each case fairly and will treat all states equally. However, Timmermans rejected the EP's demands for additional instruments.

V   Conclusion

Solid normative reasons recommend an increased role for the EU in monitoring member states compliance with the Rule of Law. Mutual recognition and mutual trust demand that EU member states scrupulously comply with the Rule of Law. The all affected principle justifies an interest from all EU citizens and member states in maintaining healthy Rule of Law systems in each state. Finally, a consistency requirement adds weight to the normative case which goes beyond punctual episodes. Despite several institutional proposals, the EU has settled for the softest of all. This new EU mechanism contains a number of strong limitations and thus a strong intergovernmental bias. It also lacks specific content leaving how, what, when and whether to act to the complete discretion of the Member States. It has no coercive value, and it fails to add a new stage harnessed to the already existing preventive and corrective phases of Article 7 TEU. Under these conditions, no significant addition has emerged after intense demands on the issue. In any case, crafting a procedure for Rule of Law compliance scrutiny (and this applies to Article 7 TEU) requires a cautious construction of its design in order to avoid unexpected and unwanted effects.

2

Beyond Legality – Before Democracy

Rule of Law Caveats in the EU Two-Level System

GIANLUIGI PALOMBELLA[*]

I Introduction

If one seeks a distinctive notion of the Rule of Law relevant to the European Union as an autonomous entity, the main and current meaning which can be found is that it coincides with the idea of a legal order, in its existence and operation. In truth, the very fact of Europe as a legal order of its own *is* an achievement, and it has meant the overcoming of an indefinite number of political, social and legal obstacles. At the same time, it posited the premises for a progressive *iter*, heading towards unique features, neither of a state nor of a common international law entity. The institution of a specific organisation of legality meant the framing of new forms of relationships, ordered through the law, among the European states. However, it is not only a new interface between pre-existing orders, it is a new level of order with the ambition to govern states, peoples and individuals.[1]

The Rule of Law has been always a *fil rouge* in the history of the European project, even before[2] its first appearance in the Treaty of Maastricht,[3]

---

[*] Professor of Law, University of Parma and Scuola Superiore Sant'Anna, Pisa.
[1] For this, see Case 26/62 *NV Algemene Transporten Expeditie Onderneming van Gend en Loos* v. *Nederlandse Administratie der Belastingen* ECLI:EU:C:1963:1 [1963] ECR 1 (special English edition). See also R. Schütze, *From Dual to Cooperative Federalism* (Oxford: Oxford University Press, 2009).
[2] G. Bebr, *Rule of Law within the European Communities* (Brussels: Université Libre de Bruxelles, 1965); A. Arnull, 'The Rule of Law in the European Union', in A. Arnull, and D. Wincott (eds.), *Accountability and Legitimacy in the European Union* (Oxford: Oxford University Press, 2002).
[3] See the Preamble 'CONFIRMING their attachment to the principles of liberty, democracy and respect for human rights and fundamental freedoms and of the Rule of Law' and Art. J(1) '[. . .] to develop and consolidate democracy and the Rule of Law, and respect for human rights and fundamental freedoms'.

and eventually in the present form provided by Article 2 TEU: 'The Union is founded on the values of respect for human dignity, freedom, democracy, equality, the Rule of Law and respect for human rights, including the rights of persons belonging to minorities'. Its landmark invocation – and judicial application – in the ECJ *Les Verts* judgment famously explains that 'the EEC Treaty, albeit concluded in the forms of an international agreement, none the less constitutes the constitutional charter of a Community based on the Rule of Law'.[4] The import of such an assumption is that the Community is 'based on the Rule of Law, inasmuch as neither its Member States nor its Institutions can avoid a review of the question whether the measures adopted by them are in conformity with the basic constitutional charter, the Treaty. [...] [T]he Treaty established a complete system of legal remedies and procedures designed to permit the Court of Justice to review the legality of measures adopted by the institutions'.[5] Unsurprisingly, the connection has been made between this meaning of the Rule of Law and the doctrines of direct effect[6] and supremacy,[7] at least insofar as a community legal order with a two-level system could hardly be expected to work without them. This means that both supremacy and direct effect are being interpreted as pillars of a full-fledged order whose instruments enable legality to work. In the ECJ's words in Costa: 'the law stemming from the treaty, an independent source of law, could not, because of its special and original nature, be overridden by domestic legal provisions, however framed, *without being deprived of its character as community law and without the legal basis of the community itself being called into question*'.[8] The main sense of the Rule of Law thereby achieved at the level of the European Union revolves around the value of legality including judicial review as a tool *vis-à-vis* non-compliance.[9] It must be noted that the strength of these concurring doctrines is supported and reinforced by the

---

[4] Case 294/83 *Partie Ecologiste 'Les Verts'* v. *Parliament* ECLI:EU:C:1986:166 [1986] ECR 1339, para. 23. Cf. Opinion 1/91 *EEA Agreement* ECLI:EU:C:1991:490 [1991] ECR I-6097.
[5] *Les Verts*, para. 23.   [6] *Van Gend en Loos*.
[7] Case 6/44 *Flaminio Costa* v. *ENEL* ECLI:EU:C:1964:66 [1964] ECR 585.
[8] Emphasis added. *Costa* v. *ENEL*, p. 594.
[9] This can also be read in *Kadi*: Joined Cases C-402 and 415/05P *Kadi & Al Barakaat International Foundation* v. *Council & Commission* ECLI:EU:C:2008:461 [2008] ECR I-6351, para. 281: 'it is to be borne in mind that the Community is based on the Rule of Law, *inasmuch as* neither its Member States nor its institutions can avoid review of the conformity of their acts with the basic constitutional charter, the EC Treaty, which established a complete system of legal remedies and procedures designed to enable the Court of Justice to review the legality of acts of the institutions (Case 294/83 *Les Verts* v. *Parliament* [1986] ECR 1339, paragraph 23)' (emphasis added). In this same sense, see D. Kochenov,

institution of the 'preliminary reference'. With regard to *Van Gend en Loos*, Joseph Weiler notes the importance of 'the confluence of the doctrine of direct effect with the (unintended and at the time unappreciated) genius of the preliminary reference system. Take away the preliminary reference and direct effect and a transnational system loses much of its impact'.[10]

II   What Rule of Law?

The ideal evoked as the Rule of Law in such an order – gathering diverse peoples reasonably jealous of their own normative sovereignty – has been essentially identified with the aspiration of becoming a community of law, well established, effective and obeyed.

Legality, certainty and predictability encapsulate the sense of this kind of conception of the Rule of Law. However, in one venerable version, the 'Burkean' mode, respect for the law is also more than mere formalism and is held to protect the substantive values, a nation's achievements. It relies on the link between constituencies, their ethos and the law. It conceives of the Courts as reflecting the whole experience of a nation.[11] Similarly, lessons from de Montesquieu's *Esprit des Lois* cherish the laws as necessary relations among things.[12] The law has to correspond to what it must regulate, not *vice versa*. To protect the 'Rule of Law in this jurisdiction', as the Supreme Court (in the US) usually solemnly calls it, means to abide by 'our' law *vis-à-vis* external or internal threats to our social, moral and political achievements.

For this conception of the Rule of Law to be credibly at the basis of the European emphasis on 'a community based on the Rule of Law', a

---

'The EU Rule of Law: Cutting Paths through Confusion', 2(1) (2009) *Erasmus Law Review* 5.

[10] And: 'Put differently, there is I contend a huge difference between, say, a ruling of the International Court of Justice (ICJ, the World Court) that a certain international norm at issue before it produces direct effect, but this ruling takes place in the normal procedural and substantive context of intergovernmental litigation and state responsibility, and an identical ruling of the ECJ (the European Court) within the procedural context of the preliminary reference'. (J. H. H. Weiler, 'Van Gend en Loos: The Individual as Subject and Object and the Dilemma of European Legitimacy', 12 (2014) *IJCL* 94, 95).

[11] O. W. Holmes, in *Missouri* v. *Holland* (1920) 252 U.S. 416, 433; and see R. Post, 'The Challenge of Globalization to American Public Law Scholarship' 2 (2001) *Theoretical Inquiries in Law* 323, 326 et seq.

[12] C. L. de Secondat, Baron de Montesquieu, *The Spirit of Laws* (Cincinnati: Thomas Nugent, R. Clarke & Co., 1873), Preface at p. XXXII.

fabric of feelings and shared values should develop at the European level, one which might even approximate the sense of legal patriotism which once stemmed from the unity of a nation. Nonetheless, and even in such a case, this conception would simply mean to require that law and order be obeyed, either for their own sake, like in some formalist conceptions, or because of the community values which they can safeguard.

This way of thinking essentially shifts the issue from the Rule of Law to the respect for the laws of a legal system mentioned. However, the two things should not be conceived of as merely coincident. The Rule of Law cannot mean just the self-referentiality of a legal order.

The risks of such a view can be observed in a famous example, the judgement of the former Court of First Instance in *Kadi*, which maintained that the Rule of Law, prevailing in the International Law jurisdiction, required the European institutions to abide by the UN Security Council (UNHCR) resolution depriving Mr Kadi of his rights to defence, to a judge and to property, and failed to think of the Rule of Law as an independent criterion for scrutinising the international legal order itself.[13] The same stance, *mutatis mutandis*, was adopted by the ECJ, when it carefully assumed that 'any judgment given by the Community judicature deciding that a Community measure intended to give effect to such a [UNSC] resolution is contrary to a higher Rule of Law in the Community legal order would not entail any challenge to the primacy of that resolution in international law'.[14]

The invocation of the Rule of Law is at risk of being transformed into an opportunity for making 'our' own legal system a fragment of a pluralist Babel of meanings, and such an invocation would then support a case for separation and autonomy.

This fate is inherent to any circumstances where different legal orders, however integrated they may be – even within the European Union – diverge, for example on the interpretation of the soundness and legality of their legislative or constitutional norms. It is rather naïve or disingenuous to assume that some invocations of 'our own' Rule of Law are credible and others are not; it is rather contingent on how many or how few 'essential values' one system thereby locks from external intrusion. The

---

[13] General Court (then CFI) *Kadi* v. *Council of the EU and Commission of the EC* (T-315/01) [2005] ECR II-3649. See also G. Palombella, 'The Rule of Law Beyond the State: Failures, Promises and Theory' 7 (2009) *I-CON* 442–67.

[14] Joined Cases C-402 and 415/05P *Kadi & Al Barakaat*, para. 288.

point is instead the nature and the content of a Rule of Law principle, regardless of where it is predicated – in the EU law or elsewhere – and despite the fact that in most occasions, as said above, the EU has not done much to elaborate the notion in a more mature mode, the existence and functioning of a legal order is only the precondition for the ideal of the Rule of Law to be pursued.[15] Although compliance and certainty are necessary for a legal order to exist, they are hardly sufficient for the Rule of Law to be achieved.

Consequently, the Rule of Law requires something that apparently goes beyond the requisites for efficient legality standards, and its ideal hints to a notion which – although capable of elaboration by the concurrence of many – cannot be simply reduced to a jurisdiction or a system relative meaning. On this premise, the Rule of Law should fit the transnational level, inasmuch as it can afford the transitive nature of its features.

***

We should neither rely on the belief that the Rule of Law is already universally agreed upon nor accept that its pretensions are unbounded. Some, albeit briefly sketched, reconstruction of the Rule of Law ideal, its meaning and import is therefore in order. As I argued elsewhere,[16] the Rule of Law means more than compliance with rules.[17] Such a conception as 'a law of rules' to be complied with bears however the principled fight against arbitrary power. At this level of meaning, as it is commonly noted, Joseph Raz enriched the set of Rule of Law requirements by elaborating on those first suggested by Lon Fuller, regardless of the moral value which the latter recognised in their resulting effect.[18] But it is true that

---

[15] See, in this regard, D. Kochenov, G. de Búrca and A. Williams (eds.), *Europe's Justice Deficit* (Oxford: Hart Publishing, 2015).

[16] G. Palombella, 'The Rule of Law as an Institutional Ideal' in L. Morlino and G. Palombella (eds.), *Rule of law and Democracy: Internal and External Issues* (Leiden and Boston: Brill, 2010).

[17] For such a view, see instead A. Scalia, 'The Rule of Law as a Law of Rules', 56 (1989) *University of Chicago Law Review* 1175.

[18] Generality, clarity, promulgation, stability, consistency between rules and behaviours, non-retroactivity, non-contradictory rules, and not requiring the impossible: L. Fuller, *The Morality of Law*, 2nd edn (Yale: Yale University Press, 1969), Chapter 2. About the moral value implied in Fullerian requirements see, A. Marmor, 'The Rule of Law and Its Limits', 23 (2004) *Law and Philosophy* 1, 39 et seq. See also N. MacCormick, 'Natural Law and the Separation of Law and Morals' in R. P. George (ed.), *Natural Law Theory: Contemporary Essays* (Oxford: Clarendon Press, 1992), p. 123 et seq.

the Rule of Law is conceived of differently on a scale of degrees, and sometimes we are recommended to extend the concept to include the protection of fundamental rights or the full content of a liberal democratic or welfare state, etc.[19] However, on one hand, as Martin Krygier remarked, this 'anatomic'[20] hypothesis overlooks the central point of the Rule of Law, which is its teleology instead of its alleged requisites; on the other hand, listing requirements, be they formal, procedural or substantive constitutionalist and democratic, seems questionable, partly because they can either end up equating the Rule of Law with the *functional* efficiency of a legal order *as such*, or on the contrary, because they require the Rule of Law ideal to match one of its possible historical and institutional incarnations, in order to incorporate some extraneous, though valuable, objectives, such as the democratic control of power or the satisfaction of the material needs of individuals and the like. The pursuit of extraneous goals which typically inspire different spheres such as politics, ethics and economy is what Joseph Raz probably had in mind when he distinguished the Rule of Law from the 'rule of the good law', as he aptly dubbed the stance taken by Hayek in conflating his liberal market economy ideal with the very definition of the Rule of Law.[21]

The Rule of Law prescribes only *legal* features. It does not ask for the law to bear some specific content, the good law, nor does it claim to dictate the internal form of the realm of power (for example that power be democratically organised). The Rule of Law means respect for a legally desirable situation, in which – in the pursuit of the fundamental aspiration of liberty which is the root of the notion – dominating law appears to be contestable, as a matter of law, on the basis of some independent legal force and institutional structures in the interests of everyone. Let me briefly explain this assumption.

In general, an enlightening route should be a faithful reflection of the history of the 'Rule of Law' ideal and the ways down which it has developed at least since the thirteenth century, through say, A.V. Dicey's influential

---

[19] See P. P. Craig, 'Formal and Substantive Conceptions of the Rule of Law: An Analytical Framework' (1997) *Public Law*, 467; and also T. R. S. Allan, *Constitutional Justice* (Oxford: Oxford University Press, 2001).

[20] M. Krygier, 'The Rule of Law: Legality, Teleology, Sociology', in G. Palombella and N. Walker (eds.), *Relocating the Rule of Law* (Oxford: Hart Publishing, 2009).

[21] J. Raz, 'The Rule of Law and Its Virtue', in J. Raz (ed.), *The Authority of Law: Essays on Law and Morality* (Oxford: Clarendon Press, 1979), p. 227; F. Hayek, *The Road to Serfdom* (London: Routledge, 1944); F. Hayek, *The Constitution of Liberty* (Chicago: Chicago University Press, 1960); and W. Scheuermann, 'The Rule of Law and the Welfare State: Toward a new Synthesis', 22 (1994) *Politics and Society* 195.

account in the nineteenth century to the present debate:[22] as a general
caveat it should be born in mind that the Rule of Law ideal through this
itinerary refers to features which the law is desired to embody, mainly in
order to ensure protection from a monopolising legal power and on the
basis of some positive law which is factually and legally located beyond
the reach of the sovereign and his whim. What the English tradition provided, by counterbalancing sovereign law with judicial precedents, the
common law, *consuetudo* and conventions belonging to the law of the
land, had been barely available in the European continent, where it had
been substantively erased by the experience of codification and the dogma
of legislative supremacy. Records can be found which show the Rule of
Law rationale as one referred to (and based on) a *duality of law*, where
some other *positive* law, beyond the sovereign's law, exists and escapes the
purview of the dominant exercise of sovereign jurisgenerative power. In its
medieval roots, the law was deemed to be only partly 'gubernaculum', that
is, under the will of the sovereign. It was also partly 'jurisdictio', where the
fundamental laws of the land lie beyond the sovereign's reach, as Charles
McIlwain reminded us.[23] That *duality* is visible in later times, mainly
in the constitutional couple of rights and legislation as terms endowed
with equal standing. We can safely state in continental Europe that this
achievement, the granting of equal force to rights before legislation, was
achieved only recently, following the constitutional restructuring of the
legal state in the latter half of the twentieth century. However, this rationale reveals a *fil rouge*, a scheme of balance, of legal non-domination,
which can have varied institutional incarnations. The pre-constitutional
nineteenth and twentieth century *Rechtsstaat* in continental Europe can be
shown as in itself a non-arbitrary, rule-based, hierarchically rigorous one
where the administration of power was submitted to legislation alone, and
nonetheless far from the distinctive rationale of the English 'Rule of Law'
root.[24] The latter in turn prevents sovereign legislation from being the
sole source of the law, compared to the legislative power of the continental
European state. The true reason why a sovereign's action can be neither
'unlimited' nor 'unbridled', is that beyond the free and legitimate exercise

---

[22] A. V. Dicey, *Introduction to the Study of the Law of the Constitution*, 8th edn (London: Macmillan, 1915). Cf. Palombella, 'The Rule of Law as an Institutional Ideal'.

[23] C. McIlwain, *Constitutionalism: Ancient and Modern* (Ithaca: Cornell University Press, 1947), pp. 67–92.

[24] See G. Palombella, 'The Rule of Law and Its Core', in G. Palombella and N. Walker, (eds.), *Re-Locating the Rule of Law* (Oxford: Hart Publishing, 2009).

of 'gubernaculum', a 'jurisdictio' aspect of law has developed positively and lies beyond its reach.[25]

For these very reasons, it is a likewise inadequate description of this normative ideal which quintessentially focuses on its procedural[26] quality. No doubt, procedure and non-arbitrariness could go hand-in-hand. Nonetheless, even if procedures did enable participation, empower citizens and enhance their dignity, this can hardly be different from the listing of requisites for a legal order to properly function (Fuller) or from instilling democratic presuppositions through procedures. Moreover, in the absence of the characterising feature of the Rule of Law, procedures would only achieve the good (if any) which can be provided through the substantively unbridled choices of the sovereigns.[27] If the Rule of Law does not in truth afford any specific content to its posited norms (unless it slips into being the 'rule of the good law'),[28] nonetheless, it requires another law (be it procedural or substantive, or both) where separate and independent sources can set counter-limits and guarantees. It is this equilibrium which fosters both the right and duty of the sovereign to rule, and justice, safeguards of individual expectations and minority rights. It can thus be said that the ideal refers naturally to preventing monopoly over the sources of law, and the subsequent *legal domination*. It refers to and is in need of the existence, within a legal order, of some *other* positive law which lies somehow separately to one side, either belonging, say, in the 'common law' as in the English tradition, or receiving a supra-legislative guarantee by a constitution and so forth, whatever institutional

---

[25] In the case of the constitutional liberal democratic state, owing to the equal force ultimately granted by way of a constitution to rights and other principles *and* the democratic principle of legislation.

[26] J. Waldron, 'The Rule of Law and the Importance of Procedure', in G. E Fleming (ed.), *Getting to the Rule of Law* (New York: New York University Press, 2011), p. 3.

[27] *Ibid.* (in an unobjectionable comment on Waldron's article); R. West, 'The Limits of Process', in G. E. Fleming (ed.), *Getting to the Rule of Law* (New York: New York University Press, 2011), p. 42: 'Procedural justice, in other words, can be *demoralizing*. After all, you had your day in court, what's to complain of? The procedural justice, then, strengthens the system by legitimating it, all the more so in an unjust regime. If that effect – the legitimising effect, for short – is substantial, then the procedural justice of a trial in an unjust regime may perversely increase the overall injustice of the regime, making it all the more invulnerable to change, whether through politics, revolution or subterfuge. A legal system that abides by the Rule of Law, where the latter is defined by reference to procedural criteria, is not necessarily thereby more just. When it isn't, it's not clear where the value of all that procedure lies, other than in the fodder it provides modernist writers'.

[28] J. Raz, 'The Rule of Law and Its Virtues', in J. Raz (ed.), *The Authority of Law: Essays on Law and Morality* (Oxford: Clarendon Press, 1979), p. 267.

instruments might be required from time to time for that result to be achieved. For instance, the sheer fact that some rights are actually provided by law is not determinant or decisive for the Rule of Law to be realised. The issue of the Rule of Law depends on the existence of an autonomous guarantee of rights, norms and any other principles of law, one that would defend them from being legally cancelled on the basis of some sovereign legislative authority. The point in such a tension and balance between the two sides through the existence of an 'independent' law, is to prevent the more powerful rule-maker from modifying it in a legally legitimate way.[29]

III Rule of Law in the Extra-State Setting

Of course, as the concept concerns the composition and sources of law, not the state and its scheme as such, it can be referred to in a transnational setting as readily as in the domestic order. Indeed, in the supra-state arena, its normative meaning persists, unless one does conflate an ideal concerning the law into a notion centred upon the state and some of its special characters (as it is done by translating the Rule of Law into *Stato di diritto*, and its equivalents). What is distinctive is not the limitation of the state through the law, but more properly the *limitation of law through law*.

In the supranational sphere it seems quite straightforward to assert what should be called the *Rule by law* dimension, an insistence which is premised on a sometimes justified prejudice in favour of the good values that the international order holds *vis-à-vis* reluctant states; and not much differently, the same presupposition supports the primacy of European law over its Member States, thereby simply requiring addressees, states in particular, to 'obey the law'. As suggested: 'They should treat it as authoritative and let it guide and constrain their actions'.[30] Such an interpretation possibly misunderstands the main problem of the Rule of Law and risks being unfaithful to its import, since it overlooks the contingency of the good embodied in the rulings of any supranational actor. It also sets aside

---

[29] Likewise, such a guarantee should simultaneously ensure the full jurisgenerative governmental power to pursue its political visions of the common good, without being undermined in its own sphere by some tyranny of traditional forms of inherited legality and the like.

[30] M. Kumm, 'International Law in National Courts: The International Rule of Law and the Limits of the Internationalist Model', 44 (2003) *Virginia Journal of International Law* 22.

the Hobbesian[31] truth behind the idea that the sovereign be *subject to its law*: that is, the fact that sovereigns are *ceteris paribus* entitled to make the law themselves and to change it at their will, all the more so in the international environment. In this sense, such a Rule *by* law concept hardly makes sense of the motto, *the Rule of Law, not men*.[32] If one follows the reconstruction of the concept, for instance by considering a line drawn by scholars such as Haskins, Goodhart and Reid,[33] the Rule of Law contrasts with the rule *by* law,[34] excluding thereby a simply instrumental use of law from being an appropriate interpretation. On the contrary, at issue is precisely that the law is constructed in an institutional context where it is simply not up to the most powerful Masters of Treaties, or to the omnipotent global regulators, and there is a legal aspect that the latter have no authority to reverse. This could hold true, of course, in any supranational order built upon some fundamental primary laws, principles and rights deemed of higher rank, and working in fact as criteria of recognition of legality and validity of other norms. It can at the same time appear in a two-level system, depending on the legal capacity of the plurality of the member states' orders to interact confrontationally: that is, on the basis of legal reasons, balancing, proportionality, margin of appreciation, equal protection and similar argumentative *topoi*, operating, if need be, in the place of a hierarchically ordered formalist monism. This all the more is the case, in an international environment where supranational entities – or worse still, a number of politically deracinated 'global regimes', unaccountable to their addressees[35] – purport to regulate an indefinite array of peoples, individuals and states, and pursue straightforwardly some field-related and one-sided normative power.

Of course, this claim about the logics entrenched in the Rule of Law does not match the narratives which are content with listing the features that the law needs to embody in order *to be law*, thereby overlooking much

---

[31] T. Hobbes, *Leviathan* (Oxford: Blackwell, [1651] 1946), Chapter 46, part 11.

[32] More about this in G. Palombella, 'The Rule of Law as an Institutional Ideal'.

[33] A. L. Goodhart, 'The Rule of Law and Absolute Sovereignty', 106 (1958) *University of Pennsylvania Law Review* 947; P. Reid, *Rule of Law: The Jurisprudence of Liberty in the Seventeenth and Eighteenth Centuries* (DeKalb: North Illinois University Press, 2004); G. L. Haskins, 'Executive Justice and the Rule of Law: Some Reflections on Thirteenth-Century England', 30 (1955) *Speculum* 529.

[34] Such description of the Rule of Law as a rule *by* law is common: for example, M. Kumm, 'International Law in National Courts'; or S. Beaulac, 'The Rule of Law in International Law Today', in G. Palombella and N. Walker, *Relocating the Rule of Law*.

[35] Cf. G. Palombella 'Global legislation and Its Discontents', in J. Petman and R. Livoja, *International Law Making* (London: Routledge, 2013).

of the issue in question, not least the problem of the monopolisation and instrumentalisation of the law.

IV   Diagnoses and Justification

Although in the records of the European Union there is scant trace of such a complex manifestation of the Rule of Law, its attachment to it should be taken seriously, as should the autonomy of the Rule of Law within a provision like Article 2 TEU, which mentions the Rule of Law alongside human rights and democracy. Of course, a Rule of Law crash in a Member State is correctly identified through structural deficiencies. However and accordingly, their repair is impossible *only* thanks to the diligence of a Court, a supranational commission, and the like. It can affect the identity of a legal order, and as a consequence, liberty, democracy, rights and everything else. Although the cure and the pursuit of new equilibria do not come from the simple impulse of a Court's sentencing, a Court can admittedly anticipate and foster them, and arguably, this can work directly on some of the consequences of the problem, firstly – as András Jakab[36] would have it – by protecting fundamental rights.

Serious indications of a Rule of Law crisis on the Continent have been described in some circumstances and regret has been voiced at the insufficiency of the process provided by Article 7 TEU,[37] which leaves too much to *political* discretion and negotiation; as it is claimed, the enforcement of the Rule of Law throughout the Member States lacks an efficient safeguarding tool.

It must be noted, though, that the absence, the risks or the gross violation of the Rule of Law in a country will often be more than what the EU is capable of managing as an administrative issue. It could even be considered a governance problem, of the kind that can be inquired into through a set of means-efficiency indicators which experts, committees, commissions, agencies and epistemic authorities can straightforwardly identify and apply. But simply putting a state on trial or submitting it to economic sanctions, in the neutral form of governance edicts, could be necessary perhaps, in one way or another way, but still be disappointing: does what we can expect 'our' European Union to do end here?

---

[36] See A. Jakab, 'The EU Charter of Fundamental Rights as the Most Promising Way of Enforcing the Rule of Law against EU Member States' in this volume.

[37] Accordingly, suggestions are proposed on how to resolve the issue. See for example the chapters by K. L. Scheppele, 'Enforcing the Basic Principles of EU Law through Systemic Infringement Procedures' and J.-W. Müller, 'Protecting the Rule of Law (and Democracy!) in the EU: The Idea of a Copenhagen Commission' – among others – in this volume.

Again, gross infringement of Article 2 TEU should mean that a country has lost its ability to manage the tension between *gubernaculum* and *jurisdictio*, it has caused one to prevail over the other. Not that the limitation of the sovereign power is always what is needed: it can well be the reverse. In some central European countries in the recent past, *modernisation* through the law and new parliamentary legislation have been the progressive and civilising aspects, curbing and reshaping the normative fabric of a land overwhelmed by tradition, pre-modern legal institutions, ethical barriers, economic privileges and age-old cultural prejudices.[38] This can make us more cautious in simply following stereotypes, since the Rule of Law is the search for an equilibrium which must be preserved, but it is admittedly an idiosyncratic matter, and some Rule of Law factors can of themselves remain opaque to indicators.

We should bear in mind that conservatives and neo-liberals often fear the 'injection of any substantive concerns into adjudication or discretionary authority in administration' as a threat to a full, formal idealised rule of law; while radicals complain about the de-regulatory effect of legislative indeterminacy, delegation to the Executive, and the like.[39] As Martin Krygier writes: 'That suggests that not every potential source of threat to the rule of law will be equally salient in different legal orders: some will be much threatened, others less so, by the same things. It also suggests that different threats might require different defences. Not to mention that we might want to do more than ward off threats'.[40]

The proof of a Rule of Law crisis is a high threshold. This notwithstanding, in her speech[41] of September 2013, Viviane Reding, then the EU Justice Commissioner, suggested improving EU action in reinforcing the Rule of Law by allowing the CJEU to hear cases on Article 2 TEU, that is, concerning alleged breaches of the Rule of Law principle. It has been fairly noted that according to such a proposal (along with others put forward in that speech):

> the Court could henceforward hold Member States accountable not only for the breach of concrete provisions of EU law, but also of vaguely

---

[38] For a global overview of constitutional implications of the Eastern Enlargement, see W. Sadurski, *Constitutionalism and Enlargement of Europe* (Oxford: Oxford University Press, 2012).

[39] M. Krygier, 'Transformations of the Rule of Law: Legal, Liberal, and Neo-', 21 (Working Paper available in draft at www.kcl.ac.uk/law/research/centres/kjuris/papers/Transformations-krygier.pdf).

[40] *Ibid.*

[41] V. Reding, The EU and the Rule of Law – What Next?, at http://europa.eu/rapid/press-release_SPEECH-13-677_en.htm.

defined "values", which include not only the Rule of Law, but also "non-discrimination", "pluralism", "solidarity", or "tolerance".[42]

As a consequence, the CJEU would be turned into 'a judicial super-institution with nearly unlimited powers to use those vague concepts as a pretext for interfering everywhere and at all levels. This would be the end of Member States' sovereignty'.[43] The warning and the remedies have also been criticised on the basis of the contestability of the *diagnosis* on which they are premised: that is, it appears controversial that the problems which arose in France, Hungary and Romania in recent years represent structural failures of the Rule of Law.[44]

The above considerations could well lead us to appreciate instead that the handling of Article 7 TEU, and the instruments provided therein, seem to entrust the political capacity of the EU *vis-à-vis* the Member States to achieve a solution, instead of prompting an easy and ready-made legal or technocratic guillotine. The 'infringement' of the Rule of Law requires countermeasures which should work internally at a deeper level and cannot be simply imposed from an external authority alone. In the latter case, the Rule of Law has often been understood alongside some other 'goods', whose promotion it is supposed to determine in most cases: economic development, democracy, human rights and social equation welfare.

The recent case of an overwhelming popular majority achieving the ability to alter previous constitutional structures and guarantees in Hungary could be viewed from different perspectives: on the one hand, its fidelity to a formal principle of legality; on the other, the danger presented to the political rights of minorities and the independence of the judiciary, the risk that a non-dominant social culture be oppressed or discriminated against, and the risk that constitutional checks and balances be erased and the like. The example proves, regardless of the accuracy of the diagnosis, that the Rule of Law criterion and the conception behind it largely exceed law-obedience and judicial review. The idea of legality in which the EU as an autonomous entity has been exemplary, is as yet too thin and insufficiently developed. Conceptions of the Rule of Law based on unqualified procedural requirements, even including the availability of judicial guarantees, are elusive,

---

[42] *Ibid.*

[43] J. Cornides, 'Rule of Law or Rule of Judges?', *EJIL Talk*, at www.ejiltalk.org/the-european-union-rule-of-law-or-rule-of-judges/.

[44] *Ibid.*

would capture the idea of a well-established, rule-channelled, obeyed legal order, and yet would still fall short of our intuition of a proficient Rule of Law. It is a good set of parameters or litmus tests, but one which particularly recalls pervasive corruption, the abuse of power, and the 'unconstitutional' use of a constitution:[45] properly so, since one thing which can cause the Rule of Law to disappear is a disfiguring use of legality (the 'abuse' of the power or of a right, in the pursuit of aims for which the power or the right were not meant),[46] along with the substantive immunity of normative power from those obligations and limits through other laws and guarantees which the 'sovereign' in theory cannot itself overwrite.

**

Once an agreed diagnosis is made, the next issue is the grounds on which the EU should be entitled to dictate to the people in a Member State substantive Rule of Law measures applicable to that state, which do not relate to the infringement of any other law of the EU itself.

The main, genuinely 'European', justification for such EU interference into a Member State domain should simply be in the relevance of the peoples and individuals directly to the Union as an autonomous supranational 'unity'. Admittedly, indicia for the 'Europeanisation' of problems previously understood as internal have been laid down, eminently by the ECJ, and meaningfully with regard to citizenship.[47]

The quality of a distinctive EU Rule of Law, as an ultimate safeguard and template for reference should come to the forefront. Of course, since 'being normative' (toward the Member States) implies for the EU being

---

[45] C. Closa, D. Kochenov and J. H. H. Weiler, 'Reinforcing Rule of Law Oversight in the European Union', Working Paper No. 2014/25, RSCAS, 4: 'Three profoundly interrelated criteria could be employed as key signs of which kind of problems we are witnessing. The first is Jan-Werner Müller's 'constitutional capture' – a problem, which was spreading through the region and beyond the EU as well, also characterised as unconstitutional constitutionalism or a constitutional *coup d'Etat*: a profound reshuffling and abuse of power through perfectly legal means. The second criterion is the general dismantlement or profound undermining of the liberal democratic state and the third is a reference to systemic corruption, which can be an overwhelming problem undermining Article 2 TEU compliance'.

[46] G. Palombella, 'The Abuse of Right and the Rule of Law', in A. Sajó (ed.), *The Dark Side of Fundamental Rights* (Utrecht: Eleven, 2006).

[47] D. Kochenov, 'A Real European Citizenship: A New Jurisdiction Test: A Novel Chapter in the Development of the Union in Europe', 18 (2011) *CJEL* 55; Case C-135/08 *Janko Rottmann* v. *Freistaat Bayern* [2010] ECR I-1449; Case C-34/09 *Gerardo Ruiz Zambrano* v. *Office national de l'emploi (ONEm)* [2011] ECR I-1177.

consistent between its own 'supranational' behaviour and the demands that it makes of Member States,[48] whatever is taught by EU internal practice should become the interpretive example of the Rule of Law, a judgmental criterion, for the European monitoring institutions. However, all in all, the main aspects of the Rule of Law propounded in this realm concisely amount to the idea of vertical legality in a mainly market-driven sense and to some not fully defined Rule of Law as a system-relative notion.[49] Relevant additional aspects are the following: the EU's own chronic lack of legal, let alone political, accountability, particularly in its substantive governance (especially in its well-known agency and comitology infrastructure), decision-making processes' relative independence of legal review, let alone the innovative practices – stretching the limits of its legally legitimate powers – adopted during the financial crisis. It has been remarked for some time now that the operational structure underpinning the survival of the EU's governmental strength is relying upon these varied 'modes of governance' which 'tend, albeit to varying degrees and with important differences, to cut themselves free of legal ties'.[50] All in all, it is because of this that Beck and Grande could describe the EU and the increasing weight of its executive administrative power 'as a decentralised, territorially differentiated, transnational negotiation system dominated by elites'.[51]

All the above is not in itself a better proxy for European citizens than the deficiencies or failures in the Rule of Law within the Member States. It is equally complex for the EU to propound a valued ideal, phrasing it through requirements of thicker import than that which itself has practiced on a very thin interpretation. So, a vicious circle surfaces: the deep justification for Rule of Law oversight reinforcement by the EU can be traced back to the protection of persons *as Europeans* and is predicated on the aspiration that the EU become – and mature as – an autonomous polity and an autonomous legal order. However, the Rule of Law records of such a supranational entity, made of peoples and individuals (not just by Member States), can hardly be regarded as fully credible and reliable. The EU can certainly be a Rule of Law *guardian* over its Member States

---

[48] Not by chance that this is one of Lon Fuller's eight requirements for *the law to exist* (see footnote 18 above).

[49] Compare with *Kadi* above.

[50] C. Joerges, 'How the Rule of Law Might Survive the New Turn to Governance' (2007), Working Paper No. 9, RECON, 2.

[51] U. Beck and E. Grande, *Cosmopolitan Europe* (London: Polity Press, 2007), p. 53.

due, among other reasons, to the associative obligations already agreed upon by states, but to be such a guardian is much different from itself being the *justification* and the ultimate reference, the citizenship space of its peoples and of each European, independently of the authority of their states of nationality. In this case, European citizens should see exemplary evidence of the EU's reputation in the observance of the Rule of Law: something that they would hardly find now.

V   Nature and Limits of the Democratic Caveat

Such a weakness should not be conflated with the lack of democracy in the EU: if anything it is a question of a deficit in matching up to the ideal and practice of the Rule of Law. Indeed, for normative and historical reasons, there is no necessary coincidence between the two ideals nor between the two deficits, and it is true that recent events such as those in Hungary are thought of as a *contrast* between democratic power and the guarantees of the Rule of Law. Even in the EU, the two are dissociated: we may consider that democracy has faded while the Rule of Law is in the ascendant,[52] although for independent reasons, this is disputable, as recalled above. Nonetheless, the foregoing considerations pave the way to questions about the democratic problem and its relationship to a European Rule of Law enforcement, a controversial subject where understandably opposite stances are confronted. In response to comprehensive theories of the Rule of Law as embodying every kind of goods, from rights to democracy, welfare and social guarantees, it is worth repeating that the Rule of Law and democracy are different things, and if the first concerns the organisation of legality in a given context, democracy concerns the organisation of the political power of the sovereign. Indeed, to put it bluntly, the Rule of Law might even be followed by states where political authority is not democratically organised: so it has been in the past, and can be in the future as well. However, let me first recall – before the questions of democratic caveats be put the forefront – that the Rule of Law issue in a supranational entity or a two-level system on the one hand means an interference in the autonomy of a Member State, because it requires that the domestic legal configuration conforms to some externally defined Rule of Law template. On the other hand, it demands consistency between the two levels. It is naturally a reflexive instance of

---

[52] J. H. H. Weiler's contribution to this volume.

the notion of the Rule of Law.[53] Since the Rule of Law is itself a constitutional domestic 'value', a state can argue that it *is* complying with its
'internal' Rule of Law even if it is blamed for not complying with international law or European law. This hypothesis has often had currency in
the *sui* generis relations between powerful countries, such as the United
States and the rule of *international* law.[54] However, Article 2 TEU has the
special characteristic of obliging Member State respect for the very Rule
of Law that is relevant *inside* the domestic domain, that is, the content
of the European law to be complied with (Art. 2 TEU) *is the domestic*
Rule of Law itself. In fact, Article 2 TEU – in conjunction with Article 7
TEU – amounts to a meta-norm whose infringement arises precisely in
the two levels simultaneously. The only way to avoid an instrumental use
of the Rule of Law as a self-protecting shield lies in a convergence upon a
'transitive' meaning of the Rule of Law as a common denominator among
the two levels, like the one I have suggested above.

   In general, there is a familiar trend within these circumstances: constitutional arrangements regulating the connection between one legal
system (a country) and a supranational order lay down a kind of pre-
commitment: as has been particularly evident in the Central Eastern
European states involved in EU enlargement, such a pre-commitment
to the EU norms and values is expected to work in the same way as a
Constitution on the whole does: that is, by defending ourselves domestically even from our own changes of opinion, majorities and contingent
political oscillations. In this sense, the constitutional domestic *acquis* providing for a commitment to European or international law turns out to be
'a means of locking in policies'.[55] The expression was also used to explain
how new European democracies entered into international treaties with
a view to pre-committing themselves (domestically) to protecting, or in
other words, 'locking in' human rights.[56]

---

[53] I am not suggesting here that for the Rule of Law to be respected in the Member States, the
    EU needs to be better founded on a democratic basis. As I shall remark later on, depending
    on the conception of the Rule of Law, it can be a shared value regardless of the democratic
    nature of a supranational organisation.

[54] Cf. my comments on the U.S. Supreme Court decision *Hamdan* v. *Rumsfeld* (2006):
    G. Palombella, *The Rule of Law beyond the State: Failures, Promises and Theory*, footnote 13
    above.

[55] T. Ginsburg, 'Locking in Democracy: Constitutions, Commitment, and International
    Law', 38 (2006) *NYU Journal of International Law and Politics* 707–60, 757.

[56] According to Andrew Moravcsik, the origins of the European Convention on Human
    Rights lie in 'self-interested efforts by newly established (or re-established) democracies

On the other hand, it should be noted that distinct from the case in international law, Member States in the EU have no room to choose which varied forms of allegiance and what interfacial rules of validity, direct effect, incorporation and the like should channel their external commitments *vis-à-vis* the supranational order, and they cannot make use of interfacial devices which allow them, say, to postpone incorporation[57] or limit it to only those issues capable of easier appropriation.

The reflexive nature of the EU *Rule of Law* problem is located in this context, one which necessarily has to revolve around some continuity of meaning between the two levels at which the Rule of Law applies. Tensions in the Rule of Law in the two-level context might certainly stem from gross infringements and violation, but they can as equally originate from an oblique use of the concept and an unshared understanding of it. It should be pointed out that, to a certain extent, the authority to scrutinise and order compliance with the Rule of Law to a member country, is not founded upon the internal democratic nature of the EU (although it could well be highly supportive), but before that, on the credibility of the EU as a Rule of Law actor, as I submitted *supra*.

***

Now, however generated, those tensions, all the more if not solved by calling upon the authority and credibility of the EU, inevitably face a democratic caveat, one difficult to manage since the EU itself is regarded today as being in 'democratic default'[58] (the current version of the democratic deficit). Notably, paradoxes are stressed which arise from the effect of Rule of Law stringency in conjunction with democratic weakness in the EU: in other words, the Rule of Law 'has the paradoxical effect of objectifying [the individual] him or her – an object of laws over which one has no effective democratic control. [...] the Rule of Law underpins, supports and legitimates a highly problematic decisional process'.[59] While the Rule of Law in the EU works substantively by supporting individual economic rights ('in some measure at the expense of democratic

---

to employ international commitments to consolidate democracy, "locking in" the domestic political status quo against their non-democratic opponents'. ('The Origins of Human Rights Regimes: Democratic Delegation in Postwar Europe', 54 (2000) *International Organizations*, 217–52, 243–4).

[57] Think of the UK Human Rights Act 1998.

[58] G. Majone, 'From Regulatory State to a Democratic Default' 52 (2014) *JCMS* 1216.

[59] Weiler in C. Closa, D. Kochenov and J. H. H. Weiler, 'Reinforcing Rule of Law Oversight in the European Union', Working Paper No. 2014/25, RSCAS, 28.

legitimation'), procedurally this is reinforced through the 'genius' of the Preliminary Reference, allowing individuals to resort to the EU to contest domestic decision-making.[60]

These comments on the paradoxes of the *combined effect* of Rule of Law effectiveness and the political/democratic deficit are (a) underpinned by the general idea of Rule of Law as a principle requiring obedience to law and to the Courts' decisions; and (b) presuppose that – reflecting the Rule of Law centred on legality and compliance – it cannot rest on sheer coercion but needs a *political* culture, that is, a sound democracy to sustain it. Within this line of reasoning, the EU's scant democratic credentials are pointed to when it asks states to respect Rule of Law values.

Despite the intuitive soundness of this narrative, some further considerations are however needed.

Let us ask whether, in principle, democracy can definitely solve the Rule of Law problem. In some views, this holds true simply because the Rule of Law is just a consequence: it all depends on whether a poliarchic[61] society or a republican[62] polity is established. Legal features add nothing decisive, they are the epiphenomenon. This amounts to saying that the service provided by the Rule of Law has no special legal quality, nor a distinctive normative resilience even when other non-legal determinants fade, since it derives as an automatic result of political sovereignty and its organisational structure. Accordingly, the sovereign is bridled (Rule of Law) if it is organised through ultimately *political* constraints, otherwise the Rule of Law would simply mean to serve a law that it can change for the worse at its whim (the Hobbesian paradox); the Rule of Law is still in the sovereign's hands instead of being, as I have submitted, a balance of dual-sided legality,

---

[60] *Ibid.*, 29: 'Preliminary reference always posits an individual vindicating a personal, private interest against the national public good'.

[61] S. Holmes writes: 'the degree of justice or injustice depends on who wields power and for what ends', 'Lineages of the Rule of Law', in J. Maravall and A. Przeworski, (eds.), *Democracy and the Rule of Law* (Cambridge: Cambridge University Press, 2003), p. 51. Here I do *not* mean that Weiler's considerations, resumed above, maintain this view, nor that they assume the ancillary or merely consequential nature of the Rule of Law.

[62] Likewise, it is remarkable that even in P. Pettit, 'Law and Liberty', in S. Besson and J. L. Marti (eds.), *Legal Republicanism* (Oxford: Oxford University Press, 2009)), the reason for legislation not to dominate (as a *fil rouge* with Pettit's republican theory) is not traced back to the existence of some law or legal device which accomplishes its own separate task. On the contrary, it is derived directly from the transformation of law into a faithful instrument of societal ruling. Once the ruling power is democratic in the recommended sense, then this turns out to be fortunate and produces good law.

a limitation of *rule-making* by another positive law that the holder of ruling power cannot overwrite. In such a view, a Rule of Law ideal means a
political culture, *not* a distinct culture *of legality* which locates jurisgenerative authority in more sources than just sovereignty (whoever holds it).
Here the circle comes to close on the kind of illusory Rule of Law which
can be used to provide legitimation through lip service and enhance whatever good or bad a political fabric provides. Such a notion of the Rule of
Law can thus end up as a matter of procedural regularity, judicial review
and obedience.

Although Weiler's caveat implies the relative autonomy of the Rule of
Law from political democracy, nonetheless it is itself likely to presuppose
this latter conception of the Rule of Law, one which is an individualistic
resource that can trigger anti-democratic consequences. This explains the
perverse effect mentioned which is allegedly generated by the combination
of democratic failure and legal–Rule of Law efficiency.

As I argue, regardless the democracy deficit, there is nothing to be
gained in overlooking the potential of a different, sound and mature
conception of the Rule of Law, since what this should be contrasted against
first is the chronic downplaying of its normative ideal, a downplaying
which is the best means to reduce the Rule of Law to merely being an
instrumental shield of power.

Moreover, and back to the democratic problem itself, how far is it true
that whatever idea of Rule of Law is applied in a two-level system and
elsewhere, it can justify itself and its viability only on the condition that
it has some democratic basis? This assumption might be seen as implied
in the concern regarding the imposition on a Member State of Rule of
Law compliance from an undemocratic European Union: 'Those living
in glass houses should be careful when throwing stones'.[63]

In my view the caveat would be more apposite with reference – and as
one addressed – to the *Rule of Law deficiencies* of the EU itself, as recalled
above. As for the 'democratic' deficiencies, if we scratch the surface, the
answer might be less certain. Let me clarify this point.

Needless to say, insofar as democracy and the Rule of Law can support and mutually strengthen each other, they are both desirable and
largely compatible. Nonetheless, the Rule of Law requires some law to
confront, limit and counterbalance the holding of jurisgenerative power,
regardless of its political forms and structures, and of those who wield

---

[63] J. H. H. Weiler in C. Closa, D. Kochenov and J. H. H. Weiler 'Reinforcing Rule of Law
Oversight in the European Union'.

it. Accordingly, the Rule of Law is also endowed with a conceptual independence from democracy. It applies to and confronts any form of power and government.

Now, what would a full EU democracy do? First, and of itself, it will make political accountability real: a Member State, for instance, would have its say in making or changing its representatives in the EU's government. Second, that would make the EU an entity at least in part politically homologous with the democratic standards of, say, a federal state, or put differently, would make the walls of the edifice of the EU be viewed by its peoples from an *internal* perspective. If those living in this house should throw a stone, they would throw it at themselves. Completing the metaphor, making the political individual a subject not an object, and realising a democratic union conceived of as a true common weal, thus activating the democratic reflexivity (governing–governed) would not simply reinforce the glass to infrangibility, it would make a real difference within the building: turning a gross violation occurring in one country into one felt to occur in the whole EU polity. That said, the two-level system structure, a unique feature of the EU, would not disappear. The question of Articles 2 and 7 TEU would remain because potential Rule of Law infringements would be located in that other nature of the composite EU order where the dialectic between the inside and the outside, the distinction between Member state and the EU, resurface, due to the much valued *unitas in pluralitate*. It is especially in this point that the mentioned 'legal non-domination' and balance, quintessential features of the Rule of Law organisation of legality, would provide a relevant service. The Rule of Law should be cooperatively improved to reflect a transitive criterion between the two levels, to connect multiple orders whose legally ostensible arguments are equally required of supranational and national actors and eventually to replace, at least in part, a top-down authoritative integration among legalities.

Of no less importance, the fully democratic *control* over the EU establishment and decision-making by perhaps some Member States does not in principle imply either a better quality of Rule of Law *in the EU* or minor political resistance by states against the potential intention of the supranational institutions to raise a Rule of Law issue against them. Whether the outcome be better or worse is unpredictable.

At this point, the issue of the EU as a credible *Rule of Law actor in its own right* comes again to the forefront, as we know that democratic organisations are as likely as democratic states to show deep deficiencies in their Rule of Law records, and not just in principle.

VI   Conclusion

The moral is that caring about the quality of legality and the Rule of Law in the EU has to be a primary concern in times when the Rule of Law is being used opportunistically, objectionably and is exposed to double standards. In such circumstances, it can be presumed that the struggle for definitions is itself a matter of power and imposition. However, things could be different. The ideal of the Rule of Law requires institutional settings which can be time and context dependent, but they must share coherence with the normative objective that the ideal evokes. As it concerns *the law*, not directly power or social organisation, it concerns the adequacy of legal institutions to prevent *the law* from turning itself into a mere tool, a malleable servant to political monopoly and instrumentalism, at home and abroad, in Member States and the Union. The Rule of Law rests on a resilient normative structure, one that is often overlooked by scholarly debates, which embodies the 'duality of law', institutional equilibrium, to be conceived as relevant features bearing on a distinctive *legal* plane. From this point on, the tensions in a two-level system should first be managed by developing a shared understanding of the core material of the Rule of Law, fostering consistency and banning double standards.

Without displacing the debate about which devices to activate for Rule of Law oversight to be reinforced, a further comment is needed. As we have seen, to defend the Rule of Law is not like getting to repair a single rule, or a single right, although this can be implied. The Rule of Law is the entire picture, seen through the lens of the quality of legality. If a Member State is confronted with the charge of infringing Article 2 TEU – formally a single 'norm' – it cannot just respond by fixing some of its own 'rules', but in doing so, it has to revise its legal system rationale and rebalance it differently. This cannot be a question that a strict legal syllogism can channel through individual cases either. In this regard, the experience of the ECtHR can show instances of the reverse: when the Court has had to adjudicate some individual rights (a well-circumscribed and defined issue compared to the Rule of Law), whose violation by a Member State appeared repeatedly as the superficial symptom of a much deeper systemic problem within the country, such circumstances led the Court itself to start a dialogue, step-by-step, something like a trial-and-error process.[64] Although matters

---

[64] Examples of ongoing refinements and dialogued assessments come from the practice of the ECtHR, for instance, in the instructive saga of the Polish rent-control cases concerning

of human rights are distinct from the wider questions of the Rule of Law, it is worth recalling how the Court handled the issue firmly and with clarity but at the same time with patient 'political' sensitivity. In my view the example can be of assistance, as a start, for our European institutions to understand that a Rule of Law problem is one which always requires considering *how to become the one who can cast the first stone,* and how to cure something which in principle exceeds the capacities of techno-administrative governance and strictly judicial weapons.

property rights under rent-control legislation, which involved an ongoing process of moves and dialogues among the Polish Constitutional Court, the ECtHR and the Parliament: see L. Garlicki, 'Cooperation of Courts: The Role of Supranational Jurisdictions in Europe', 6 (2008) *I-CON* 514 et seq. Lech Garlicki considered the communication among courts, both horizontally and vertically, an essential aspect of rights protection in a 'triangle of cooperation' which should be carefully nurtured: 'there is always a potential for collisions, and then the triangle of cooperation may degenerate into a 'Bermuda triangle', in which individual rights and liberties might simply disappear' (*Ibid.,* 512).

3

Overseeing the Rule of Law in the EU

Legal Mandate and Means

CHRISTOPHE HILLION[*]

I intend to make use of the prerogatives of the Commission to uphold, within our field of competence, our shared values, the rule of law and fundamental rights, while taking due account of the diversity of constitutional and cultural traditions of the 28 Member States.

Jean-Claude Juncker, 2014

I Introduction

There is growing concern about some EU Member States' disregard for the Rule of Law. Various schemes have been put forth in an attempt to remedy the situation. Following a call for a 'new and more effective mechanism to safeguard fundamental values in Member States',[1] the European Commission established an 'EU framework to strengthen the Rule of Law',[2] while the Council and Member States have initiated an annual 'dialogue to promote and safeguard the Rule of Law'.[3] This chapter discusses the

---

[*] I am grateful to the participants of the 2014 EUI seminar for their comments on the original presentation, and to Anne Myrjord for her limitless support.

[1] See the letter of the Foreign Ministers of Denmark, Finland, Germany and the Netherlands, of 6 March 2013, to the President of the European Commission. The letter can be found at www.rijksoverheid.nl/bestanden/documenten-en-publicaties/brieven/2013/ 03/13/brief-aaneuropese-commissie-over-opzetten-rechtsstatelijkheidsmechanisme/ brief-aan-europese-commissieover-opzetten-rechtsstatelijkheidsmechanisme.pdf.

[2] Communication from the Commission to the Council and the European Parliament, 'A New EU Framework to Strengthen the Rule of Law', COM(2014) 158 final.

[3] Conclusions of the Council of the European Union and the Member States meeting within the Council on Ensuring Respect for the Rule of Law, General Affairs Council meeting, Brussels, 16 December 2014. Different proposals have also been made within the European Parliament, for example the 'Copenhagen Commission' (see European Parliament, Tavares report on the situation of fundamental rights: standards and practices in Hungary (pursuant to the European Parliament resolution of 16 February 2012) (2012/2130(INI)), 24.06.2013); and the 'EU Democratic Governance

underlying question of what the Union is legally entrusted to do on this rather slippery terrain. What legal mandate does it have to protect and promote the Rule of Law? And importantly, what are the means to fulfil such a mandate?

II Mandate

The Rule of Law features prominently in EU primary law. It is listed both among the founding *values* of the Union (a), and as an *objective* that EU institutions are specifically mandated to pursue (b).

(a) Respect for the Rule of Law as Condition for EU Membership

According to Article 2 TEU, the EU is founded on a set of values, one of which is the Rule of Law. Further, the Preamble of the EU Charter of Fundamental Rights (CFR) mentions the Rule of Law as a founding *principle* of the Union, while Article 21(1) TEU establishes that it has inspired the EU's 'own creation, development and enlargement'.

The values of the Union are 'common to the Member States',[4] and as such they must be respected for states to maintain their membership rights intact. Thus, a 'clear risk of a serious breach' of those common values can be reprimanded by the Council on 'a reasoned proposal' by the Commission, the Parliament or other Member States, while 'a serious and persistent breach' can lead to a suspension, by the Council, of 'certain' of the prevaricating state's 'rights deriving from the application of the Treaties [...], including the voting rights of the representative of the government of that Member State in the Council'.[5] Similarly, any country aspiring to become a member of the Union must respect and promote these values in accordance with Article 49 TEU.[6]

Two rationales stand out to explain why the Treaties make EU membership rights contingent upon state observance of the common values. First, a Member State contravening such values would endanger the legitimacy of EU decision making as a whole, and possibly impede the lawfulness of

---

Pact' proposed by the ALDE group (www.alde.eu/event-seminar/events-details/article/an-eu-democratic-governance-pact-44603/).

[4] Article 2 TEU.   [5] Article 7 TEU. The provision is further examined below.

[6] According to Article 49(1) TEU: 'Any European State which respects the values referred to in Article 2 and is committed to promoting them may apply to become a member of the Union'.

subsequent EU decisions.[7] Second, Rule of Law deficiencies potentially disrupt the very functioning of the Union legal order, based as it is on mutual legal interdependence and mutual trust among its members.[8] This argument has been made by both Member States and EU institutions,[9] including the European Court of Justice:

> [...] essential characteristics of EU law have given rise to a structured network of principles, rules and mutually interdependent legal relations linking the EU and its Member States, and its Member States with each other, which are now engaged, as is recalled in the second paragraph of Article 1 TEU, in a 'process of creating an ever closer union among the peoples of Europe.

This legal structure is based on the fundamental premise that each Member State shares with all the other Member States and recognises that they share with it a set of common values on which the EU is founded, as stated in Article 2 TEU. That premise implies and justifies the existence of trust between the Member States that those values will be recognised and, therefore, that the law of the EU which implements them will be respected.[10]

(b) Respect for the Rule of Law as an EU Objective

The Rule of Law must not only be respected for a state to become and remain a member of the EU, it must also be actively promoted. Accordingly, Article 3(1) TEU foresees that the Union exists to '*promote* [...] *its values and the well-being of its peoples*' (emphasis added). Article 13(1) TEU reiterates this broadly defined EU value-promotion

---

[7] Further on the all-affected principle: for example J.-W. Müller, 'Should the EU Protect Democracy and the Rule of Law inside Member States', 21 (2015) *ELJ* 141, esp. 144–5; C. Closa, D. Kochenov and J. H. H. Weiler, 'Reinforcing Rule of Law Oversight in the European Union', EUI Working Papers, RSCAS 2014/25, 5.

[8] See a discussion of this argument in Carlos Closa's chapter in this volume; see also A. von Bogdandy and M. Ioannidis, 'Systemic Deficiency in the Rule of Law: What It Is, What Has Been Done, What Can Be Done' 51 (2014) *CMLRev.* 59.

[9] See, for example, the Commission in its Communication to the Council and the European Parliament on Article 7 of the Treaty on European Union, 'Respect for and Promotion of the Values on which the Union is Based', COM(2003) 606; also see Note from the Presidency to the Council, 'Ensuring Respect for the Rule of Law in the European Union', doc. 15206/14, Brussels, 14 November 2014.

[10] See Opinion 2/13 *ECHR II* ECLI:EU:C:2006:81, paras 167–168; European Commission, 'A New EU Framework to Strengthen the Rule of Law', 2; European Commission, 'Article 7 of the Treaty on European Union', 10.

mandate, by stating that the EU institutional framework 'shall aim to pro-mote [the Union's] values'. As in Article 3(1) TEU, value-promotion spear-heads the list of the institutions' duties, preceding that of advancing the Union's objectives, serving its interests, those of its citizens and those of its Member States.

In other words, ensuring respect for the Rule of Law in the EU legal order is not exclusively a judicial task.[11] It is mainstreamed into the activities of *all* EU institutions.[12] Thus, the protection and promotion of EU values (including the Rule of Law) inform and determine how the EU pursues its objectives and uses its competences, and how its institutions exercise their powers.[13] The 2014 Conclusions of the Council and Member States on ensuring respect for the Rule of Law recognised this when emphasising 'that the European Union and its institutions are *committed* to promoting EU values, including respect for the Rule of Law as laid down in the Treaties' (emphasis added).[14]

As an objective of the Union, and as a cardinal aim of its institutional framework, respect for the values of Article 2 TEU in general, and of the Rule of Law in particular, entails further obligations on the Mem-ber States. Following the principle of sincere cooperation enshrined in Article 4(3) TEU, they must 'facilitate the achievement of the Union's tasks and refrain from any measure which could jeopardise the attain-ment of the Union's objectives'. Such an obligation of cooperation is all the more significant since the European Court of Justice acknowledges it as a self-standing requirement, which applies irrespective of the nature of EU

---

[11] At the judicial level, guaranteeing the Rule of Law in the EU entails, as held repeatedly by the Court of Justice, that 'the acts of its institutions are subject to review of their compatibility with, in particular, the Treaties, general principles of law and fundamental rights', see for example Case C-583/11P *Inuit Tapiriit Kanatami and Others* v. *Parliament and Council* ECLI:EU:C:2013:625.

[12] On the involvement of political institutions in the safeguarding of EU fundamental values: see P. Alston and J. H. H. Weiler, 'An "Ever Closer Union" in Need of a Human Rights Policy', in P. Alston (ed.), *The EU and Human Rights* (Oxford: Oxford University Press, 1999), p. 627.

[13] See in this respect: Council conclusions on the Commission 2013 report on the application of the EU Charter of Fundamental Rights and the consistency between internal and external aspects of human rights' protection and promotion in the European Union, Justice and Home Affairs Council meeting, Luxembourg, 5 and 6 June 2014. Also, the guidelines on methodological steps to be taken to check fundamental rights compatibility in the Council's preparatory bodies, 10140/11; Communications from the Commission on the Strategy for the effective implementation of the Charter of Fundamental Rights by the European Union (COM(2010) 0573); and the Operational Guidance on taking account of Fundamental Rights in Commission Impact Assessments (SEC(2011) 0567).

[14] Council of the European Union and the Member States meeting within the Council, 'Ensuring Respect for the Rule of Law', 16 December 2014.

and Member States' competence.[15] In other words, even when Member States exercise their residual competence, they should ascertain that their actions do not impede the EU's fulfilment of its tasks. In practical terms, this entails not only that constitutional initiatives in the Member States cannot disregard EU values, but that they should also assist the Union in fulfilling its value promotion mandate.[16] It is therefore arguable that national specificities, safeguarded under Article 4(2) TEU, cannot permit a member's disrespect of the values of Article 2 TEU.[17]

EU institutions are equally bound to cooperate. According to the second sentence of Article 13(2) TEU, they must '*practice* mutual sincere cooperation' (emphasis added). They must therefore assist one another to ensure that the Union in general, and its institutional framework in particular, fulfil their value promotion aims. Here too, the obligation of cooperation is increasingly significant. It was recently codified in EU primary law, and as a result the Court of Justice has played an active role in enforcing it.[18]

The foregoing indicates that EU primary law provides a solid constitutional basis for active EU *engagement* to ensure compliance with the values of Article 2 TEU in general, and the Rule of Law in particular. Member States are bound to respect the EU's values, not only to keep their membership rights intact but also because as Member States, they must assist the Union and its institutions effectively to fulfil their joint

---

[15] See, for example, Opinion 1/03 *Lugano* ECLI:EU:C:2006:81, para. 119, Case C-266/03 *Commission* v. *Luxembourg* ECLI: EU:C:2005:341, para. 58; Case C-433/03 *Commission* v. *Germany* ECLI:EU:C:2005:462, para. 64. Further: see for example E. Neframi, 'The Duty of Loyalty: Rethinking Its Scope through Its Application in the Field of EU External Relations', 47(2010) *CMLRev.* 323.

[16] The respective Rule of Law initiatives of the Commission and Council have indeed acknowledged the significance of the obligation of cooperation. The Commission thus expects 'that the Member State concerned cooperates throughout the process and refrains from adopting any irreversible measure in relation to the issues of concern raised by the Commission, pending the assessment of the latter, in line with the duty of sincere cooperation set out in Article 4(3) TEU. Whether a Member State fails to cooperate in this process, or even obstructs it, will be an element to take into consideration when assessing the seriousness of the threat'. The Council and Member States conclusions on the Rule of Law dialogue emphasised, more ambiguously, that while respecting Member States' national identity in line with Article 4(2) TEU, their dialogue approach 'should be brought forward in light of the principle of sincere cooperation'.

[17] In this sense, see F. Timmermans, First Vice-President of the Commission, 'EU Framework for Democracy, Rule of Law and Fundamental Rights', European Parliament (Strasbourg: 11 February 2015); and Editorial Comments: 'Safeguarding EU Values in the Member States – Is Something Finally Happening?', 52 (2015) *CMLRev.* 619.

[18] See e.g. Case C-65/93 *Parliament v.Council (GSP)* ECLI:EU:C:1995:91; Case C-409/13 *Council* v. *Commission* ECLI:EU:C:2015:217.

and overriding aim of value-promotion, as enshrined notably in Article 3(1) TEU.[19]

Having established this twofold EU mandate as regards the Rule of Law, the following sections turn to the question of the Union's means to fulfil it. However prominent the mandate may be, its fulfilment is, like any other EU activity, governed notably by the principles of conferral, subsidiarity and proportionality, enshrined in Article 5 TEU. In the same vein, how EU institutions achieve their aims (including the promotion of the Rule of Law) is subject to the general principle of institutional balance. Thus, as recalled in Article 13(2) TEU, each institution 'shall act within the limits of the powers conferred on it in the Treaties, and in conformity with the procedures, conditions and objectives set out in them'.

Section II discusses the EU competence to *sanction* Member State breaches of the Rule of Law, while Section III examines possible *preventive* competence, namely to *promote* the Rule of Law, against the backdrop of the recent initiatives by the Commission and the Council, mentioned earlier.

III   Means to Sanction Breaches of the Rule of Law

Two complementary means can be used legally to compel Member States to respect the Rule of Law as a value of the Union: first the specific sanction mechanism of Article 7 TEU (a), and second, the general enforcement procedure of Articles 258–260 TFEU.

(a) Article 7 TEU

Introduced by the Treaty of Amsterdam, Article 7 (2)–(4) TEU endows the EU with a power to tackle situations where Member States are

---

[19] It should be noted that the aims of Article 3(1) TEU appear to have a distinct nature and function in the EU legal order. Declaration 41 on Article 352 TFEU, annexed to the EU treaties, points out that: 'the reference in Article 352(1) of the Treaty on the Functioning of the European Union to objectives of the Union refers to the objectives as set out in Article 3(2) and (3) of the Treaty on European Union and to the objectives of Article 3(5) of the said Treaty with respect to external action under Part Five of the Treaty on the Functioning of the European Union. It is therefore excluded that an action based on Article 352 of the Treaty on the Functioning of the European Union would pursue only objectives set out in Article 3(1) of the Treaty on European Union' (emphasis added). Therefore, like CFSP objectives, these aims cannot *alone* activate the residual competence to the same degree as other EU tasks and objectives. Instead, they may be pursued only through other specific competences and legal bases expressly provided in or implied from treaty provisions, if any.

in 'serious and persistent breach' of EU values, including the Rule of Law.[20]

It is up to the European Council to determine that such a serious and persistent breach exists. The decision is made unanimously,[21] following a proposal by the Commission or one third of the Member States. The consent of the European Parliament is also required.[22] First, however, the Member State in question must be invited to submit its observations. If the European Council determines that a serious breach exists, the sanction foreseen in Article 7(3) TEU involves the suspension of 'certain of the rights deriving from the application of the treaties to the Member State in question'. The Council decides the suspension, acting by qualified majority.

This sanction mechanism is a particularly meaningful tool considering the function it plays in relation to the prominent EU value-promotion mandate, but also in view of its scope. The Council Legal Service regards it as a 'Union competence to supervise the application of the Rule of Law, as a value of the Union, in a context that is not related to a specific material competence or that exceeds its scope'.[23] In other words, contrary to the CFR,[24] the mechanism is not confined to situations where Member States

---

[20] On the background to the inclusion of this mechanism and its early misfortunes, see B. de Witte, 'The Impact of Enlargement on the Constitution of the European Union' in M. Cremona (ed.), *The Enlargement of the European Union* (Oxford: Oxford University Press, 2003), p. 209, esp. pp. 227 et seq.; W. Sadurski, 'Adding a Bite to a Bark? A Story of Article 7, the EU Enlargement, and Jörg Haider', 16 (2010) *CJEL* 385; F. Hoffmeister, 'Enforcing the EU Charter of Fundamental Rights in Member States: How Far Are Rome, Budapest and Bucharest from Brussels?', in A. von Bogdandy and P. Sonnevend (eds.), *Constitutional Crisis in the European Constitutional Area: Theory, Law and Politics in Hungary and Romania* (Oxford: Hart Publishing, 2015), p. 195; J.-W. Müller, 'Should the EU Protect Democracy and the Rule of Law inside Member States' 21 (2015) *ELJ* 141; L. F. M. Besselink, 'The Bite, the Bark and the Howl: Article 7 and the Rule of Law Initiatives', in A. Jakáb and D. Kochenov (eds.), *The Enforcement of EU Law and Values* (Oxford: Oxford University Press), forthcoming.

[21] Though without the participation of the Member State concerned, in line with Article 7(5) TEU and Article 354 TFEU.

[22] Rule 83 of the rules of procedure of the EP (July 2014) entitled 'breach by a Member State of fundamental principles foresee that the EP may vote on a proposal calling on the Commission or the Member States to submit a proposal pursuant to Article 7(2) TEU.

[23] Council Legal Service Opinion on Commission's Communication on 'A New EU Framework to Strengthen the Rule of Law' – Compatibility with the Treaties (doc. 10296/14).

[24] It will be recalled that according to Article 51(1) CFR, 'The provisions of this Charter are addressed to the institutions, bodies, offices and agencies of the Union with due regard for the principle of subsidiarity and *to the Member States only when they are implementing Union law*. They shall therefore respect the rights, observe the principles and promote the application thereof in accordance with their respective powers and respecting the limits of the powers of the Union as conferred on it in the Treaties'.

'implement EU law'. The fact that *all* actions or inactions of Member States can be considered for the purpose of the sanctions mechanism may indeed explain its stringent procedural requirements and thresholds for sanctioning breaches.

(b) Classic Infringement Mechanism

While Article 7 TEU establishes a specific EU competence to tackle certain breaches of the Rule of Law, the classic infringement mechanism of Article 258–260 TFEU arguably has a role to play in this respect too.

Legally, the Commission must ensure the application of the EU Treaties and 'oversee the application of Union law under the control of the Court of Justice'.[25] Nothing in EU primary law appears to exclude the provisions of Article 2 TEU from this supervisory remit. Indeed, Article 258 TFEU refers to the 'treaties' denoting the horizontal scope of application of the procedure it establishes, in line with the 'depillarisation' of the EU initiated by the Lisbon Treaty.[26] The only express limitation to the Commission's enforcement powers concerns the Common Foreign and Security Policy (CFSP), as set out in Article 24(1) TEU.

In the same vein, the Treaties neither restrain nor exclude the European Court of Justice's jurisdiction over Article 2 TEU. Had such restriction been intended, the primary lawmakers would have made it explicit, as they did in relation to the CFSP,[27] or indeed with respect to Article 7 TEU, when they limited the Court's control to the provision's procedural stipulations.[28] Article 19 TEU has certainly been understood as entrusting the Court with general jurisdiction, from which derogations must be interpreted narrowly.[29]

In principle therefore, the EU should also be able to enforce the provisions of Article 2 TEU through the classic infraction mechanism.[30] Two

---

[25] Article 17(1) TEU.

[26] Indeed, since 1 December 2014, the powers of the Commission under Article 258 TFEU and the powers of the Court of Justice have become applicable to EU acts in the field of police and judicial cooperation in criminal matters, adopted before the entry into force of the Lisbon Treaty. See Article 10(3), Protocol 36 to the Treaties, on Transitional Provisions.

[27] Article 275(2) TFEU.   [28] Article 269 TFEU.

[29] See in this respect, Case C-658/11 *European Parliament* v. *Council* ECLI:EU:C:2014: 2025, esp. paras 69–74.

[30] Similarly, any Member State could in principle activate the enforcement procedure envisaged in Article 259 TFEU if another Member States is deemed to be violating the provisions of Article 2 TEU.

general questions nevertheless arise when it comes to *exercising* either of the two sanctioning powers.

First, Article 2 TEU is substantively vague.[31] Some indeed doubt that it imposes any obligations at all,[32] even if the EU-specific competence to ensure its observance, discussed above, suggests otherwise.[33] It remains the case that the substantive and thus operative content of the 'EU's values' is ambiguous. A 'serious and persistent' *breach* of the Rule of Law for the purpose of the Article 7(2) TEU sanction mechanisms, or a *failure* to comply, warranting an enforcement procedure, is therefore difficult to establish. This in turn makes the efficacy and the very relevance of these mechanisms questionable. Genuine EU oversight of Member State observance of Article 2 TEU would therefore require the clarification of the latter's substance, for instance in the form of operative standards.[34] Surely the Rule of Law must be monitored in accordance with Rule of Law standards, including legal certainty![35]

In effect, EU values in general, and the Rule of Law in particular, *have* been incrementally articulated, notably in the context of EU enlargement policy. This has been deemed necessary to ensure that the substantive conditions of Article 49(1) TEU are fulfilled. In particular, EU institutions and Member States have to ascertain that the candidate state respects and

---

[31] This was recalled at point 9 of the COREPER doc. 10168 on the Council Conclusions on fundamental rights and the rule of law and on the Commission's 2012 Report on the Application of the Charter of Fundamental rights of the European Union, 6–7 June 2013. See also Address given by Ireland's Minister of State for Disability, Older People, Equality and Mental Health, Kathleen Lynch TD at 4th Annual FRA Symposium: *Promoting the Rule of Law in the EU*, 7 June, Vienna, p. 6 – Ireland then held the Presidency of the EU Council.

[32] See Müller, 'Should the EU Protect Democracy and the Rule of Law inside Member States'.

[33] In its opinion on the Commission's Rule of Law Framework, the Council Legal Service recognised that 'a violation of the values of the Union, including the Rule of Law, may be invoked against a Member State [adding that] Article 7 TEU provides for a Union competence to supervise the application of the rule of law, as a value of the Union, in a context that is not related to a specific material competence or that exceeds its scope', see doc. 10296/14, at paras 16 and 17.

[34] The Commission's Rule of Law Framework Communication does contain clues about the core meaning of the rule of law, making references to the case law of the European Courts, and documenting expertise from the Council of Europe and the Venice Commission. See 'A New EU Framework to Strengthen the Rule of Law', 4 and esp. Annex I.

[35] As recalled by the European Court of Justice's judgment in Case C-147/13 *Spain* v. *Council* ECLI:EU:C:2015:299 at para. 79: 'the principle of legal certainty requires that rules of law be clear and precise and predictable in their effect, so that interested parties can ascertain their position in situations and legal relationships governed by EU law'; see also the judgments in cases C-81/10P *France Télécom* v. *Commission* ECLI:EU:C:2011:811, para. 100; and C-643/11 *LVK* ECLI:EU:C:2013:55, para. 51.

promotes the values of Article 2 TEU, for its membership application to be admissible. Indeed, the content of Article 2 TEU has been further developed in the context of the constantly evolving 'pre-accession strategy', whereby the Commission reports to the Council and European Council on the candidates' progress in fulfilling the accession criteria.[36]

Articulated notably by reference to constitutional and international sources, EU membership conditions have been formally *endorsed* by the Member States. Recall for instance that the latter must unanimously agree on the 'benchmarks' proposed by the Commission for opening and closing the accession negotiations regarding the Rule of Law (Chapter 23, Judiciary and Fundamental Rights), before they are presented to the candidate. In the same vein, the Commission's annual progress reports, which have elaborated on the substance of *inter alia* the Copenhagen political criteria,[37] are submitted to and subsequently discussed and upheld by the Council and European Council, while the candidate's eventual *qualification* as member, in the sense of its fulfilment of the membership requirements, must be approved by all Member States by ratifying the Accession Treaty on the basis of their domestic constitutional requirements.

With the blessing of the Member States, the Commission has thus elaborated the content of Article 2 TEU, substantively and normatively, *vis-à-vis* candidate states.[38] These conditions have become part of EU

---

[36] Thus the Commission's 'Progress reports' and 'Screening reports' have given some indications as to what the rule of law requirement may amount to and how it may be operationalised. In normative terms, the Commission's 2013 Strategy Report on enlargement, entitled 'Copenhagen Twenty Years on: Fundamentals First – Rule of Law, Democracy and the Economy', clearly emphasised the significance of the Rule of Law in the accession process, notably by including 44 references to the notion. In substantive terms, several pages are specifically devoted to the Rule of Law in the 2014 progress report on Serbia; with the first subsection under the heading 'political criteria' devoted to 'democracy and rule of law' being one of the longest subsections in the entire document. Also note the so-called New Approach introduced by the EU in relation to Chapter 23 of the accession negotiations, devoted to Fundamental Rights and the Judiciary. Through this New Approach, the EU institutions articulate the specific EU *acquis* in those areas which a candidate country must adopt and implement before accession.

[37] Namely, the stability of institutions guaranteeing democracy, the Rule of Law, human rights and respect for and protection of minorities. Further: M. Cremona, 'Accession to the European Union: Membership Conditionality and Accession Criteria', 25 (2001) *Polish Yearbook of International Law* 219; C. Hillion, 'The Copenhagen Criteria and Their Progeny', in C. Hillion (ed.), *EU Enlargement: A Legal Approach* (Oxford: Hart Publishing, 2004), pp. 1–23.

[38] While those membership conditions have been criticised: see, for example, D. Kochenov, *EU Enlargement and the Failure of Conditionality* (Alphen aan den Rijn: Kluwer Law International, 2008); J.-W. Müller, 'Should the EU Protect Democracy and the Rule of Law'; compare K. Smith, 'The Evolution and Application of EU Membership Conditionality',

customary law on membership.[39] Since respect and promotion of the values of Article 2 TEU, including the Rule of Law, is an essential element of membership as argued above, these standards could equally be used as yardsticks for ascertaining states' *continuing* observance of Article 2 TEU *within* the EU,[40] for example, both for the purpose of Article 7 TEU and of Article 258 TFEU procedures.

We can also envisage that the EU judicature would play a role in clarifying the content of Article 2 TEU.[41] Given its jurisdiction as defined in Article 19 TEU and informed by the aims of Article 13(1) TEU, the Court of Justice could thereby progressively codify the membership standards discussed above. After all, the Court did spell out the whole body of General Principles of EU law. It did so without elaborate substantive foundations in EU primary law, but by reference to international and other national constitutional sources.[42] This remains also true for the content of the Charter of Fundamental Rights, which partly finds its roots in the General Principles. The Court could thus use similar inspirations to articulate the Rule of Law as per Article 2 TEU. The Commission appears to support this reasoning in its Rule of Law Framework Communication:

> the case law of the Court of Justice of the European Union [. . .] and of the European Court of Human Rights, as well as documents drawn up by the Council of Europe, building notably on the expertise of the Venice Commission, provide a non-exhaustive list of [the] principles [and standards stemming from the Rule of Law] and *hence define the core meaning of the rule of law as a common value of the EU in accordance with Article 2 TEU* (emphasis added).[43]

in M. Cremona (ed.), *The Enlargement of the European Union* (Oxford: Oxford University Press, 2003), p. 105. Indeed, their content and use have been significantly amended in the light of experience.

[39] The principle introduced in Article 49(1) TEU by the Lisbon Treaty that the 'conditions of eligibility agreed upon by the European Council shall be taken into account' confirms the constitutional nature of such conditions.

[40] See C. Closa, 'Reinforcing EU Monitoring of the Rule of Law' on temporal consistency in this volume.

[41] The ECJ has already been invited to do so, for instance, in Case C-505/13 *Levent Redzheb Yumer* ECLI:EU:C:2014:2129. In this case, the Court declined jurisdiction to interpret Art. 2 TEU not because it considered itself unable in principle to provide such an interpretation, but because the referring court had failed to explain why that interpretation was relevant to the pending case. Article 2 TEU was also invoked by Spain, though unsuccessfully in Case C-146/13 *Spain v. European Parliament and Council* ECLI:EU:C:2015:298; see also, Opinion of Advocate General Yves Bot of 18 November 2014, esp. paras 35–38.

[42] In this respect, see T. Tridimas, *The General Principles of EU Law* (Oxford: Oxford University Press, 2006).

[43] European Commission, 'A New EU Framework to Strengthen the Rule of Law' (COM (2014)158, p. 4.

Indeed, the Annex to the Communication refers to several judgments of the European Court of Justice establishing various General Principles and touching on provisions of the Charter of Fundamental Rights, to spell out the core elements of the Rule of Law.[44]

This articulation exercise thus raises the thorny question of how the values of Article 2 TEU, binding Member States in all situations, interact with the General Principles of EU law and the Charter of Fundamental Rights, whose application is limited to Member States 'acting in the scope of Union law'.[45] Given that the General Principles and the Charter cover aspects of the Rule of Law, could they inform the interpretation of the values of Article 2 TEU, despite their circumscribed application? Alternatively, should the values be interpreted differently, by reference to other sources, considering the distinct function of Article 2 TEU? In other words, should the Court introduce a differentiation between the values applicable to Member States in general, and the founding principles applicable to Member States when implementing EU law; or should the interpretation of the notions of 'implementing EU law' and 'acting in the scope of Union law' be revisited?

These are not purely theoretical questions. Indeed, the discussion about the possible reintroduction of the death penalty in Hungary illustrates well the difficulty resulting from the present system of differentiated application of the Charter[46] and of the General Principles, on the one

---

[44] See Annex I of European Commission, 'A New EU Framework to Strengthen the Rule of Law'. For instance, the Court referred to Joined cases 46/87 and 227/88 *Hoechst* v. *Commission* ECLI:EU:C:1989:337 [1989] ECR 2859, establishing the protection against arbitrary or disproportionate intervention as a general principle of Union law, and to Case C-550/07P *Akzo Nobel Chemicals and Akcros Chemicals* v. *Commission* ECLI:EU:C: 2010:229 [2010] ECR I-8301 on the principle of equal treatment, as general principles enshrined in Articles 20 and 21 CFR.

[45] Article 51 CFR in the case of the Charter and case law in the case of the General Principles: see, for example, Case C-555/07 *Küçükdeveci* ECLI:EU:C:2010:21 [2010] ECR I-365.

[46] According to the explanations relating the Charter of Fundamental Rights (OJ 2007 C303/17), Article 51(1) ought to be understood in the light of the following elements: as regards the Member States, it follows unambiguously from the case law of the Court of Justice that the requirement to respect fundamental rights defined in the context of the Union is binding on the Member States only when they act in the scope of Union law (Case 5/88 *Wachauf* ECLI:EU:C:1989:321 [1989] ECR 2609; Case C-260/89 *ERT* ECLI:EU:C:1991:254 [1991] ECR I-2925; Case C-309/96 *Annibaldi* ECLI:EU:C:1997:631 [1997] ECR I-7493). The Court of Justice confirmed this case law in the following terms: 'In addition, it should be remembered that the requirements flowing from the protection of fundamental rights in the Community legal order are also binding on Member States when they implement Community rules' (Case C-292/97 ECLI:EU:C:2000:202 [2000] ECR I-2737, para. 37 of the grounds). Of course this rule, as enshrined in the Charter,

hand, and of Article 2 TEU, on the other. Applied strictly, the current regime means that one could only invoke the prohibition of the death penalty deriving from Article 2(2) CFR against Hungary when 'acting in the scope of Union law'. As submitted by von Bogdandy, such a reading would deprive the CFR provision of actual meaning, in turn suggesting that the provisions of the Charter could be used as inspiration for interpreting Article 2 TEU[47] and as a yardstick for its enforcement.[48] Indeed, the Preamble of the Charter points towards such a connection when declaring that 'The peoples of Europe, in creating an ever closer union among them, are resolved to share a peaceful future based on *common values*' (emphasis added), insofar as the purpose of the Charter is arguably to articulate such values.

At the very least, the broad EU value-promotion mandate noted earlier should inform the scope of application of the Charter and of the General Principles. In particular, the limits to their application should not be interpreted in such a way as to inhibit the fulfilment of the Union's aim of value promotion. In particular, Article 51(1) CFR should not be read and applied in a way that would frustrate the respect and promotion of the values of Article 2 TEU, and in turn make Article 7 TEU inoperative, nor should it be read and applied in a way that would deprive the provisions of the Charter of actual meaning.[49]

In addition to the substantive vagueness of Article 2 TEU, the other question which arises in the exercise of EU sanctioning powers is that of the interaction between the specific procedures of Article 7 TEU and the general enforcement mechanism of Articles 258–260 TFEU. As rightly mentioned by Hoffmeister, 'there is nothing in the treaty which informs us about the relationship between the two procedures'.[50] Should Article 7 TEU operate as a *lex specialis* to sanction breaches of the Rule of Law as per Article 2 TEU, thereby excluding the application of the classic infraction procedure (Article 258 TFEU)?

applies to central authorities and to regional or local bodies, and to public organisations, when they are implementing Union law.

[47] In this sense: 'Juncker droht Ungarn mit Rausschmiss', *Süddeutsche Zeitung* (31 May 2015), at www.sueddeutsche.de/politik/europaeische-union-juncker-droht-ungarn-mit-rausschmiss-1.2501777.

[48] See A. von Bogdandy, 'The European Union as a Human Rights Organization? Human Rights and the Core of the European Union', 37 (2000) *CMLRev.* 1307, 1309 and 1319; Hoffmeister, 'Enforcing the EU Charter of Fundamental Rights in Member States'.

[49] Another option would be to suppress Article 51 altogether: see speech by then Vice-President of the European Commission, EU Justice Commissioner Viviane Reding, 'The EU and the Rule of Law – What Next?' (Brussels: 4 September 2013), Speech/13/677.

[50] Hoffmeister, 'Enforcing the EU Charter of Fundamental Rights in Member States'.

On the one hand, we could consider that Article 7 TEU sets out a specific arrangement in relation to Article 2 TEU, given that the Court has only limited jurisdiction over its provisions.[51] We could also argue that the very relevance of Article 7 TEU could brought into question if the Commission were allowed to trigger the enforcement procedure to tackle alleged breaches of the Rule of Law. Indeed, it could lead to the circumvention of the specific limits to the Court's jurisdiction. On the other hand, it can be argued that Article 7 TEU ought to be triggered only where the classic enforcement procedure of Articles 258–260 TFEU is inadequate to address what is becoming a *systematic* threat to the Rule of Law. In other words, the issue at stake would have to be something more than circumstantial failure to fulfil an obligation under the Treaties. This, it seems, is the approach adopted by the Commission in its Rule of Law framework.[52]

Arguably, an exclusion based on the *lex specialis* argument of the classic enforcement mechanism to address breaches of the Rule of Law enshrined in Article 2 TEU, would seem unjustified. First, and as recalled earlier, it finds no supported in the text of the EU Treaties. Second, such an exclusion would sit uneasily with the institutional balance guaranteed under Article 13(2) TEU, in that it would encroach upon the general supervisory powers of the Commission. Third, preventing the Commission from exercising its supervisory task in relation to the Rule of Law would also depart from the aims of the EU's institutional framework, of which it is part, to promote the values of Article 2 TEU (as per Article 13(1) TEU), and to assist the Union in fulfilling this cardinal objective in all its actions (as per Article 3(1) TEU read in combination with Article 13(2) TEU). Restricting the EU's ability to safeguard its values to the mechanisms of Article 7 (i.e. cases of *serious* breaches) would impede the fulfilment of the

---

[51] Article 269 TFEU foresees that: 'The Court of Justice shall have jurisdiction to decide on the legality of an act adopted by the European Council or by the Council pursuant to Article 7 of the Treaty on European Union solely at the request of the Member State concerned by a determination of the European Council or of the Council and in respect solely of the procedural stipulations contained in that Article. Such a request must be made within one month from the date of such determination. The Court shall rule within one month from the date of the request'.

[52] See European Commission, 'A New EU Framework to Strengthen the Rule of Law', 5. Further: Hoffmeister, 'Enforcing the EU Charter of Fundamental Rights in Member States', 195, 204; K.L. Scheppele, 'What Can the European Commission Do When Member States Violate Basic Principles of the European Union? The Case for Systemic Infringement Actions', at http://ec.europa.eu/justice/events/assises-justice-2013/files/contributions/45.princetonuniversityscheppelesystemicinfringementactionbrusselsversion_en.pdf; see also K.L. Scheppele, 'Enforcing the Basic Principles of EU Law through Systemic Infringement Procedures' in this volume.

EU's value-promotion aim, especially in view of the Article's particularly demanding requirements. Conversely, the possibility of enforcing Article 2 TEU through the classic infringement procedure would allow the EU to intervene at an earlier stage, that is, before the breach becomes serious and persistent, and thus far more damaging to the EU legal order.

For sure, the substantial differences between the two mechanisms reflect the distinct yet arguably *complementary* function they fulfil in the Treaties system. First, they are deemed to respond to different types of Member State deviance from Article 2 TEU. While the infraction procedure purports to tackle *any* failure, the Article 7 TEU sanctions mechanism is crafted specifically to address a 'serious and persistent' breach of Article 2 TEU, whose effect is more corrosive of the EU legal order as a whole. In the case of the infraction procedure, the failure is more limited and circumstantial, whereas in the context of Article 7 TEU, the breach becomes systematic, denoting that the State's contentious behaviour is of a systemic character.

Second, and as a result, the Union's responses vary under each mechanism. In the context of the infraction procedure, a state's failure to fulfil an obligation can lead to a judicial sanction, and eventually to the payment of a lump sum and/or a penalty payment, if the state concerned fails to comply with the Court's judgment. The purpose is to respond to a contentious *action* (or omission). By contrast, the 'persistent and serious' breach under Article 7 TEU, if established by the European Council, leads to the suspension of some of the prevaricating state's membership rights, including its participatory rights. Thus, the target is the state's overall *behaviour*, by way of *quarantine*,[53] to protect the functioning of the Union.

The notion of the complementarity of the procedures under Article 258 TFEU and Article 7 TEU, respectively, appears to be endorsed by the Council and the Member States. Their joint Conclusions not only suggested that the Rule of Law could be safeguarded through the two procedures, they also indicated that the infraction procedure is not excluded from the 'field of the Rule of Law' where it coexists with the Article 7 procedure.[54]

---

[53] As aptly put by J.-W. Müller, 'Should the EU Protect Democracy and the Rule of Law inside Member States', 144.

[54] 'The dialogue established by the conclusions *complements* the existing means which the EU might use in the field of Rule of Law, namely the infringement procedure in the case of a breach of EU law and the so-called Article 7 procedure of the Lisbon Treaty, which allows for the suspension of voting rights in the case of a serious and persistent breach of

Provided the obligations deriving from Article 2 are articulate enough, as discussed above, the Commission should therefore be able to enforce the values of Article 2 TEU in the event of a state's failure, *before* it becomes severe enough to qualify for an Article 7 procedure. Whether it would be an enforcement of Article 2 TEU alone would depend on the specific factual situation, but also on the degree of intelligibility of Article 2 itself. Accordingly, it would be possible to invoke a failure of Article 2 alongside other, more specific failures, for example, non-compliance with a directive, to indicate clearly that the latter also amount to a violation of an EU *value*. The recent infraction cases against Hungary would have been good candidates for such a combined approach.[55] In sum, the application of the classic enforcement procedure to Article 2 TEU could help *prevent* the deterioration of the Rule of Law situation.[56]

IV   Means to Promote the Rule of Law

While the EU can sanction Member States' breaches of the Rule of Law, it is also entrusted with *preventing* them. This is the specific purpose of Article 7(1) TEU (a). As illustrated by several recent initiatives, the EU institutions appear to be more active on this preventive front compared to sanctions, albeit mainly *outside* the particular framework of Article 7(1) TEU (b). This phenomenon is partly explained by the disagreement among institutions as to the role the Union should play in this domain.

(a)   Article 7(1) TEU

Introduced by the Treaty of Nice, the main preventive mechanism is contained in Article 7(1) TEU. It foresees that the EU can act where there is a 'clear *risk* of a serious breach' by a Member State of the values of Article 2 TEU. The procedure is triggered by submission from the

---

EU values'. Conclusions, General Affairs Council, 16 December 2014, doc. 16936/14, at p. 21.

[55] See Case C-286/12 *Commission v. Hungary* ECLI:EU:C:2012:687; and Case C-288/12 *Commission v. Hungary* ECLI:EU:C:2014:237. Other cases can also be mentioned, for example, against Romania: see Hoffmeister, 'Enforcing the EU Charter of Fundamental Rights in Member States', 195, 210 et seq.; Scheppele, 'What Can the European Commission Do When Member States Violate Basic Principles of the European Union?'.

[56] Several issues would need to be addressed for the Commission to oversee compliance with the values of Article 2 effectively: See C. Hillion, 'Enlarging the European Union and Its Fundamental Rights Protection', in S. Adam et al. (eds.), *The European Union in the World* (Leiden/Boston: Brill, 2013), p. 557.

Commission, the European Parliament, or by one third of the Member States, of a 'reasoned proposal' to the Council. The latter may then decide by a majority of four-fifths of its members and with the consent of the Parliament, that this 'clear risk' does exist. However, it should first hear the Member State concerned, and possibly address recommendations to it, following the same procedure. Once the determination is made, the Council is then required to verify 'regularly' that 'the grounds on which such a determination was made continue to apply'.

This provision was introduced to 'giv[e] the Union the capacity to act preventively in the event of a clear risk of a serious breach of the common values, [thereby] greatly enhanc[ing] the operational character of the means already available under the Amsterdam Treaty, which allowed only remedial action after the serious breach had already occurred'.[57] The mechanism has never been activated, although developments in some Member States could have justified it. One reason could be the unfortunate tendency to assimilate this *preventive* mechanism with the separate *sanction* mechanism of paragraphs 2–4, under the repellent label of the 'nuclear option'.[58]

Granted, the substantive and procedural requirements are also demanding for the Council to establish the 'clear risk' and to make recommendations. Yet the initial submission of a 'reasoned proposal' by the Commission or the European Parliament, in itself an important element to draw attention to a contentious situation, is by contrast uncomplicated. It is not dependent on Member State support, and again it is distinct from the much more politically sensitive sanction mechanism. Conversely, it is an express competence to fulfil the value-promotion mandate of Article 13(1) TEU and should thus be exercised accordingly.

Following the entry into force of the Treaty of Nice, the Commission argued that the new paragraph constituted a legal basis for the establishment of regular monitoring of Member State compliance with the founding principles of the Union, then enshrined in Article 6(1) TEU.[59]

---

[57] See European Commission, 'Article 7 of the Treaty on European Union', 3. Further Sadurski, 'Adding a Bite to a Bark?'; See, for example, Besselink, 'The Bite, the Bark and the Howl'.

[58] See the 2012 State of the Union speech of then Commission President Barroso, at http://europa.eu/rapid/press-release_SPEECH-12-596_en.htm.

[59] See European Commission, 'Article 7 of the Treaty on European Union', 3; Compare European Parliament, Voggenhuber Report on the Commission communication on Article 7 of the Treaty on European Union: 'Respect for and Promotion of the Values on which the Union is Based' (COM(2003) 606 – C5-0594/2003 – 2003/2249(INI)), 1 April 2004.

In its 2003 Communication on the amended Article 7 TEU, it considered that the provision 'confers new powers on the Commission in its monitoring of fundamental rights in the Union and in the identification of potential risks [adding that it] intends to exercise its new right in full and a clear awareness of its responsibility'. More generally, it pointed out that Article 7(1) TEU 'places the institutions under an obligation to maintain constant surveillance',[60] adding that 'the legal and political framework for the application of Article 7 [...] based on prevention, requires practical operational measures to ensure thorough and effective monitoring of respect for and promotion of common values'.[61] However, this dimension of Article 7(1) TEU never materialised either, despite initial attempts,[62] and notwithstanding valid legal arguments to support such a development.[63]

Since the Treaty of Lisbon, Article 7(1) TEU foresees that the Council 'may address recommendations' to the prevaricating state following a 'reasoned proposal', and *prior* to the determination of the 'clear risk'. The EU is thus endowed with competence to monitor the state concerned *prior to* the risk determination.[64] The Council is also entrusted, after having established the 'clear risk of a serious breach', to '*verify regularly* that the grounds on which such a determination was made continue to apply' (emphasis added). That the Council should have this express power does not mean that the Commission and the European Parliament have no implied ability to undertake their own monitoring, notably to be able to produce a '*reasoned* proposal' (emphasis added). This would indeed be in line with their duty of sincere cooperation to provide adequate assistance to the Council, as it has itself occasionally requested.[65] For the

---

[60] See European Commission, 'Article 7 of the Treaty on European Union', 7.   [61] *Ibid.*, 8.

[62] As analysed by Sadurski, 'Adding a Bite to a Bark?' Some degree of EU monitoring of Member States, partly related to the rule of law, has recently appeared in the form of the EU Anti-Corruption Report (e.g. Report from the Commission to the Council and the European Parliament, COM(2014) 38) and the annual EU Justice Scoreboard (Communication from the Commission to the European Parliament, the Council, the European Central Bank, the European Economic and Social Committee, and the Committee of the Regions, COM(2015) 116).

[63] As early as 2000, Armin von Bogdandy considered that the power to establish monitoring mechanisms of the general human rights records of Member States was inherent in the EU's tasks and competences under Article 7 TEU, in its pre-Nice version: A. von Bogdandy, 'The European Union as a Human Rights Organization? Human Rights and the Core of the European Union', 37 (2000) *CMLRev.* 1307, 1309. See also, for example, Hoffmeister, 'Enforcing the EU Charter of Fundamental Rights in Member States', 195.

[64] Besselink, 'The Bite, the Bark and the Howl'.

[65] See, for example, Council conclusions on the Commission 2013 report on the application of the EU Charter of Fundamental Rights and the consistency between internal and

Commission in particular, this derives from its general power to ensure the application of the Treaties, and to oversee the application of Union law.[66]

For sure, the Council could certainly invite the Commission to produce preliminary studies to assist it in the performance of its tasks, using other legal powers if need be. For instance, Article 337 TFEU foresees that the Commission may collect any information and carry out any checks required for the performance of the tasks entrusted to it. This must be done within the limits and under the conditions laid down by the Council acting by a simple majority in accordance with the provisions of the Treaties. In this context, the Commission could assess potential risks of serious breach, and if needed, submit 'reasoned proposals' to the Council. Moreover, under Article 241 TFEU, the Council could also ask the Commission to undertake any studies it considers desirable for the attainment of common objectives. Given that promoting EU values is a primary objective of the Union, the studies in question could regularly report on Member State compliance with the values of Article 2 TEU, the way it has been asked to do it in relation to candidates for membership in the context of Article 49(1) TEU.[67] Finally yet importantly, the residual competence of Article 352 TFEU[68] could also be used, in combination with Article 7(1) TEU.[69]

---

external aspects of human rights' protection and promotion in the European Union Justice and Home Affairs Council meeting, Luxembourg, 5 and 6 June 2014; point 7 of the COREPER doc. 10168 on Council Conclusions on fundamental rights and Rule of Law and on the Commission 2012 Report on the Application of the Charter of Fundamental Rights of the European Union, 6–7 June 2013.

[66] Thus, the Commission publishes an annual Single Market Scoreboard which includes an evaluation of the Member States' performance in transposing internal market rules, at http://ec.europa.eu/internal_market/scoreboard/index_en.htm.

[67] Moreover, in the specific context of the Area of Freedom, Security and Justice, monitoring compliance with the Rule of Law could be based on Article 70 TFEU, according to which, without prejudice to Articles 258, 259 and 260 TFEU, the Council may, on a proposal from the Commission, adopt measures laying down the arrangements whereby Member States, in collaboration with the Commission, conduct objective and impartial evaluation of the implementation of the Union policies referred to in Title V on the Area of Freedom, Security and Justice by Member States' authorities, in particular in order to facilitate full application of the principle of mutual recognition. The European Parliament and national Parliaments must be informed of the content and results of the evaluation.

[68] It should be recalled that Article 352 TFEU (or Article 308 EC, as it then was) was used as legal basis for the establishment of the EU Fundamental Rights Agency; see Regulation (EC) No 168/2007 establishing a European Union Agency for Fundamental Rights; OJ 2007 No. L53/1.

[69] Some of these legal bases have been envisaged and discussed by L. Moxham and J. Stefanelli, 'Safeguarding the Rule of Law, Democracy and Fundamental Rights: A Monitoring Model for the European Union', Bingham Centre for the Rule of Law, 15 November 2013; they

Be that as it may, the preventive mechanism of Article 7 TEU has thus far remained a dead letter. Instead, faced with deteriorating compliance with the Rule of Law in the Union, alternative preventive mechanisms have been set up.

(b)   Prevention outside Article 7 TEU

The Commission's 'EU Framework to strengthen the Rule of Law'[70] thus displays a slight change of approach in the prevention of breaches of EU values. Not only does it refrain from reviving the idea of regular monitoring based on Article 7(1) TEU, but the proposed framework is also set to operate *outside* of the mechanisms of Article 7 TEU altogether.

The mechanism consists of a three-stage structured dialogue, to be initiated in case of 'clear indications of a systematic threat to the rule of law in a Member State'. The process begins with the Commission sending a 'Rule of Law opinion' to the Member State in question, which substantiates the Commission's concerns and gives the national authorities the option to respond. Should the matter not be resolved satisfactorily, the Commission issues a 'Rule of Law recommendation'. This spells out the reasons for its concerns, possible solutions and a deadline within which the Member State has to remedy the identified issues and inform it of the steps taken. If unsatisfied by the Member State's efforts, the Commission may decide to activate the Article 7 TEU mechanisms.

The Communication further explains that the framework aims to trigger a dialogue between the Commission and the Member State concerned to address 'threats to the rule of law [...] which are of systemic nature [...] *before* the conditions for activating the mechanisms foreseen in Article 7 TEU [are] met' (emphasis added). It is not conceived as 'an alternative to [the latter], but rather [as] preced[ing] and complement[ing] [its] mechanisms'.[71] In other words, the Commission Rule of Law Framework

---

were also examined, though not in detail, in the Opinion of the Council Legal Service on the Commission proposal for a new Rule of Law framework (doc. 10296/14).

[70] European Commission, 'A New EU Framework to Strengthen the Rule of Law'. For the background to this initiative, see Commission President's 'State of the Union' speeches of 2012 and 2013, and Discussion Paper 4: Rule of Law, Assises de la Justice, Conference (Brussels: 21–22 November, 2013), at www.ec.europa.eu/justice/events/assises-justice-2013/files/rule_of_law_en.pdf.

[71] Communication, 'A New EU Framework to Strengthen the Rule of Law', p. 3; also the preamble of the Commission Recommendation of 27 July 2016 regarding the Rule of Law in Poland, C(2016) 5703, pp. 2–3.

represents an additional pre-preventive procedure[72] operating between the classic infringement procedure and the Article 7 TEU mechanisms.

On the part of the Council it was decided to 'establish [. . .] a dialogue among all Member States within the Council to promote and safeguard the rule of law in the framework of the Treaties'.[73] While acknowledging the Council's role in 'promoting a culture of respect for the rule of law within the European Union', the hybrid 'Conclusions *of the Council and the Member States meeting in the Council'* (emphasis added) foresee that the dialogue be held annually at the General Affairs Council, and that it is prepared by the Presidency and the COREPER. The first dialogues took place under the Luxembourg (2015) and Netherlands (2016) presidencies of the EU Council, respectively.

The two initiatives confirm that, as EU institutions, both the Commission and the Council (and the Member States) are committed to promoting EU values. The Commission has indeed activated its Rule of Law Framework in relation to Poland. They also suggest that prevention could take other forms than the specific mechanism of Article 7(1) TEU. The initiatives thus constitute new tools and approaches for the protection and safeguarding of EU values, and could help prevent or distract from the activation of Article 7 TEU.

That said, the two approaches differ significantly. One reason for this is the institutions' distinctive powers in general, and in the context of Article 7 TEU in particular. The differences also appear to express an underlying divergence of views as to the role the EU should play in safeguarding the Rule of Law. Thus, the *object* of the two undertakings is not the same. The Commission intends has established a 'framework'

---

[72] The new Commission 'First Vice-President' in charge of 'Better Regulation, Interinstitutional Relations, the Rule of Law and the Charter of Fundamental Rights', would presumably have an active role to play in this framework, as the incumbent has made clear. See hearing at the European Parliament, at www.ec.europa.eu/commission/sites/cwt/files/commissioner-ep-hearings/2014-ep-hearings-reply-timmermans-en.pdf; and debate on EU framework for democracy, rule of law and fundamental rights (11 February 2015), at www.europarl.europa.eu/sides/getDoc.do/pubRef=-//EP//TEXT+CRE+20150211+ITEM-017+DOC+XML+V0+/EN&language=EN; meeting at EP Committee on Civil Liberties, Justice and Home Affairs (30 March 2015), at www.europarl.europa.eu/news/en/news-room/content/20150326IPR38564/html/Committee-on-Civil-Liberties-Justice-and-Home-Affairs-meeting-30032015.

His title and place in the hierarchy signal that safeguarding the values of the Union, and particularly the Rule of Law and fundamental rights, are a top priority for the new College.

[73] Council of the European Union and the Member States meeting within the Council, 'Ensuring Respect for the Rule of Law', 16 December 2014.

to 'strengthen' the Rule of Law and to '*resolve future threats* to the rule of law in Member States before conditions for activating the mechanism (of Article 7) would be met' (emphasis added).[74] In contrast, the Council and the Member States have established a 'dialogue' to '*promote a culture of respect for the rule of law*' (emphases added).

Moreover, the approaches differ in *nature*. While the Commission proposes a dialogue between itself and a prevaricating Member State in an *EU*-driven process, the Council and Member States envisage a dialogue 'among' peers, pointing towards a more restricted EU involvement. Indeed, while the Communication suggests that the EU (notably the Commission), has the appropriate *competence* to set out a framework to strengthen the protection of the Rule of Law, the Conclusions clearly indicate that the Council, and indirectly the EU, is not considered legally competent to establish even an annual Rule of Law *dialogue* on its own.[75] It is symptomatic of this belief that the Conclusions of the Council and Member States emphasise that their approach is 'without prejudice to the principle of conferred competences, as well as the respect of national identities of Member States inherent in their fundamental political and constitutional structures',[76] without mentioning any provision of the EU Treaties. The document does not refer to the Commission's Communication either, instead mentioning a note from the *Presidency* on 'Ensuring respect for the Rule of Law'.[77] Seemingly, the Conclusions of the Council and Member State are not based on, and are not meant to be a follow-up of the Commission's initiative, suggesting instead that the latter does not have the power to take such an initiative with respect to the Member States.

This position reflects, although only partly, the views of the Council Legal Service that Article 7 TEU itself does not constitute a basis to further develop or amend the procedure which it establishes. It also implies that additional monitoring and dialogue, involving the Commission as envisaged in the 2003 Communication, would also be impossible:

---

[74] Communication, 'A New EU Framework to Strengthen the Rule of Law', p. 3; Recommendation, 'Regarding the Rule of Law in Poland', Preamble.

[75] Though interestingly, the Presidency note referred to in the Conclusions (Note from the Presidency to the Council, 'Ensuring Respect for the Rule of Law', 14 November, 2014) did not mention the possible need for formal support of the Member States to establish an annual Rule of Law dialogue.

[76] For more on the interaction between Article 4(2) TEU and Article 2 TEU, see Editorial Comments, 'Safeguarding EU Values in the Member States'.

[77] Note from the Presidency to the Council, 'Ensuring Respect for the Rule of Law', 14 November, 2014.

> there is no legal basis in the treaties empowering the institutions to create a new supervision mechanism of the respect of the rule of law by the Member States, additional to what is laid down in Article 7 TEU, neither to amend, modify or supplement the procedure laid down in this Article. Were the Council to act along such lines, it would run the risk of being found to have abused its powers by deciding without a legal basis.

Instead, the Council Legal Service recommended that the Member States establish a mechanism through an intergovernmental agreement, potentially involving the institutions for some tasks.[78]

In sum, while there is agreement on the notion that institutions must promote the Rule of Law as a founding value of the Union, there is a clear divergence regarding the extent and nature of this preventive role, both in the context of Article 7(1) TEU, and outside of it. Clearly, the interinstitutional sincere cooperation called for in Article 13(2) TEU, to ensure that EU fundamental rights and values are safeguarded in line with the strong mandate of Article 13(1) TEU, has yet to materialise.

V   Conclusion

Envisaged as one of the Union's values, the Rule of Law is the keystone of the EU edifice. This chapter has argued that EU primary law bestows a strong and multi-layered mandate on the Union to ensure its observance. While the treaties foresee increased EU preventive and sanctioning competences for that purpose, they also entail duties of sincere cooperation on Member States and the institutions to assist the Union in promoting the Rule of Law, defined as one of its objectives. The combination of EU competence and Member States obligations, though far from flawless, could partly nuance the view that the Union lacks adequate mechanisms to address assaults on its values. The fact that little use if any has been made of available mechanisms is indeed indicative that the weakness could lie outside the current legal arrangements.

---

[78] Doc. 10296/14.

4

Protecting Democracy inside the EU

On Article 7 TEU and the Hungarian Turn to Authoritarianism

BOJAN BUGARIČ*

I Introduction

The European Union is facing a unique historical situation: a political club of democratic regimes established primarily to promote peace and prosperity in post-Second World War Europe is confronted with the first EU Member State ever to slide into an authoritarian illiberal political regime. The Fidesz government achieved the fundamental revision of the rules of the constitutional and political order in Hungary. In only five years (from 2010 to 2015), it has managed to transform Hungary from one of the success stories of the transition from Communism to democracy into a semi-authoritarian regime based on an illiberal constitutional order by systematically dismantling checks and balances, undermining the rule of law, limiting the independence of judiciary, almost destroying press freedom, attacking civil society and increasing executive power. Such a 'constitutional revolution' produced a nominally democratic constitution, but, as Miklós Bánkuti, Gábor Halmai and Kim Lane Scheppele argue, Hungary 'can no longer be described substantively as a republican state governed by the Rule of Law'.[1] The major 'deficiency' of the new

---

* Visiting Scholar, Center for European Studies at Harvard University; Associate Professor, Ljubljana Faculty of Law. I have benefited from commentary and advice on earlier drafts from Ivan T. Berend, Marco Dani, Tom Ginsburg, Wojciech Sadurski, Kim Lane Scheppele, Roberto Toniatti, Jan-Werner Müller, and the editors of this book, Dimitry Kochenov and Carlos Closa. The chapter draws in part on an earlier paper 'Protecting Democracy and the Rule of Law in the European Union: The Hungarian Challenge', LEQS – LSE 'Europe in Question' Discussion Paper Series, No.79/2014, at www.lse.ac.uk/europeanInstitute/LEQS/LEQSPaper79.pdf.

[1] M. Bánkuti, G. Halmai and K. L. Scheppele, 'From Separation of Powers to a Government without Checks: Hungary's Old and New Constitution', in G. A. Toth (ed.), *Constitution*

constitutional structure is that it vests so much power in the centralised executive that no real checks and balances exist to restrain this power.[2]

After Victor Orbán's speech in July last year in Tusnádfürdő, it became more than clear that he wants to create an illiberal state, a different kind of constitutional order from a liberal democracy. In his speech, he denounced a decadent and money-based West and outlined a future Hungarian state, based on 'a work based society [...] of a non-liberal nature'.[3]

As a consequence, the new Hungarian constitutional order is in a direct conflict with the 'fundamental values' of the EU 'political' constitution, such as democracy, the Rule of Law and respect for human rights. These values are protected by Article 2 TEU.[4] One of the most important legal questions facing Europe today is how well is the EU equipped, legally and politically, to defend democracy and the Rule of Law in its member states?

While EU constitutional law contains a legal provision designed to deal with such a situation, this provision is often criticised as being largely inadequate to provide a toolkit with which to intervene effectively in the internal matters of Member States.[5] Article 7 TEU, often described as a 'nuclear option',[6] establishes a legal mechanism which aims to protect EU fundamental values. Article 7 contains an early warning mechanism in case of a clear risk of a serious breach of the values under Article 2 and a sanctions mechanism in the event of a serious and persistent breach of EU values by a Member State. In order to employ the preventive mechanism, Article 7 requires a four-fifths majority of the Council and assent of the European Parliament.[7] The sanctioning mechanism, on the

---

for a Disunited Nation: On Hungary's 2011 Fundamental Law (Budapest: CEU Press 2012), p. 268.

[2] Ibid.

[3] K. Edy, 'EU Urged to Monitor Hungary as Orbán Hits at "Liberal Democracy" ', Financial Times (30 July 2014), at www.ft.com/cms/s/0/0574f7f2-17f3-11e4-b842-00144feabdc0.html#axzz3j4Qp6p00.

[4] The values protected by Article 2 TEU include respect for human dignity, freedom, democracy, equality, the Rule of Law and respect for human rights, including the rights of persons belonging to minorities. The same article (Article 2 TEU) declares that these enumerated values are common to the Member States 'in a society in which pluralism, non-discrimination, tolerance, justice, solidarity and equality between women and man prevail'.

[5] J.-W. Müller, 'Safeguarding Democracy Inside the EU: Brussels and the Future of Liberal Order' (2012/13) Transatlantic Academy Paper Series, No. 3, 1.

[6] The term 'nuclear option' was first used by M. Barosso, the President of the European Commission, see Ibid., 17.

[7] According to Article 354 TFEU, an absolute majority (a two-thirds majority) of members in the EU Parliament is required for 'assent'.

other hand, requires unanimity in the Council and assent of the European Parliament. In the latter case, the Council can even suspend certain rights of the Member State, including its voting rights in the Council.

The essentially 'political' nature of the Article 7 mechanism (the ECJ does not have any role in this procedure) led some authors to argue that its use would be catastrophic and would undo the fabric of the Union.[8] Furthermore, since the enforcement of this article depends upon a strong political consensus, other authors argue that a procedural requirement of unanimity or super-majority (four-fifths) makes it almost impossible to use.[9] As these authors explain, the required majority voting involves 'considerations of political opportunity', which could lead to a 'habit of mutual indulgence', already apparent in the states' unwillingness to sue each other (i.e. initiate the Article 259 TFEU procedure). They also point to the negative experience of the Haider affair, which led to an unwillingness to use this mechanism in the future. As a consequence, a range of proposals have been put forward, which basically take it for granted that the drawbacks of Article 7 make this provision practically unusable and argue that instead of a political approach, as devised in Article 7, it might be more appropriate to use a legalistic approach via infraction procedures pursuant to Article 258 TFEU.[10]

In Section II, I argue that Article 7 is too quickly dismissed as an inadequate and too overtly political tool, before even being used in practice. Moreover, a major problem surrounding the debate on whether to use Article 7 for Hungary has less to do with the legal intricacies of Article 7 than with the absence of the political will to use it. Hence, I argue that the crucial problem is not the legal structure of Article 7 but a lack of political will on the part of all the key political actors legally entitled to intervene in such a situation. With some further improvements, particularly with enlarging the list of possible sanctions (including a possibility of financial

---

[8] A. Williams, 'The Indifferent Gesture: Article 7 TEU, the Fundamental Rights Agency and the UK's Invasion of Iraq', 31 (2006) *ELRev.* 27.

[9] A. von Bogdandy et al., 'A Rescue Package for EU Fundamental Rights-Illustrated with Reference to the Example of Media Freedom', at http://ukconstitutionallaw.org/2012/02/18/a-rescue-package-for-eu-fundamental-rights/.

[10] While some of the proposals try to offer innovative modifications of the infringement procedure (see, e.g. K. L. Scheppele, 'Enforcing the Basic Principles of EU Law through Systemic Infringement Procedures' and G. N. Toggenburg and J. Grimheden, 'The Rule of Law and the Role of Fundamental Rights: Seven Practical Pointers' in this volume), others look for reformed versions of pre-article 7 procedure (See e.g. the chapters by J.-W. Müller, 'Protecting the Rule of Law (and Democracy!) in the EU: The Idea of a Copenhagen Commission' and K. Tuori, 'From Copenhagen to Venice' in this volume).

sanctions[11] and ultimately, the expulsion of a member state from the EU) and by slightly lowering a required majority for the approval of the sanctions, the Article 7 mechanism could become truly workable. However, even if imperfect, the Article 7 mechanism still offers a better prospect for dealing with situations such as in Hungary than a legalistic approach. The current legal actions against Hungary illustrate the limits of such an approach. While the Commission was quite successful and imaginative in its legal argument, skilfully using the previous case law of the ECJ to press Hungary on certain less secure legal grounds, all the cases ultimately failed to address broader, legally more difficult to define, issues such as judicial independence.[12] Therefore, judicial action may be useful, but only as a complement to the Article 7 TEU mechanism.

However, in terms of the potential effectiveness of the use of Article 7, we also need to examine the political economy of the use of Article 7. In Section III, I argue that the current EU economic and political crises have weakened the ability of the EU institutions to effectively tackle the Hungarian problem. With trust in EU at an all-time low and with the unwillingness of the EU political elites to adequately acknowledge the gravity of the Hungarian problem, it is quite unlikely that sanctions, even if imposed, would actually achieve the desired results. Moreover, even if there is a strong consensus for sanctions, the literature on sanctions shows that 'the effects of sanctions are often fairly disappointing'.[13] Finally, the presence of Putin's assertive Russia in the East, spreading its influence among the 'ostracised' EU countries such as Hungary, Greece and Cyprus, is likely to further undermine the effectiveness of sanctions against Hungary.

II   Does EU Law Protect Democracy and the Rule of Law Inside Member States?

Quite paradoxically for the organisation created in the wake of the Second World War, the EU's concern for democracy and the Rule of Law is relatively recent. When the EEC was founded, the assumption was

---

[11] See K. L. Scheppele's 'Enforcing the Basic Principles of EU Law'.

[12] Case C-286/12 *Commission* v. *Hungary* ECLI:EU:C:2012:687 (the radical lowering of the retirement age for Hungarian judges constitutes unjustified discrimination on grounds of age); Case C-288/12 *Commission* v. *Hungary* ECLI:EU:C:2014:237 (independence of the Data Protection Supervisor).

[13] G. C. Hufbauer, J. J. Schott, K. A. Elliott and B. Oegg (eds.), *Economic Sanctions Reconsidered*, 3rd edn (Washington, DC: Peterson Institute, 2008).

that Member States were 'trusted to be respectful of the common values of the liberal tradition'.[14] It was the anticipation of its eastward enlargement in the 1990s that prompted the EU to grant the Copenhagen criteria for EU accession constitutional status in the Treaty of Amsterdam.[15] Despite some early attempts in the 1950s to bring protection of human rights within the ambit of European integration,[16] the EEC Treaty remained silent on the subject of human rights and democracy. The original deal reached at Messina established a dual European constitutional order: the supranational economic constitution on the one hand and the intergovernmental political order on the other.[17] The hope of the founding fathers of the European project was that the economic constitution would provide functionalist pressure for an 'ever closer union', eventually leading to a stronger political union. With the subsequent amendments to the original Rome Treaty, the EU developed some important elements of a political constitution.[18] Nevertheless, the development of an elaborate and strong economic constitution has not been paralleled by an equivalent pace and depth of political integration.[19] As Joseph Weiler argues, democracy was simply not in the DNA of the European integration project.[20]

EU law currently offers two different legal options for dealing with cases like Hungary's: the Article 7 procedure and the infraction procedure under Article 258 TFEU. The first has a legal base in Articles 2 and 7 TEU. While Article 2 defines the basic values of the Union, Article 7

---

[14] Editorial Comments, 'Hungary's New Constitutional Order and "European Unity"' 49 (2012) *CMLRev.* 882.

[15] W. Sadurski, 'Adding Bite to a Bark: The Story of Article 7, E.U. Enlargement, and Jörg Haider' 16 (2010) *CJEL* 387.

[16] As de Búrca explains, with the failure of the European Defence Treaty in the early 1950s, the idea of a European political community and a strong protection of human rights suffered a strong setback. As a consequence, protection of human rights was deliberately removed from the agenda of the Spaak Report, which led to the drafting of the EEC Treaty. G. de Búrca, 'The Evolution of EU Human Rights Law', in P. Craig and G. de Búrca (eds.), *The Evolution of EU Law*, 2nd edn (Oxford: Oxford University Press, 2011), pp. 474, 475.

[17] For the historical account see A. S. Milward, *The European Rescue of the Nation State*, 2nd edn (London: Routledge 2000), p. 216; for a legal account see S. Giubboni, *Social Rights and Market Freedom in the European Constitution* (Cambridge: Cambridge University Press, 2006), pp. 29–30.

[18] C. Joerges, 'Rechtsstaat and Social Europe: How a Classical Tension Resurfaces in the European Integration Process', 9 (2010) *Comparative Sociology* 72.

[19] W. Sadurski, 'Democratic Legitimacy of the European Union: A Diagnosis and Some Modest Proposals', (2013) Sydney Law School Legal Studies Research Paper 13/29, Polish Yearbook of International Law.

[20] J. H. H. Weiler, 'In the Face of Crisis: Input Legitimacy, Output Legitimacy and the Political Messianism of European Integration', 34 (2012) *Journal of European Integration* 825.

provides for legal remedies to sanction violations of Article 2. Article 7 defines the standard to be used when violations of Article 2 occur. When there is 'a clear risk of a serious breach' of principles mentioned in Article 2 by a member state, the Council could issue appropriate recommendation to that State. This is the *preventive mechanism* described in Article 7(1) TEU, which was introduced with the Treaty of Nice in 2001 after lessons from the Haider affair. In 2000 EU leaders resorted to fourteen bilateral coordinated Member State government actions to sanction Austria's coalition government, including Haider's FPÖ party. The sanctions included the suspension of contacts with Austrian government officials, the withdrawal of EU support for Austrian applications for senior positions in international organisations, and the absence of contacts with Austrian ambassadors.[21] Even though Haider's Freedom Party (FPÖ), a coalition junior partner of the People Party (ÖVP), had political views which trivialised or even idealised certain features of the National Socialist past, the fact was that the Austrian government had not violated any EU rules. Thus, the bilateral 'sanctions' were primarily invoked by Haider's political statements and justified as a response to them.[22] The *sanctioning mechanism* in Article 7(2) TEU was introduced with the Treaty of Amsterdam in 1997. The use of sanctions, which include a suspension of certain membership rights of the Member State in question, including voting rights in the Council, is triggered by the existence of 'a serious and persistent breach' of Article 2 (TEU) by a Member State.

The first question is whether the Hungarian 'illiberal democracy' represents a clear risk of a serious breach or even a serious and persistent breach of principles from Article 2. As I argue throughout this chapter, there is little doubt that the new Hungarian constitutional order, particularly those provisions which *systematically* undermine or even remove the independence of the judiciary, media and other independent bodies, basically undermine the very foundations of the Rule of Law in Hungary.

Jan-Werner Müller argues that in Hungary and some other Eastern European countries 'something new is emerging: a form of illiberal democracy in which political parties try to capture the state for either ideological purposes or, more prosaically, economic gains'.[23] He points to an alarming similarity in these new forms of 'democracy' with Putin's 'managed' democracy: 'Like Moscow, the governments of these

---

[21] W. Sadurski, 'Adding Bite to a Bark', 405.   [22] *Ibid.*, 405.

[23] J.-W. Müller, 'Eastern Europe Goes South: Disappearing Democracy in the EU's Newest Member States', 932 (2014) *Foreign Affairs* 15.

countries are careful to maintain their democratic façades by holding regular elections. But their leaders have tried to systematically dismantle institutional checks and balances, making real turnovers in power increasingly difficult.[24] At the moment, the Hungarian version of 'illiberal democracy' represents the most problematic example of this trend.[25]

A recent Editorial Comment in one of the most prestigious European academic journals argues that this threshold was met in the Hungarian case.[26] This *Common Market Law Review* editorial also argues that the Hungarian constitution, which in its preamble contains a nationalistic conception of nation, distinguishing between 'real' and 'other Hungarians' and 'sits uneasily with the model of an open and inclusive society promoted in article 2 of the TEU'.[27]

Wojciech Sadurski argues that we have a case where Hungary 'blatantly and clearly' violates principles of democracy and human rights and that Article 7 presents a toolkit to deal with 'precisely such occasions'.[28] Finally, in its comprehensive Opinion[29] the Council of Europe's Venice Commission produced a 'harsh review' of the new Hungarian Constitution.[30] Moreover, criticism has increased after the adoption of the Fourth Amendment to the Hungarian Constitution, leading Human Rights Watch, the EU Commission and the Council of Europe to ask the Hungarian government to bring its legislation in line with the human rights standards of the EU and the Council of Europe.[31] On 11 March 2013, the Hungarian Parliament adopted the so-called 'Fourth Amendment',[32] an amalgam of various constitutional provisions seeking to limit the independence

---

[24] *Ibid.*

[25] B. Bugarič, 'A Crisis of Constitutional Democracy in Post-Communist Europe: "Lands In-Between" Democracy and Authoritarianism', 13 (2015) *I-CON* 219.

[26] Editorial Comments, 'Hungary's New Constitutional Order', 878.   [27] *Ibid.*, 874, 875.

[28] W. Sadurski, 'Rescue Package for Fundamental Rights: Comments by Wojciech Sadurski', Verfassungsblog, 24 Februrary 2012, at http://verfassungsblog.de/rescue-package-fundamental-rights-comments-wojciech-sadurski/.

[29] CDL-AD(2011)016-e Opinion on the new Constitution of Hungary adopted by the Venice Commission at its 87th Plenary Session (Venice, 17–18 June 2011), at www.venice.coe.int/webforms/documents/CDL-AD(2011)016-E.aspx.

[30] E. K. Jenne and C. Mudde, 'Can Outsiders Help? 23 (2012) *Journal of Democracy* 150.

[31] Human Rights Watch, 'Wrong Direction on Rights: Assessing the Impact of Hungary's New Constitution and Law' (2013) 3, at www.hrw.org/sites/default/files/reports/hungary0513_ForUpload.pdf.

[32] The 'fourth amendment' represents the fourth set of amendments to the Hungarian Constitution since its entry into force in 2011. See Fourth Amendment to Hungary's Fundamental Law, Office of the Parliament, Document number T/9929, Budapest, February 2013, at http://lapa.princeton.edu/hosteddocs/hungary/Fourth%20Amendment%20to%20the%20FL%20-Eng%20Corrected.pdf.

of the judiciary,[33] bringing universities under even more governmental control,[34] opening the door to political prosecution,[35] criminalising homelessness,[36] making the recognition of religious groups dependent on their cooperation with the government[37] and weakening human rights guarantees across the board.[38] However, the most problematic are the amendments in Articles 12 and 19, which drastically limit the jurisdiction of the Constitutional Court, one of the last defenders of the Rule of Law in Hungary. The two amendments repeal all of the decisions made by the Court before January 1, 2012 (when the new Hungarian Constitution entered into force) so that they have no legal effect. As a result, no previous precedents of the Court may be invoked in new cases based on the new Constitution. Second, the Court is prevented from reviewing constitutional amendments for substantive conflicts with constitutional principles. From now on, the Court is allowed only to review the procedural validity of new amendments.[39]

The strongest critique of the new Hungarian constitutional order so far came from the Tavares report[40] adopted by the European Parliament in July 2013. The Tavares Report harshly criticises the state of fundamental rights in Hungary, and it recommends the establishment of an independent mechanism to follow the development of fundamental rights in Hungary. Based on Müller's idea,[41] the Report envisages the establishment of a

---

[33] Article 13/1 Fourth Amendment gives the president of the National Judicial Office an exclusive power to 'manage the central administrative affairs of the courts'.

[34] Article 6 Fourth Amendment passes financial management of the universities to the government. In combination with Article 9(4) of the new Constitution giving the President of the Republic the power to appoint both university presidents and professors, Article 6 thus represents a direct threat to the independence of universities.

[35] Article 14 Fourth Amendment entrenching the right of the head of the National Judicial Office to take any legal case and move it to a different court for decision.

[36] Article 8 Fourth Amendment declares that 'law or local government decree may outlaw the use of certain public space for habitation in order to preserve the public order, public safety, public health and cultural values'.

[37] Article 4 (2) Fourth Amendment.

[38] See Human Rights Watch Report, 'Wrong Direction on Rights', 1, stressing that the new constitutional provisions 'undermine human rights protection in the country'.

[39] See Paul Blokker's chapter (Chapter 12) in this volume.

[40] The Report is named after Rui Tavares, the Portuguese Green MEP, who was the rapporteur. EU Parliament, REPORT on the situation of fundamental rights: standards and practices in Hungary (pursuant to the European Parliament resolution of 16 February 2012) (2012/2130(INI)) Committee on Civil Liberties, Justice and Home Affairs, Rapporteur: Rui Tavares, 24 June 2013 (A7-0229/2013).

[41] J.-W. Müller, 'Safeguarding Democracy Inside the EU', 25; see also J.-W. Müller, 'Protecting the Rule of Law (and Democracy!) in the EU: The Idea of a Copenhagen Commission' in this volume.

'Copenhagen Commission' as a high-level expert body which would review continued compliance with the Copenhagen criteria used for admission to the EU on the part of any Member State. This non-political body would issue recommendations to EU institutions and Member States on how to respond and remedy any deterioration in EU values.[42] Shortly afterwards, the Commission followed this lead and put forward a new 'Pre-Article 7 Procedure'.[43] According to Kochenov and Pech, this new mechanism represents only 'a timid step in the right direction',[44] because 'the Commission's "light-touch" proposal falls short of what is required to effectively address ongoing and serious threats to the rule of law within the EU'.[45]

Despite the fact that Hungary obviously violates Article 2 TEU, the EU institutions have failed so far to utilise the Article 7 TEU mechanism. While the possibility to use the Article 7 TEU procedure was contemplated by the European Parliament, the European People's Party, a centre-right coalition of different European parties controlling the majority in the Parliament, expressed its reluctance to take action on this ground.[46] When the European Parliament attempted to take action against Hungary, it became apparent that EU officials and MPs are internally divided over the priority and severity of the situation. Again, the largest party in the European Parliament, the European People's Party, opposed the proposal. It is important to add that Fidesz belongs to the same political bloc and that Orbán has many friends among the European Peoples' Party members. As a result, many doubt that either the European Parliament or the Council would be willing to resort to the Article 7 TEU mechanism. Most recently, when the EP debated the proposal of the Orbán government to reintroduce the death penalty in Hungary, Manfred Weber, the chair of the EPP in the EP, sought to talk about Hungary as an economic driving force[47] and was unwilling to follow a more critical response from the Commission, which threatened to use Article 7 if Hungary decided to enact the death penalty.[48]

---

[42] EU Parliament, Tavares Report, para. 80.

[43] European Commission, 'A New EU Framework to Strengthen the Rule of Law', COM(2014) 158 Final, 11 March 2014.

[44] D. Kochenov and L. Pech, 'Monitoring and Enforcement of the Rule of Law in the EU: Rhetoric and Reality', 11 (2015) *EUConst* 512.

[45] *Ibid.*   [46] Editorial Comments, 'Hungary's New Constitutional Order', 878.

[47] See www.europarl.europa.eu/plenary/de/debate-details.html?date=20150519&detailBy= date.

[48] N. Nielsen, 'Hungarian PM Defends Death Penalty Debate', *EU Observer* (19 May, 2015), at https://euobserver.com/justice/128762.

The unwillingness of the EU institutions to use the Article 7 procedure shows how difficult it is to use this essentially political mechanism. Mattias Kumm, for example, criticises the unanimity required for the sanctioning mechanism.[49] Kumm has a point, but as Sadurski responds, the preventive mechanism, on the other hand, requires 'only' a supermajority.[50] There is nothing wrong if Article 7 requires such a supermajority among Member States when it comes to triggering the preventive mechanism. A strong consensus among Member States would only strengthen the legitimacy of their action. It would be wrong and politically dangerous if 'only' a smaller majority of countries could launch such a mechanism. Nevertheless, to improve the Article 7 procedure, unanimity for the sanctioning mechanism should be replaced with a supermajority. Both prongs of the Article 7 procedure would thus require a 'workable' majority, which would then make Article 7 easier to use in practice.

Not only is the Article 7 mechanism politically very demanding, but the EU's political ability to protect democracy among its members is also more-or-less untested.[51] Before the Hungarian case, it was only during the Haider affair in 2000 that the use of such drastic measures was contemplated by EU political leaders. Although such moves were unprecedented in EU history, what is more interesting is that there was a strong split between the centre-left and centre-right parties in the European Parliament concerning the legitimacy of the Austrian government. Thus, the only way for the EU Council to adopt these measures was to bypass the Parliament and the Commission. The EU Presidency of the Council thus issued a declaration[52] without consulting the two institutions representing the Union's interests. Another flaw of the Declaration was that the sanctions were imposed regardless of any explicit violation of EU rules by the Austrian coalition government. No surprise then that without using an appropriate legal basis and without support of the two key EU institutions, the sanctions were doomed to fail. In fact, they were lifted only a few months later. Today, it is almost unanimously agreed that imposing

---

[49] M. Kumm, 'Rescue Package for Fundamental Rights: Comments by Mattias Kumm' Verfassungsblog, 21 Februrary 2012, at http://verfassungsblog.de/rescue-package-fundamental-rights-comments-mattias-kumm/.

[50] W. Sadurski, 'Rescue Package for Fundamental Rights'.

[51] E. K. Jenne and C. Mudde, 'Can Outsiders Help?', 147.

[52] Statement from the Portuguese presidency of the EU on behalf of XIV Member States, Lisbon, 31 January 2000, at http://ec.europa.eu/dorie/fileDownload.do;jsessionid=Ng8KStTVk5CvsXhnJGcm4q8Rry89P6cT8bs35h08fhpvFPssDYGc!1615003456?docId=84237&cardId=84237. The 'bilateral measures' are detailed above.

sanctions on Austria was highly questionable.[53] Hence, the lessons from
the Haider affair cast a serious doubt on whether Brussels has 'any leverage
over a member country once it gains admission to the European club'.[54]

After the Haider affair, the Hungarian case represents the EU's first real
case of one of its Member States so clearly violating certain principles
of democracy and the Rule of Law that even considerations of use of
Article 7 TEU provisions are not entirely excluded.[55] In order to make
the EU intervention into Hungary's largely 'domestic affairs' legitimate,
Müller argues that in addition to existing Union law, the EU also needs
a principled and systematic way of thinking about the legitimacy of such
interventions. As he forcefully argues, they have to rely on a broader
concept of the EU, which is not only an economic union but also a
political community of non-negotiable values.[56]

Müller employs here a powerful historical argument to support his
claims. He basically argues that it can be shown that post-war Europe
opted, in reaction to the political catastrophes of mid-century Europe, for
a 'Madisonian model' of democracy. This model, defined by Loewenstein,
of so-called militant democracy[57] is based on a series of constitutional
innovations aimed at providing a new balance of democracy and liberalism, 'but with both liberalism and democracy redefined in the light of the
totalitarian experience of mid-twentieth century Europe'.[58] The essential
elements of this new concept of 'militant' or 'constraining' democracy
were new unelected institutions with explicitly delegated powers to monitor the 'excesses' of parliamentary democracy. The most notable example
was a constitutional court with extensive powers to review the constitutionality of acts of parliament. The ethos of this new constitutional order
was a distrust of unrestricted parliamentary sovereignty. European integration, Müller argues, was part of this new constitutional model, with

---

[53] E. K. Jenne and C. Mudde, 'Can Outsiders Help?' 147; J.-W. Müller, 'Defending Democracy
within the EU', 139.

[54] E. K. Jenne and C. Mudde, *Ibid.*, 147.

[55] The Tavares Report does not rule out the use of the 'nuclear option' if the Hungarian
government does not comply with the monitoring program (EU Parliament Report, para.
86).

[56] J.-W. Müller, 'Europe's Perfect Storm: The Political and Economic Consequences of the
Eurocrisis', 59 (2012) *Dissent* 53.

[57] The concept of a militant democracy has a more specific German component. On this, see
J.-W. Müller, *Constitutional Patriotism* (Princeton, NJ: Princeton University Press, 2007),
pp. 15–45. I would like to thank Marco Dani for making this point.

[58] J.-W. Müller, *Contesting Democracy: Political Ideas in Twentieth-Century Europe* (New
Haven and London: Yale University Press, 2011), p. 129.

its inbuilt distrust of popular sovereignty and the delegation of powers to independent bodies.[59] So, the argument goes, if the EU is more than just a single market, then it is essential that it protects its distinctive model of democracy and the Rule of Law. In this sense, the values of Article 2 TEU and the procedure provided in Article 7 express obligations on Member States 'as members of the Union', as famously argued by Advocate General Poiares Maduro in the *Centro Europa* case.[60] In that sense, the values and procedures under Articles 2 and 7 are more than just a political declaration left to the political discretion of the Member States to decide.

It is therefore crucial that in the Hungarian case the European institutions, seeking to learn from past mistakes, avoid the main flaw of the EU response to the Haider affair, which sanctioned Austria only for Haider's words and not his acts.[61] Despite Haider's regrettable apologism for Nazism and his unwillingness to distance himself clearly from fascist heritage, there was no track record of any concrete violations of human rights in Austria at that time.[62] As several authors have argued, in such cases the EU first and foremost needs to stick to clear standards allowing fair and objective evaluation of the country in question. Second, the EU should look for 'a clear case of a breach', consisting not only of individual, sporadic measures but of a well-documented 'track record' of

---

[59] Even though I am largely sympathetic towards Müller's argument, I think that it is only partially correct. The model of 'constrained' democracy was not applied to the EU with the same purpose as to a nation state. In the former, the main aim of constraint was to limit the discretion of economic policymaking without simultaneously precluding other forms of democratic policymaking at a Member State level. For a similar critique of Müller, see J. Komárek, 'The EU is More Than a Constraint on Populist Democracy', Verfassungsblog, 25 March 2013, at www.verfassungsblog.de/en/the-eu-is-more-than-a-constraint-on-populist-democracy/#.UX06IqO2g5s; and P. Anderson, 'After the Event', 73 (2012) *New Left Review* 54.

[60] Opinion in Case C-380/05 *Centro Europa 7* ECLI:EU:C:2008:59 [2008] ECR I-349, para. 20.

[61] In their statements, the EU leaders condemned Haider's 'naked appeal to xenophobia' (Cook) and argued that FPÖ does not share the EU 'shared values' (Schöder), and 'essential values of the European family' (Gutteres). See M. Merlingen, C. Mudde and U. Sedelmeier, 'The Right and the Righteous? European Norms, Domestic Politics and the Sanctions against Austria', 39 (2001) *JCMS* 65. Even though their statements were not far from the truth, they did not mention a single example of concrete violations of such core EU values.

[62] This was also a major conclusion of the 'Three Wise Men Report' in September 2000 which prompted lifting of the sanctions against Austria. See C. Leconte, 'The Fragility of the EU as "Community of Values": Lessons from the Haider Affair', 28 (2005) *West European Politics* 640.

such violations. Here the EU could also rely on the Commission's Communication of 2003 explicitly defining 'the conditions' for application of Article 7.[63]

There are two important points in this Communication which help to set clear standards for the future application of Article 7. First, the Communication clearly indicates that what is at stake are not only separate violations of Union law but a breach of the 'very foundations of the Union'. Second, the Commission emphasises that such a breach must be serious and persistent, going beyond 'isolated violations of human rights', resulting in a 'systematic problem'.[64] Furthermore, attempting to clarify a clear risk of a serious breach, the Commission argued that 'purely contingent risks' should be excluded. Here the Commission used the example of legislation adopted in wartime abolishing procedural guarantees. This example drew heavy criticism from other EU institutions.[65] But more important are further clarifications dealing with the seriousness of the breach: both the purpose and effect of such acts have to be considered. As far as the second prong of this test is concerned, the Commission argues that a breach must in its effect have implications for one or more of the fundamental values from Article 2. The new Rule of Law Framework adopted last year did not add much to these standards.[66] As I argue in this chapter, the Hungarian case represents a clear violation of these standards and in that respect cannot be compared to the Austrian case. Hence, the EU institutions should not have a problem with identifying clear standards and sticking to these standards when evaluating Hungary's violations of Article 2 TEU.

Due to the political reasons explained above, none of the institutions entitled to initiate the Article 7 procedure (the Commission, the European Parliament, or one third of the Member states) has decided to activate this mechanism so far. First, in January 2011 the Vice-President of the European Commission Neelie Kroes expressed her concern about the December 2010 media laws. Later, Hungary addressed some of the concerns identified about banned content and balanced reporting requirements,

---

[63] EU Commission, Communication to the Council and the European Parliament on Article 7 of the Treaty on European Union: Respect for and Promotion of the Values on Which the Union is Based, COM(2003) 606 final, 15 October 2003.

[64] *Ibid.*

[65] The main objection to such an example was that a higher standard of protection of fundamental rights is needed. W. Sadurski, 'Adding Bite to a Bark', 416.

[66] See Kochenov and Pech, 'Monitoring and Enforcement of the Rule of Law in the EU'.

leading the Commission to drop the proceedings.[67] But the narrow focus of the Commission's intervention left the main problems with media freedom unaddressed. For example, Dawson and Muir criticise the Commission for using arguments based on the internal market to address restrictions on media freedom. As they argue, the Commission should rather resort to Article 11 of the Charter of Fundamental Rights of the European Union protecting the freedom and pluralism of the media in the EU.[68] In other words, Dawson and Muir argue that the Commission should address the violation of fundamental rights more directly.

Instead of using the Article 7 procedure, the Commission decided to initiate several separate legal actions against Hungary on more narrow legal grounds. The most interesting among them was the case involving an alleged violation of the independence of judiciary caused by a provision in the Transitional Act (a supplement to the Constitution intended to explain how the new Constitution should be implemented) lowering the retirement age of judges from 70 to 62 years, which as a consequence would lead to the retirement of 274 judges and public prosecutors in a very short period.[69] The most problematic aspect of this new rule is that among the judges who would retire were most of court presidents responsible for assigning cases. Even though the new Constitution contains several other provisions which are even more problematic from the perspective of judicial independence,[70] the Commission decided to use very narrow legal grounds to deal with the case: it relied exclusively on Directive 2000/78/EC on equal treatment in employment, which prohibits discrimination on the grounds of age.[71] On the other hand, many more contentious issues affecting the independence of the judiciary were not raised in this case. In November 2012, the Court of Justice ruled that the radical reduction of the retirement age for Hungarian judges constitutes unjustified discrimination on grounds of age, thus violating Council

---

[67] See Press Release: 'Media: Commission Vice-President Kroes Welcomes Amendments to Hungarian Media Law', Memo/11/89, Brussels, 16 February 2011, at http://europa.eu/rapid/press-release_MEMO-11-89_en.htm.

[68] M. Dawson and E. Muir, 'Enforcing Fundamental Values: EU Law and Governance in Hungary and Romania', 19(4) (2012) *Maastricht Journal of European and Comparative Law* 472.

[69] Act CLXII of 2011 on the legal status and remuneration of judges, Section 230.

[70] Among the most problematic are provisions limiting the independence of the Constitutional Court and provisions granting the president of the National Judicial Office almost complete discretion to choose which judge will hear a case.

[71] Editorial Comments, 'Hungary's New Constitutional Order', 880.

Directive 2000/78/EC.[72] Despite this legal victory, the judges were never comprehensively re-instated, and Fidesz' loyalists basically remained in place. As Jan-Werner Müller argues, '[despite] its nominal legal success, Europe appeared impotent in getting at the real issue, which was political and had nothing to do with the discrimination of individuals'.[73] What is clear from these separate legal proceedings is that despite certain important legal victories, they ultimately fail to address broader institutional issues which threaten the very foundations of the Rule of Law and liberal democracy in Hungary,[74] namely, in that the main aim of the infraction procedure is not to target the constitutional order of a State. In other words, the judicial proceedings addressed the issues of violations of fundamental values from Article 2 only *indirectly*.[75]

Moreover, as Sadurski argues under the orthodox account of the EU law, the Union lacks any general competence in the field of human rights. Its competence is limited to specific areas explicitly governed by European law, such as a limited range of external policies and anti-discrimination policy. Further, the Member States are subject to the European Court of Justice (E.C.J.) in the domain of human rights only insofar as they are implementing EU law.[76]

Since the most problematic aspects of the new Hungarian constitution are those where the Constitution does not implement EU Law, it is therefore not surprising that individual legal actions fail to redress the real problems. These represent, legally speaking, the entirely 'internal' affairs of a Member State, if judged upon the rules defining the ECJ's jurisdiction in this area.[77] As Article 51(1) CFR explicitly states, the EU's protection of human rights under the CFR applies to the Member States 'only when they are implementing Union Law'.[78]

Therefore, judicial action may be useful, but only as a complement to the Article 7 TEU mechanism. There are many other controversial issues in Hungary in addition to dismantling democracy, the Rule of Law, and checks and balances, which can hardly be addressed through purely judicial means. As I mentioned above, the Orbán government implemented many questionable anti-Semitic, anti-Roma and other nationalist

---

[72] Case C-286/12 *Commission* v. *Hungary*.
[73] J.-W. Müller, 'Should the EU Protect Democracy and the Rule of Law Inside Member States?', 21(2) (2015) *ELJ* 148.
[74] Editorial Comments, 'Hungary's New Constitutional Order', 877, 878.
[75] Dawson and Muir, 'Enforcing Fundamental Values', 471.
[76] W. Sadurski, 'Adding Bite to a Bark', 419.   [77] *Ibid.*
[78] But see A. Jakab, 'The EU Charter of Fundamental Rights as the Most Promising Way of Enforcing the Rule of Law against EU Member States' in this volume.

policies, the combined effect of which is to produce an authoritarian regime. Agreeing with several authors[79] who point to the limits of a purely legalistic approach, with its institutional constraints embedded in a narrow and technical framing of broad political issues in the legalistic jargon, I argue that a *direct approach* provided by the Article 7 mechanism[80] offers a better opportunity to address the breaches of the fundamental values of Article 2 TEU. It is very unfortunate that many other legal scholars too easily dismiss the value of Article 7 procedure by questioning the utility of an essentially political procedure and calling it a 'dead letter'.[81] As I argue in this chapter, the real problem is not Article 7 *per se* but the political unwillingness of the EU institutions to realise that Hungarian authoritarianism poses a very serious threat to the EU integration process. I therefore cannot agree more with Leonard Besselink, who argues that 'the legal possibilities offered under Article 7 are insufficiently explored, both by the institutions and in the literature'.[82]

If violations of EU fundamental values are not sanctioned, that has severe repercussions for the functioning of European integration. Sadurski argues that if the EU does not resort to these measures now, no one will take them seriously in the future.[83] As an editorial in the New York Times argues, 'failure to take steps against the Orbán government would be abdicating the values that form the foundation of the European Union'.[84]

III   The Politics of the EU Intervention: On the Limits of the European Political Constitution

In order to make the Article 7 procedure more effective, Müller suggests some important changes to this mechanism. As a last resort, he proposes

---

[79] W. Sadurski, D. Thym and P. Lindseth have been sceptical about addressing fundamentally political problems through legal means. See debate 'Rescue Package for Fundamental Rights', on Verfassungsblog, at www.verfassungsblog.de/en/category/schwerpunkte/rescue-english/#.UilTBEa2iM8.

[80] M. Dawson and E. Muir distinguish between indirect judicial approaches and a direct political approach provided by Article 7 TEU, see M. Dawson and E. Muir, 'Enforcing Fundamental Values', 471.

[81] S. Greer and A. Williams, 'Human Rights in the Council of Europe and the EU: Towards "Individual", "Constitutional" or "Institutional" Justice?', 15(4) (2009) *ELJ* 474.

[82] L.F.M. Besselink, 'The Bite, the Bark, and the Howl: Article 7 TEU and the Rule of Law Initiative', in A. Jakab and D. Kochenov (eds.), *The Enforcement of EU Law and Values* (Oxford: Oxford University Press, 2017, forthcoming).

[83] W. Sadurski, 'Rescue Package for Fundamental Rights'.

[84] Editorial, 'Hungary's Dangerous Slide', *The New York Times* (5 November 2014).

the expulsion of a Member State from the EU. Such a sanction would apply only when 'democracy is not just slowly undermined or partially dismantled, but where the entire edifice of democratic institutions is blown up or comes crashing down, so to speak'.[85] As we know, EU law currently does not envisage expulsion of a Member State. Here I agree with Müller that the EU, as a political community, has outer and inner boundaries. Adding the most extreme sanction, expulsion, to the existing EU toolkit helps define more clearly the boundaries of the EU. In other words, there is no place in the EU for a country where 'liberal democracy and the rule of law cease to function'.[86]

Furthermore, Müller suggests a system of gradated sanctions, which include cutting EU cohesion funds or imposing significant fines. This proposal, envisioning sanctions different from those envisaged in Article 7, is a good idea. One of the problems of the Article 7 mechanism is that it leaves only a 'nuclear option' to the Council, that is, a suspension of voting rights. One of the possible problems of this powerful sanction is that it could very easily even further alienate the Orbán government from the EU and push it even more firmly towards Putin's sphere of influence.[87] If other, primarily financial sanctions, are added, this should make the Article 7 system more effective. While the suspension of voting rights sends a powerful message to a violating country, it nevertheless remains more symbolic in nature, particularly in the case of a smaller, less influential EU country like Hungary. Economic sanctions, on the other hand, are more likely to have a more direct and stronger effect, particularly in a country like Hungary, which is currently heavily dependent on EU structural funds. While Hungary's Prime Minister Viktor Orbán has declared at mass rallies that 'we won't be colonies [of the EU]', he had no qualms about signing a 2014–2020 budget agreement with the EU that will provide nearly EUR 35 billion of aid for Hungary, a country with an annual GDP of EUR 111 billion. But as Kenneth Rogoff argues, economic sanctions do not always work.[88] A strong international consensus to impose sanctions makes them more likely to work. And conversely, '[one] of the major reasons economic sanctions have fallen short in the past is that not all countries have complied. Indeed, significant differences of domestic

---

[85] J.-W. Müller, 'Safeguarding Democracy Inside the EU', 23.   [86] *Ibid.*, 26.

[87] R. Lyman and A. Smale, 'Defying Soviets, Then Pulling Hungary to Putin', *The New York Times* (7 November 2014).

[88] K. Rogoff, 'Do Economic Sanctions Work, Project Syndicate', at www.project-syndicate .org/print/do-economic-sanctions-work-by-kenneth-rogoff-2015-1.

opinion in the imposing country often undermine sanctions as well'.[89] This aspect turns out to be critical in the current EU context, where the EU institutions cannot find a common language regarding the Hungarian case.

The next important issue which needs to be considered is under which political conditions are such outside interventions most likely to succeed. Here it is useful to be reminded about the political sensitivity of such 'external' interventions. More recent literature on the development of modern liberal and accountable government is informative on this point. As Fukuyama and Birdsall argue, effective institutions have to evolve indigenously: 'Institutions such as the rule of law will rarely work if they are simply copied from abroad, societies must buy into their content'.[90] Accordingly, before resorting to an intervention, the EU institutions should consider the political situation in the country in question. This point is explained by Müller, who argues that 'as long as there is some reasonable hope that national politics will be self-correcting, outside intervention would be illegitimate. It could look like Brussels picking a winner in a domestic power struggle'.[91] For example, Jenne and Mudde observe some positive developments within Hungarian civil society, while acknowledging the political weakness of most of the opposition parties, except Jobbik, a far-right proto-Fascist party which is gaining in popularity. They argue that the outside pressure must be accompanied by sufficient political resistance from below to contain the Fidesz government.[92] Democracy could not simply be imposed from the outside. There are very few examples in history of authoritarian regimes being brought to their knees by the outside interventions.

While I basically agree with the point that EU intervention should be a last resort, the situation in Hungary clearly indicates that the situation there is far from 'self-correcting'. On the contrary, the Fidesz government seems to be determined to continue with the constitutional revolution.

---

[89] Ibid.

[90] N. Birdsall and F. Fukuyama, 'The Post-Washington Consensus: Development After the Crisis', 90(2) (2011) Foreign Affairs 52.

[91] J.-W. Müller, 'Should Brussels Resist Hungary's "Putinization"? Or Do EU Member States Have a "Democratic Over-Ride"?', Open Democracy, at www.opendemocracy.net/jan-werner-mueller/should-brussels-resist-hungarys-%E2%80%98putinization%E2%80%99-or-do-eu-member-states-have-%E2%80%98democ.

J.-W. Müller uses the example of Berlusconi's Italy as a case in point. While Berlusconi tried to remove checks and balances and to introduce a presidential regime, the opposition and the judiciary remained strong. Therefore, Brussels was right in not intervening in Italy.

[92] E. K. Jenne and C. Mudde, 'Can Outsiders Help?', 154.

While the EU intervention so far has brought some minor changes to Hungarian legislation, it remains a long way from preventing Fidesz from continuing to undermine the Rule of Law and checks and balances in the country.

The political context of the EU intervention in Hungary reveals another very important aspect of these actions. The EU and other international organisation are far more likely to exert pressure on a Member State in cases of economic and judicial issues which directly impact foreign interests. But, they are:

> far less confrontational over matters that undermine the internal func-tioning of democracy, such as curtailment of press freedoms, corruption in public administration, and the centralization of power in the hands of the ruling party – partly because of their over-riding interest in ensuring fiscal stability, but also because they have a limited mandate to intervene in political matters.[93]

For example, while we are witnessing unprecedented encroachments of the sovereignty of the Member States by the EU in fiscal matters, there is great reluctance among the EU bodies for such a vigilant approach in more sensitive social or political matters.[94] The EU has adopted a series of measures (the Fiscal Compact, the European Stability Mechanism and the 'Six Pack') which cut directly through the most sensitive aspects of Member State sovereignty in fiscal matters.[95] This contrast between fiscal and social/political measures reflects the limits of EU integration towards a stronger political union. While the spillover effect works quite strongly in economic matters, it is far more benign when the EU tries to protect its fundamental political values. In other words, when it comes to funda-mental values like democracy and the Rule of Law, the EU institutions and elites seem to lack political enthusiasm and the will which they otherwise express when dealing with the Eurozone crisis. We should not be surprised then that Article 7 has not yet been used for Hungary. With trust in EU at an all-time low and with the unwillingness of the EU political elites adequately to acknowledge the gravity of the Hungarian problem, it is quite unlikely that sanctions, even if imposed, would actually achieve the desired results. Therefore, ultimately the real problem is not Article 7, but a lack of political legitimacy and will in the EU institutions to deal with

---

[93] *Ibid.*, 151.   [94] Editorial Comments, 'Hungary's New Constitutional Order', 878.
[95] See A. J. Menéndez, 'The Existential Crisis of the European Union', 14 (2013) *German Law Journal* 453. M. Dawson and F. de Witte, 'Constitutional Balance in the EU after the Euro-crisis', 76(5) (2013) *Modern Law Review* 817.

cases like Hungary. Moreover, this political impotency of the EU institutions very clearly reveals the discrepancy between, on the one hand, the self-understanding of the Union as founded on universal values and as the guarantor of their protection within the Union's territory and, on the other hand, the limited capacities of the European Union to involve itself and intervene in the internal orders of its Member States.[96]

IV Conclusion

The rise of illiberal authoritarianism in Hungary is reminiscent of the dramatic events in Europe's most awful century. Rupnik sees a worrisome resemblance between Orbán's rhetoric and the pre-communist authoritarian regime of Miklós Horthy. Imre Kertézs, a Nobel laureate, for example thinks that there are many parallels between the situation in the 1930s and the present. Even if the existence of the EU makes the danger of rising authoritarianism less dramatic, there are still reasons to be concerned at the authoritarian illiberal attacks on liberal democracy. As the Hungarian case shows, the EU has quite limited powers to effectively prevent the slide to authoritarianism. The irony is that conditionality, so powerful before the CEE countries joined the EU, loses much of its teeth once countries become Member States of the EU. Yet the discussion of the EU instruments to contain such slides into illiberalism has also shown that they are not totally unimportant and that they can be further improved. What is less clear is how to 'reform' the European elites, unwilling to take the Hungarian case more seriously.

---

[96] Editorial Comments, 'Hungary's New Constitutional Order', 877.

PART II

Proposing New Approaches

5

Enforcing the Basic Principles of EU Law through Systemic Infringement Actions

KIM LANE SCHEPPELE[*]

I Introduction

The European Union is experiencing a crisis of values because some Member States are faltering in their commitment to the basic principles which were supposed to be secured by EU membership.[1] Between the financial crisis and the rise of nationalist and far-right parties across the EU, Member State governments have found domestic support both for bashing the EU and for questioning the democratic rotation of power, the unflinching protection of human rights and the security of the Rule of Law. In this chapter, I will propose one way that the European Commission could respond to this backsliding by changing how it deploys infringement procedures.

While the EU has acted quickly over the last few years to respond to the Euro crisis,[2] the *moral* crisis has received far less urgent attention and

[*] Princeton University. I would like to thank Gábor Halmai, Dimitry Kochenov, Jan-Werner Müller, Dan Keleman, the participants in the EUI workshop on 'Reinforcing Rule of Law Oversight in the European Union' in January 2014 in Florence, as well as many commentators who have addressed an earlier version of this proposal with such enthusiasm and seriousness. This chapter builds on my prior proposals for the systemic infringement action: K. L. Scheppele, 'The EU *Commission* v. *Hungary*: The Case for the "Systemic Infringement Action,"' Assises de la Justice, European Commission, November 2013, at http://ec.europa.eu/justice/events/assises-justice-2013/files/contributions/45.princetonuni versityscheppelesystemicinfringementactionbrusselsversion_en.pdf and K. L. Scheppele, 'Making Infringement Procedures More Effective: A Comment on Commission v. Hungary, Case C-288/12' Eutopia Law, 29 April 2014, at http://eutopialaw.com/2014/04/29/making-infringement-procedures-more-effective-a-comment-on-commission-v-hungary-case-c-28812-8-april-2014-grand-chamber/.

[1] Admission to the EU requires that prospective Member States show commitment to these values upon entry. C. Hillion (ed.), *EU Enlargement: A Legal Approach* (Oxford: Hart Publishing, 2004).

[2] R. Smits, 'Crisis Response in Europe's Economic and Monetary Union: Overview of Legal Developments', 38 (2005) *Fordham Int'l LJ* 1135; F. Fabbrini, E. H. Ballin and H. Somsen

has caught European institutions largely unprepared. Prospective Member States were required to run the gauntlet of the Copenhagen Criteria to be admitted to the EU, but the Treaties never adequately anticipated that commitments to the values in Article 2 of the Treaty of the European Union (TEU)[3] might be substantially weakened after a Member State gained entry. As a result, the Treaties have no mechanism for throwing out a state which persistently fails to respect the values of democracy, the Rule of Law and human rights.[4] The 'nuclear option'[5] – Article 7 TEU – permits the EU to remove a Member State's vote in the European Council.[6] But Article 7 TEU is more of a quarantine mechanism for the healthy states to avoid being affected by the pariah state than it is a mechanism for restoring Member State compliance with EU values.[7] Besides, Article 7 TEU has been widely thought to be unworkable as a practical sanction, because supermajorities in the Council and Parliament are required for the success of this option and party alignments at the EU level prevent the key parties from criticising governments from allied states.[8] Seeing the problem, the European Commission proposed a new 'rule of law mechanism' in March 2014 which provides a roadmap for gathering and assessing evidence which could lead to an Article 7 TEU procedure,[9] but the

---

(eds.), *What Form of Government for the European Union and the Eurozone?* (Oxford: Hart Publishing, 2015); A. J. Menéndez, 'The Existential Crisis of the European Union', 14 (2004) *German Law Journal* 453.

[3] 'The Union is founded on the values of respect for human dignity, freedom, democracy, equality, the rule of law and respect for human rights, including the rights of persons belonging to minorities. These values are common to the Member States in a society in which pluralism, non-discrimination, tolerance, justice, solidarity and equality between women and men prevail'. Consolidated Version of the Treaty on European Union, Article 2 (hereinafter TEU).

[4] There is, of course, now a procedure for Member States to leave the EU of their own volition: Art. 50 TEU. For an analysis: A. Łazowski, *Withdrawal from the European Union: A Legal Appraisal* (Cheltenham: Edward Elgar Publishing, 2015).

[5] Commission President, José Manuel Barroso, called Article 7 the 'nuclear option' in his State of the Union Speech in 2012, at http://europa.eu/rapid/press-release_SPEECH-12-596_en .htm.

[6] See C. Hillion, 'Overseeing the Rule of Law in the EU: Legal Mandate and Means' in this volume; W. Sadurski, 'Adding Bite to the Bark: The Story of EU Enlargement, Article 7 and J. Haider', 16 (2010) *CJIL* 385.

[7] I am indebted to J-W. Müller for this idea.

[8] R. D. Kelemen, 'Epp ♥ Orbán: Leading Figures in the European People's Party Are Sheltering the Orbán Regime in the Name of Partisan Politics', Politico.EU, 18 June 2015, at www .politico.eu/article/epp-defends-hungary-orban-against-criticism/.

[9] Communication from the European Commission to the Council and the Parliament, A New EU Mechanism to Strengthen the Rule of Law, COM(2014) 158 final/2, 19 March 2014.

European Council's legal service almost immediately opined that this simple mechanism exceeded the powers of the Commission.[10] Nonetheless, the Commission seems determined to go ahead in theory, though nothing has yet followed in practice.[11] The other key proposals on the table – for example a 'Copenhagen Commission' to review Member States for their continued compliance with the Copenhagen Criteria[12] – are widely assumed to require Treaty change.[13] Not only would Treaty change take a long time but it would require unanimity. Any Member State which saw itself in the crosshairs of such a proposal would have every incentive to veto the change.

What then can be done with the tools at hand? I propose a new approach which is a simple extension of an old mechanism: the infringement procedure created in Articles 258 and 260 of the Treaty on the Functioning of the European Union (TFEU).[14] The Commission could signal *systemic breach* of fundamental Treaty obligations by a Member State by *bundling a group of specific alleged violations together* to argue before the Court of Justice of the European Union (ECJ) that the infringement of EU law in a Member State is not minor or transient, but systemic and persistent. Unlike the usual infringement procedure in which narrowly focused elements of Member State action are singled out for attention one at a time,[15] a *systemic infringement procedure* would identify a pattern of state practice

---

[10] Opinion of the Council Legal Service, Commission's Communication on a New EU Mechanism to Strengthen the Rule of Law, at http://data.consilium.europa.eu/doc/document/ST-10296-2014-INIT/en/pdf.

[11] Commission Statement: EU Framework for Democracy, Rule of Law and Fundamental Rights, Speech of First Vice-President, Frans Timmermans, to the European Parliament, Strasbourg, 12 February 2015, at http://europa.eu/rapid/press-release_SPEECH-15-4402_en.htm. The Commission in January 2016 invoked this mechanism against Poland.

[12] The Copenhagen Commission was first proposed by my Princeton colleague J-W. Müller, 'Should the EU Protect Democracy and the Rule of Law within Member States?', 21 (2015) *ELJ* 141. See also Chapter 10 in this volume.

[13] C. Closa, D. Kochenov and J. H. H. Weiler, 'Reinforcing the Rule of Law Oversight in the European Union', EUI Working Papers No. 2014/25, RSCAS.

[14] P. Craig and G. de Búrca, *EU Law: Texts, Cases Materials*, 6th edn (Oxford: Oxford University Press, 2015), pp. 431–53; S. Andersen, *The Enforcement of EU Law: The Role of the European Commission* (Oxford: Oxford University Press, 2012).

[15] Wennerås has noted that the Commission seems to prefer bringing multiple separate smaller-bore actions rather than one larger action putting the pieces of a broader puzzle together. This piecemeal approach has made it more difficult for the Commission to win substantial remedies at the compliance and sanctioning stage. P. Wennerås, 'Making Effective Use of Article 260 TFEU' in A. Jakab and D. Kochenov (eds.), *The Enforcement of EU Law and Values: Methods against Defiance* (Oxford: Oxford University Press, 2017, forthcoming).

that, when the individual elements are added up, constitute an even more serious violation of a Member State's fundamental EU obligations than the individual elements, taken separately. It is this *pattern* that would give rise to the finding of a *systemic* breach. By using the common infringement procedure in new ways, the Commission would be deploying a tried and true instrument but using this familiar method to achieve a more ambitious purpose.

As I will argue below, an ECJ finding of systemic violation could open up a space for the Commission to require systemic compliance with EU values, something a Member State would find more difficult to evade than compliance with a more narrowly expressed judgment and something that would be more likely to ensure accomplishment of the goals of the Union.[16] When a Member State then fails to comply with a systemic infringement, the Commission should propose a system of sanctions to restore EU values by suspending EU funds until compliance is achieved.

II   Rethinking the Ordinary Infringement Procedure

Infringement actions under Article 258 TFEU are typically brought by the Commission to challenge a specific and concrete violation of EU law by a Member State. They carry the assumption that these violations occur in a Member State that is otherwise generally compliant.[17] But what if the conduct of a Member State raises serious questions about its more general willingness to observe EU law, particularly when a Member State threatens basic EU principles of democracy, Rule of Law and protection of human rights,[18] or persistently undermines the enforcement of EU law within its jurisdiction?[19]

---

[16] Hillion has argued that the desiderata contained in Article 2 TEU are not just vague orienting principles of the Union but common values that Member States have obligations – even legal obligations – to internalise and promote. Hillion, 'Overseeing the Rule of Law in the EU'.

[17] This assumption is reinforced by the principle of sincere cooperation in Article 4(3) TEU. A. Fuerea, 'Brief Considerations on the Principles Specific to the Implementation of the European Union Law', 21 (2014) *Lex ET Scientia International Journal* 49.

[18] A. Williams, *The Ethos of Europe: Values, Law and Justice in the EU* (Cambridge: Cambridge University Press, 2010); E. Herlin-Karnell, 'EU Values and the Shaping of the Global Context', in D. Kochenov and F. Amtenbrink (eds.), *The European Union's Shaping of the International Legal Order* (Cambridge: Cambridge University Press, 2013), p. 89.

[19] M. Klamert, *The Duty of Loyalty in EU Law* (Oxford: Oxford University Press, 2014); A. Hatje, *Loyalität als Rechtsprinzip in der Europäischen Union* (Baden-Baden: Nomos, 2001).

Ordinary infringement actions are important, but they are often too narrow to address the structural problems which persistently noncompliant states pose. To take one example, consider the infringement action that the Commission brought against Hungary when it suddenly lowered the judicial retirement age and removed from office the most senior ten percent of the judiciary.[20] This action permitted the Hungarian government to replace many judicial leaders with judges more to their liking and thereby threatened the independence of the judiciary which, in addition to enforcing national law, is crucial to the enforcement of EU law. The Commission brought an infringement action in the matter, claiming age discrimination.[21] While the Commission expedited the case and won a resounding victory at the ECJ,[22] the Hungarian government was able to avoid restoring the most important judges to their prior jobs.[23] The

---

[20] For the facts giving rise to the case, see K. L. Scheppele, 'How to Evade the Constitution: The Constitutional Court's Decision on the Judicial Retirement Age', Verfassungsblog, 9 August 2012, at www.verfassungsblog.de/evade-constitution-case-hungarian-constitutional-courts-decision-judicial-retirement-age/ and www.verfassungsblog.de/evade-constitution-case-hungarian-constitutional-courts-decision-judicial-retirement-age-part-ii/.

[21] Case C-286/12 *Commission* v. *Hungary* ECLI:EU:C:2012:687 [2012] ECR.

[22] U. Belavusau, 'On Age Discrimination and Beating Dead Dogs: Commission v. Hungary', 50 (2013) *CML Rev.* 1145; T. G. and N. Hôs, 'Retirement of Hungarian Judges, Age Discrimination and Judicial Independence: A Tale of Two Courts', 42 (2013) *Indiana LJ* 289; A. Vincze, 'The ECJ as the Guardian of the Hungarian Constitution: Case C-286/12 Commission v. Hungary', 19 (2013) *European Public Law* 489; K. L. Scheppele, 'Constitutional Coups and Judicial Review: How Transnational Institutions Can Strengthen Peak Courts at Times of Crisis (With Special Reference to Hungary)', 23 (2014) *Transnational Law and Contemporary Problems*, 51, 75–8, 105–7.

[23] After an amendment to the law on the judiciary in March 2013, permitting previously retired judges to return to work, the Hungarian government reported that 152 judges had been reinstated although only 21 returned to their original high court administrative positions. Fifty-six chose lump sum compensation, one reached age 70, which was the original retirement age, and another died. U.S. Department of State, Bureau of Democracy, Human Rights and Labor, Country Reports on Human Rights Practices for 2014, Report on Hungary, at www.state.gov/j/drl/rls/hrrpt/humanrightsreport/index.htm?year=2014&dlid=236532. The Hungarian government's figures indicate that three-quarters of the judges were reinstated, which may have been why the European Commission eventually found that Hungary had complied with the judgment of the ECJ, but these official statistics do not square with other sources of information about the fate of the judges. First, a number of judges seem to be missing from this report. The government's numbers only cover 210 judges, when the Venice Commission estimated that the number might have been as high as 270. Venice Commission, *Opinion on Act CLXII of 2011 on the Legal Status and Remuneration of Judges and Act CLXI of 2011 on the Organisation and Administration of Courts of Hungary*, adopted by the Venice Commission at its 90th Plenary Session (Venice, 16–17 March 2012), CDL-AD(2012)001-e, 27, at

government offered the judges compensation instead, a reasonable remedy in a discrimination case.[24] Unsurprisingly, many of the judges reportedly chose to take the compensation and collect their pensions, rather than return to new jobs in the judiciary. In the end, the Commission had to declare victory and say that the Hungarian government had complied with the ECJ decision,[25] even though the government had nonetheless been able to engage in a major reshuffle of Hungary's judicial leadership. This was a conventional infringement action – successful in legal terms, but it changed very little in the troubling situation on the ground.

If a Member State threatens the basic values of the Treaties or casts doubt on the legal guarantees presumed by EU law, it is probably violating more than one precise part of EU law. Under present practice, the Commission picks its battles, so it currently fails to bring many actions that it might otherwise be justified in launching. As Wennerås notes, the Commission lacks the resources to monitor the application of all EU law across twenty-eight states. However, as he also points out, the

---

www.venice.coe.int/webforms/documents/?pdf=CDL-AD%282012%29001-e. The International Bar Association thought the number was larger than 270. International Bar Association, *Courting Controversy: the Impact of the Recent Reforms on the Independence of the Judiciary and the Rule of Law in Hungary* Article 35 (September 2012), at www.ibanet.org/Document/Default.aspx?DocumentUid=89D4991A-D61F-498A-BD21-0BAFFA6ABF17. The Hungarian government's figures do not seem to account for almost one quarter of the judges who were probably affected by the policy.

    The official statistics on the number of judges who returned to their jobs also contrasts sharply with detailed reports about the reinstatement of judges on particular courts, particularly the most important general court in Budapest, the Metropolitan Court. Gergely Mikó, court president, said that 14 of the 70 judges on his court were forced to retire by the change in the retirement age, but only one was reinstated. 'Efficiency of criminal procedures increased, Metropolitan Court leader says', MTI (Hungarian News Agency), 21 July 2013, at www.politics.hu/20130721/efficiency-of-criminal-procedures-increased-metropolitan-court-leader-says/. So, on that particular key court the reinstatement rate was only 7% instead of the 72% the government claimed overall. For these reasons, I suspect that the Hungarian government's numbers may not be reliable.

[24] European law requires that Member States ensure that people who experience discrimination have 'real and effective judicial protection', which has generally been interpreted to require individualised remedies rather than collective solutions. E. Ellis and P. Watson, *EU Anti-Discrimination Law*, 2nd edn (Oxford: Oxford University Press, 2013), pp. 246–54, 301–15; Directive 2006/54/EC of the European Parliament and of the Council of July 5 2006 on the Implementation of the Principle of Equal Opportunities and Equal Treatment of Men and Women in Matters of Employment and Occupation Art. 4, OJ 2006 No. L204/23, Art. 18 (requiring that states ensure that individual remedies for sex discrimination be 'dissuasive and proportionate to the damage suffered').

[25] European Commission, Press Release, 'European Commission Closes Infringement Procedure on Forced Retirement of Hungarian Judges', 23 November 2013, at http://europa.eu/rapid/press-release_IP-13-1112_en.htm.

Commission has a tendency to see problems as individual trees rather than as larger forests and to bring larger numbers of small cases rather than smaller numbers of large cases.[26] The ECJ has encouraged the Commission to consolidate actions to highlight more 'general and persistent' violations, but the Commission uses this option infrequently.[27] As current Commission practice stands, only some violations – and not necessarily the most substantial ones – are raised in infringement procedures, giving rise to the under-enforcement of EU law.

One remedy to the under-enforcement problem would urge the Commission simply to increase the number of individual infringement actions against persistently violating states. But even if the Commission were to multiply narrowly tailored infringement actions to signal greater concern about a particular Member State, the ECJ is not institutionally able to see the patterns in question if the cases are filed as they presently are: one by one and separately, if at all.[28] The Court of Justice has many panels of judges in its normal operation, so it is quite possible that an otherwise related set of discrete infringement actions could be considered by different panels at the Court and without any individual judge ever having the opportunity to observe patterns specific to a particular Member State which would indicate a more serious threat to the basic values of the Treaties. The ECJ, unlike the European Court of Human Rights, does not have the principle that the national judge must sit on every case from her home country (and therefore, in practice, that the same panel of judges would hear all the current cases from the same state). Instead, the ECJ assigns cases to panels of judges randomly. Moreover, the caseload is sufficiently high so that one panel may not know that another panel within the same Court is hearing a case from the same country, which raises some of the same rule-of-law issues unless the cases are on the same narrow doctrinal point.[29]

---

[26] Wennerås, 'Making Effective Use'.   [27] Ibid., see footnotes 51–60.

[28] Only very occasionally has the Commission filed several cases which link a variety of infringements in a particular area of EU law together to show a pattern of violation. And in some of these cases, the Court has confirmed the patterned violations: Case C-494/01 Commission v. Ireland [2005] ECR I-3331; Case C-135/05 Commission v. Italy [2007] ECR I-3475; Case C-88/07 Commission v. Spain [2009] ECR I-1353. However, this strategy of identifying broader patterns of violation is not a general practice, nor have the cases taken on the more ambitious task of revealing persistent violations of core EU values.

[29] For the structure of the Court, the composition of the Chambers and the system of assignment of opinions, see K. Lenaerts, I. Maselis and K. Gutman, in J. T. Nowak (ed.) EU Procedural Law (Oxford: Oxford University Press, 2014), paras 2.04, 2.10–2.13 (hereinafter Lenaerts, EU Procedural Law).

The Commission could overcome some of this fragmentation by requesting that the Court of Justice assemble a Grand Chamber[30] to hear the most important complaints against a particular Member State, but these individual infringement actions would still not give the Court of Justice the scope to consider an overall pattern of noncompliance as an important fact in and of itself, because such evidence would be beyond the bounds of any specific case. The Court must have a wider field of vision to see what is happening within a persistently violating state to assess the legal situation adequately. A different strategy for framing cases seems called for, a strategy which places specific violations in a broader perspective and which sets the stage for the sort of remedies that would be necessary to bring a Member State back into line with basic values. For that, the Commission needs the option of a systemic infringement procedure.

A systemic infringement procedure could be launched if the Commission identifies that a Member State is engaging in a systemic violation of EU principles and is not just violating a particular narrow provision of EU Law. A systemic infringement action would aim directly at the systemic nature of the violation by compiling a single legal action from a set of troubling laws, decisions and actions. Bundling together a pattern of violations which adds up to more than the sum of its parts would allow the Commission to capture a whole concerning practice and not just a component part of that practice. That said, the systemic infringement action needs to be more than simply a bundle of unrelated complaints, linked only by virtue of their common origin in a single Member State. The case should be tied together with an overarching legal theory which links the allegations together, making the systemic violation clear and pointing to a systemic remedy.

Bundling together a set of violations to demonstrate a larger pattern is hardly radical: in fact, the Commission has already tried it and the Court has confirmed the practice.[31] In *Commission* v. *Ireland*,[32] the Commission provided evidence that twelve different waste disposal sites in Ireland had been allowed to operate in flagrant violation of the Waste Directive.[33] The

---

[30] "'The Court shall sit in a Grand Chamber when a Member State or an institution of the Communities that is party to the proceedings so requests'. Statute of the Court of Justice, Chapter II, Article 16.

[31] See the discussion of this issue in Lenaerts, EU Procedural Law, at s. 5.11, pp. 166–7 (with many examples in the notes).

[32] Case C-494/01 *Commission* v. *Ireland* [2005] ECR I-3331.

[33] Council Directive 75/442/EEC on Waste, OJ 1975 No. L194.

number mattered: one or two sites might have been the fault of specific local governments or site operators. Twelve sites, located all over the country, spoke of a general lack of enforcement of a Directive which had been in force for nearly twenty-five years at the time that the Commission brought its action. 'This tolerant approach [to the enforcement of the Directive]', wrote the Court, 'is indicative of a large-scale administrative problem [. . .] and it was sufficiently general and long-lasting to enable the conclusion to be drawn that a practice attributable to Irish authorities existed'.[34] As the Court argued, one instance of violation would have disguised the systematic nature of the problem and would not alone have been enough for the Court to attribute the failure to the Member State. While the Court did not outline a general standard for determining when the sum of individual violations would add up to more than the sum of the parts, AG Geelhoed opined that a 'structural infringement' required demonstration that the violations were of sufficient duration, persisted over a range of particular examples and demonstrated sufficient seriousness to warrant a finding of a pattern of infringement.[35]

The Court gave a similar judgment against Italy, also for violation of the Waste Directive, after the Commission documented 4,866 illegal tips, located all over the country.[36] The Commission referred to its approach in that case as 'horizontal', enabling it to 'identify and correct more effectively the structural problems'.[37] The Court agreed, finding that the Italian government had 'generally and persistently, failed to fulfil its obligations'.[38]

'General and persistent' violations have been found in a number of cases where the Commission has brought together evidence of a pattern of violation.[39] But there are also a depressingly large number of cases in which the Commission's 'general and persistent' violation cases were not affirmed by the Court. In each case, however, the Court asserted its willingness to hear 'bundled' cases; the cases collapsed over the proof

---

[34] Case C-494/01 *Commission* v. *Ireland* [2005] ECR I-3331, para. 133.

[35] AG Geelhoed, Opinion in Case C-494/01 *Commission* v. *Ireland* [2005] ECR I-3331.

[36] Case C-135/05 *Commission* v. *Italy* [2007] ECR I-3475, para. 10.

[37] Case C-135/05 *Commission* v. *Italy* [2007] ECR I-3475, para. 19.

[38] Case C-135/05 *Commission* v. *Italy* [2007] ECR I-3475, para. 44.

[39] See for example Case C-88/07 *Commission* v. *Spain* [2009] ECR I-1353 (finding Spain in violation of the Directive on medicinal products for human use because it withdrew more than 200 products which were in circulation in other Member States if they were not specifically listed in a national law that did not assess on a case-by-case basis whether the items were dangerous to human health; the case depended on challenging not only the limiting law but also the 200 examples of substances actually removed from pharmacy shelves).

of the pattern, because not enough instances were investigated, because the duration of the violations was not clear or because the instances investigated did not add up to a pattern on a common subject.[40] The problem, therefore, seems to be evidentiary and not jurisprudential.

As these examples indicate, bundling a series of specific violations together to demonstrate a larger pattern is no longer a radically novel idea in the Court's jurisprudence. However, the use I propose is different from the uses we have seen thus far. Instead of simply documenting a pattern that shows EU law has been violated, the systemic infringement procedure would focus on claims which raise questions of a more fundamental sort, where the Member State's commitment to European values would be raised by the way the action is framed. The systemic infringement procedure would therefore be distinguished from the pattern-based cases by the seriousness of the violations alleged in European constitutional terms.

Systemic infringement procedures before the Court could be structured doctrinally in one of several ways. First, and perhaps most ambitiously, they could directly allege that a pattern of Member State conduct violates one or more of the basic principles outlined in Article 2 TEU. This would have the disadvantage of being a novel form of legal action. A number of commentators believe that Article 2 TEU can be enforced only through Article 7 TEU, a distinctly political procedure,[41] which may make judges from the ECJ believe that they are treading in territory that is not theirs to police. However, an increasing chorus of voices is starting to argue

---

[40] Case C-34/11 *Commission* v. *Portugal* ECLI:EU:C:2012:712, paras 41–50 (Commission failed to establish air pollution violations for a sufficient number of locations or over a long enough span of years); Case C-68/11 *Commission* v. *Italy* [2012] ECLI:EU:C:2012:815, paras 49–57 (Commission failed to specify locations and duration of air pollution); Case C-160/08 *Commission* v. *Germany* [2010] ECR I-3713, paras 113–123 (Commission failed to show that the lack of public tenders was widespread in a particular substantive field); Case C-416/07 *Commission* v. *Greece* [2009] ECR I-5703, paras 44–49 and 97–100 (Commission failed to provide adequate proof that Greece had failed its obligations to protect animals during transport to slaughter); Case C-342/05 *Commission* v. *Finland* [2007] ECR I-4713, paras 32–39 (administrative practice can be a violation of EU law, but it must be shown to be consistent and general); Case C-156/04 *Commission* v. *Greece* [2007] ECR I-4129, paras 44–53 (establishing an administrative practice requires more than two cases); Case C-441/02 *Commission* v. *Germany* [2006] ECR I-3449, paras 44–56 (Commission failed to establish an administrative practice of a consistent and general nature).

[41] M. Avbelj, 'The Inherent Limits of Law – the Case of Slovenia', Verfassungsblog, 6 December 2013, at www.verfassungsblog.de/en/the-inherent-limits-of-law-the-case-of-slovenia-2/ and P. Blokker, 'Systemic Infringement Action: An Effective Solution or Rather Part of the Problem?' Verfassungsblog, 5 December 2013, at www.verfassungsblog.de/en/systemic-infringement-action-an-effective-solution-or-rather-part-of-the-problem-2/.

that ECJ enforcement of Article 2 TEU should be contemplated. For example, former Commission Vice President Viviane Reding, while still in office holding the Justice portfolio, suggested that the Commission could consider grounding an infringement action in Article 2 TEU.[42] Christophe Hillion's chapter in this volume makes the case more strongly, arguing that the Commission as guardian of the Treaties should be able to enforce Article 2 TEU to ward off more serious violations.[43] He envisions judicial enforcement of Article 2 as a precautionary measure seeking to dissuade an offending Member State from engaging in conduct which could ground an Article 7 TEU procedure. Most recently, the 'Editorial Comments' in the Common Market Law Review noted that 'the Treaties neither restrain nor exclude the Court of Justice's jurisdiction in relation to Article 2 TEU. Had such limitation been wanted, the primary law-makers could have made it explicit'.[44]

A novel action would take some serious work to put together. In particular, many of the Article 2 values are stated very broadly, and critics say it would be difficult to create workable definitions of those general terms to make Article 2 legally enforceable.[45] But you could start with the Rule of Law, which is not a mysterious concept to a judge. Surely, it includes the idea of judicial independence, and the ECJ already has jurisprudence specifying what it means for other important EU institutions to be independent.[46] Using these standards, the ECJ could easily assess whether the independence of a Member State's judiciary had been compromised, something that would raise serious questions about the Member State's commitment to the Rule of Law as an Article 2 principle.

Take Hungary for example. As we have seen, the ECJ already found that the government of Hungary had committed unlawful age discrimination

---

[42] 'We could go further, by creating a new specific procedure to enforce the rule of law principle of Article 2 TEU against Member States by means of an infringement procedure brought by the Commission or another Member State before the Court of Justice'. V. Reding, Vice-President of the European Commission, 'The EU and the Rule of Law: What Next?' Speech given 4 September 2013, at http://europa.eu/rapid/press-release_SPEECH-13-677_en.htm.

[43] Hillion, 'Overseeing the Rule of Law in the EU'.

[44] Editorial Comments, 'Safeguarding EU Values in the Member States – Is Something Finally Happening?', 52 (2015) CMLRev. 619, 622.

[45] Ibid., at 625. But the authors then went on (at 626) to argue that the EU judiciary could also contribute to the clarification of Article 2 TEU.

[46] See, for example, the cases on the independence of data protection commissioners: Case C-288/12 Commission v. Hungary ECLI:EU:C:2014:237; Case C-518/07 Commission v. Germany ECLI:EU:C:2010:125; Case C-614/10 Commission v. Austria ECLI:EU:C:2012:631.

when it suddenly lowered the judicial retirement age and dismissed the most senior ten percent of its judiciary.[47] But surely the problem was not *just* age discrimination. When the criteria for holding office can be changed so that current judges can be suddenly removed from office, this is also an infringement of the independence of the judiciary. In assessing what it means for an institution to be independent, the ECJ could take a page from its own jurisprudence on the independence of data protection officers in Member States. Hungary had just such a case before the Court when the office of data protection ombudsman was reorganised and the incumbent dismissed before the end of his term. In that case, the ECJ said:

> 54. If it were permissible for every Member State to compel a supervisory authority to vacate office before serving its full term, in contravention of the rules and safeguards established in that regard by the legislation applicable, the threat of premature termination to which that authority would be exposed throughout its term of office could lead it to enter into a form of prior compliance with the political authority, which is incompatible with the requirement of independence.[48]

If we were simply to substitute the word 'judge' for 'supervisory authority' in that paragraph, we would have a strong argument that the lowering of the judicial retirement age was not just age discrimination but also a violation of judicial independence. The Court already has the tools, the standards and the existing jurisprudence to do this.

Finding that a country had altered qualification criteria for sitting judges could be enough for a systemic infringement action, since it would mean establishing that it was not just one judge but fully ten percent of the judiciary that had been dismissed in this way, clearly a pattern of practice. But in the Hungarian case, there is much more. When the retirement age was lowered, the sitting president of the Supreme Court – too young to be affected by this change – was removed because the government changed the qualifications for his job and applied the changes immediately to him. Former Supreme Court President András Baka has since won a case at the European Court of Human Rights over his dismissal.[49] While the Hungarian government was providing for a high level of turnover at the highest levels of the judiciary, it also radically overhauled the system of

---

[47] See text at footnote 20.
[48] Case C-288/12 *Commission* v. *Hungary* ECLI:EU:C:2014:237.
[49] ECt.HR *Baka* v. *Hungary* (App. no. 20261/12, Grand Chamber, 23 June 2016).

judicial appointments,[50] granting the power to appoint, promote, demote, reassign, discipline and remove judges to a single political official close to the government who, for two years, also had the power to move cases from the courts to which they were assigned by law to other courts around the country.[51] The Venice Commission[52] and the International Bar Association[53] found that these measures endangered the independence of the judiciary.

A systemic infringement procedure could bring together this set of changes – the lowering of the retirement age and the consequent termination of judicial appointments, the change of qualifications for judges already in office, the new system for appointing judges which concentrated power in the hands of one political official and the power of this political official to move cases around the court system on her own remit – and allege that the independence of the judiciary had been infringed by each item separately but even more comprehensively when all are taken together. Article 2's Rule of Law provision could provide a doctrinal anchor for this action. It is not necessary to have a precise definition covering all cases at the margins to identify a case which goes to the heart of a principle and it is not necessary to have a precise definition of every single term in Article 2 to be able to enforce the terms more amenable to adjudication.

But legally enforcing the broad principles of Article 2 TEU is not the only theory under which a systemic infringement action could be framed.

[50] K. L. Scheppele, 'First, Let's Pick All the Judges', in Paul Krugman, Conscience of a Liberal Blog, 12 March 2012, at http://krugman.blogs.nytimes.com/2012/03/10/first-lets-pick-all-the-judges/.

[51] J. Rozenberg, 'Meet Tünde Handó: In Hungary, One Woman Effectively Controls the Judiciary, and She Happens to Be Married to the Author of Its Constitution', *The Guardian* (20 March 2012), at www.theguardian.com/law/2012/mar/20/tunde-hando-hungarian-judges.

[52] European Commission for Democracy through Law (Venice Commission), *Opinion on Act CLXII of 2011 on the Legal Status and Remuneration of Judges and Act CLXI of 2011 on the Organisation and Administration of Courts of Hungary*, adopted by the Venice Commission at its 90th Plenary Session (Venice, 16–17 March 2012), CDL-AD(2012)001-e, at www.venice.coe.int/webforms/documents/?pdf=CDL-AD%282012%29001-e and *Opinion on the Cardinal Acts on the Judiciary that were amended following the adoption of Opinion CDL-AD(2012)001 on Hungary*, adopted by the Venice Commission at its 92nd Plenary Session (Venice, 12–13 October 2012), CDL-AD(2012)020-e, at www.venice.coe.int/webforms/documents/?pdf=CDL-AD%282012%29020-e.

[53] International Bar Association's Human Rights Institute (IBAHRI), *Courting Controversy: the Impact of the Recent Reforms on the Independence of the Judiciary and the Rule of Law in Hungary* (September 2012), at www.ibanet.org/Document/Default.aspx?DocumentUid=89D4991A-D61F-498A-BD21-0BAFFA6ABF17.

A systemic infringement procedure could argue, alternatively, that a systemic violation of the basic principles of EU law puts a Member State in violation of Article 4(3) TEU. This is familiar ground to the ECJ, which has already developed extensive jurisprudence in 'sincere cooperation' or loyalty.[54] Using this rubric, the Commission would argue that the laws and practices of the Member State challenged systematically interfere with the operation of EU law in the Member State's jurisdiction and thus violate the Member State's obligations of loyalty.

To see how this might work, consider reframing the proposed infringement procedure on the independence of the judiciary in Hungary as an Article 4(3) TEU action. National courts are, of course, also Union courts, since they are primary enforcers of EU law. If the national courts have been fundamentally reorganised in a Member State to be structurally dependent on political will, then the ability of the national courts to independently assess violations of EU law may be called into question. The laws themselves could be given as evidence that the judiciary has fallen under political influence.

To make the case under Article 4(3) TEU, and to tie the matter more directly to the dangers of mistaken application of EU law, some concrete examples of political pressure being successfully applied to politically vulnerable judges would strengthen the case. Unfortunately, there are already such examples from Hungary, where political officials publicly attacked judicial decisions in cases involving EU law and judges afterwards changed their minds. A tragic car accident in which a drunk driver from Slovakia fell asleep at the wheel and crashed into a car on a Hungarian highway, killing four, may not sound like an EU law case. But when the Slovakian driver was sentenced to six years in prison and given a suspended sentence pending the government's appeal against the judge's leniency, an EU law issue emerged. The head of the governing party's fraction in the Parliament, Antal Rogán, publicly attacked the judge for not jailing the woman immediately, arguing that the Slovakian woman would flee back to Slovakia. That afternoon, another court revoked the suspended sentence and sent the woman to jail. However, the European arrest warrant provides a remedy in case a criminal suspect flees to another EU member state, so citizens of other EU Member States should be treated no differently than citizens of the country where the criminal sentence was issued.[55] In

---

[54] For a comprehensive account of the loyalty principle in EU law, see M. Klamert, *The Principle of Loyalty in EU Law* (Oxford: Oxford University Press, 2014).

[55] For a detailed account of the case, see É. Balogh, 'Political Interference with the Hungarian Judiciary', *Hungarian Spectrum*, 5 December 2013 (hereinafter Political

another recent case, a Roma school run by the Greek Catholic Church was challenged because it included only Roma children, after a decision from the European Court of Human Rights had found that Hungarian schools were engaged in pervasive discrimination.[56] The lower courts that heard the case noted that the church operated parallel segregated Hungarian and Roma schools, and found the schools in violation of both the ECtHR decision and the Equal Treatment Act.[57] These decisions outraged Education Minister Zoltán Balog, who publicly attacked the courts and threatened to change the law. The Supreme Court (*Kúria*) then reversed the decisions and upheld the government's position, despite the obvious conflict with both an ECtHR judgement and the statute transposing the EU Directive.[58] The strong attacks in the public press by governing party officials against the particular judges who made these decisions and then the later compliance of other judges in the system with these partisan demands have given rise to the public view that the judiciary is now subject to political pressure.[59] A Member State in which judges publicly change their minds under political pressure cannot be said to have an independent judiciary. It becomes an EU law matter under Article 4(3) when national legal changes substantially infringe the independence of the judiciary and when the pressure extends to wrongly deciding cases in EU law.

In a third variant of the systemic infringement procedure, the Commission could allege that a Member State has engaged in a systemic violation of a particular substantive area of EU law through a pattern of conduct which adds up to more than the sum of its parts. As we have seen, the Commission has already done this with its 'general and persistent' jurisprudence.[60] But a systemic infringement procedure could elevate the existing practice to permit it to reach cases which challenge the EU values

---

Interference), at http://hungarianspectrum.org/2013/12/05/political-interference-with-the-hungarian-judiciary/.

[56] *Horváth and Kiss* v. *Hungary* (application no. 11146/11).

[57] The Equal Treatment Act, Act CXXV of 2003 on Equal Treatment and the Promotion of Equal Opportunities, transposed Council Directive 2000/43/EC of 29 June 2000 Implementing the Principle of Equal Treatment Between Persons Irrespective of Racial or Ethnic Origin, OJ 2000 No. L180/22.

[58] É. Balogh, The Hungarian Supreme Court Decided: Segregation Is Lawful in Parochial Schools, Hungarian Spectrum blog, 28 April 2015, at http://hungarianspectrum.org/2015/04/28/hungarian-supreme-court-decided-segregation-is-lawful-in-parochial-schools/.

[59] Both the Hungarian Association of Judges and the President of the Hungarian Supreme Court have issued warnings that incidents like this make it appear that judges are politically controlled. Balogh, 'Political Interference with the Hungarian Judiciary'.

[60] See text at footnotes 35–40.

contained in Article 2 TEU, which include protection of human rights. Instead of using Article 2 TEU directly, the Commission could allege that a Member State's infringement of EU law rose to the level of violating individual rights under the EU Charter of Fundamental Rights (CFR).

Article 51 CFR limits the scope of the Charter to EU institutions and 'to the Member States only when they are implementing Union law'.[61] However, if a Member State's systemic violation of EU law is sufficiently extreme, then the rights of EU citizens within that Member State can be endangered. Perhaps a critic might argue that the Charter should not apply where a Member State misapplies or does not apply EU law when it should, but that is a formalism bound to fail.[62]

If the Commission is the guardian of the Treaties – all Treaties, including the Charter – then it has an obligation to ensure that fundamental rights are protected when violated by Member States implementing EU law. Here, the Commission would not be bringing a case against a Member State which infringed a particular individual's right but would instead bring an Article 258 TFEU action for situations in which the regular misapplication of EU law itself generated a practice of widespread rights violation.

It is easier to see how this new form of action would work with an example. The Commission could focus on Hungary's persistent violations of the Data Protection Directive.[63] Since 2011, the Hungarian government has repeatedly gathered the personally identifiable political opinions of individuals through mass surveys ('social consultations') without legal limitations on how the data may be used or how long it might be kept.[64] This is not just a violation of Article 8(1) of the Directive, which directly bans government collection of individually identifiable political opinion, but it is also a violation of Article 6(1) of the Directive, which requires clear legal limits on the collection and use of personal data. These social

---

[61] Art. 51(1) CFR.

[62] See K. Lenaerts, 'Exploring the Limits of the EU Charter of Fundamental Rights', 8 (2012) *EUConst* 375 (arguing that the Charter should apply to Member States' actions even when they have derogated from EU law). Surely, under this logic, Charter rights should apply to Member States misapplying EU law.

[63] Directive 95/46/EC of the European Parliament and of the Council of 24 October 1995 on the Protection of Individuals with Regard to the Processing of Personal Data and on the Free Movement of Such Data, *OJ 1995 No. L281/31*.

[64] I have documented these assertions more fully in K. L. Scheppele, 'Making Infringement Procedures More Effective: A Comment on Commission v. Hungary, Case C-288/12' *Eutopia* Law, 29 April 2014, (hereinafter Scheppele, More Effective), at http://eutopialaw.com/2014/04/29/making-infringement-procedures-more-effective-a-comment-on-commission-v-hungary-case-c-28812-8-april-2014-grand-chamber/.

consultations might also be in violation of Article 28(2) of the Directive, which requires the data protection officer to be involved in all personal data collection efforts, as the data protection ombudsman was dismissed when he brought legal action against this data collection activity, claiming among other things that he had not been consulted before the question-naires went out. The Court has already established that the prior data protection ombudsman had been dismissed in violation of the Directive, which requires his complete independence.[65] It could examine the inde-pendence of the new data protection officer, who is currently housed in an agency nestled within a government ministry, and who has not objected to the practice of social consultation. He dropped the case started by his predecessor challenging these data collection practices, and a new social consultation was issued in spring 2015.[66] The European Parliament reso-lution against Hungary passed in June 2015 specifically criticised Hungary on the data protection issues, including the requirement that people pro-vide personally identifiable information in response to questions about immigration.[67]

The collection of personally identifiable political opinions without legal limit is not just a violation of the Data Protection Directive, but it is also a violation of the individual right of data privacy protected by Article 8 CFR.[68] If Hungary were to be found not just to have infringed EU law but also to have violated the fundamental rights of its citizens in doing so, then the shadow of Article 2 TEU would fall over the case. However, if the case were brought as a systemic violation of the Directive plus an allegation of the infringement of a particular right in the Charter, then the ECJ would not have to rule directly on Article 2. In fact, the same logic would apply to our earlier example of judicial independence, because the Commission could add to the bundled set of complaints mentioned there an allegation that these practices caused a violation of Article 47 CFR, the right to an effective remedy and a fair trial.[69]

---

[65] Case C-288/12 *Commission* v. *Hungary* ECLI:EU:C:2014:237.

[66] European Commission, 'Hungary: Government's National Consultation on Immi-gration and Terrorism Creates Widespread Debate', European Website on Integra-tion, at https://ec.europa.eu/migrant-integration/news/hungary-governments-national-consultation-on-immigration-and-terrorism-creates-widespread-debate?pdf=1.

[67] European Parliament Resolution of 10 June 2015 on the Situation in Hungary (2015/2700(RSP)), para. 5, at www.europarl.europa.eu/sides/getDoc.do?pubRef=-//EP// TEXT+TA+P8-TA-2015-0227+0+DOC+XML+V0//EN&language=EN.

[68] Art. 8 CFR.

[69] Art. 47 CFR. While this chapter was in press, the Commission brought an infringement action against Hungary alleging a violation of Art. 47 CFR together with a number of *acquis* violations in its treatment of refugees'.

Systemic infringement procedures identify the seriousness of violations committed by persistently challenging states by raising important
EU principles in addition to more technical violations. They therefore
also open up a different conversation about what compliance means. By
grouping a set of laws, decisions and practices together to make a more
general case, the Commission would be laying the ground for arguing
that systemic violations of Member State obligations must be met with
systemic compliance actions.

Regardless of how that it is ultimately grounded in EU law, a systemic
infringement procedure would enable the Commission to signal to the
Court of Justice a more general concern about deviation from core principles than a more narrowly tailored infringement action would allow.
It would also have the advantage of putting before the ECJ consolidated
evidence of a *pattern* of violation so that the overall situation in a particular Member State is not lost in a flurry of individual complaints, each of
which might go to a different panel of judges. The ECJ could then either
agree with the Commission that the set of allegations packaged together
amounts something more systemic which violates basic EU values, or it
could find that only some of the allegations within the set violate particular aspects of EU law. Just as with the 'general and persistent' cases,
the ECJ would ultimately have to determine whether the larger pattern of
infringement were proved by the Commission.

III   Reframing Compliance under the Systemic
Infringement Procedure

If the ECJ agrees that a Member State's conduct rises to the level of a
systemic violation, then compliance with the Court's judgment should
also be systemic. A Member State should be required to fix not just
small technical violations in its implementation of EU law, but it should
also be required to fix the systemic threat to EU principles. Compliance
should therefore be assessed differently than in a more highly tailored
infringement actions. A systemic infringement action should therefore
open up a wider range of options for what would count as compliance,
something to which the ECJ would contribute by finding a range of linked
practices to be violations of EU law.

Pål Wennerås has noted that the Commission often seems not to
be looking ahead to the compliance and sanctions phases when it files

infringement procedures under Article 258 TFEU.[70] As a result, the Commission sometimes finds that it must file a fresh Article 258 TFEU action to mop up the spillover from its initial action to make the sanctions effective. If the Commission returns to the ECJ to assess a fine for failing to comply with the Court's initial decision under Article 260 TFEU, the sanctions must be limited to assessing whether a Member State has failed to do what the ECJ had ordered. If the ECJ found no violation of a neighbouring provision or practice which would need to be changed in order to achieve full compliance with its ruling, then the ECJ will not approve of sanctions which target a provision or practice which was not raised in the initial action. This problem, which becomes particularly apparent under Article 260 TFEU, no doubt blows back on the ability of the Commission to enforce a judgment effectively in the first place as it seeks initial compliance. If an infringing Member State can see that the Commission's hands are tied, enforcing the Court's precise ruling and no more, the Member State can evade systemic compliance by limiting its responses as narrowly as possible to those specific items. If infringement of EU law extends to the infringement of EU principles, however, a narrowly drafted ECJ ruling may not provide enough leeway to the Commission to ensure full compliance.

Take the Hungarian judicial age discrimination case, for example. Instead of bringing the case as a matter of age discrimination, suppose the Commission had brought the question of judicial independence before the ECJ in a systemic infringement procedure, claiming that Hungary was violating the Rule of Law under Article 2 TEU or that it was infringing the loyalty principle under Article 4(3) TEU. If the ECJ confirmed the systemic infringement, then the Hungarian government would have had to address more than the wishes of the specific judges affected by the one-off lowering of the retirement age, unlike in the simple discrimination case. With a more systemic framing, compliance could require measures to ensure that faith in the neutrality and objectivity of the judiciary was restored. This could include ensuring in law and practice that judges were secure in their positions and could not be arbitrarily dismissed, demoted or disciplined if they ruled against the government. If the prematurely retired judges no longer wanted to return to their jobs, then compliance could consider the difference it had made that they had been removed.

In this example, and in fact in almost any case one can imagine that would rise to this level of seriousness, the Commission will probably not

---

[70] Wennerås, 'Making Effective Use'.

be the first institution to take note of the problems and to assess both what is happening and what should be done to correct the problem. In the Hungarian case, the Venice Commission had reviewed the country's judicial reforms twice. It had found fault with the political nature of the judicial appointments and had argued for a stronger role for the National Judicial Council in personnel matters so that judges' careers would be largely controlled by judges.[71] Moreover, the Venice Commission disapproved of the system in which all Hungarian judges were reviewed by the presidents of their courts,[72] many of whom had themselves been appointed in this political process. The Hungarian government made some minor changes in response to the Venice Commission's report, but the Venice Commission assessed those changes and argued that they did not go far enough to guarantee the independence of the judiciary.[73] There were other specific recommendations in the two Venice Commission reports on the Hungarian judiciary that the Hungarian government never acted upon; the European Commission could start with those recommendations as a way of ensuring the independence of the judiciary. Of course, the point of requiring reform would not be just to have the right structures on paper but to ensure the independence of the judiciary in daily practice, so a monitoring mission could be created to ensure that the reforms worked.[74] Obviously having the Venice Commission reports and other expert assessments of the problem would be helpful in designing what compliance with EU principles should look like. The general point, however, is that a finding of the ECJ that there has been a systemic violation should be followed by a plan for systemic compliance.

---

[71] European Commission for Democracy through Law (Venice Commission), *Opinion on Act CLXII of 2011 on the Legal Status and Remuneration of Judges and Act CLXI of 2011 on the Organisation and Administration of Courts of Hungary*, adopted by the Venice Commission at its 90th Plenary Session (Venice, 16–17 March 2012), CDL-AD(2012)001-e, para. 65, at www.venice.coe.int/webforms/documents/?pdf=CDL-AD%282012%29001-e.

[72] *Ibid.*, para. 53.

[73] European Commission for Democracy through Law (Venice Commission), *Opinion on the Cardinal Acts on the Judiciary that were amended following the adoption of Opinion CDL-AD(2012)001 on Hungary*, adopted by the Venice Commission at its 92nd Plenary Session (Venice, 12–13 October 2012). CDL-AD(2012)020-e, paras 35, 44, at www.venice .coe.int/webforms/documents/?pdf=CDL-AD%282012%29020-e.

[74] The European Parliament called for just such a monitoring mechanism to be created as an 'Article 2 TEU/Alarm Agenda', European Parliament, Resolution of 3 July 2013 on the Situation of Fundamental Rights: Standards and Practices in Hungary (Pursuant to the European Parliament Resolution of 16 February 2012) (2012/2130(INI)), para. 70, at www.europarl.europa.eu/sides/getDoc.do?type=TA&language=EN&reference=P7-TA-2013-315.

Some might object that the European Commission has no power to micromanage the detailed institutional arrangements of Member States, a very sensitive subject. The internal political structures of Member States are broadly protected by Article 4(2) TEU, which requires that the Union respect Member States' 'national identities, inherent in their fundamental structures, political and constitutional'. But surely the constitutional arrangements of Member States have to be broadly compliant with the values listed in Article 2. Is there really to be no remedy in EU law if a Member State government permitted its Prime Minister to dismiss any judge who sided with the EU against the government in a matter of EU law? What if a Member State government engaged in widespread human rights violations while implementing EU law? If the answer is that 'this is what Article 7 is for', then that presupposes that legal violations have only political remedies. While Article 7 is ultimately the only way to launch political sanctions, such as removing a Member State's vote in European institutions, there is surely a place for legal sanctions to attempt to prevent a Member State's violations from reaching that point. Giving the Commission the power to require that a Member State should follow the recommendations of the Venice Commission, for example, would be one way to do that.

As this example illustrates, the point of a systemic infringement action ultimately is to bring the Member State into compliance with European principles. Given this goal, the Commission should decide how to frame a systemic infringement action from the start by thinking ahead to what it would need to accomplish in the compliance phase to achieve that goal. The Commission should therefore include in the systemic infringement action the changes to laws and practices which would be required to fix the systemic problem, if the ECJ confirms the systemic infringement. Challenging a broader set of laws, practices and outcomes would enable the Commission to fashion a remedy which would permit the key principles of the EU to be realised in practice. In fact, the systemic infringement action's primary rationale is that it focuses attention on compliance with the principles underlying EU law rather than simply fixing one-off complaints with patches.

IV Suspending EU Funds as a New Approach to Fines

What if a state remains in systemic and persistent noncompliance in violation of a decision of the ECJ? In an ordinary infringement action, the Commission would go back to the ECJ for assessment of a fine under

Article 260(2) TFEU for general violations of ECJ decisions[75] or Article 260(3) TFEU for failures to transpose directives. The same options would be open to the Commission in a systemic infringement procedure if the Member State did not engage in systemic compliance. However, I would argue that these cases should be accompanied by a new fining option. Instead of charging a fine to be paid from the Member State's treasury, the Commission should instead seek to suspend payment of EU funds to the offending Member State in the value of the fine.

Why seek fines at all? At the moment, the only sanction available under Article 260 TFEU is the payment of fines. But as the comprehensive study by Brian Jack has concluded,[76] the threat of fines rarely results in the actual payment of fines, because states typically comply at the last minute before the payments must be made. However, such compliance is achieved only after substantial delays, regardless of whether the fines are charged per day or charged in a lump sum. Since the average time between an adverse judgment against a Member State in an infringement procedure under Article 258 TFEU and the subsequent judgment about penalties under Article 260 TFEU is nine years: 'In truth, the EU lacks an effective mechanism to prevent Member States from using penalty payments to "purchase" continued noncompliance or indeed from simply ignoring both Court judgements'.[77]

Revisions in the Lisbon Treaty were designed to streamline the Article 260 proceedings. Now the Commission can seek sanctions for failure to transpose directives directly under Article 260(3) TFEU and no longer needs to produce a separate reasoned opinion for the sanctions sought in other cases under Article 260(2) TFEU.[78] Jack's investigation shows that these adjustments worked: fines are being requested and granted faster now than before the Lisbon amendments.[79] Nonetheless, Member States still drag their feet and stall recognition of the judgment – and then when Member States finally come into compliance, the sums they owe are completely forgiven.[80] Jack concluded that the sanctions available are not

---

[75] Wennerås suggests that Article 260 TFEU might not be limited to enforcement only in Article 258 TFEU procedures, but argues that it might also be used with actions brought under Article 108(2) TFEU, Article 114(9) TFEU and Article 348(2) TFEU. Wennerås, 'Making Effective Use'.

[76] B. Jack, 'Article 260(2) TFEU: An Effective Judicial Procedure for the Enforcement of Judgements?', 19 (2013) ELJ 404 (hereinafter Jack, Effective Judicial Procedure).

[77] Ibid., 421.   [78] Wennerås, 'Making Effective Use'.

[79] Jack, 'Effective Judicial Procedure'.

[80] In actions under Article 260(2) TFEU, fines are rarely if ever collected because there is usually some accommodation before the fines are due. See D. Kochenov, 'On Policing

doing the work that they should because Member States suffer no penalty for delaying compliance for years and years. While this already seems a persistent problem, it is an even more serious problem with persistently and pervasively violating states because their non-compliance is a more substantial threat to the operation of the European Union as well as to the realisation of rights for EU citizens. A more effective sanction is needed in these extreme cases.

In March 2013, the foreign ministers of Germany, the Netherlands, Finland and Denmark[81] wrote to the European Commission suggesting that new tools were needed to bring persistently deviant Member States into line:

> At this critical stage in European history, it is crucially important that the fundamental values enshrined in the European Treaties be vigorously protected. The EU must be extremely watchful whenever they are put at risk anywhere within its borders. And it must be able to react swiftly and effectively to ensure compliance with its most basic principles. We propose addressing this issue as a priority and believe that the Commission has a key role to play here.[82]

In particular, they proposed that 'as a last resort, the suspension of EU funding should be possible'.[83]

This linking of persistent and systemic noncompliance with the suspension of EU funding makes perfect sense. Withholding funds can act as a powerful motivator for a Member State to come into line with European principles, even more than the prospect of paying a fine in some distant future.[84] If a Member State continues to refuse to comply with systemic infringement judgments once EU funds are withheld, it will be clear that the European Union cannot always make a Member State change its ways,

---

Article 2 TEU Compliance: Systemic Infringements and Reverse Solange Analyzed', 33 (2014) *Polish Yearbook of International Law* 145.

[81] I. Traynor, 'Hungarian Prime Minister Warned over Moves to Increase His Power' The Guardian (8 March 2013), at www.theguardian.com/world/2013/mar/08/hungarian-prime-minister-warned-power.

[82] The text of the letter is at www.rijksoverheid.nl/bestanden/documenten-en-publicaties/brieven/2013/03/13/brief-aan-europese-commissie-over-opzetten-rechtsstatelijkheidsmechanisme/brief-aan-europese-commissie-over-opzetten-rechtsstatelijkheidsmechanisme.pdf.

[83] *Ibid.*

[84] Behavioural economics research has long shown that subjects will feel the loss of what they clearly expected more acutely than an equal sanction which is not immediate. For the classic source, see D. Kahneman and A. Tversky, 'Choices, Values, and Frames', 39 (1984) *American Psychology* 341–50.

but at least Europe will not continue to subsidise a Member State which flaunts the EU's basic values.

Attaching suspension of EU funds to a judgment of noncompliance by the ECJ has the virtue of making such a sanction a multi-institutional process, something true of other serious EU sanctions. The usual Article 258 infringement procedure requires the ECJ to agree with the Commission before a Member State can be instructed to comply. The Excessive Deficit Procedure permits cutting Cohesion Funds for violation of fiscal rules but requires ECOFIN to agree with the Commission before the funds are cut.[85] Article 7 requires both the Council and the Parliament to agree before sanctions take effect. As a result, attaching EU funding cuts to a process initiated by the Commission that must first generate two adverse ECJ judgments (the initial finding of a violation and the subsequent finding of noncompliance) has the requisite safeguards against arbitrariness. Cutting EU funds should not simply be a matter at the discretion of the Commission but should be built into an inter-institutional process like other EU sanctions.

The Commission already has in place a system for calculating fines under Article 260 TFEU[86] and, in the case of the systemic noncompliance, it could use the same formula so that the freezing of EU funds would be made proportionate to the seriousness of the violation of EU law. The only new twist would be that the Commission would then request that the fines be collected by deducting this amount from the money that the EU would otherwise pay to the offending Member State. Rather than waiting to extract a fine from a Member State while it delays compliance, the Commission would be able to carry out sanctions immediately by suspending the payment of EU funds to the amount which would otherwise have been sought as a fine. This gets the incentives right: the persistently violating Member State would have to prove its compliance in order to release the funds rather than being able to stall in violation until the fines

[85] Council Regulation (EC) 1466/97 on the Strengthening of the Surveillance of Budgetary Positions and the Surveillance and Coordination of Economic Policies, as amended by Council Regulation (EC) 1055/2005 of 27 June 2005 and Regulation (EU) No 1175/2011.

[86] For the Commission's method of calculating fines, see Communication from the Commission, Application of Article 258 of the EC Treaty, SEC(2005) 1658, at http://ec.europa.eu/atwork/applying-eu-law/docs/sec_2005_1658_en.pdf and Communication of the Commission, Implementation of Article 260(3) of the Treaty, 2011/C 12/0, at http://eur-lex.europa.eu/legal-content/EN/TXT/PDF/?uri=CELEX: 52011XC0115%2801%29&from=EN, with the most recent updated financial calculations (for 2014), at http://ec.europa.eu/atwork/applying-eu-law/docs/c_2014_6767_en.pdf.

are finally demanded. Suspending the payment of EU funds changes the baseline against which the State is acting, and it would provide much greater incentives for early compliance. Right now, as Jack's study shows, a state has nothing to lose when it waits as long as it can to comply – which is often from years to decades.

If the Commission sought suspension of EU funds as a sanction, then the suspension should be timed to occur as soon as the ECJ issues an Article 260 TFEU judgment. It is a trickier problem to figure out – when the sanctions should cease, as Wennerås notes.[87] If the Commission wants to maintain sanctions because it feels that the Member State has not yet complied, while the Member State claims that it has, then this conflict must be resolved by the ECJ. However, Wennerås's worry that the Commission might be tempted to continue sanctions after a Member State has complied applies not just to cases where EU funds might be cut, but equally to determining when daily penalties assessed by the ECJ must cease.[88] In both cases the question is what happens to the sanctions while the ECJ is resolving the conflict between the Member State and the Commission. With fines, the question does not arise in practice because the fines are not collected until the end, if at all. However, with funding streams, the penalties could be ongoing until they are halted.

An option is that, upon a credible demonstration of compliance to the ECJ in a proceeding such as that required in an 'interim measures' case,[89] the Member State could access these funds until a final judgment is made by the ECJ. Then, if the final ruling went against the Member State, it would have to pay the funds back. At that point, the problem already identified with Article 260 sanctions would appear – that Member States do not pay while the non-compliance continues and all fines are ultimately forgiven. Therefore, perhaps the funds to be returned in cases such as this should be deducted from ongoing funding streams. This is a technical issue to be resolved with this new sanctions mechanism, but nothing new in theory.

---

[87] Wennerås, 'Making Effective Use'.

[88] Case T-33/09 *Portugal* v. *Commission* ECLI:EU:T:2011:127, paras 69–72.

[89] The rules of the ECJ already allow applications to suspend the operation of judgments in other cases pending a final hearing, but at present these rules do not cover cases brought under Article 258. Rules of Procedure of the Court of Justice of 25 September 2012 (OJ 2012 No. L265/1), as amended on 18 June 2013 (OJ 2013 No. L173/65). Chapter X. An amendment to the rules would have to be made to permit interim measures to be available in these cases.

If a Member State were found in a systemic infringement procedure to have violated its obligations, full compliance would require serious changes and may take some time to accomplish. This is all the more reason for the *status quo* to be accompanied by incentives to change quickly. If the Member State faces an immediate freeze on funds from the EU, this will focus the government's attention on compliance as a high priority. Once the Member State complies, it can be rewarded by the release of the funds which were suspended. Ultimately, the result will be the same as under the current system: the Member State would end up paying nothing once it complies. But the interim situation is quite different under the two systems. Under this proposal, the Member State would bear the burden until compliance is assured, while under the current situation, the EU would suffer from non-compliance for years.

How would a suspension of funds be possible under EU law? The major sanctioning mechanisms are generally provided in the Treaties, and Treaty change – with a persistently non-complying Member State holding a veto – does not seem very likely.

I believe that this change would not require Treaty change, or even secondary legislation. The language of Article 260 TFEU already contemplates a monetary penalty for violation of a ECJ decision under Article 258 TFEU without specifying how the fine should be paid. In particular, the language of Article 260(2) TFEU does not say that the fine must be paid from the treasury of the Member State to the EU. The precise language of Article 260(2) says, 'If the Court finds that the Member State concerned has not complied with its judgment it may impose a lump sum or penalty payment on it'. It does not specify *how* the penalty should be collected. It seems a matter of interpretation of Treaty language to find that the money could be withheld from payments already committed from the EU to the Member State treasury rather than being paid from the Member State treasury to the EU. In both cases the fine is the same, since money is fungible. The only difference is that the Commission could immediately create stronger incentives for compliance by suspending payment of EU funds to the Member State without waiting for the Member State to pay the EU.

If this seems an interpretation too far and the Commission wanted unquestioned legal permission, it could seek secondary legislation to make this option clear. In other contexts, most notably the Excessive Deficit Procedure (EDP), secondary legislation has already permitted funds allocated for one purpose (e.g. Cohesion) to be docked for failure to comply with the requirements of another part of EU law (e.g. Stability and Growth).[90] The same sort of secondary legislation could be proposed to deal with Member States that persistently refuse to remedy systemic infringements, allowing EU funding streams to be cut for infringement of basic EU values.

The reversal of systemic injury to EU values by a Member State could require substantial reforms, and if a Member State presented serious and realisable plans for engaging in systemic reform, EU funds could then be gradually released to enable the Member State to carry out this plan. The point, as with ECJ fines more generally, is not to hurt the country and especially not its citizens, but to encourage compliance at the earliest possible moment and to provide assistance for projects that demonstrate solidarity with EU principles.

V   Conclusion

The European Union is experiencing a crisis of values, as some Member States are openly flouting the basic principles of EU law. This could be regarded as a political crisis to be addressed by EU political bodies invoking Article 7. However, even if it represents a political crisis, it is also simultaneously a legal crisis, as key provisions of EU law are being violated systematically without a meaningful attempt to address the violations. When violations are not neat and singular but plural and complex, the Commission needs to rise to the occasion and adapt the instruments at its disposal to meet the new challenges.

The systemic infringement procedure could provide a mechanism for the Commission to act alongside the Court of Justice to ensure that Member States that persistently and pervasively violate EU law meet their legal obligations. By identifying a pattern of Member State conduct as the subject of a single infringement action and demonstrating to the ECJ that the pattern constitutes a systemic violation of EU principles, the Commission could be given the tools to develop a programme of systemic remedy. If a Member State can play cat and mouse with the Commission by changing its infringement practices just enough to meet the narrow tests of narrow decisions, or if the Commission fails to anticipate the remedies that would follow as it designs infringement actions in the first place, then the principles of EU law will devolve into petty legalisms

---

[90] N. de Sadeleer, 'The New Architecture of the European Economic Governance: A Leviathan or a Flat-Footed Colossus', 19 (2012) *Maastricht Journal of European and Comparative Law* 354.

which are honoured only superficially. Something more needs to be done if we are to avoid a moral crisis in Europe. In this chapter, I have tried to sketch out a way to motivate the Commission and the Court to act by ensuring that the basic principles of EU law are honoured in all Member States.

6

Mutual Trust

The Virtue of Reciprocity – Strengthening the Acceptance of the Rule of Law through Peer Review

ERNST HIRSCH BALLIN*

I Introduction

All relations between persons require their reciprocal acceptance as legal subjects, which is possible only if they trust that the law will bind them together. The European Union (EU) is a polity which expresses itself in a legal order built on a diversity of national legal orders. Since it is neither possible nor desirable to replace national legal acts of any kind – be they administrative decisions or court rulings – with European legal acts, their mutual recognition is a cornerstone of the cohesion and functioning of the Union. Both the area of freedom, security and justice[1] and the internal market[2] are built on mutual recognition, that is, legal reciprocity. The Rule of Law is one of the foundational values of the Union.[3]

That is embryonically why the EU must be built on the Rule of Law. Aristotle saw that the reciprocal nature of the law is a part of the foundations of a well-ordered society. 'The public-spirited acts of a citizen motivated by a sense of justice and civic friendship are not purely altruistic or beneficent: they are based on [...] an expectation of reciprocal benefits'.[4] The great philosopher recognised that 'the rule of men over

---

* Professor of Dutch and European Constitutional Law (Tilburg University) and Human Rights Law (University of Amsterdam). He served as Minister of Justice of the Netherlands (1989–1994 and 2006–2010) and is now *inter alia* a member of the Netherlands Advisory Council on International Affairs. The author thanks Caia Vlieks LL.M. (Tilburg University) for her valuable editing work and comments.
[1] Art. 3(2) TEU.   [2] Art. 3(3) TEU.
[3] Compare Art. 2 and the Preamble of the Treaty on the European Union.
[4] D. Morrison, 'The Common Good', in M. Deslauriers and P. Destré (eds.), *The Cambridge Companion to Aristotle's Politics* (Cambridge: Cambridge University Press, 2013), pp. 176, 194.

men is less desirable than the rule of law':[5] 'man is, when perfected, the best of animals, but, when separated from law and justice, he is the worst of all'.[6]

Democracy in the EU also depends on the veracity of its aspiration, that is, to create a method of decision-making on the legal rules governing the communities and policies in which a majority under the conditions of respect for minorities decides on the realisation of shared values. One cannot have a democratic and legitimate EU if the Rule of Law is absent or fading. The Rule of Law implies that the law is the same for all. Reciprocity is a virtue in how people or entities behave towards each other. Fidelity depends on reciprocity:[7] it is an indispensable prerequisite for the acceptance of obligations.

With respect to the operations of the EU institutions, the Rule of Law is firmly rooted in the Treaties and the case law of the Court of Justice of the European Union (ECJ). It includes the principle of legality, legal certainty, fair application of the law, the principle of equality, the obligation to state the specific legal basis and the reasons for legal acts, effective legal protection and that of effective enjoyment of rights under EU law, including fundamental rights.[8] However, the constitutional system of the EU depends on a much wider and more complicated framework of institutions in the Member States which – in accordance with the principle of subsidiarity and decentralised enforcement[9] – also expresses its weakest link, precisely because of its encompassing nature. Specific legislative acts on procedural rights (e.g. on access to legal assistance and interpreters) contribute to it and the ECJ oversees its implementation.

The Rule of Law is more than a rule or even a principle (which can be balanced against other principles).[10] Article 2 TEU rightly calls it a founding value. National and international political credibility and social cohesion depend on the acceptance of this principle. The Rule of Law

---

[5] C. Horn, 'Law, Governance, and Political Obligation', in: M. Deslauriers and P. Destré, *The Cambridge Companion to Aristotle's Politics*, pp. 223, 234.

[6] Aristotle, *Politics*, I 2, 1253a31–33, quoted in Horn, 'Law, Governance, and Political Obligation', 234.

[7] J. Brunnée and S. Toope, *Legitimacy and Legality in International Law: An Interactional Account* (Cambridge: Cambridge University Press, 2010), pp. 38–9.

[8] M.L. Fernández Esteban, *The Rule of Law in the European Constitution* (The Hague: Kluwer Law International, 1999), Chapter 5.

[9] R. Schütze, *European Constitutional Law* (Cambridge: Cambridge University Press, 2012), p. 250.

[10] On the difference between principles and values, see Fernández Esteban, *The Rule of Law in the European Constitution*, pp. 39–42.

in the EU is however continuously challenged by tensions between the realisation of the values enshrined in Article 2, as well as the human rights norms and principles confirmed in Article 6, and 'contemporary understandings of "law as a means to an end"'.[11] A lack of respect for independence of the courts or citizens' rights is difficult to redress. This is a question of political and administrative culture beyond enforcement of specific legal obligations.

Kochenov convincingly argues that 'the concept of the Rule of Law to be used in European law should also acquire a substantive dimension, to add substance to its procedural aspects. This substance is nothing other than the objectives of integration'.[12] In view of its relationship with reciprocal respect among institutions and citizens for human dignity, the close relationship between the Rule of Law and human rights should also become a part of our understanding of the Rule of Law. In other words: what counts is not the rule of any 'law', irrespective of its content, but law in a democratic constitutional framework which contributes to the realisation of human rights. The opponents of enhanced Rule of Law supervision refer to the diversity between the Member States, but the Rule of Law is part of the indispensable homogeneity of values within the Union.[13] The Rule of Law has – in the words of Abdullahi Ahmed An-Na'im – a universal significance, both in international relations and domestically in view of the 'liberation from all forms of fear, including human domination'.[14]

II The Economic and Political Relevance of the Rule of Law

The Rule of Law is not only a condition for trust among citizens, but also for trust in economic life. After the collapse of the Warsaw Pact,

---

[11] M. Krygier, 'Rule of Law', in M. Rosenfeld and A. Sajó (eds.), *The Oxford Handbook of Comparative Constitutional Law* (Oxford: Oxford University Press, 2012), pp. 233, 247; B. Z. Tamanaha, *Law as a Means to an End: Threat to the Rule of Law* (Cambridge: Cambridge University Press, 2006).

[12] D. Kochenov, 'The EU Rule of Law: Cutting Paths through Confusion', 2(5) (2009) *Erasmus Law Review*, p. 24.

[13] S. Mangiameli, 'The Union's Homogeneity and Its Common Values on the Treaty on European Union', in H.-J. Blanke and S. Mangiameli (eds.), *The European Union after Lisbon* (Heidelberg: Springer, 2012), pp. 21–46.

[14] A. A. An-Na'im, 'Transcending Imperialism: Human Values and Global Citizenship', in S. Young (ed.), *The Tanner Lectures on Human Values*, Vol. 30 (Salt Lake City: Utah University Press, 2011), p. 143, at http://tannerlectures.utah.edu/_documents/a-to-z/a/An-Naim_10.pdf.

many Western European politicians deceived themselves and others with the idea that a multiparty system and economic liberalisation would be sufficient for freedom and democracy to flourish. Economic prosperity depends on reliable institutions, including the Rule of Law.[15] The Rule of Law 'implies that laws cannot be simply used by one group to encroach upon the rights of another'.[16] The four economic freedoms of the European Communities and today of the EU – the free movement of goods, capital, services and people – require access to administrative and judicial proceedings on an equal footing for a Member State's own citizens and other European citizens.

The enlargement of the EU in the first ten years of the twenty-first century with twelve Member States was, much more than Eurosceptics try to make us believe, the result of a coherent view on Europe's future. The EU wanted to bring stability across Europe, based on shared values through the irreversible inclusion of the – mostly post-communist – societies which had emerged from the former Soviet Union in a moral, economic and legal commonwealth. (That the Baltic states were treated the same way harks back to their firm westward orientation and their independence until their brutal occupation by the Soviet Union in 1940.)

According to the so-called Copenhagen criteria, admission to full membership depended not only on their adoption of the *acquis communautaire* into their laws but also on the other 'Copenhagen criteria', defined by the European Council in 1993, summarised as:

Countries wishing to join need to have:

– stable institutions guaranteeing democracy, the Rule of Law, human rights and respect for and protection of minorities;
– a functioning market economy and the capacity to cope with competition and market forces in the EU;
– the ability to take on and implement effectively the obligations of membership, including adherence to the aims of a political, economic and monetary union.[17]

Candidate Member States had to play their own part first, albeit with expensive assistance from the EU and the Western European Member

---

[15] D. Acemoglu and J. A. Robinson, *Why Nations Fail: The Origins of Power, Prosperity, and Poverty* (London: Profile Books, 2012).

[16] *Ibid.*, 327.

[17] European Commission, 'Conditions for Membership' *Europa.eu* (19 November 2014), at http://ec.europa.eu/enlargement/policy/conditions-membership/index_en.htm.

States. The policymakers knew of the risks of societies backsliding into autocratic and illiberal forms of governance. They estimated that inclusion in the EU would offer the best possible protection against such risks. Contrary to a widespread belief at that time, they did not expect that the European policymaking process would easily assimilate its extended membership. With so many new Member States, the EU needed to change its decision-making processes and to create a direct bond of trust with its citizens. The decisions taken by the heads of state and government around the turn of the century aimed to achieve the latter through the adoption of a Charter of Fundamental Rights of the European Union (CFR), and initially through a profound overhaul of the Union's setup through a constitutional treaty. Some politicians tried to preserve old ideas of national sovereignty with rearguard actions against the CFR and judicial cooperation, but overlooked the cultural dimension of integration[18] with as much naiveté as the proponents of constitutional pomp and circumstance for the constitutional treaty. The core question is trust in institutions which are not easily recognisable as the people's own institutions. This is much more a question of living values than of European legality.

Strengthening and upholding the trust of the citizens requires much more than the enforcement of European law in the courts, and breaching their trust cannot wait to be cured until the conditions for application of Article 7 TEU are met. It is, as Article 2 TEU rightly says, a question of *values*: 'the values of respect for human dignity, freedom, democracy, equality, the Rule of Law and respect for human rights, including the rights of persons belonging to minorities'. The question of how a public authority can promote its values – such as the Rule of Law – has been discussed in different contexts, for example, in ombudsmen reports. The United Nations (UN) human rights enforcement system uses peer review as one of its instruments, partly because of the absence of an international human rights court in the foreseeable future. The 'Universal Periodic Review' (UPR), established by the Human Rights Council in Resolution 5/1 of 18 June 2007, gained high acclaim. The UPR is based on self-reporting by the UN member states in multi-year cycles about the protection of human rights in their jurisdictions, alongside reports from the UN High Commissioner for Human Rights, independent reports and information from non-governmental organisations and national human

---

[18] P. Lindseth, 'Constitutionalism Beyond the State? The Administrative Character of European Governance Revisited', 33 (2012) *Cardozo Law Review*, pp. 101, 107.

rights institutions. It encourages member states to take action to improve their record. In this peer-review mechanism:

> Council members ask questions and make recommendations to reporting states. Innovative features are: (i) universality and equal treatment among all member states [...]; and (ii) interstate, interactive dialogue between the country under review and other UN member states.[19]

The UPR was one of the sources of inspiration for proposals to bolster the promotion of the Rule of Law in the EU.

III   The Stockholm Programme

Article 67(4) TFEU requires the development of mutual recognition in the area of freedom, security and justice. The Hague Programme endorsed in 2004 envisaged 'carry[ing] further the mutual recognition of judicial decisions and certificates both in civil and in criminal matters'.[20] In the preparations for 'The Stockholm Programme: An Open and Secure Europe Serving and Protecting Citizens' 2010–2014,[21] a Dutch initiative played a significant role, which was described and evaluated by the Inspection for Development Cooperation and Policy Evaluation of the Netherlands Ministry of Foreign Affairs.[22] The Dutch initiative aimed to strengthen trust through Rule of Law evaluations, based on reciprocity. It was launched at a symposium in December 2007 in Brussels with a speech by the then Minister of Justice, followed by discussion and subsequent promotion in coalition, first with Belgium and Luxemburg, later with France and Germany. Their shared interest was to create a positive context for the further advancement of the principle of mutual recognition and to respond to feelings of unease at the application of this principle. Negative experiences with pre-trial detention after the issuance of a European

---

[19] G. Gori, 'Compliance' in D. Shelton (ed.), *The Oxford Handbook of International Human Rights Law* (Oxford: Oxford University Press, 2013), pp. 893, 896.

[20] Council of the European Union, 'Note of the General Secretariat to the Delegations on the Hague Programme: Strengthening Freedom, Security and Justice in the European Union', 16054/04, Brussels, 13 December 2004.

[21] European Council, 'The Stockholm Programme – An Open and Secure Europe Serving and Protecting Citizens' [2010] OJ No. C115/1.

[22] M. van den Berge and B. Limonard, *Nederland en de onderhandelingen over het Stockholm Programma. Casestudie 3 bij IOB Evaluatie nr. 395: Strategie bij benadering. Nederlandse coalitievorming en de multi-bi benadering in het kader van de EU-besluitvorming (2008–2012)* (Inspectie Ontwikkelingssamenwerking en Beleidsevaluatie (IOB), Ministerie van Buitenlandse Zaken 2014), available in Dutch at www.iob-evaluatie.nl/sites/iob-evaluatie.nl/files/Casestudie%203%20bij%20IOB%20395_Stockholm%20Programma%20DEF_2014.pdf.

Arrest Warrant or hurdles in judicial protection for investors from other Member States illustrated the need for improvement. The lengthy pre-trial detention in some Member States after the execution of an Arrest Warrant had been criticised in legal research and by parliamentarians as a shortcoming of the blanket reliance on the judicial system elsewhere in the European Union.[23] The division of responsibility for dealing with requests for asylum under the Dublin system was stymied if a Member State failed to comply with Rule of Law-related requirements in their procedures.[24] In the wake of the Swedish presidency, the Dutch initiative was discussed with specialists from several Member States and the European institutions at a conference in Maastricht in June 2009.[25]

The Stockholm Programme was proposed by the Justice and Home Affairs Council under the Swedish presidency in 2009 and decided by the European Council on December 11, 2009. The Programme included the following decision on this subject:

> The European Council invites the Commission to [...] submit one or several proposals under Article 70 TFEU concerning the evaluation of the Union policies referred to in Title V of TFEU. That proposal (or proposals) should, where appropriate, include an evaluation mechanism based on the well-established system of peer-evaluation. Evaluation should be carried out periodically, should include an efficient follow-up system, and should facilitate better understanding of national systems in order to identify best practice and obstacles to cooperation. Professionals should be able to contribute to the evaluations. The Council should, in principle, have a leading role in the evaluation process, and in particular in its follow-up. Duplication with other evaluation mechanisms should be avoided, but synergies and cooperation should be sought, in particular with the work of the Council of Europe. The Union should take an active part in and should contribute to the work of the monitoring bodies of the Council of Europe.[26]

---

[23] R. Blekxtoon, Checks and Balances van het Kaderbesluit Europees aanhoudingsbevel 43 (2004) *Delikt en Delinkwent*, pp. 572–89. On the application by Poland also see the highly critical questions from Members of Parliament and the Dutch Minister of Security and Justice's reply in parliamentary documents: Second Chamber 2011–2012, *Aanh.* 614 (9 November, 2011).

[24] ECtHR case *M.S.S.* v. *Belgium and Greece* [2011] App. No. 30696/09 and Joined cases C-411/10 *N.S.* v. *Secretary of State for the Home Department* and C-493/10 *M.E. and Others* v. *Refugee Applications Commissioner and Minister for Justice, Equality and Law Reform* ECLI:EU:C:2011:865.

[25] Conference on Monitoring and Evaluation Mechanisms in the Field of EU Judicial Cooperation in Criminal Matters at Maastricht University, Faculty of Law, 2 and 3 June 2009. See C. Fijnaut and J. Ouwerkerk (eds.), *The Future of Police and Judicial Cooperation in the European Union* (Leiden: Martinus Nijhoff, 2010).

[26] European Council, 'The Stockholm Programme'.

Peer evaluation, as foreseen in the Stockholm Programme, can be viewed as a behavioural approach to the realisation of values in public law. Behavioural approaches have recently attracted more attention, for example, through 'nudging' – but may themselves raise concerns as to their compatibility with the Rule of Law.[27] Nudging can be applied by public authorities, but also in confrontation with them.[28] Naming and shaming is the opposite technique.

Nudging and naming and shaming are basically the aim behind techniques such as a 'scoreboard'. That is also the essence of the 'Justice Scoreboard', introduced by the erstwhile European Commission Vice-President Viviane Reding in March 2013 and since then published annually. According to the present Commissioner for Justice, Consumers and Gender Equality Vera Jourová in her preface to the 2015 edition, the Justice Scoreboard

> provides an overview of the quality, independence and efficiency of EU Member States' justice systems. Together with individual country assessments, the EU Justice Scoreboard helps to identify possible shortcomings or improvements and to regularly reflect on progress.[29]

This statement appears to be overly optimistic. The scoreboard method has an unavoidably narrow scope: it has to focus on more-or-less external criteria, which are definitely important but do not cover the development of a truly supportive culture of values. Statistical data are not well suited for comparative evaluation, even leaving aside the almost complete absence of data for the United Kingdom and partially from other Member States. To achieve an effective comparison, efforts would have to extend beyond justice and police cooperation policy. Peer evaluation requires a conversation, in which a scoreboard can play a useful role if combined with other sources of information.

IV   From Scoreboard to Political Dialogue

With a new coalition of states, the Dutch government took up the gauntlet again. In a joint letter dated 6 March 2013 to the President of the Commission, the Ministers of Foreign Affairs of Denmark, Finland,

---

[27] Wetenschappelijke Raad voor het Regeringsbeleid (WRR), *Met kennis van gedrag beleid maken* (WRR-rapport nr. 92, Amsterdam: Amsterdam University Press, 2014), p. 69.

[28] A. Meuwese, *Gedragsgericht publiekrecht* (inaugural address, Tilburg: Tilburg University, 2014), p. 7.

[29] European Commission, 'The 2015 EU Justice Scoreboard' COM (2015) 116 final, p. 3.

Germany and the Netherlands called for more European safeguards to ensure compliance with the fundamental values of the Union in the Member States. Their main argument emphasised the importance of the cultural dimension of the founding values of the EU:

> The EU should place greater emphasis on promoting a culture of respect for the rule of law in Member States. In its recent Annual Growth Survey for 2013 the Commission identifies the quality, independence and efficiency of judicial systems as a means of reducing costs for businesses and increasing the attractiveness of countries for foreign investment. Further ways to promote the rule of law within the framework of the European semester should be explored. While it is right to highlight the economic benefits of the rule of law, its significance obviously goes far beyond that.[30]

One month later, following up on its own initiative, the Dutch Government asked the Advisory Council on International Affairs (AIV or Advisory Council) to produce an advisory report on the functioning of the Rule of Law in the EU Member States of the EU. In January 2014, the AIV presented an extensive report on the Rule of Law, the existing mechanisms in the EU and the Council of Europe, and the desirability of additional instruments.[31] In the Advisory Council's view, any new mechanism should build on the insights available in the case law of domestic and EU courts as well as the European Court of Human Rights and the reports of other bodies, including the EU Fundamental Rights Agency (FRA) and the Council of Europe's Venice Commission. It recommended the active use of infraction procedures by the European Commission with a view on the complete realisation of the Rule of Law, but it also recommended that a monitoring and evaluation procedure be established by the Member States through consultations and agreement in the Council and the European Council. A more effective use of this procedure was also recommended by Kim Lane Scheppele.[32] The peer-review procedure as proposed in the report consists of three phases:[33]

---

[30] Letter of 6 March 2013 from four Ministers of Foreign Affairs to the President of the European Commission, at www.rijksoverheid.nl/bestanden/documenten-en-publicaties/brieven/2013/03/13/brief-aan-europese-commissie-over-opzetten-rechtsstatelijkheidsmechanisme/brief-aan-europese-commissie-over-opzetten-rechtsstatelijkheidsmechanisme.pdf.

[31] Advisory Council, 'The Rule of Law: Safeguard for European Citizens and Foundation for European Cooperation' (No. 87, January 2014), at http://aiv-advies.nl/download/57da03fa-3410-4aba-af05-663cb780df72.pdf.

[32] For a detailed analysis, see K. L. Scheppele, 'Enforcing the Basic Principles of EU Law through Systemic Infringement Procedures' in this volume.

[33] Compare: Advisory Council, 'The Rule of Law', pp. 36–7.

1. A committee of experts prepares a report based on consultations with organisations possessing relevant information on each Member State, and which considers a number of evaluation points and specific points of concern for each Member State. The European Commission would provide the secretariat for these expert committees.
2. The report is discussed by representatives of the Member States at the official level (the actual peer review), which leads to draft operational conclusions.
3. These conclusions are discussed and adopted by the Council in the form of Council Conclusions. The results of the reviews are also submitted to the Justice and Home Affairs Council, which oversees the follow-up. The recommendations and follow-up should be reported to the European Parliament.

V   A New EU Framework and the Council's Response

In March 2014, in its last year under the presidency of José Manuel Durão Barroso, the European Commission presented 'a new EU Framework to strengthen the Rule of Law',[34] which is supposed to fill the gap between the infraction procedure (Article 258 TFEU) in cases of alleged breach of EU law and the most drastic measures against a Member State under Article 7 TEU. The legal nature of the framework is merely a Communication from the Commission to the European Parliament and the Council.

In her explanation, Vice-President and Justice Commissioner Viviane Reding[35] nicknamed the proposal 'a *pre*-Article 7 procedure', consisting of three stages. Whenever the Commission arrives at the conclusion that in a Member State 'a systemic threat to the rule of law' exists, it will give it a 'rule of law warning'. The Commission listed in the Communication the following principles on to the Rule of Law:

> legality, which implies a transparent, accountable, democratic and plural-
> istic process for enacting laws; legal certainty; prohibition of arbitrariness
> of the executive powers; independent and impartial courts; effective judi-
> cial review including respect for fundamental rights; and equality before
> the law.[36]

---

[34] European Commission, 'A New EU Framework to Strengthen the Rule of Law' COM(2014) 158 final/2.

[35] V. Reding, 'A new Rule of Law Initiative' (Speech 14/202, Strasbourg, 11 March 2014), at http://europa.eu/rapid/press-release_SPEECH-14-202_en.htm.

[36] European Commission, 'A New EU Framework to Strengthen the Rule of Law', p. 4.

If the Member State fails to remedy its shortcomings, the warning will be followed by a 'Rule of Law recommendation'. Assuming that the Member State responds to this recommendation, the Commission will in the third stage 'monitor *how* the Member State is implementing the recommendation'.[37] If not, Article 7 is the fallback position with respect to the Member State concerned. The dialogue between Commission and Member State will, according to the text of the Communication, be based on 'an objective and thorough assessment of the situation at stake'.[38]

The threshold for applying the new framework is quite high. According to the Communication, the 'main purpose of the Framework is to address threats to the Rule of Law [...] which are of a systemic nature'.[39] On its webpage, the Commission offered two examples of the 'challenges to the Rule of Law on several occasions in recent years', although the 'systemic nature' is not apparent in the first example: France's Roma crisis in 2010 and threats to the independence of the judiciary during Romania's 2012 political crisis.[40] In its press release, the bar is raised further to the level of a 'systemic breakdown':

– The framework can be activated in situations where there is a *systemic breakdown* which adversely affects the integrity, stability and proper functioning of the institutions and mechanisms established at national level to secure the rule of law. The EU framework is not designed to deal with individual situations or isolated cases of breaches of fundamental rights or miscarriages of justice.
– *Equality of Member States*: the framework will apply in the same way in all Member States and will operate on the basis of the same benchmarks as to what is considered a systemic threat to the rule of law.[41]

These conditions made it quite unlikely that the framework would be applied anytime soon. The Hungarian situation – changes in the constitution, including the early retirement of a large group of judges with a negative impact on judicial independence – was for instance not mentioned

[37] Reding, 'A new Rule of Law Initiative'.
[38] European Commission, 'A New EU Framework to Strengthen the Rule of Law', p. 4.
[39] *Ibid*.
[40] European Commission, 'EU Takes Action to Protect Rule of Law', *Europa.eu* (12 March 2014), at http://ec.europa.eu/news/justice/140312_en.htm.
[41] European Commission, 'European Commission Presents a Framework to Safeguard the Rule of Law in the European Union', Press Release, *Europa.eu* (11 March 2014), at http://europa.eu/rapid/press-release_IP-14-237_en.htm.

as an example, although a further deterioration could have triggered a change of direction.[42]

Sooner than expected though, the new Commission, which was appointed in late 2014 under the presidency of Jean-Claude Juncker and which has endorsed the procedure laid down in the Communication, felt the need to activate the Rule of Law Framework in response to the constitutional crisis in Poland. It is the First Vice-President Frans Timmermans who is, inter alia, in charge of the Commission's policy with respect to the Rule of Law and the Charter, who is currently engaged in a dialogue with Poland.

In its response to the AIV Report, sent to Parliament on 24 April 2014,[43] the Dutch government endorsed most of its recommendations. It recognised that the Commissions' initiatives and the peer-review proposal go very well together, complementing each other in various contexts.[44] Peer review under the aegis of the Council appears to be better suited to a process of gradual enculturation of the Rule of Law.

In its meeting of 16 December 2014, the Council of the European Union (General Affairs Council) embarked on an initiative on its own. Based on the Italian Presidency note on 'Ensuring Respect for the Rule of Law',[45] it 'adopted conclusions on respect for the Rule of Law, establishing a political dialogue among member states to promote and safeguard the Rule of Law within the EU'.[46] The purpose of the conclusions is 'a dialogue among all Member States within the Council' that would promote 'a culture of respect for the Rule of Law within the European Union'.[47]

---

[42] B. Bugarič, 'Protecting Democracy and the Rule of Law in the European Union: The Hungarian Challenge' (2014) LEQS Paper No. 79/2014, at www.lse.ac.uk/europeanInstitute/LEQS/LEQSPaper79.pdf; see also D. Kochenov, 'Europe's Crisis of Values', 48 (2014) *Revista catalana de dret públic*, p. 160.

[43] Parliamentary Papers II 2013/14, 33877, 19.

[44] *Ibid.*, available in Dutch at www.rijksoverheid.nl/bestanden/documenten-en-publicaties/rapporten/2014/04/24/gecombineerde-kabinetsreactie-aiv-advies/gecombineerde-kabinetsreactie-aiv-advies.pdf; and available in English at the webpage of the Advisory Council: http://aiv-advies.nl/6d4/publications/advisory-reports/the-rule-of-law-safeguard-for-european-citizens-and-foundation-for-european-cooperation#government-responses.

[45] Council of the European Union, 'Note from the Presidency to the Council on the Subject of Ensuring the Respect for the Rule of Law in the European Union' (16862/14, Brussels, 12 December 2014).

[46] Council of the European Union, '3362nd Council Meeting – General Affairs' (Press Release, 16936/14, *Europa.eu* (16 December 2014), at www.consilium.europa.eu/en/workarea/downloadasset.aspx?id=40802192315.

[47] Council of the European Union, 'Conclusions of the Council of the EU and the Member States meeting within the Council on ensuring the respect for the rule of law' (17014/14, Brussels, 16 December 2014), para. 1.

> The dialogue will take place once a year in the Council, in its General Affairs configuration, and be prepared by the COREPER (Presidency), following an inclusive approach. The Council will consider, as needed, to launch debates on thematic subject matters.[48]

The issue was thus effectively taken out of the hands of the Justice and Home Affairs Council, who had dealt with the subject in previous years. Any relationship with the Commission's framework is not visible, which gives the impression that the Council wanted to create an alternative.

The Ministers of Foreign Affairs also emphasised

> that such an approach will be without prejudice to the principle of conferred competences, as well as the respect of national identities of Member States inherent in their fundamental political and constitutional structures, inclusive of regional and local self-government, and their essential State functions, including ensuring the territorial integrity of the State, maintaining law and order and safeguarding national security, and should be brought forward in light of the principle of sincere cooperation.[49]

Even before any controversial issues related to the Rule of Law could be raised, the Ministers already appeared to be accepting excuses for illiberal democracies. Much will depend on how the Council will prepare its annual 'dialogue'. Only if the debate is prepared, possibly with the assistance of the FRA, with a substantive analysis of the Rule of Law situation, will it prove useful in truly promoting the Rule of Law.

VI   The Way Ahead

The real significance of the Council's conclusions will largely depend on how the recent decisions in the Council are implemented. Whether the introduction of peer evaluation can be viewed as effective will depend on the climate in and between the Member States. If a Member State's government steadfastly undermines the Rule of Law, the review procedure will not be sufficient. From that point of view, it is understandable that Kochenov and Pech view the recent decisions as 'grossly inadequate to tackle the problem of "Rule of Law backsliding post EU accession"'.[50] Rule of Law enforcement can only take the form of direct, legally binding interventions in situations of serious shortcomings – in other words, when trust has already been undermined. Concerns such as those expressed by

---

[48] *Ibid.*, para. 6.   [49] *Ibid.*, para. 4.

[50] D. Kochenov and L. Pech, 'Upholding the Rule of Law in the EU: On the Commission's "Pre-Article 7" Procedure as a Timid Step in the Right Direction', EUI Working Papers No. 2015/24, RSCAS.

Sionaidh Douglas-Scott[51] and Kochenov on Europe's 'justice deficit'[52] relate to such situations.

The Rule of Law initiative, however, is meant to *prevent* such situations. The importance of peer review is tailored for prevention and growth in the virtue of reciprocity, that is, as a stimulus for a growing acceptance of the value of the Rule of Law. Peer-review procedures should definitely not be viewed as an alternative for political or legal actions against Member States that disregard the founding values of the European Union. Once a political system has drifted away from the Rule of Law, it is too late to rely on dialogue between justice systems representatives. However, if we wish to prevent such situations and reverse negative developments, it remains worthwhile to strive for the enculturalisation of Rule of Law principles in the attitudes and practices of professionals and officials. Ultimately, these professionals and officials are those who can make a difference, not only for the citizens of their own state but also for other European citizens who – as a result of the mutual recognition of judicial decisions and arrest warrants, or when they avail themselves of the economic freedoms of the Union – have to rely on the Rule of Law in other Member States.

Bringing a value to life is first a matter of developing attitudes and virtues. The Rule of Law depends on reciprocal respect and mutual trust, which could very well start with how we promote it.

---

[51] S. Douglas-Scott, 'Justice, Injustice and the Rule of Law in the EU' in D. Kochenov, G. de Búrca and A. Williams, *Europe's Justice Deficit?* (Oxford: Hart Publishing 2015), p. 51.

[52] D. Kochenov and A. Williams, 'Europe's Justice Deficit Introduced', in D. Kochenov, G. de Búrca and A. Williams, *Europe's Justice Deficit?*, p. 1.

7

The Rule of Law and the Role of Fundamental Rights

Seven Practical Pointers

GABRIEL N. TOGGENBURG* AND JONAS GRIMHEDEN**

I How Much Heterogeneity Can European Unity Afford? The Argument for Minimum Constitutional Cohesion

The EU is known to export what are often described as 'European' values to the outside world. At the same time the 'Copenhagen dilemma' became a catchword for those who want to stress that the EU lacks the legal means and/or political will to fight for the same values vis-à-vis its own Member States. The EU is well aware of this challenge. Indeed, the European Commission and the High Representative of the European Union for Foreign Affairs and Security Policy underline that the 'EU must lead by example [as it] is under severe scrutiny for what are perceived as discrepancies in its approach to human rights issues [double standards and internal/external inconsistencies]'.[1] The EU's commitment to these shared values cannot be viewed in isolation from the commitment of its Member States to the same values.

It is well recognised that the EU provides a very unique and close form of integration which brings together national constitutional systems in a shared constitutional space. National constitutional traditions influence the body of law which has developed under the umbrella of the

---

* Senior Legal Advisor with the EU Agency for Fundamental Rights (FRA) and Visiting Professor at the Faculty of Law, University of Graz. The authors wrote this chapter in private capacity, expressing strictly personal views which cannot be attributed to the Agency.
** Head of Sector Access to Justice, FRA and Associate Professor of Law (*Docent*) at the Faculty of Law, Lund University.
[1] Action Plan on Human Rights and Democracy (2015–2019) 'Keeping Human Rights at the Heart of the EU Agenda', Joined Communication to the European Parliament and the Council JOIN(2015) 16 final.

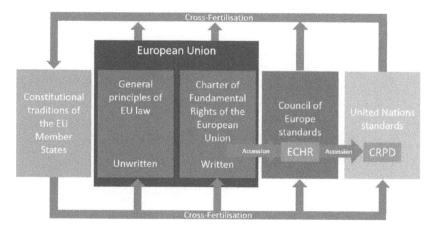

Figure 1   Interlinks between the sets of standards in the European Union.[2]

European Union. EU law in turn influences and shapes national systems (international law is also part of this cycle of cross-fertilisation, as illustrated in Figure 1). Under the principle of loyalty, the Member States are obliged to 'facilitate the achievement of the Union's tasks and refrain from any measure which could jeopardise the attainment of the Union's objectives'.[3] Among the objectives of the Union is to promote the founding values prominently listed in Article 2 Treaty on European Union (TEU), which it shares with its Member States. Moreover, the Treaty underlines that other objectives of the EU include promoting the 'well-being of its people',[4] to 'offer its citizens an area of freedom, security and justice without internal frontiers'[5] and to 'combat social exclusion and discrimination, and [. . .] promote social justice and protection, [. . .] economic, social and territorial cohesion, and solidarity among Member States'.[6] In this sense it is not surprising that terms such as the 'integrated state'[7] or 'Verfassungsverbund'[8] became natural parts of the academic discourse on the European Union.

---

[2] According to the European Union Agency for Fundamental Rights, Fundamental Rights: Challenges and Achievements in 2011 – Annual Report 2011 (2012), 18.

[3] Art. 4 (3) TEU.   [4] Art. 3 (1) TEU.   [5] Art. 3 (2) TEU.   [6] Art. 3 (3) TEU.

[7] M. Nettesheim and P. Schiera, *Der integrierte Staat* (Berlin: Duncker & Humbold, 1999).

[8] I. Pernice, 'Theorie und Praxis des Europäischen Verfassungsverbundes', in C. Calliess (ed.), *Verfassungswandel im europäischen Staaten- und Verfassungsverbund* (Tübingen: Mohr Siebeck, 2007), p. 61; I. Pernice, 'La Rete Europea di Costituzionalità – Der Europäische Verfassungsverbund und die Netzwerktheorie', 70 (2010) *Zeitschrift für ausländisches und öffentliches Recht* 51.

From a more practical perspective, the EU and its Member States are also tied together in such a way that major changes to the political system in one Member States can easily have spill-over effects in other states and in the working of the EU as a whole. Consider, for instance, the impact that a Member State government and its members in the European Parliament can have on EU policymaking, which again affects the other Member States. Or think of the obligation to mutually recognise across borders judgments in criminal matters or judicial and extrajudicial decisions in civil matters. In fact, mutual cooperation among Member States and the overall functioning of the EU are built on the assumption that all Member States remain within the 'constitutional bow' as drawn by Article 2 TEU.[9] Where Article 2 values are compromised in a way which threatens the functioning of the EU, there is no way that this could be justified by having recourse to the 'national identity' the European Union has to respect. Firstly, 'national identities' as set out in Article 4(2) TEU is a term of EU law which cannot be interpreted by the respective Member States alone.[10] Secondly, the identity of an 'integrated state' is co-defined by its very membership in the EU. Even where a national system is tempted to put EU-induced developments under a sort of 'national identity impact assessment', designating constitutional zones immune to integration, the reach of such an approach would be limited by the fact that an integrated state cannot unilaterally escape the value dialogue established by the EU treaties.[11]

There is hence no need to change the Treaties by adding 'a new clause to oblige the Member States to respect the constitutional identity of the European Union, not least in terms of its values and principles'.[12] The

---

[9] For instance, Protocol 24 on asylum from nationals of Member States of the EU states: 'Given the level of protection of fundamental rights and freedoms by the Member States of the European Union, Member States shall be regarded as constituting safe countries of origin in respect of each other for all legal and practical purposes in relation to asylum matters'. According to the Protocol, applications for asylum made by a Member State national may be taken into consideration when that state is being subjected to an Article 7 TEU procedure.

[10] See in detail A. von Bogdandy and S. Schill, 'Die Achtung der nationalen Identität unter dem reformierten Unionsvertrag', 70 (2010) *Zeitschrift für ausländisches und öffentliches Recht* 701, 713–5.

[11] Compare the 'Identitätskontrolle' as developed in the judgment of the German Constitutional Court in BVerfGE 123. It was argued that the practical relevance of this doctrine is limited to moments of treaty change. See A. Putler, Art. 4 EUV, in C. Callies and M. Ruffert (eds.), *EUV AEUV Kommentar*, 4th edn (Munich: Verlag CH Beck, 2011), p. 62.

[12] What a prominent former member of the European Parliament, Andrew Duff calls the 'Viktor Orban Clause'. See A. Duff, 'EU in Deep Trouble with Top Court',

challenge is rather to operationalise Articles 2 (shared values), 3 (EU objectives), 4 (cooperation between EU and Member States), 5 (exercise of EU competencies), 6 (fundamental rights obligations) and 7 (sanctions for violation of values) TEU in a way which takes the shared values seriously without overstretching the EU's role and competencies.

The semi-constitutional nature of the European Union (EU) is reflected, for instance, in the EU's ambition to sanction those Member States which threaten an assumed EU-wide 'constitutional homogeneity'[13] expressed in the shared values listed in Article 2 TEU. A '*clear risk* of a serious breach' of these values can be addressed by the EU under the Article 7(1) TEU procedure. In more troublesome cases, 'the *existence* of a serious and persistent breach' by a Member State can officially be determined and commented upon by the EU in the Article 7(2) procedure. The EU can even proceed to imposing political sanctions against the respective Member State via the Article 7(3) TEU procedure. These three steps represent a spectrum of increasingly severe political responses provided for in the Treaties.

The Article 7 procedures are reactive rather than preventive in nature and have so far not gained much practical relevance, which has attracted some criticism. First, the *substantial* thresholds in Article 7 are very high (only persistent and systemic threats to the shared values are addressed). Second, the *procedural* hurdles are equally high as the various stages of the Article 7 procedure can be activated only by the political actors and need qualified majority in the Council (or, for the procedure declaring the existence of a serious and persistent breach of constitutional values: unanimity in the European Council). Thirdly, the procedure only partly falls within the jurisdiction of the Court of Justice of the European Union, thereby further underlining the impression that addressing values violations is a matter of politics rather than constitutional consideration and expert assessment.[14]

A variety of considerations will motivate the decision to activate Article 7. Admittedly, given the current nature of the procedure, power relations and party politics might play a role. Nevertheless, the question of deviation is decided by the following consideration: is the Member

Euractiv (8 January, 2015), at www.euractiv.com/sections/justice-home-affairs/eu-deep-trouble-top-court-311090.

[13] F. Schorkopf, *Homogenität in der Europäischen Union – Ausgestaltung und Gewährleistung durch Art. 6 Abs, 1 und Art. 7 EUV* (Berlin: Duncker & Humbold, 2000).

[14] Art. 269 TFEU.

State perceived by its peers as clearly departing from the shared values in a manner which seriously threatens the consensus of 'who we are' in the EU community of states? Similar processes can occur at a national level. In Italy and Austria, a telling term was coined in this regard: the '*arco costituzionale*' or the '*Verfassungsbogen*' draws a dividing line between what a constitution accepts and what is beyond the constitutionally accepted.[15]

For the EU we can say that the contours of this 'constitutional bow' are less than crystal-clear, typically even more blurred than at the national level.[16] This is despite the fact that the drafters of the EU Treaty, when formulating Article 2 TEU, wanted to select:

> a hard core of values meeting two criteria at once: on the one hand, they must be so fundamental that they lie at the very heart of a peaceful society practicing tolerance, justice and solidarity; on the other hand, they must have a clear non-controversial legal basis so that the Member States can discern the obligations resulting therefrom which are subject to sanction.[17]

Considering these two criteria, it appears debatable whether Article 2 as such clearly signals what sort of behaviour can be sanctioned under Article 7 TEU and what cannot.

This is even more so given that within the EU, the ambition to be united is set into perspective by the condition to preserve diversity, as is succinctly symbolised by the European motto 'united in diversity'.[18] The treaties allow for supranational intervention by the 'centre' to protect shared values, but they also protect 'the periphery' by shielding national identities against European intervention. There is thus an ambivalence as the centripetal provision of Article 2 (the shared values) is counterbalanced by more centrifugal provisions such as the one in Article 4(2) TEU, underlining that the EU has to respect the 'national identities, inherent in their fundamental structures, political and constitutional, inclusive

---

[15] G. N. Toggenburg, 'Was soll die EU können dürfen um die EU-Verfassungswerte und die Rechtsstaatlichkeit der Mitgliedstaaten zu schützen? Ausblick auf eine neue Europäische Rechtsstaatshygiene' (2013) *Policy Brief der Österreichischen Gesellschaft für Europapolitik* No. 2013/13, at www.oegfe.at/cms/uploads/media/OEGfE_Policy_Brief-2013.10.pdf.

[16] For a variety of different perspectives, see for example D. Kochenov and A. Williams, 'Europe's Justice Deficit Introduced' in D. Kochenov, G. de Búrca and A. Williams (eds.), *Europe's Justice Deficit?* (Oxford: Hart Publishing, 2015), p. 1.

[17] See Annex 2 of CONV 528/03 as of 6 February 2003, 11.

[18] Whereas the Treaty of Lisbon avoided the incorporation of semi-constitutional 'symbols' in the text of the treaties (including the European motto of unity in diversity), declaration number 52 underlines that for more than half of the Member States these symbols continue 'to express the sense of community of the people in the European Union and their allegiance to it'. See OJ C 326 as of 26 October 2012, 357.

of regional and local self-government'.[19] In light of these forces driving towards unity while allowing for a wide degree of diversity, a number of key questions must be asked, and attempts must be made to respond to them: to what degree can national autonomy be invoked to justify a deviant non-mainstream reading of the assumedly shared values in Article 2 TEU? How much diversity can European unity afford?

Against the background of this particular and densely integrated 'constitutional space' the EU and its Member States have built in co-ownership, we will in the following address the 'Rule of Law debate' through the lenses of fundamental rights. We argue that it would be advisable to take fundamental rights as the starting point of the value debate (Section II). Building on objective and 'three-dimensional' rights-based indicators (Section III) – including the EU's own performance in this respect – and instilling a culture of peer review and exchange of promising practices (Section IV) would allow for a more objective form of value-control which is owned equally by all actors. In addition, we argue for avoiding a top-heavy approach by putting the situation on the ground at the centre (Section V). The overall ambition is to arrive at a permanent and preventive fundamental rights culture. One way forward is a strategic framework for the protection and promotion of fundamental rights (Section VI) which could assign tasks and responsibilities in a way which combines intergovernmental and supranational elements (Section VII).

II   How to View the Rule of Law Debate? The Argument for a Fundamental Rights Perspective

Assuming that the 'Rule of Law debate' is in essence about finding ways to best protect the values which are, according to Article 2 EU Treaty, shared between the EU and its Member States, there is something strange with the heading 'Rule of Law debate', as the Rule of Law is only one out of six[20] elements mentioned in Article 2 TEU. This provision lists the values which on the one hand are the value foundation of the Union ('founded on'), and on the other hand build the shared core of values offered by the national constitutional systems ('common to the Member States'). These values therefore form the normative backbone linking the national level with the EU level and provide guidance in both directions. That only one, admittedly horizontal value, namely the Rule of Law, has been singled out in most of the political debate can be explained by the specific nature of the 'Hungarian crisis' sparking the Rule of Law debate, which

---

[19] Art. 4 (2) TEU.   [20] Or, depending on how one counts, thirteen elements.

indeed centres on prominent Rule of Law elements such as the role of the judiciary or of constitutional legislation.

However, beyond its name, the ensuing political debate was not always a fortunate one. On the one hand, the debate became politicised in some corners (the more aggressive reaction) and ignored the fact that a solid debate on systemic deficiencies cannot focus on individual legalistic elements in isolation but has to look at the 'combined effects of many developments' (the more defensive reaction), on the other.[21] Against a specific political background, various legal development can lead to a situation where 'the whole is greater than the sum of its parts'.[22] For instance, it would not be sufficient to look in isolation at the appointment of judges. Other developments, such as the introduction of new majorities to elect public officials, or new standard employment terms for public officials or new electoral laws should be included in the assessment.

In this sense it is positive to note that there are at least three ways in which the debate has developed for the better.[23] It has moved from a country-specific Article 7 emergency context to a shared concern about how to better uphold values in all EU Member States.[24] Secondly, it has moved from a reactive containment approach to exploring ways for the EU itself to promote its values proactively.[25] Thirdly, the debate moved from focusing on the Rule of Law to a much wider reading of the shared values which more squarely reflects Article 2 TEU and the Charter of Fundamental Rights of the European Union.[26] In fact, a closer look reveals that most of the Article 2 values are covered by the Charter and

---

[21] M. Kjærum, Director of the FRA, speech given in the European Parliament on the situation in Hungary, 9 February 2012, at http://fra.europa.eu/sites/default/files/fra_uploads/1945-MK-speech-hearing-on-Hungary_09-02-12.Brussels.pdf.

[22] *Ibid.*

[23] For the development of the political positions, see for instance the selection of documents provided in Democracy Reporting International (2013), Proposals for New Tools to Protect EU Values: An Overview, Briefing Paper 43, at http://democracy-reporting.org/publications/thematic-papers/briefing-paper-43-november-2013.html. For the academic discussion, see amongst many A. von Bogdandy and M. Ioannidis, 'Systemic Deficiency in the Rule of Law: What It Is, What Has Been Done, What Can Be Done', 51(1) (2014) *CMLRev.* 59.

[24] See, for example, European Commission, 'A New Framework to Strengthen the Rule of Law', COM (2014)158 final.

[25] See, for example, the Conclusions of the Council of the European Union and the member states meeting within the Council on ensuring respect for the rule of law, 16 December, 2014. They aim to promote the Rule of Law via an 'evidence-based' approach also through the means of an annual 'dialogue' in the Council.

[26] See, for example, the European Union Agency for Fundamental Rights, Fundamental Rights: Challenges and Achievements in 2013 – Annual Report 2013 (2014), pp. 7–20.

Values as listed in Article 2 TEU	Equivalence in the Charter (shaded Charter titles cover the corresponding Article 2 values only partly)
Human dignity	Human dignity (Title I)
Freedom	Freedoms (Title II)
Democracy	Citizens' rights (Title V)
Equality	Equality (Title III)
The Rule of Law	Justice (Title VI); Citizens' rights (Title V)
Respect for human rights	All titles of the Charter
Rights of persons belonging to minorities	Equality (Title III)
Pluralism	Equality (Title III)
Non-discrimination	Equality (Title III)
Tolerance	Equality (Title III)
Justice	Justice (Title VI)
Solidarity	Solidarity (Title IV)
Equality between women and men	Equality (Title III)

Figure 2   Comparison between Article 2 TEU values and the Charter of Fundamental Rights of the European Union.[27]

indeed are reflected there in more detailed and rights-based language, as Figure 2 shows.

Values like dignity, equality between women and men, freedom and non-discrimination are simply more specific expressions of the value 'respect for human rights'. Two other values, namely 'the Rule of Law' and 'democracy' appear – next to the 'respect for human rights' – equally able to encompass other Article 2 values such as 'justice', 'equality', 'pluralism' and 'tolerance'. It has been argued that the relationship between the three elements of Rule of Law, fundamental rights and democracy is co-constitutive and that like the legs of a three-legged stool, 'if one is missing the whole is not fit for purpose'.[28] This being correct, we can still

---

[27] *Ibid.*, p. 10.

[28] S. Carrera, E. Guild and N. Hernanz, 'The Triangular Relationship between Fundamental Rights, Democracy and the Rule of Law in the EU: Towards an EU Copenhagen Mechanism' (2013) CEPS.

argue that fundamental rights cover the spectrum of Article 2 to a wider degree compared to democracy and the Rule of Law.

Moreover, the EU possesses a detailed Charter of Fundamental Rights of the European Union, transparently drafted fifteen years ago by government officials and mainly national and European Parliamentarians, partly based on civil society input. There is no similarly comprehensive written catalogue of the elements which form the EU *acquis* for the Rule of Law, let alone democracy, as there is in the area of individual rights.

Arguably, the EU's normative expectation under Article 2 TEU is more legitimate and can be followed up more efficiently if exercised through the lens and in the language of fundamental rights. Systematic engagement with – such as monitoring of – fundamental rights, implementing a shared fundamental rights culture and developing an inter-institutional framework for the protection and promotion of fundamental rights would cover most of Article 2. As even a very 'thin' notion of the Rule of Law covers certain (especially judicial) fundamental rights,[29] taking fundamental rights as the starting point means also to directly address elements of the Rule of Law. Moreover, indirectly, the protection and promotion of fundamental rights helps prevent systemic Rule of Law crises. In fact, a trustworthy system which protects the fundamental rights of its residents and citizens can be considered one of those 'societal conditions'[30] which are necessary for a country to function as a state governed by the Rule of Law.

III   How to Ensure Rights-Based Performance? The Argument for Fundamental Rights Indicators

What can such a more systematic engagement achieve? Multinational companies know well how to focus on essential figures. Many have subsidiaries in several parts of the world, operations in even more, with different types of activities, expenditures and income which they manage to focus on what sometimes is referred to as Key Performance Indicators

---

[29] See, for example, L. Pech, 'The Rule of Law as a Constitutional Principle of the European Union', Jean Monnet Working Paper No. 04/09, 27, at www.jeanmonnetprogram.org/papers/09/090401.html.

[30] Advisory Council on International Affairs, 'The Rule of Law: Safeguard for European Citizens and Foundation for European Cooperation', (2014) No. 87, at http://aiv-advies.nl/6d4/publications/advisory-reports/the-rule-of-law-safeguard-for-european-citizens-and-foundation-for-european-cooperation.

(KPIs). Similarly, international organisations use indicators to measure progress, for instance the Millennium Development Goals;[31] and states apply indicators, for example as part of their national human rights action plans to bring focus to their activities and enable assessment of progress.[32]

The EU also uses indicators in a number of settings, such as when examining Member States progress in the Single Market Scoreboard or the EU Justice Scoreboard.[33] These distilled overviews of the actual situation help the EU focus on aspects deemed to be important, just as multinationals do using KPIs. The European Union Fundamental Rights Agency (FRA), for instance, has developed indicators in a number of areas, such as the rights of the child and the rights of persons with disabilities.[34] At the request of the European Commission, the FRA is developing and populating indicators on the rights of Roma in partnership with Member States, feeding into EU policy and follow-up.[35]

Various models or frameworks are available to capture different aspects of the actual situation using indicators. Those used by the United Nations Office of the High Commissioner for Human Rights, and also by the FRA, seek to capture three modes: commitment, effort and results (see Figure 3).[36] This corresponds in the framework to the three categories of structural, process and outcome indicators. What exactly goes into each of these is less relevant, as what matters is that not only the situation on paper is taken into account, but also the situation on the ground, irrespective of

---

[31] See www.un.org/millenniumgoals/.

[32] See, for example, Finland, Ministry of Justice, National Action Plan on Fundamental and Human Rights 2012–2013, 2012, 16 et seq.

[33] See, respectively, at http://ec.europa.eu/internal_market/scoreboard/performance_by_governance_tool/infringements/index_en.htm. European Commission, 'A New EU Framework to Strengthen the Rule of Law', COM(2014) 158 final, 11 March, 2014, at http://ec.europa.eu/justice/effective-justice/files/com_2014_158_en.pdf. For an overview of initiatives in the EU, see FRAME (FP7 project), Baseline Study on Human Rights Indicators in the Context of the European Union, Work Package No. 13 – Deliverable No. 1, 24 December 2014, at www.fp7-frame.eu/wp-content/materiale/reports/12-Deliverable-13.1.pdf.

[34] European Union Agency for Fundamental Rights, 'Developing Indicators for the Protection, Respect and Promotion of the Rights of the Child in the European Union' (2009); and European Union Agency for Fundamental Rights, 'The Right to Political Participation for Persons with Disabilities: Human Rights Indicators' (2014), pp. 2–14.

[35] See http://fra.europa.eu/en/project/2013/multi-annual-roma-programme/member-states.

[36] Office of the High Commissioner for Human Rights, 'Human Rights Indicators: A Guide to Measurement and Implementation', 16, at www.ohchr.org/Documents/Publications/Human_rights_indicators_en.pdf.

Figure 3 The 'structural – process – outcome' indicator framework.[37]

the efforts of government – something which tries to capture the spectrum between the extremes of the legislation in place and actual enjoyment of rights. Indicators in such a framework can therefore also capture where a problem may lie and what needs to be done, by making it clearer, for instance, what policy measures at the process level appear to lead to better outcomes. This approach thus has both preventive and reparative advantages.

To be as pertinent and credible as possible, indicators should be identified in broad consultation with experts, government and civil society representatives. Once indicators have been agreed on, they need to be given life – data and information are required to populate them, and there may be a need to set standards or benchmarks for what should be viewed as 'compliant'. There is a great deal of data and information from international monitoring bodies, but this tends to focus on the structural and process levels. Statistics showing actual enjoyment – outcome level – are harder to come by, but surveys do exist which provide a comparative perspective across countries.[38]

---

[37] European Union Agency for Fundamental Rights, Fundamental Rights: Challenges and Achievements in 2014 – Annual report 2014 (2015), based on Human Rights Indicators – A Guide to Measurement and Implementation, OHCHR (2012), at www.ohchr.org/EN/Issues/Indicators/Pages/documents.aspx.

[38] See for instance, FRA surveys: Jewish people's experiences and perceptions of discrimination and hate crime in European Union Member States; EU LGBT survey; Survey on gender-based violence against women; Roma pilot survey; Racism and social marginalisation survey; Racism and social marginalisation survey; EU-MIDIS: European Union Minorities and Discrimination Survey; all available at http://fra.europa.eu/en/research/surveys.

With indicators which capture the right aspects in place, and with agreement on data and information to populate the indicators, an organisation is well equipped to analyse the situation, assess what seems to work and what not, develop strategy and take informed decisions and steps. It is however important to recall that indicators indicate, so the results must always be viewed with a sufficient extent of context, which may or may not justify deviances, say, from a pattern across states. Indicators of fundamental rights in the EU, as elsewhere, bring clarity to discussions and action – and ensure that debates on the core values of the EU are based on objective and pre-determined criteria which capture intent, efforts and the situation on the ground.

IV   How to Move Beyond the Rhetoric of Sanctions: The Argument for Leading by Example and Learning from Peers

Indicators and other forms of monitoring and review tend to be regarded as 'finger-pointing' and even as sanctions for failure. A system can certainly be designed and conceived in this way but this is not essential. A 'sunshine policy' which engages and involves rather than paralyses and excludes is often more effective. What is important for the credibility of the EU is to include in any assessment of the values of the EU, not only the Member States but also the EU itself.

Considering the value commitment of the Member States alongside that of the EU would underscore that the Article 2 values are shared between the two layers of governance. Since all the Article 2 values are of a horizontal nature, they should reasonably be mainstreamed across all the EU's activities. Fundamental rights are thus at the core of an integrated Europe. In its 2013 Annual Report, FRA stressed that 'fundamental rights should not be reduced to a function of imposing limits on legislation and public administration'[39] but have an enabling character that 'can point towards the design, adoption and implementation of certain initiatives'.[40] In some areas the Treaties make this explicitly obligatory, such as in the case of equality between men and women, as well as when combating discrimination based on, for instance, ethnic origin or disability.[41] The same is true for an issue such as data protection.[42]

---

[39] European Union Agency for Fundamental Rights, Fundamental Rights: Challenges and Achievements in 2013 – Annual Report 2013 (2014), p. 12.
[40] *Ibid.*   [41] Treaty on the Functioning of the European Union (TFEU), Arts. 8 and 10.
[42] Art. 16 TFEU.

Mainstreaming these horizontal fundamental rights obligations appears to merit complete integration into key policy cycles. Restricting fundamental rights to non-discrimination policies, for instance, would not unlock the full capacity of fundamental rights and would indeed not fully respect the obligations of the EU and its Member States under the Treaties. Fundamental rights should thus be included in key policy cycles, such as the European Semester.[43] Efforts to establish a link between the European Semester and social investment as well as fundamental rights intensified in 2012–2013. The European Commission makes repeated calls for respect of the Charter of Fundamental Rights,[44] and the European Parliament argues for improved assessment of the fundamental rights impact of fiscal and structural reforms.[45] In its Resolution of 22 October 2014, it welcomed the revised employment and social scoreboard[46] and called for the inclusion of additional indicators – such as quality of work, child poverty levels, access to healthcare and homelessness – in the scoreboard. The Resolution then called for these indicators to have a real influence on the European Semester process given that the 'economic and social aspects of the EU are two sides of the same coin, both of which play a key role in the EU's development'.[47]

This renewed fundamental rights orientation in EU policies is likely to impact on the EU Member States realities on the ground. For instance, making the use of EU funds (such as Structural and Investment Funds) dependent on fundamental rights (so called *ex ante* conditionalities) is an example of how mainstreaming fundamental rights can trickle down and ensure that Member States, when implementing the relevant EU regulations, stick to the Charter.[48] The introduction of this new fundamental rights–oriented spending policy was considered by

---

[43] See for example European Union Agency for Fundamental Rights, Fundamental Rights: Challenges and Achievements in 2014 – Annual Report 2014 (2015).

[44] European Commission, 'Towards Social Investment for Growth and Cohesion – Including Implementing the European Social Fund 2014–2020', COM(2013) 83 final, 2.

[45] European Parliament resolution of 22 October 2014 on the European Semester for economic policy coordination: implementation of 2014 priorities (2014/2059(INI)).

[46] The second edition of the scoreboard of key employment and social indicators was introduced to strengthen the social dimension of the Economic and Monetary Union by gaining a better understanding of the labour market and social developments at risk. The indicators are presented in the Commission's Communication of 2 October 2013 on Strengthening the Social Dimension of the Economic and Monetary Union.

[47] Motion for a European Parliament Resolution on the European Semester for economic policy coordination: implementation of 2014 priorities (2014/2059(INI)).

[48] See details at http://ec.europa.eu/regional_policy/index.cfm/en/funding/.

some not just as desirable but mandatory under current legal requirements.[49]

A Union leading by example is a good starting point, but to ensure that
the EU's community of values does not only rely on European oversight
but strongly builds on shared ownership by and mutual trust among its
Member States, it is important to enhance the transnational exchange of
experience, views and promising practices with regard to the protection
and promotion of the Article 2 values. This exchange could be organised
in a variety of contexts and formats. It could encompass government
bodies and judicial organs. For instance, the Association of the Council of
State and Supreme Administrative Jurisdictions of the European Union
(ACA Europe) could further enhance their cooperation to deal more
systematically with questions of how Article 2 values are upheld in the
different national systems. Something similar could be said for specialised
bodies such as the Data Protection Authorities and the like. Working
Parties bringing together the relevant administrations are another avenue
for pooling knowledge and expertise from different Member States. For
instance, the FRA has established two Working Parties with Member
States on hate crime and on Roma integration which are bearing fruit. For
example, the Hate Crime Working Party is developing a simple reporting
tool for victims to report hate crime incidents. Not addressing hate crime
is a factor in the radicalisation that we see in Europe today.

A variety of practical tools could be developed further. For instance,
the European e-justice portal could prove an effective access point for
promising practices on how best to meet EU justice standards. It could,
for instance, offer a search function for vetted practices. FRA initiated a
modest attempt in this regard with an online toolkit for public officials,
which includes examples under various headings of how better to join up
fundamental rights initiatives.[50] The identification of such practical tools
should again be based on an open exchange of experience. An example

---

[49] See, for example, for the argument of the CRPD that was ratified by the EU: G. Quinn,
'Getting a Life – Living Independently and Being Included in the Community. A Legal
Study of the Current Use and Future Potential of the EU Structural Funds to Contribute to
the Achievement of Article 19 of the United Nations Convention on the Rights of Persons
with Disabilities', OHCHR (2012), at www.europe.ohchr.org/Documents/Publications/
Getting_a_Life.pdf.

[50] European Union Agency for Fundamental Rights, 'Making Rights R – A Guide for
Local and Regional Authorities' (2014), at http://fra.europa.eu/en/publication/2014/
making-rights-real-guide-local-and-regional-authorities.

from the area of home affairs is the collaboration Member State experts and the European Commission developed with the FRA to produce concrete practical guidance on apprehension practices in the form of 'dos and don'ts' for immigration law enforcement officials.[51]

Cooperation can not only be renewed at the technical level but also at the political level. Here, channels could be established through intergovernmental fora and platforms and also through supranational groups such as the Council FREMP Working Group (on fundamental rights, citizens' rights and free movement of persons within the EU). Ideally, these different exchange platforms would inform the discussion in the Council of the European Union which has so far not dedicated specific meetings to the protection and promotion of the Article 2 values. On 16 December 2014, the Council agreed on the establishment of 'a dialogue among all Member States within the Council to promote and safeguard the rule of law in the framework of the Treaties'. This new framework complements the existing Article 7 procedures and the EU's infringement procedures. The Council underlined that the dialogue will be based on the principles of objectivity and equality and that it will be 'conducted on a non-partisan and evidence-based approach'. It will respect national identities and should be 'brought forward in light of the principle of sincere cooperation'. Finally, the Council stressed that this process should avoid duplication and take 'into account existing instruments and expertise in this area'. The Presidency of the EU is tasked with ensuring that all these principles are respected. The dialogue will be held once a year in the Council's General Affairs configuration, and be prepared by COREPER (Presidency), 'following an inclusive approach'. The Council also stated that it might, in case of need, also 'launch debates on thematic subject matters'.[52] The dialogue could be conducted as a self-standing event, but could also be linked effectively to the subsequent year's dialogue, where promising practices and topics could be further explored, possibly even on the basis of further experience during the year. The annual dialogues could thus serve to steer progress politically in this area. In order to be

---

[51] European Union Agency for Fundamental Rights, 'Twelve Operational Fundamental Rights Considerations for Law Enforcement When Processing Passenger Name Record (PNR) Data' (2014), at http://fra.europa.eu/sites/default/files/fra-2014-fundamental-rights-considerations-pnr-data-en.pdf.

[52] See Council of the European Union, Conclusions of the Council of the European Union and the member states meeting within the Council on ensuring respect for the rule of law, 16 December 2014. The Council will 'evaluate, by the end of 2016, the experience acquired on the basis of this dialogue'.

based on evidence, and given the necessary political will, the debate could also be underpinned by expert input from outside the Council, including for instance an annual synthesis report based on the 'Union core' of data, information and analysis drawn from all the different actors in the relevant fields, including at UN and Council of Europe levels.

V   How to Make Fundamental Rights a 'Joined-Up' Mission? The Argument for a Bottom-Up Approach

Engaging Article 7 TEU could result in sanctions such as the withdrawal of a Member State's voting rights. This measure risks aggravating the situation by increasing exclusion from 'the core' of states.[53] Such sanctions could then also alienate the population of the Member State being targeted (a phenomenon that could already be observed back in 2000 during the so-called Austrian crisis).[54] As argued above, a Member State spiralling away from the values of the EU should be swayed to return to the fold by the power of attraction and peer pressure. To prevent such spiralling, the values must also be well-grounded in society – in the full range of actors from regional and local government to civil society organisations.

Ideally, any EU Article 7 activity should build on evidence collected at the national level and open up channels of communication with relevant civil society organisations in the country concerned. For instance, the European Parliament could reflect the European Commission's Rule of Law framework by adopting procedures which mirror the different procedural steps in the Commission' new Rule of Law framework. Accordingly, if the European Commission launches a 'Commission assessment' (the first step of the new framework), the European Parliament could invite key civil society organisation across the full spectrum of civil society for a LIBE Committee hearing.[55] If the Commission begins the second step of its procedure (Commission recommendation), the Parliament's rules could

---

[53] See, for example, G. N. Toggenburg, 'La crisi austriaca: delicati equilibrismi sospesi tra molte dimensioni', 2 (2001) *Diritto pubblico comparato ed europeo* 735.

[54] See M. Dani, 'Opening the Enforcement of EU Fundamental Values to European Citizens', Verfasssungsblog, 7 April 2013, at www.verfassungsblog.de/opening-the-enforcement-of-eu-fundamental-values-to-european-citizens/#.Vdzfp_lViko.

[55] The Committee for Civil Liberties, Justice and Home Affairs appears well placed for such a task as it is responsible not only for Article 7 procedures but also for fundamental rights in general, as well as transparency data protection; the area of freedom, security and justice; entry and movement of persons, asylum and migration; and police and judicial cooperation in criminal matters, including terrorism; etc.

allow for a Parliamentary fact-finding mission to the country concerned and, based on that visit, a Parliamentary draft report to be discussed in the Parliament. This would help prevent the alienation of the Member State population and further spiralling away from EU values. Article 7 sanctions as foreseen lack 'local ownership' (they are imposed by European institutions) and this therefore calls for special emphasis on involvement of civil society.

However, it is probably even more important that the EU and its Member States take the local level into account beyond such Article 7 scenarios. Fundamental rights, like other obligations under international human rights law, are mainly for the central government of a state to ensure. However, the government's practical and everyday responsibility for fundamental rights lies rather at the regional and local levels.[56] This need for a vertically 'joined-up' approach should also be coupled with a horizontal approach, which goes beyond involving governmental institutions at the various levels in the work on fundamental rights. For example, civil society organisations and human rights bodies active at the various levels should be engaged and fully joined up. Cooperation between government institutions and civil society organisations (CSOs) and cooperation among CSOs could be enhanced by establishing fundamental rights platforms in line with the experience collected at EU level with the FRA's Fundamental Rights Platform (bringing together around 400 relevant organisations).[57]

To emphasise the developments at national and local levels and ensure that these are linked with EU level developments does justice to the fact that 'normative prescription'[58] is not unidirectional in the EU system, since the EU's values (especially those reflected in the general principles of law) strongly build on the constitutional traditions of the Member States (see Figure 1). In fact, a serious debate on the level of commitments

---

[56] For a discussion of this, see A. Accardo, J. Grimheden and K. Starl, 'The Case for Human Rights at the Local Level: More Than an Obligation?', in *European Yearbook on Human Rights* (2012).

[57] See M. Kjærum and G. N. Toggenburg, 'The Fundamental Rights Agency and Civil Society: Reminding the Gardeners of their Plants' Roots', 2 (2012) *European Diversity and Autonomy Papers*, at www.eurac.edu/en/research/institutes/imr/activities/Bookseries/edap/Documents/2012_edap02.pdf.

[58] See for instance R. Toniatti who speaks of 'una sorta di inversione di direzione della prescrittività': R. Toniatti, 'La carta e i 'valori superiori' dell'ordinamento comunitario', in R. Toniatti (ed.), *Diritto, diritti, giurisdizione* (Cedam: Padova, 2002), pp. 7, 23.

and efforts undertaken as well as the results realised with regard to the Article 2 values requires consideration also of the regional and local governance levels as these are the layers which most directly impact on the lives of the people. Moreover, it is precisely the facts and experiences characterising the local level which should inform any policymaking at national and EU levels. The challenge lies in making sure that there is sufficient communication, coordination and cooperation between the different actors at different governance levels. Against this background, it is worth exploring how best to establish an overall strategic framework for the protection and promotion of the Article 2 values within the EU.

VI   How to Move the Values Debate from Extreme Scenarios to Business as Usual? The Argument for a Strategic Framework

Since Article 7 TEU addresses quite extreme situations and given that the Article 7 procedures are initiated and implemented by political actors, the ensuing debates can be expected to be political in nature and not necessarily strictly objective and rational in all respects. Politicised (in terms of party politics or other partisan motivations) debates risk focusing on identifying the 'perpetrator', rather than on remedying the situation which is perceived as problematic. Moreover, *ad hoc* debates on a single Member State accused of violating Article 2 are reactive and risk provoking defensive reactions by the state concerned. On the contrary, regular discussions of problematic phenomena arising over the year in different EU Member States would permit the preservation of a 'group-spirit' and could instil mutual learning. Such a pre-emptive approach would also be beneficial in terms of preserving and further developing mutual trust among the Member States. A regular exchange on how best to promote shared values within the EU would function most effectively if organised in a framework which allows the identification of EU-wide priorities, to pursue coherent objectives and to increase efficient mainstreaming and coordination.

Joining up all dots, including the mainstreaming efforts in the EU institutions (Section IV) or the various efforts by national human rights bodies and civil society organisations (Section V) would create a framework which provides a shared underlying structure so that the different existing elements can be brought together more synergistically and strategically. Such a 'strategic framework' would not necessarily have to take the shape of an explicit EU policy document. It could adopt an incremental approach, building up momentum through transnational cooperation and development of concrete steps over time. It could combine more formal EU elements with developing forms of transnational cooperation as well as fresh momentum for exploring new avenues at the national level (Section VII).

More formal EU-level elements could include the annual dialogue which is supposed to be conducted in the Council or the European Commission's justice scoreboard as well as the annual hearing in the European Parliament before it adopts its report on the fundamental rights situation within the EU. Transnational exchange mechanisms are found for instance within the various networks the FRA brings together, such as the network of Ombudspersons, the network of Equality Bodies and National Human Rights Institutions, the network of fundamental rights experts (FRANET), the Fundamental Rights Platform and the just established network of contact points in national Parliaments. Based on a mapping of all relevant institutions and mechanisms, a strategic framework for the protection and promotion of fundamental rights could renew existing levels of cooperation and exchange of experience and knowledge in a strategically relevant manner: relevant information shared at the right time in the right format.

Such a strategic framework would aim at two things. First, it would aim to make sure that various legislative and programmatic decisions taken at the EU level are based on fundamental rights-relevant evidence as produced by various actors and mechanisms at the EU level (horizontal coordination and mainstreaming). Secondly, it would aim at ensuring that EU-level developments occur in full awareness and consideration of fundamental rights-relevant developments at national and local levels (vertical coordination and mainstreaming). This would also ensure that experiences gained with EU legislation and EU policies feed into the evaluation of existing EU instruments as well as into the new proposals on how the EU level can best contribute to a flowering of the Article 2 values at the national level. This ambition would be best fulfilled if the strategic framework provided a fundamental rights policy cycle (see Figure 4) which puts the various EU-level elements (such as reports or events) in a chronological order so that they can build on each other and hence create synergies.

The European Parliament proposed that such a policy cycle should also include a programming moment: the cycle should detail 'on a multiannual and yearly basis the objectives to be achieved and the problems

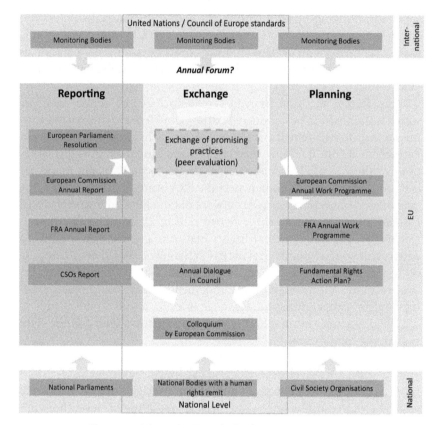

Figure 4   Schematic view of a fundamental rights cycle.

to be solved' considering that this cycle should foresee a framework for institutions and the FRA, as well as Member States, to work together by avoiding overlaps, building on each other's reports, taking joint measures and organising joint events with the participation of NGOs, citizens, national parliaments, etc.[59]

This, however, raises issues of legal competence and inter-institutional power allocation[60] – the elephant in the room in the Rule of Law debate.

---

[59] European Parliament, Resolution of 12 December 2012 on the situation of fundamental rights in the European Union (2010–2011), para. 20.
[60] See for example G. Schusterschitz, 'Rule of Law within the EU – The Unavoidable Question of Who Controls It?', in W. Schroeder (ed.), *Strengthening the Rule of Law in Europe* (Oxford: Hart Publishing, 2016).

VII   Who Does What? Addressing the 'Elephant in the Room' through a Hybrid Approach Incorporating Supranational and Intergovernmental Elements

There is a risk that in trying to protect democracy and the Rule of Law within the EU, the European Union could overstep the limits of the European political constitution and thereby risk undermining democracy and the Rule of Law within the EU.[61] Using the EU as a unidirectional and monolithic actor could indeed encounter limitations. However, viewing the EU as an integrated forum interacting with the other layers of governance as discussed above opens as yet untapped potential for the EU to have increased influence in fostering shared values as enshrined in the Charter of Fundamental Rights, without risking tipping the 'federal balance'.

The limits posed by the treaties were often interpreted narrowly. The procedure in Article 7 TEU is often read as building an exclusive monopoly for supervising the Article 2 performance of the EU Member States which prohibits the EU institutions from supplementing the Article 7 procedures under other competence bases. In some corners it is argued that not even the flexibility clause in Article 352 TFEU offers a competence base to establish mechanisms to further protect the Article 2 values, because the respect for the values of the EU was not one of the 'policies defined in the Treaties'.[62] Such a reading misunderstands the constitutional value commitment in Article 2, which by its very nature is not a 'policy'. Rather, the value commitment in Article 2 makes the values listed therein an integral part of all EU policies defined in the EU Treaties. Article 352 TFEU allows the EU to take action where there is a need to attain 'within the framework of the policies defined in the Treaties' one of the objectives of the Treaties. The promotion of the Article 2 values is one of the objectives of the EU.[63] To deny the possibility of using Article 352 TFEU to enhance the protection of fundamental rights by arguing that fundamental rights are not a self-standing 'policy' assigned by the Treaties to the EU is far from convincing. 'Fundamental rights' do not constitute a legislative policy field at the national level capable of being assigned to one rather than another governance level either.

---

[61] B. Bugarič, 'Protecting Democracy and the Rule of Law in the European Union: The Hungarian Challenge', LEQS Paper No. 79/2014, at www.lse.ac.uk/europeanInstitute/LEQS/ LEQSPapers.aspx.

[62] See text of Art. 352 TFEU.   [63] Art. 3(2) TEU.

However, Article 352 TFEU so far remains of more theoretical relevance as it requires unanimity in the Council and consent by the Parliament (and Member States such as the United Kingdom and Germany require special involvement of the national Parliaments). Moreover, Article 352 TFEU would not permit extending the framework to areas where the EU has no legislative competences whatsoever. Therefore, if a strategic framework were developed with an action plan requiring work in areas not covered by EU competence, this framework would be needed to be agreed on an intergovernmental basis. An annual meeting outside the EU institutional framework could bring together national and European institutions and relevant actors from civil society. Such an intergovernmental approach could also help avoid the momentum created in the discussion as it unfolded evaporating once the question of 'who does what' within the EU framework arises.

An Annual Forum could be placed outside the EU's institutional framework and still focus on, interact with and inform the EU (see insert at the centre of Figure 4). It could agree on a few priorities for the upcoming year and assign who is best placed to focus on what. This exchange of views and the different forms of evidence presented at that forum (which could also be available electronically so as to be even more accessible) would be of obvious relevance to the EU and its policymaking but stand as an equally relevant asset for the Council of Europe and national actors. The EU institutions could commit themselves in an annual[64] action plan to what they think falls within their competences and form an efficient contribution to the shared values. These commitments would form the supranational or 'Union core' part of the action plan. In addition, other actors, including the Member States, networks of human rights bodies and Council of Europe bodies could commit to actions or ideas also falling outside the 'Union core', thus outside EU competence.

This would reflect the fact that a decade ago the Heads of States and Government has already agreed in Warsaw that the EU should 'strive to transpose those aspects of Council of Europe Conventions within its competence into European Union Law'.[65] Arguably every international human rights commitment has a 'Union core' to which the EU can contribute to make the rights concerned real. Such a Union core was identified for instance with regard to the European Social Charter, and we would argue

---

[64] Or 2.5 years each, so that an action plan could be adopted at the beginning and the middle of a legislative cycle.
[65] Warsaw Action Plan, Guideline No. 5.

that a mapping exercise could identify a 'Union core' for all Council of Europe or UN human rights agreements.[66] The EU institutions could identify fields where they are, politically speaking, ready and, legally speaking, competent to commit themselves to specific action to complement and strengthen the Member States' international commitments. Nonetheless, the action plan would be an intergovernmental document agreed outside the EU's institutional framework, as it would also bring together actors that are not integral parts of the EU's structures (such as national human rights bodies and CSOs) and deal with issues which are beyond the EU's legislative competences (such as prison conditions or the question of whether to establish national fundamental rights platforms etc.). It would renew the synergies between the EU and the Council of Europe and UN bodies as it would at regular intervals inform the EU institutions about human rights developments outside the EU's remit and offer channels for the EU to actively support these bodies within its remit. Whereas the implementation of commitments outside the Union core would happen outside the EU institutional framework through local, regional and national institutions, commitments within the Union core would be coordinated within the EU system. The European Parliament, the Council of the European Union and the European Commission would obviously play core roles in this context.

In terms of providing relevant evidence and analysis for these political processes, the FRA could prepare a synthesis report[67] based on the various EU-relevant findings (the 'Union core') presented under the various Council of Europe[68] and UN[69] monitoring bodies as well as the FRA's own research and data. This would guarantee that the strategic framework made full use 'of existing mechanisms and [...] other relevant EU and

[66] See the action plan for the Turin process, in M. Nicoletti, (PACE Vice-President) (2014), 'High-Level Conference on the European Social Charter: General Report', Council of Europe, Italian Presidency of the EU and City of Turin, 17–18 October 2014, 49, at www .coe.int/T/DGHL/Monitoring/SocialCharter/TurinConference/Turin-General-Report_EN .pdf. For the Framework Convention for the Protection of National Minorities, see G. N. Toggenburg, 'Das Recht der Europäischen Union und das Rahmenübereinkommen zum Schutz nationaler Minderheiten', in R. Hofmann et al (eds.), *Das Rahmenübereinkommen zum Schutz nationaler Minderheiten Handkommentar* (Baden-Baden: Nomos, 2014).

[67] See also Bingham Centre for the Rule of Law, 'Safeguarding the Rule of Law, Democracy and Fundamental Rights: A Monitoring Model for the European Union' (2013).

[68] For 2013, the FRA lists 46 monitoring reports issued over the year on EU Member States. See FRA, Annual Report 2013, 236 and 237.

[69] For 2013, the FRA lists 25 monitoring reports issued over the year on EU Member States. See FRA, Annual Report 2013, 244 and 245, at http://fra.europa.eu/sites/default/files/ fra-2014-annual-report-highlights-2013-0_en_0.pdf.

international bodies' and ensure that the framework 'would apply in a transparent manner, on the basis of evidence objectively compiled, compared and analysed and on the basis of equality of treatment as between all Member States'.[70] Proposals to create new institutions (such as a Copenhagen Commission alongside the Venice Commission and the Agency in Vienna) or new monitoring mechanisms appear unnecessary. The Agency combines a flexible mandate which permits a very wide range of activities including country reports. For instance, in the context of Article 7, the Council declared that 'neither the Treaties nor the Regulation establishing the European Union Agency for Fundamental Rights precludes the possibility for the Council to seek the assistance [. . .] when deciding to obtain from independent persons a report on the situation in a Member State within the meaning of Article 7 TEU'.[71] More importantly, the Agency is an independent expert body which is – as an EU body – aware of the EU's specificities but at the same through a range of networks institutionally linked to the realities of the national legal systems. This outreach, which expert bodies would normally lack, is complemented by a high level Scientific Committee which brings together renowned experts with a proven record of solid judgment (composed of, *inter alia*, members of Constitutional Courts, a former Vice President of the ECtHR, as well as members of UN, Council of Europe and national monitoring bodies). All this is not to say that the mandate of the Agency cannot be improved,[72] but to make the point that the EU's fundamental rights body is well-equipped to play a relevant role in any future framework addressing the Rule of Law debate.

VIII   Conclusion

To conclude, for the EU to lead by example when defending its founding values is not easy, but it is possible. Admittedly, its factual and legal position is very different *vis-à-vis* third countries from what it is *vis-à-vis*

---

[70] Council of the European Union, Conclusions of 6 June 2013 on Fundamental Rights and Rule of Law and on the Commission 2012 Report on the Application of the Charter of Fundamental Rights of the European Union, para. 9 lit. iii and vi.

[71] Declaration by the Council on proceedings under Article 7 of the Treaty on European Union, Council document 6396/07 ADD 1 as of 27 February 2007, see also COM(2003) 606 final, section 2.1., 10.

[72] See on this G. N. Toggenburg, 'The EU Fundamental Rights Agency and the Fundamental Rights Charter: How Fundamental Is the Link between Them?', in S. Peers et al. (eds.), *The EU Charter of Fundamental Rights: A Commentary* (Oxford: Hart Publishing, 2013), p. 1613.

its own Member States. Nevertheless, there are avenues to provide for increased levels of consistency in the EU's commitment to its founding values. We argue that viewing the founding values in Article 2 through the prism of the Charter is a promising approach to identify areas where the EU has much to offer. Moving the Rule of Law debate from a punitive, unilateral EU intervention to something that deals with all the founding values, applies to all actors equally and becomes a normal element of a regular exercise outside extreme situations seems a promising direction to take. Admittedly, not everything in such a 'strategic framework' could be offered by the EU. This should not be regarded as a weakness but rather as a hook to provide for increased interaction and coordination among all the relevant actors within and outside the EU institutional asset.

8

The Potential of the EU Charter of Fundamental Rights for the Development of the Rule of Law Indicators

MARTIN SCHEININ[*]

I Introduction

The proposition made in this chapter is that the relevance of the EU Charter of Fundamental Rights (CFR) for an EU-level Rule of Law mechanism should not be dismissed or underestimated too easily. If used systematically and using methodologically rigorous indicators, the Charter has potential as an important component of a Rule of Law mechanism, either as a trigger for its initiation or as a normative yardstick in its implementation. The legal basis for a mechanism, or for action by the EU institutions or Member States, is not the topic of this chapter.[1] Neither will it be necessary here to determine whether the Charter and Charter-based indicators should be used as triggers or as normative yardsticks. My claim is that the Charter could serve either function.

This chapter draws upon experience of developing indicator tables to assist monitoring of state human rights treaty compliance by United Nations human rights treaty bodies. I will argue that the straightforward dismissal of the Charter as an important normative source for a Rule of Law mechanism rests on a lack of understanding of what indicators are and how they could be used, and also rests on what is referred to below as 'Strasbourg Myopia'.

To say that the Charter should be seen 'as an important normative source' could mean that Charter provisions, or some of them, are interpreted as expressing the legal obligations of Member States.[2] But this

---

[*] European University Institute, Florence.
[1] See Chapter 3 by Christophe Hillion in this volume.
[2] See the chapter by András Jakab (Chapter 9) in this volume, a contribution which attributes an important and strong role to the Charter in enforcing the Rule of Law.

position is not necessary for adopting the suggestion made in this chapter that Charter provisions could be used to develop a set of Rule of Law indicators. Indicators are primarily empirical in nature, and even when there is a normative dimension to them, they are used more as rules of thumb than as *per se* legally binding rules. The EU Charter of Fundamental Rights is a normative catalogue of the rights of individuals. However, the use of its provisions to develop a set of indicators does not constitute a process of applying those norms as legal norms. Rather, they are used a source of inspiration and guidance for conducting legal assessments under Articles 2 and 7 TEU, which then would be the applicable legal norms, informed and applied in the light of the empirical information an indicator-based approach to the Charter can provide.

The position criticised in this chapter from the EUI Working Paper on Rule of Law oversight, which is the precursor to this volume, is expressed as follows:

> Moreover, crucially, it should not be forgotten that the drawback of any approach based on the Charter of Fundamental Rights, consists in the very starting assumption behind looking in the direction of the Charter in the first place, namely that the values of Article 2 TEU are about – or can always be approached through – human rights or fundamental freedoms. That this is not the case can be illustrated by the situation in the non-complying countries themselves. A strong agreement emerged in Florence that fundamental rights are only part of the problem and the focus should be on the wider Rule of Law and democracy concerns. Both on substance and also institutionally – i.e. through the Fundamental Rights Agency of the European Union – there are limits to what can be achieved by only focusing on fundamental rights.[3]

Yes, there are limits, but there is also great potential, and this chapter seeks to explain why.

As Gabriel Toggenburg and Jonas Grimheden point out in their own chapter in this volume,[4] the Charter actually offers a fairly broad coverage of the founding values listed in Article 2 TEU. They also defend the view that the EU Fundamental Rights Agency (FRA) and its Scientific Committee should have a role in a Rule of Law Mechanism. I support these positions. The main point to be made below is also mentioned by Toggenburg and Grimheden, but worthy of further elaboration: the

---

[3] C. Closa, D. Kochenov and J. H. H. Weiler, 'Reinforcing Rule of Law Oversight in the European Union', EUI Working Paper RSCAS No. 2014/25, p. 12.
[4] See Chapter 7 by Gabriel Toggenburg and Jonas Grimheden in this volume.

Charter could be made good use of in the Rule of Law Mechanism through the identification and use of *indicators* based on its provisions.

II   The Problem of Strasbourg Myopia

It would be an overstatement to suggest that the EU Charter of Fundamental Rights could *alone* provide the normative framework for assessing a Member State's substantive compliance with Rule of Law. That said, the current discussion, including as reflected in the quote presented above, appears to suffer a reverse problem of *understating* the relevance of the Charter. I will argue that this tendency flows from a methodological error which can be termed *Strasbourg Myopia*. The symptoms of this Myopia are: (i) over-emphasis of certain selected *traditional liberty rights* enshrined in the fairly old-fashioned ECHR, to the detriment of a holistic approach which would seek to address all fundamental rights interdependently, (ii) over-emphasis of *negative obligations* on the EU or Member States, to the detriment of the full recognition of a whole range of positive obligations; (iii) over-emphasis of the *individualistic nature* of fundamental rights, to the point where the population is reduced to atomistic individuals which can each have their separate case with respect to a Member State and (iv) over-emphasis of a *violations approach*, establishing high substantive and procedural standards for any determination by an authoritative European court that a fundamental rights-related problem exists. These features of Strasbourg Myopia can be explained by reference to a European human rights culture which has been formed and informed by the huge – but nevertheless relative – success of the ECHR as an instrument of constitutional significance for the States and peoples of Europe. The symptoms of Strasbourg Myopia relate to and result from how the ECHR works in practice, through individual complaints, through the requirement of exhausting domestic remedies, and through authoritative determinations that a violation of the ECHR has occurred and is attributable to a specific State. These are all important characteristics of a strong human rights monitoring mechanism based on the operation of a single authoritative Court which can be directly accessed by aggrieved individuals and which has the power to issue legally binding judgments upon States. That said, these features should not prejudge and limit the potential role of the Charter in a totally different legal and institutional framework.

I suggest that instead of this individualistic and violation-based approach, Rule of Law assessment could rely on the Charter's provisions through an *indicator-based* approach. Indicators would need to be developed to identify system-level issues which are simultaneously related to specific provisions of the Charter and able to provide meaningful guidance as to whether the Rule of Law in a particular Member State is in good shape or showing pathological symptoms. Specifically, indicators would need to be found which are capable of serving as early warning signs of the deterioration of Rule of Law. This does not exclude their usefulness also in the determination of actual breaches of Rule of Law, but it does not conceptually require the latter, as early warning on its own would be a valuable enough goal to strive for.

An indicator-based approach should not be overly ambitious. It would not be realistic to expect that it could provide actual answers regarding compliance or non-compliance with Rule of Law. However, indicators could merely be exactly what the term suggests, evidence-based categories of data capable of giving indications of the existence or non-existence of a problem or an emerging problem. Such indicators could also act as triggers for other mechanisms – including political ones – to take over.

III   Learning from the UN Human Rights Indicator Project

Meaningful Rule of Law indicators can be developed. In 2005–2012 this author had the pleasure of being involved in and chairing a series of expert consultations convened by the Office of the United Nations High Commissioner for Human Rights, aiming to complement the traditional monitoring of United Nations human rights treaties with an indicator-based assessment (referred to below as the OHCHR Indicator Project).[5] The primary purpose of the exercise was to assist the human rights treaty bodies – independent expert panels acting under each respective human rights treaty – in their examination of periodic reports by States Parties. The periodic reporting procedure is the only mandatory monitoring mechanism under the UN human rights treaties, where mechanisms of individual complaint remain formally optional, even if they are accepted today by a majority of world States. The outcome of the periodic reporting procedure is a 'Concluding Observations' document in which the treaty body assesses the human rights situation in the country concerned, performing a normative assessment under the treaty in question and usually including recommendations how the situation could be improved.

---

[5] *Human Rights Indicators: A Guide to Measurement and Implementation*, United Nations Office of the High Commissioner for Human Rights, 2012.

Generally, the Concluding Observations do not address individual cases and do not make pronouncements about violations but rather express 'concern' about an insufficient degree of compliance or that the situation is in some respect 'incompatible' with the provisions of the treaty. The latter idea implies that the State Party in question is in breach of its international treaty obligations, while the former wording can relate to various levels of misgivings about the human rights situation or its deterioration.

The issuing of Concluding Observations by a treaty body is ultimately a matter of treaty interpretation. But before that, the process requires a great deal of preparatory work, including the systematic collection of information, the formulation of written and oral questions to a State Party, and an analysis of the responses received through a dialogue with State Party representatives. The OHCHR Indicator Project emerged from the need to assist the task of the treaty bodies through the development of human rights indicators which would not replace treaty interpretation as a task of the treaty bodies but systematise the collection and analysis of information needed for that task.

The key elements of the methodology of the OHCHR Indicators Project were: (i) to develop indicator tables for the human rights recognised in the 1948 Universal Declaration of Human Rights and subsequently in legally binding human rights treaties, including the two Covenants of 1966,[6] by seeking to cover as many of these articles as possible;[7] (ii) to identify the main substantive dimensions – called attributes – of each of these rights, based on how each right has been addressed in the institutional practices of interpretation under the respective human rights treaty;[8] (iii) to identify and list under each attribute three types of indicators, namely structural indicators, process indicators and outcome indicators, selected for their ability to provide indications of varying levels of compliance or non-compliance[9] and (iv) to rely as far as possible on indicators which represent quantitative data available under pre-existing statistical categories.[10]

Of these steps, item (iii) requires some explanation. Structural indicators relate to the existence of laws and institutions which enable and

---

[6] The International Covenant on Economic, Social and Cultural Rights and the International Covenant on Civil and Political Rights.

[7] The main report from the project (see *Human Rigths Indicators*) includes fourteen indicator tables for a fairly wide selection of rights, providing balanced cover of civil and political rights and economic, social and cultural rights.

[8] *Ibid.*, pp. 30–2.   [9] *Ibid.*, pp. 33–8.   [10] *Ibid.*, Chapter III.

secure compliance with the human right in question.[11] Process indicators seek to measure ongoing efforts towards that aim.[12] Outcome indicators are also about achievements, mapping the facts on the ground, the actual effective delivery of human rights enjoyment.[13] There may be some overlap between structural and process indicators, as for instance a specific national strategy document may have features of the two. Likewise, a process indicator for one right may sometimes be suitable as an outcome indicator of another human right.[14]

IV Selecting the Most Pertinent Provisions of the EU Charter of Fundamental Rights

I argue that applying the same methodology as was used in the OHCHR Indicator Project but using the Charter would allow for the development of uniform Rule of Law indicators both capable of providing early warning of a deterioration of the situation in a Member State and of acquiring data to assess whether a situation is in actual breach of the normative requirements on Member States stemming from the EU's commitment to Rule of Law. Three specifications are offered below to substantiate this assertion.

(1) *It is necessary to identify a set of selected provisions of the Charter that are most relevant for the exercise.*

All fundamental rights are relevant to securing the Rule of Law and in assessing whether it is being honoured. However, some rights are more pertinent than some others for this task. Below is a non-exhaustive list of Charter rights recommended to establish a Rule of Law indicator process.

Article 19(1) CFR: Prohibition against collective expulsions.
Article 20 CFR: Equality before the law.
Article 21 CFR: The prohibition against discrimination on any ground, such as sex, race, colour, ethnic or social origin, genetic features, language, religion or belief, political or any other opinion, membership of a national minority, property, birth, disability, age or sexual orientation.

---

[11] *Ibid.*, pp. 34–5. See also, Figure 3 in Chapter 7 by Toggenburg and Grimheden in this volume.
[12] *Human Rights Indicators*, pp. 36–7.   [13] *Ibid.*, pp. 37–8.
[14] *Ibid.*, p. 38. The example provided in the OHCHR Guide is that the proportion of people covered by health insurance can simultaneously be a process indicator for the right to health and an outcome indicator for the right to social security.

Article 22 CFR: Respect for cultural, religious and linguistic diversity.
Article 23 CFR: Equality between women and men.
Articles 39–40 CFR: Electoral rights.
Article 41 CFR: The right to good administration.
Article 47 CFR: The right to an effective remedy and to a fair trial, notably:
  – (2) by an independent and impartial tribunal previously established by law and
  – (3) effective access to justice.

Article 52(1) CFR: The requirement that any limitation on the exercise of the Charter must be 'provided for by law'.

(2) *For the development of Rule of Law indicators, it is necessary to look into these rights not merely as Charter provisions with a certain textual formulation, but also as value commitments by Member States, intrinsically linked to Article 2 TEU.*

The main reason why this requirement needs to be included is that some of the provisions of the Charter are formulated as EU-level rights without explicitly reaffirming that the underlying value commitments naturally require similar commitments at the national level. In the above list, for instance Articles 39–41 CFR (electoral rights and the right to good administration) have been formulated as if pertaining only to the EU level. In the development of indicators, what is decisive is the substance of those rights, not the governance level at which they are exercised.

(3) *The indicator tables as developed in the OHCHR Indicator Project were produced to measure human rights compliance as such, and using the same approach and methodology for Rule of Law assessment may require additional elements.*

Notably, the OHCHR Indicator Project produced indicator tables for the right to a fair trial and for equality and non-discrimination. They would provide a point of departure for the development of indicator tables for Articles 20, 21, 23 and 47 CFR – roughly half of the whole task. However, the new purpose of using the indicator approach for Rule of Law assessment will also require that under these rights a new attribute (a substantive dimension) is added to the existing indicator tables. We would need to identify structural, process and outcome indicators under the new Rule of Law attribute which are capable of illustrating and measuring the state of the Rule of Law in a Member State at a given time. These indicators could include some which are already being used for other attributes of the same rights, starting with indicators which have been identified as pertinent to all the attributes of a given right. Once that is done for this first subset of Charter rights, where corresponding OHCHR indicator tables already exist, the same methodology should be applied to produce indicator tables for the remaining rights, that is Articles 19(1), 22, 39–41, 47 and 52(1) CFR in the tentative list presented above.

V Structure, Process and Outcome Indicators for Rule of Law

The *structural indicators* to be selected for the new purpose of Rule of Law assessment will include a Member State's international treaty commitments, constitutional guarantees, permanent legislation and regular institutions which together amount to safeguards for compliance with the Rule of Law, including in the case of internal challenges. Participation in treaties which do not allow for unilateral denunciation, unconditional acceptance of international individual petition mechanisms, explicit inclusion of elements of the Rule of Law in national constitutions and the existence and scope of judicial review over unconstitutional laws are all strong candidates for potential structural indicators.

Process indicators seek to measure ongoing commitment, in this case towards the aspect of the Rule of Law under the Charter rights selected as the basis for the development of Rule of Law indicators. They may relate to less institutionalised governmental policy documents or to budgetary allocations (for instance to promote religious, cultural and linguistic diversity) but also to factual data – including statistics – where they serve as indicators of commitment rather than of the end result. Process indicators for the relevant aspect of the Rule of Law could include issues such as reported occurrences of government ministers publicly criticising court rulings (or alternatively publicly defending judicial independence), or the same officials publicly responding to incidents of racist violence (or alternatively not responding). Statistics on racist violence, and also surveys related to experiences of and views on xenophobia and racism, can also serve as process indicators.[15]

---

[15] For the link between hate crime and the Rule of Law, see Council Framework Decision 2008/913/JHA of 28 November 2008 on combating certain forms and expressions of racism and xenophobia by means of criminal law, where recital 1 of the Preamble spells out in explicit term: 'Racism and xenophobia are direct violations of the principles of liberty, democracy, respect for human rights and fundamental freedoms and the rule of law, principles upon which the European Union is founded and which are common to the Member States'. OJ 2008 No. L328/55.

Outcome indicators for the Rule of Law would employ a wide variety of statistics geared towards being able to provide evidence or at least presumptions of either actual compliance or non-compliance with the Charter provisions selected for exercise, here related to the actual enjoyment of those rights by the population. One of the benefits of the indicator approach is that it is not limited to this outcome dimension of compliance but can also detect trends and risks in situations which have not yet manifested themselves as actual rights violations. That said, an indicator-based approach is not complete unless it also includes the facts on the ground concerning actual enjoyment of rights. The relevant statistical parameters should be selected so that they best represent and capture the aspect of the Rule of Law of the selected rights, including equality and non-discrimination, promotion of diversity, electoral rights and the rights to a fair trial and effective remedy. Judicial statistics will play an important role when appropriate categories of cases are selected – for example, prosecutions and convictions of racist crimes and hate crimes. Statistics on judicial dismissals as a consequence of legislative amendments (e.g. by changing the retirement age) can also be relevant. Statistics on complaints of electoral fraud as such, irrespective of their outcome, may be an indication of distrust of elections in the administration and hence be a valid indicator.

One reason why a complex matrix of dozens of indicators may be required is the 'Frankenstate' problem identified by Kim Lane Scheppele: a too-simplistic list of seemingly meaningful indicators of the Rule of Law might not be able to identify an emerging 'Frankenstate', that is, an intentionally constructed constitutional aggregate composed from various individually perfectly reasonable pieces which imbue the state with its monstrous quality only because of the horrible way that those pieces interact when stitched together.[16]

Above is an initial effort to come up with illustrative examples of the kind of structure, process and outcome indicators which could be identified for a new aspect of the Rule of Law under selected Charter rights. The EU Fundamental Rights Agency (FRA) is ideally placed to conduct the actual exercise of selecting the indicators due to its status as an autonomous EU agency deploying multidisciplinary expertise, its

---

[16] K. L. Scheppele, 'The Rule of Law and the Frankenstate: Why Governance Checklists Do Not Work, Governance', 26 (4) (2013) *International Journal of Policy, Administration, and Institutions* 559–62.

experience and capacity in collecting multiple forms of data, and its multiple expert networks. FRA has already undertaken some of this work in specific areas, in particular in relation to disability, Roma and children, and it is producing surveys which will be able to contribute in particular to outcome indicators.[17] The FRA has also intentionally and systematically developed the capacity to build upon the indicators project at the OHCHR, including in some areas which would be suitable for developing Rule of Law indicators.[18] The 2013 FRA Symposium was devoted to the theme of the Rule of Law, with the clear intention that the development of appropriate indicators should be a part of its aims.[19] If the FRA were to further emulate the OHCHR Indicator Project process, it would need a key multidisciplinary team of staff experts – for example a lawyer, an economist, a political scientist and a sociologist – and a series of consultations involving external experts, including from statistical organisations, non-governmental organisations and academia. As the building of a comprehensive indicator table for a particular right – or just one aspect of a right – requires a holistic assessment of how well the suggested indicators complement each other, two-day meetings between twenty or so experts from diverse backgrounds proved to be a uniquely productive way of doing the job in the OHCHR Indicator Project.

VI   Inclusion of the 'Provided by Law' Requirement

The challenge for a Rule of Law assessment is generally not in defining the line between a violation of a right and an all-things-considered non-violation, that is, a justified interference with or limitation of a

---

[17] Concerning pertinent FRA activities, see: http://fra.europa.eu/en/project/2015/eu-midis-ii-european-union-minorities-and-discrimination-survey; http://fra.europa.eu/en/project/2015/fundamental-rights-survey; http://fra.europa.eu/en/project/2014/rights-persons-dis abilities-right-independent-living;   http://fra.europa.eu/en/project/2011/fundamental-rights-indicators; http://fra.europa.eu/en/publication/2014/right-political-participation-persons-disabilities-human-rights-indicators; http://fra.europa.eu/en/publication/2012/fra-symposium-report-using-indicators-measure-fundamental-rights-eu-challenges-and; http://fra.europa.eu/en/publication/2012/developing-indicators-protection-respect-and-promotion-rights-child-european-union;   http://fra.europa.eu/en/project/2013/multi-annual-roma-programme.

[18] See 'Using Indicators to Measure Fundamental Rights in the EU: Challenges and Solutions,' 2nd Annual FRA Symposium Vienna, FRA Symposium Report (12–13 May 2011).

[19] Promoting the Rule of Law in the European Union, 4th Annual FRA Symposium Vienna, FRA Symposium Report (7 June 2013).

fundamental right. One element of the permissible limitations test enshrined in Article 52(1) CFR was included in the above tentative list of Charter provisions to be used for the development of indicators, namely, the requirement that any limitations of fundamental rights must be provided for by law. This requirement is indeed an important component of the Rule of Law, and in mature constitutional systems it relates to the precision, clarity, foreseeability (in many areas, including of course criminal law) non-retroactivity and parliamentary status of a legal instrument which results in restrictions on a fundamental right, as well as to the availability of effective remedies in its application. As all these features are of immediate relevance for a Rule of Law assessment, they would qualify as indicators based on Article 52(1) CFR. It would probably also be possible to identify structure, process and outcome indicators here related to the 'provided by law' requirement.

As said, Rule of Law indicators would not generally be found in the elements of the permissible limitations test or, more generally, at the fine dividing line between permissible limitations and violations. Rather, they would be found at a deeper level of fundamental rights compliance, related to enabling, structural or systemic dimensions of fundamental rights which are often collective in nature and which relate much more closely to positive obligations than to negative ones. As indicated above, pessimistic accounts of the capacity of the Charter to provide proper guidance for a Rule of Law assessment result rather from a 'Strasbourg Myopia' than from the provisions of the Charter. To assess compliance with the Rule of Law, including to identify the early warning signs of when a country is drifting off course and the risk of a Rule of Law deficit is identifiable, it is important to see beyond actual violations. For this kind of a broader approach, the main challenge will be in finding the proper indicators for problems or risks with respect to the Rule of Law *before* these problems manifest themselves as violations of individual fundamental rights.

VII   Using the Resulting Indicators

In the above I suggested that the FRA would play a central role in developing the indicator tables for Charter-based Rule of Law assessment. It is also perfectly plausible that the FRA could also play a related central role in applying the indicator framework in real situations. Its multidisciplinary expertise, data collection capacity and multiple expert networks would permit the production of annual Rule of Law indicator datasheets for all Member States. Producing them non-selectively for all Member States and avoiding normative conclusions at that stage is important to develop the methodology and also to create a repository of data which could ultimately be used to determine which of the indicators are best suited to detecting actual Rule of Law issues, including early warning signs.

The FRA has highly qualified expert staff who would probably be able to handle the identification and application of attributes and indicators for use in the Rule of Law mechanism. That said, it should also be noted that the FRA also possesses a Scientific Committee which is particularly well suited to be the body responsible for the process. The FRA Scientific Committee is one of the statutory bodies of the FRA under its founding Regulation. It is composed of eleven independent persons selected according to demanding requirements concerning both their qualifications and independence. It is 'the guarantor' of the scientific quality of FRA's work, and it adopts its positions by a two-thirds majority.[20] These features make the Scientific Committee an attractive institution for depoliticising the role of the Charter and Charter-based indicators in a Rule of Law mechanism.[21]

A major role for the FRA, either involving its Scientific Committee or otherwise, fits very well into the broader framework of the Commission's Rule of Law Framework. The Framework, presented in March 2014 in a Commission Communication to the Parliament,[22] declared the creation of a framework which 'will apply in the same way to all Member States' and 'will operate on the basis of the same benchmarks'.[23] It would be geared towards 'systemic threats' instead of being 'triggered by individual breaches of fundamental rights or by a miscarriage of justice'.[24] This is

---

[20] Council Regulation EC 168/2007 of 15 February 2007 establishing a European Union Agency for Fundamental Rights, Article 14.

[21] In a critique of the OHCHR framework of human rights indicators, Margaret Satterthwaite and AnnJanette Rosga warn against reducing human rights assessment and the exercise of judgment it entails into 'solely technical measurement'. They emphasise the importance of also allowing space for democratic engagement in the overall assessment process. The proposal made in this chapter addresses this warning by emphasising the need for a proper role for the indicators-based approach within a broader assessment framework. See, A. Rosga and M. Satterthwaite, 'Measuring Human Rights: UN Indicators in Critical Perspective', in K. E. Davis, A. Fisher, B. Kingsbury and S. E. Merry (eds.), *Governance by Indicators: Global Power through Quantification and Rankings* (Oxford: Oxford University Press, 2012), pp. 297–316.

[22] 'A New EU Framework to Strengthen the Rule of Law,' Communication from the Commission to the European Parliament and the Council, COM(2014) 158 final/2.

[23] *Ibid.*, p. 6.   [24] *Ibid.*

very much in line with the foundational choices for an indicator-based approach as proposed above. In a key paragraph, the Communication also indicates a role for the FRA which is perhaps more modest than the one suggested above, but which nevertheless is fully aligned with what I propose here. According to the Communication, the Commission will collect and examine all the relevant information 'and assess whether there are clear *indications*' (emphasis added) of a systemic threat to the Rule of Law. In the same paragraph, it further stated that such an assessment could be based on 'indications received from available sources and recognized institutions, including notably the bodies of the Council of Europe and the European Union Agency for Fundamental Rights'.[25] These parameters can be included verbatim in the design of the indicator-based mechanism presented in this chapter.

After the Commission Communication of March 2014, the Council announced an annual Rule of Law Dialogue, something that is expected to be weaker and softer than the Mechanism presented by the Commission.[26] There is no need to conclude that this move by the Council has superseded the Commission's plans. Rather, it is perfectly understandable that as an intergovernmental body, the Council wants to offer its own contribution towards securing the Rule of Law in the EU, independently of what is designed by the Commission. In an important speech to the European Parliament[27] in February 2015, First Vice-President Frans Timmermans affirmed that the Commission will continue with its Rule of Law Framework, even after the Council had developed its own annual Rule of Law Dialogue. According to Timmermans, 'all institutions have important, complementary roles to play'. Underlining that the Commission has its own role, and that as a part of that role it would be for the Commission to advise the CJEU if the Rule of Law is threatened in a Member State, Timmermans affirmed that the Commission's EU Rule of Law Framework will remain in place. He even mentioned some of the issues which could move the Commission to take action, namely 'unlawful retirement of judges'

---

[25] *Ibid.*, p. 7, where footnote 20 indicates the legal basis for the role of the FRA: 'See in particular Article 4(1)(a) of Council Regulation (EC) No 168/2007 establishing a European Union Agency for Fundamental Rights (OJ L 53, p. 1)'.

[26] See D. Kochenov and L. Pech, 'Monitoring and Enforcement of the Rule of Law in the EU: Rhetoric and Reality' 11 (2015) EUConst 512.

[27] Speech by Frans Timmermans, First Vice President of the Commission on the Commission Statement: EU framework for democracy, rule of law and fundamental rights, Strasbourg, 12 February 2015, SPEECH/15/4402, at http://europa.eu/rapid/press-release_SPEECH-15-4402_en.htm.

and 'measures affecting the independence of supervisory authorities'. 'We are keeping a close eye on all issues arising in Member States relating to the rule of law, and I will not hesitate to use the Framework if this required by the situation in a particular Member State'.[28]

The determination shown by the Commission is warmly welcomed. To operationalise this determination, this chapter has proposed the development of an indicator-based approach, with an important role for the FRA as a crucial building block of the Mechanism, both in designing and implementing it. One of the merits of an indicator-based approach is that there is no automaticity between the indicators or the annual Rule of Law indicator datasheets in relation to each Member State, and subsequent action by political institutions. Multidisciplinary expertise will be important, even essential, and it will be utilised with full respect for the independence of the experts. Entrusting the FRA's Scientific Committee with the task of assessing the indicator-based data will help in depoliticising this phase of the process. However, what action will then result after such assessment will be a matter for political processes.

An indicator-based approach was also supported in the 10 June 2015 European Parliament resolution on the situation in Hungary, where Operative Paragraph 12 went beyond the specific situation in Hungary and proposed a mechanism which is broader in scope than just focusing on Rule of Law. Nevertheless, the Charter, the FRA, indicators, and annual reports on all Member States are important elements in the Parliament's position, which all coincide with what is proposed above. In its resolution the European Parliament called on the Commission 'to present a proposal for the establishment of an EU mechanism on democracy, the rule of law and fundamental rights, as a tool for compliance with and enforcement of the Charter and Treaties as signed by all Member States, relying on common and objective indicators, and to carry out an impartial, yearly assessment on the situation of fundamental rights, democracy and the rule of law in all Member States, indiscriminately and on an equal basis, involving an evaluation by the EU Agency for Fundamental Rights, together with appropriate binding and corrective mechanisms, in order to fill existing gaps and to allow for an automatic and gradual response to breaches of the rule of law and fundamental rights at Member State level'.

In addition, the Parliament instructed its own Committee on Civil Liberties, Justice and Home Affairs (LIBE Committee) to contribute to the

---

[28] See Chapter 1 by Carlos Closa in this work for a detailed discussion of the various proposals.

development and elaboration of the proposal in the form of a legislative own-initiative report to be adopted by the end of the year.[29]

VIII   Conclusion

The positions of the Commission and the Parliament reflected in the immediately preceding section appear highly promising, both in terms of providing the prospect of an evidence-based and effective Rule of Law Mechanism within the EU and through creating a much-needed window of opportunity for the inclusion of an indicator-based expert phase into the Mechanism as a necessary precursor for any action by political bodies. In their Introduction to their seminal edited volume *Governance by Indicators*, Kevin Davis, Benedict Kingsbury and Sally Engle Merry provide a concise list of features demonstrating why the use of indicators may be attractive for decision-makers as a preparatory phase: efficiency, consistency, transparency, scientific authority and impartiality.[30] Indeed, the proposal defended in this chapter follows this model faithfully.

This chapter has defended the view that selected provisions of the EU Charter of Fundamental Rights provide a proper basis for the elaboration of a set of Rule of Law indicators which should be developed and applied in the indicator-based expert phase of a Mechanism. The EU Fundamental Rights Agency and perhaps its Scientific Committee should have a leading role in that phase, to secure the utilisation of multidisciplinary scholarly expertise and independent verification by a body of independent experts already entrusted with a quality assurance function at the FRA. Ensuring that the assessments made are evidence based and represent state-of-the art methodology are important prerequisites for the Rule of Law Mechanism as a whole becoming legitimate in the eyes of European citizens and effective as to the delivery of well-founded assessments, without hesitation or bias.

---

[29] European Parliament resolution of 10 June 2015 on the situation in Hungary (2015/2700(RSP)), para. 12, Texts Adopted (provisional edition P8_TA-PROV(2015) 0227), at www.europarl.europa.eu/sides/getDoc.do?pubRef=-//EP//NONSGML+TA+P8-TA-2015-0227+0+DOC+PDF+V0//EN.

[30] K. E. Davis, B. Kingsbury and S. E. Merry, 'Introduction: Global Governance by Indicators', in Davis et al., Governance by Indicators, pp. 4–28.

9

The EU Charter of Fundamental Rights as the Most Promising Way of Enforcing the Rule of Law against EU Member States

ANDRÁS JAKAB*

I Introduction

The ambition of this chapter is to show that the best method for enforcing the Rule of Law against Member States is a creative reinterpretation of Article 51(1) of the EU Charter of Fundamental Rights (Charter, CFR), whereby the fundamental rights of the Charter are also made applicable in purely domestic cases. To support our point, we will entrench the argument in a Toynbeean approach, that is by means of 'challenge and response': the Rule of Law should be perceived as a tool which is a response to the arbitrary use of state power (originally developed against absolutism). The concept's inherently anti-sovereigntist nature should prevail whenever we interpret a legal document (such as the Charter) enacted in order to promote key aspects of the Rule of Law such as the promotion of fundamental rights. Currently, the most important historical challenge to the Rule of Law in Europe is the systematic dismantling of the Rule of Law (and democracy) in certain Member States, and for which the present chapter attempts to offer a partial cure.

* Schumpeter Fellow, Max Planck Institute for Comparative Public Law and International Law, Heidelberg; Director and Tenured Research Chair, Hungarian Academy of Sciences, Centre for Social Sciences, Institute for Legal Studies, Budapest. For critical remarks I am grateful to Paul Blokker, Carlos Closa, Bruno de Witte, Jonas Grimheden, Christophe Hillion, Michael Ioannidis, Dimitry Kochenov, Mattias Kumm, John Morijn, Jan-Werner Müller, Joakim Nergelius, Gianluigi Palombella, Jari Pirjola, Norbert Reich, Martin Scheinin, Kim Lane Scheppele, Kaarlo Tuori, Zsófia Varga, Andre Wilkens and Nele Yang.

II   A Toynbeean Approach to Constitutional Ideas

Constitutional ideas can be viewed in two different ways. First, they can be regarded as being derived from specific moral principles, such as freedom, equality or solidarity. Secondly, they can be viewed as responses to social challenges. This chapter follows the second track, and it is my belief that moral ideas can also be explained as long-term default responses to social challenges.[1] In line with Toynbee, I regard societies as regularly facing new challenges that they try to find the right solutions to.[2] By challenge, I mean a new circumstance or problem which requires a new, creatively formulated method to solve it. Such creativity can take the form of new inventions or the introduction of new ideas about how a society should be organised.[3] If a specific invention or new idea is not able to solve a particular problem (incorrect response), then the society (culture or nation) in question experiences either no progress or actual decline until the correct response is established (or it loses its distinctive identity and is dissolved in another society, culture or nation). At this point, competent lawyers, driven by their instinct to look for definitions, may be asking themselves what is actually meant by the words 'society', 'no progress' or 'decline'. This is also the case with the idea of the Rule of Law,[4] which was originally invented as a response to absolutism.[5] Over time, definitions

---

[1] R. A. Posner, *The Problematics of Moral and Legal Theory* (Cambridge, MA: Harvard University Press, 1999), p. 17.

[2] A. J. Toynbee, *A Study of History*, Vol. 1 (Oxford: Oxford University Press, 1933), p. 271. While different aspects of Toynbee's work have been subject to justified criticism (especially the role of religion, the relationship between civilisations, certain concrete historical details), his basic scheme of challenge-and-response does seem to fit the historical facts. For an account of recent literature on Toynbee see M. Perry, *Arnold Toynbee and the Western Tradition* (New York: Peter Lang, 1996), especially, pp. 103–28; for a good introduction to his work see C. T. McIntire and M. Perry, 'Toynbee's Achievement', in C. T. McIntire and M. Perry (eds.), *Toynbee. Reappraisals* (Toronto: Toronto University Press, 1989), p. 3; for classic literature on him (and some of his own methodological essays) see M. F. A. Montagu (ed.), *Toynbee and History: Critical Essays and Reviews* (Boston: Porter Sargent, 1956).

[3] See A. Sajó, *Limiting Government: An Introduction to Constitutionalism* (Budapest: CEU Press, 1999), pp. 1–7 on constitutional ideas as expressions of what kind of past experiences the constitution-giver wanted to avoid.

[4] The expressions 'Rule of Law' and *Rechtsstaat* are used synonymously in this chapter unless otherwise indicated.

[5] For more details see A. Jakab, 'Breaching Constitutional Law on Moral Grounds in the Fight against Terrorism. Implied Presuppositions and Proposed Solutions in the Discourse on "The Rule of Law vs. Terrorism"', 9(1) (2011) *I-CON* 58; A. Jakab, *European Constitutional Language* (Cambridge: Cambridge University Press, 2016).

of the Rule of Law have evolved.[6] The only key element which has never been questioned is the *limitation of or struggle against the arbitrary use of government power.*[7] In the following we will see how this idea of the Rule of Law is currently being challenged in some Member States and what the most promising way to deal with it would be.

III   A New Historical Challenge in Europe: Dismantling the Rule of Law in Member States

Recent events in Hungary and Romania have proved that it is far from obvious that once a state becomes a member of the EU it will follow the principles of the Rule of Law without any external enforcement mechanism.[8] This chapter is, however, not about these two countries but about the general legal problem convincingly put forward by Jan-Werner Müller, who basically states that the Copenhagen criteria cannot be enforced efficiently against Member States (and their enforcement was deficient even against candidate countries).[9] The requirements of the thick concept of the Rule of Law can be breached systematically, and the European Union is unable to handle this efficiently. If, however, the EU does not want to lose its credibility, it has a duty to defend the Rule of Law (see Article 2 TEU) to the greatest possible extent, at least within Europe, and especially within the European Union.[10] This tension between the

---

[6] 'Rule of Law' is often used in an expanded sense, which includes the political ideology of the respective speaker or judge, cf. J. Raz, *The Authority of Law* (Oxford: Clarendon, 1979), p. 210.

[7] In the US this abuse means abuse in the interest of particular interests instead of the aggregated interest of all citizens, see C. Möllers, *Die drei Gewalten: Legitimation der Gewaltengliederung in Verfassungsstaat, Europäischer Integration und Internationalisierung* (Weilerswist: Velbrück Verlag, 2008), pp. 29–35. In France the risk of abuse stemmed from the monarchical executive. The legislature in the US is conceived as representing lobbies or other particular interests, as opposed to France, where the legislature is the people's voice. Möllers, *Ibid.*, pp. 32, 35. On the Rule of Law as opposed to arbitrariness see M. Krygier, 'The Rule of Law: Legality, Teleology, Sociology', in G. Palombella and N. Walker (eds.), *Relocating the Rule of Law* (Oxford: Hart Publishing, 2009), p. 45. On the term as restriction of government discretion B. Z. Tamanaha, 'A Concise Guide to the Rule of Law', in Palombella and Walker, *Relocating the Rule of Law*, pp. 7–8.

[8] For more details see A. von Bogdandy and P. Sonnevend (eds.), *Constitutional Crisis in the European Union. Theory, Law and Politics in Hungary and Romania* (Oxford: Hart Publishing, 2015), pp. 5–190.

[9] See J.-W. Müller, 'Should the EU Protect Democracy and the Rule of Law inside Member States?', 21(2) (2015) *ELJ* 141; D. Kochenov, *EU Enlargement of the Failure of Conditionality* (Alphen aan den Rijn: Kluwer Law International, 2008).

[10] See C. Hillion, 'Overseeing the Rule of Law in the EU: Legal Mandate and Means' in this volume.

impotence in enforcement of the EU on the one hand, and the moral and (implied) legal duty to enhance the Rule of Law within its territory, on the other hand, lies at the heart of this chapter. The majority of the possible enforcement methods available relies on political discretion (isolation of the political party concerned within its European party family, Article 7 TEU and infringement procedures by the Commission), and therefore cannot be counted on to guarantee the aforementioned values. European politicians may (and in a matter of fact actually do) conduct themselves opportunistically: they often downplay conflicts or even pretend that conflicts do not exist. It seems that European politicians have a tendency to turn a blind eye to such problems when faced with a major crisis within the EU which seems to them to be of more importance than issues of constitutionalism in one of the Member States. While it is obvious that we should expect European politicians to believe in the values of constitutionalism, liberty is based on a distrust of politicians.[11] A mechanism which places the enforcement of constitutionalism in the hands of politicians is a useful but untrustworthy mechanism. Judicially guaranteed mechanisms represent the most trustworthy mechanisms for enabling those who are affected to enforce these values.[12] In the following we are going to argue that the most promising way to enforce the Rule of Law against Member States in which governments have been hijacked by groups which work on dismantling the Rule of Law is to widen the application of the EU Charter of Fundamental Rights (CFR) through a creative reinterpretation of its Article 51(1).

IV   Existing Interpretations of Article 51(1) CFR

Article 51(1) CFR, which limits its scope as regards the Member States: it is applicable to them '*only* when they are interpreting Union law', is viewed as being probably the most important provision or '"keystone" of the Charter'.[13] Not only does this restrictive formulation appear to contradict

---

[11]   See B. Bugarič, 'Protecting Democracy inside the EU: On Article 7 TEU and the Hungarian Turn to Authoritarianism' in this volume.

[12]   As the key question of this paper concerns the relationship between the individual and the government, we will not concentrate on issues relating to the horizontal effect of fundamental rights. On these issues under the Charter, see T. von Danwitz and K. Paraschas, 'A Fresh Start for the Charter', 35 (2012) *Fordham International Law Journal* 1396, 1423–25.

[13]   K. Lenaerts, 'Exploring the Limits of the EU Charter of Fundamental Rights', 8 (2012) *EUConst.* 375, 377. According to P. Eeckhout, 'The EU Charter of Fundamental Rights

the underlying philosophy that it is assumed inspires the Charter,[14] but it is also more restrictive than the former case law of the ECJ concerning the applicability of fundamental rights (conceptualised as fundamental principles of law).[15] The explanatory memoranda do not really provide any clarification of the situation either:[16]

> As regards the Member States, it follows unambiguously from the case law of the Court of Justice that the requirement to respect fundamental rights defined in a Union context is only binding on the Member States when they act in the scope of Union law (judgment of 13 July 1989, Case 5/88 *Wachauf* [1989] ECR 2609; judgment of 18 June 1991, ERT [1991] ECR I-2925); judgment of 18 December 1997 (C-309/96 *Annibaldi* [1997] ECR I-7493). The Court of Justice confirmed this case law in the following terms: 'In addition, it should be remembered that the requirements flowing from the protection of fundamental rights in the Community legal order are also binding on Member States when they implement Community rules ... ' (judgment of 13 April 2000, Case C-292/97, [2000] ECR 2737, paragraph 37 of the grounds). Of course this rule, as enshrined in this Charter, applies to the central authorities as well as to regional or local bodies, and to public organisations, when they are implementing Union law.

Three main interpretations can be found in the literature concerning Article 51(1) CFR: (a) A literal and rather restrictive approach which requires the actual existence of EU law in an area in order to trigger the application of the Charter.[17] This interpretation, however, not only

---

and the Federal Question', 39 (2002) *CMLRev.* 945, 954, it is paradoxical to have a general fundamental rights charter with limited scope.

[14] R. A. García, 'The General Provisions of the Charter of Fundamental Rights of the European Union', Jean Monnet Working Paper No. 4/02, at www.jeanmonnetprogram.org/archive/papers/02/020401.pdf, 5.

[15] For a detailed comparison with previous case law, see X. Groussot, L. Pech and G. T. Petursson, 'The Scope of Application of Fundamental Rights on Member States' Action: In Search of Certainty in EU Adjudication', Eric Stein Working Paper No. 1/2011, at www.era-comm.eu/charter_of_fundamental_rights/kiosk/pdf/EU_Adjudication.pdf. For the history of different draft versions of the CFR see G. de Búrca, 'The Drafting of the European Union Charter of Fundamental Rights', 26 (2001) *ELRev.* 126.

[16] Explanations relating to the Charter of Fundamental Rights (OJ 2007 No. C303/17, 32). For a critical view on these rather confusing explanations, see L. F. M. Besselink, 'The Member States, the National Constitutions and the Scope of the Charter', 8 (2001) *Maastricht Journal of European and Comparative Law* 68, 76–8. Groussot et al., 'The Scope of Application of Fundamental Rights', 19 denounce the explanations to Art. 51 as 'a mixture of various formulas'.

[17] S. Peers, 'The Rebirth of the EU's Charter of Fundamental Rights', 13 (2013) *Cambridge Yearbook of European Legal Studies* 283, 298; T. von Danwitz and K. Paraschas, 'A Fresh Start for the Charter', 35 (2012) *Fordham International Law Journal* 1396, 1409; P. M. Huber, 'Unitarisierung durch Gemeinschaftsgrundrechte – Zur Überprüfungsbedürftigkeit der

contradicts the previous case law of the ECJ (as quoted above in the explanatory memoranda), but it is also in conflict with the Charter itself, as Article 53 CFR explicitly states that the Charter cannot lead to a diminished level of fundamental rights protection.[18] If this interpretation were to be accepted, this would result in a lower level of fundamental rights protection than that which existed before the adoption of the Charter. (b) Since *Åkerberg Fransson*,[19] it seems to be clear that the former literal interpretation no longer mirrors the actual legal situation.[20] In this judgment the scope of the Charter was clarified by interpretation and the widely held view in the literature that any material link and *potential* lawmaking are sufficient for the application of the Charter was accepted.[21] This view had also been previously promoted by AG Sharpston in *Ruiz Zambrano*:[22]

> Transparency and clarity require that one be able to identify with certainty what 'the scope of Union law' means for the purposes of EU fundamental rights protection. It seems to me that, in the long run, the clearest rule would be one that made the availability of EU fundamental rights protection dependent neither on whether a Treaty provision was directly

ERT-Rechtsprechung', (2008) *Europarecht* 190, 196; M. Borowsky, 'Artikel 51 – Anwendungsbereich', in J. Meyer (ed.), *Charta der Grundrechte der Europäischen Union*, 3rd edn (Baden-Baden: Nomos, 2011), pp. 642, 653–4; Z. Varga, 'Az Alapjogi Charta alkalmazási köre I', 5 (2013) *Európai Jog* 17, 19 with further references. See also P. Yowell, 'The Justiciability of the Charter of Fundamental Rights in the Domestic Law of Member States', in P. M. Huber (ed.), *The EU and National Constitutional Law* (Stuttgart: Boorberg, 2012), pp. 107, 114–23.

[18] C. Nowak, 'Grundrechtsberechtigte und Grundrechtsadressaten', in F. Sebastian, M. Meselhaus and C. Nowak (eds.), *Handbuch der Europäischen Grundrechte* (Munich: Beck, 2006), pp. 212, 244–5.

[19] Case C-617/10 *Åkerberg Fransson* ECLI:EU:C:2013:105, judgement of 26 February 2013.

[20] F. Fontanelli, 'Hic Sunt Nationes: The Elusive Limits of the EU Charter and the German Constitutional Watchdog', 9(2) (2013) *EUConst.* 315; A. Ward, 'Article 51 – Scope', in S. Peers, T. Hervey and J. Kenner (eds.), *The EU Charter of Fundamental Rights. A Commentary* (Oxford: Hart Publishing, 2014), pp. 1413, 1433–37. On the conflict between the wide Fransson doctrine and the strict approach of the German FCC to Art. 51 see D. Thym, 'Separation versus Fusion – or How to Accommodate National Autonomy and the Charter? Diverging Visions of the German Constitutional Court and the European Court of Justice', 9(3) (2013) *EUConst.* 391.

[21] Eeckhout, 'The EU Charter of Fundamental Rights', 993; H. Kaila, 'The Scope of Application of the Charter of Fundamental Rights of the European Union in the Member States', in P. Cardonnel, A. Rosas and N. Wahl (eds.), *Constitutionalising the EU Judicial System* (Oxford: Hart Publishing, 2012), p. 291; J. Kokott and C. Sobotta, 'The Charter of Fundamental Rights of the European Union after Lisbon', EUI Working Papers No. 2010/6, 7, at http://cadmus.eui.eu/bitstream/handle/1814/15208/AEL_WP_2010_06.pdf?sequence=3.

[22] Opinion of AG Sharpston in Case C-34/09 *Ruiz Zambrano* ECLI:EU:C:2010:560, para. 163.

applicable nor on whether secondary legislation had been enacted, but rather on *the existence and scope of a material EU competence.* To put the point another way: the rule would be that, provided that the EU had competence (whether exclusive or shared) in a particular area of law, EU fundamental rights should protect the citizen of the EU *even if such competence has not yet been exercised.*

According to this interpretation, however, is also the idea that the Charter cannot be engaged unless there is a link to the material scope of an EU competence.[23] This means that the application of the Charter is therefore still viewed as collateral, and its rights are not viewed as being freestanding rights.[24] While some call for a further clarification of this interpretation in order to make its application easier for national judges, it probably conforms with both the actual ECJ case law[25] and the dominant opinion in the literature.[26] (c) The emergence of a possible third, more liberal, interpretation which suggests that the Charter is also applicable outside of the scope of EU law was the result of recent events, especially in Hungary, Italy and Romania.[27] The legal justification offered for such an interpretation is that Union citizenship must entail a guarantee of last resort for fundamental rights in cases of systemic failure in a Member State.[28] This reverse *Solange* approach has been advanced by Armin von Bogdandy and his colleagues.[29] The approach has been met with criticism for a

---

[23] On the different definitions of the general concept 'scope of EU law' see S. Prechal, S. de Vries and H. van Eijken, 'The Principle of Attributed Powers and the "Scope of EU Law"', in L. Besselink, F. Pennings and S. Prechal (eds.), *The Eclipse of the Legality Principle in the European Union* (Alphen aan den Rijn: Kluwer Law International, 2011), p. 213; Eeckhout, 'The EU Charter of Fundamental Rights', 993; Opinion of AG Sharpston, para. 173.

[24] An expression borrowed from Groussot, Pech and Petursson, 'The Scope of Application…', 22.

[25] Recently confirmed by Case C-206/13 *Siragusa* ECLI:EU:C:2014:126, para. 24.

[26] M. Borowsky, 'Artikel 51 – Anwendungsbereich', in J. Meyer (ed.), *Charta der Grundrechte der Europäischen Union,* 4th edn (Baden-Baden: Nomos, 2014), pp. 743, 758–60; E. Hancox, 'The Meaning of "Implementing" EU Law under Article 51(1) of the Charter: Åkerberg Fransson', 50 (2013) *CMLRev.* 1411, 1418–27; F. Fontanelli, 'National Measures and the Application of the EU Charter of Fundamental Rights – Does curia.eu Know iura.eu?', 14 (2014) *Human Rights Law Review* 231, 263–5.

[27] See for example www.verfassungsblog.de/category/schwerpunkte/rescue-english/.

[28] For an early iteration of this idea in the context of free movement of persons, see Case C-380/05 *Centro Europa 7* ECLI:EU:C:2008:59 [2008] ECR I-349, Opinion of AG Poiares Maduro, paras 20–22.

[29] A. von Bogdandy et al., 'Reverse *Solange* – Protecting the Essence of Fundamental Rights against EU Member States', 49(2) (2012) *CMLRev.* 489. The concept had been previously used in a similar sense (without a specific use of Union citizenship, however) by D. Halberstam, 'Constitutional Heterarchy: The Centrality of Conflict in the European

number of reasons: for being too dramatic and stigmatising (and therefore contradicting the principle of mutual respect provided in Article 4(3)
TEU) instead of concentrating on actual fundamental rights protection,
for requiring a systemic failure of fundamental rights protection for the
establishment of which the procedures necessarily contain a decision by
a political body (thus leaving fundamental rights protection at the mercy
of politicians),[30] and also for using the *Solange* formula, which is considered to be a potential face-saving excuse for inaction.[31] To avoid these
objections (but possibly resulting in others) we are going to develop a
different approach in this chapter: an approach which would elevate the
Charter into a real and fully fledged bill of rights in the European Union
via creative reinterpretation.[32]

V   For a Creative Reinterpretation of Article 51(1) CFR

If we aim for a fully fledged values community which benefits all its citizens
equally, then the Charter should gain as such full applicability in every
case, even in purely domestic cases in domestic courts and even if there is
no systemic failure of fundamental rights protection at a domestic level.
This means that with the additional assistance of the supremacy of EU law
(more precisely here: of the Charter) fundamental rights-based judicial
review would be introduced across Europe. The type of judicial review
envisioned would be decentralised in the sense that local courts would
be able to exercise it, but its unified application would be ensured by the
preliminary procedure: it could therefore also be labelled semi-centralised
judicial review.

Such an approach would enable the European Union to become a
'community of fundamental rights' where nobody would be left behind.
The idea of excluding a Member State because of fundamental rights
violations is an appalling and unacceptable denial of a European moral

Union and the United States', in J. L. Dunoff and J. P. Trachtman (eds.), *Ruling the World?
Constitutionalism, International Law, and Global Governance* (New York: Cambridge University Press, 2009), p. 326.

[30] For a detailed explanation of the concept and of different procedures see A. von Bogdandy
and M. Ioannidis, 'Systemic Deficiency in the Rule of Law: What It Is, What Has Been
Done, What Can Be Done', 51(1) (2014) *CMLRev*. 59.

[31] D. Kochenov, 'On Policing Article 2 TEU Compliance – Reverse Solange and Systemic
Infringements Analyzed', 33 (2014) *Polish Yearbook of International Law* 145, 156.

[32] It seems that after Opinion 2/13 ECJ, the ECHR will not become the bill of rights of the
EU. See editorial comment: 'The EU's Accession to the ECHR – a "NO" from the ECJ!',
52(1) (2015) *CMLRev*. 1.

community: the citizens of the excluded country would be left to suffer, whereas the rest of Europe would save itself.

This would be especially important in cases where, sacrilegiously, violations of fundamental rights are entrenched in constitutions and where constitutional courts have been stuffed with party apparatchiks who do not care about constitutional arguments. Ordinary courts have the advantage of existing in great numbers in each country, meaning that it is difficult to replace their staff to suit party political lines, and even a single ordinary judge can cry for help through a preliminary reference to the ECJ.

In the following subsections, I will counter the likely objections to my proposal concerning its efficiency (including alternative routes for the better protection of fundamental rights) and its doctrinal or moral justification.

(a)   Doctrinal Triggers: Articles 2 and 7 TEU vs. Union Citizenship

The proposed reinterpretation contradicts both the literal meaning of Article 51(1) CFR, its current interpretation by the ECJ and most of the literature.[33] Consequently, in order to support my idea, it is necessary to provide some solid doctrinal arguments in support. There seem to be two possible parallel ways to justify this extensive interpretation of the scope of the Charter: one is to use the concept of Union citizenship, the other is to use Articles 2 and 7 TEU as triggers. While the two justifications do not exclude each other, I feel that the second option has more potential. Union citizenship is generally viewed as consisting of a bundle of rights,[34] and as an 'autonomous' legal status it also seems to replace the ideology of cross-border effects, as it triggers the application of EU law even in cases where there is no cross-border element,[35] and has developed into being able to protect citizens from their own Member States.[36]

---

[33] See Groussot et al., 'The Scope of Application of Fundamental Rights', 23: 'it is simply wrong to affirm that natural and legal persons, following the entry into force of the Lisbon Treaty, have gained the right to institute judicial proceedings on the basis of any provision of the Charter, in any situation, against any national (or EU) public authorities'.

[34] G. Palombella, 'Whose Europe? After the Constitution: A Goal-Based Citizenship', 3 (2005) *I-CON* 357, 377–82.

[35] P. Van Elsuwege, 'Shifting the Boundaries? European Union Citizenship and the Scope of Application of EU Law', 38 (2001) *Legal Issues of Economic Integration* 263 (analysing *Ruiz Zambrano*). See also the opinion of AG Poiares Maduro in Case C-135/08 *Janko Rottmann* ECLI:EU:C:2009:588 [2010] ECR I-1449, para. 23.

[36] D. Kochenov, 'The Essence of EU Citizenship Emerging from the Last Ten Years of Academic Debate: Beyond the Cherry Blossoms and the Moon?', 62 (2013) *ICLQ* 37, 135.

A further step in the same direction would be to state that Union citizenship can trigger the application of the Charter.[37] However, this approach is a substantial departure from the traditional one, which views the scope of the Charter as defined *ratione materiae*.[38] Another way to justify the wide application of citizenship while retaining the requirement of *ratione materiae* would be to use Article 7. Article 7 TEU provides that in the case of a 'clear risk of a serious breach' of the core values laid down in Article 2 TEU (which includes the respect for human rights) a special procedure can be initiated. Article 7 has never been applied but if we use the formula developed in *Fransson* ('if it is *capable of indirectly affecting* EU law')[39] then – with reference to Articles 2 and 7 read together – basically *all human rights violations* can trigger the application of Article 51(1) CFR.[40]

(b)   Formal Modification of Article 51(1) CFR?

Some who might otherwise agree with the reasoning behind my proposal, might also argue that it would be *contra legem* without formal amendment of the Charter (and of TEU), and thus unacceptable.[41] In general, treaty

---

[37] S. Iglesias Sánchez, 'Fundamental Rights and Citizenship of the Union at a Crossroads: A Promising Alliance or a Dangerous Liaison?', 20 (2014) *ELJ* 464 (arguing for an extension of the scope of the Charter in order to solve the problem of reverse discrimination). Contrast with F. Schulyok, 'The Scope of Application of EU Citizenship and EU Fundamental Rights in Wholly Internal Situations' (2012) *Europarättslig Tijdskrift* 448.

[38] M. Safjan, 'Areas of Application of the Charter of Fundamental Rights of the European Union: Fields of Conflict?', EUI Working Papers – Law No. 2012/22, at http://cadmus.eui .eu/bitstream/handle/1814/23294/LAW-2012-22.pdf, 2. See, on the dilemma F. Fontanelli, 'The European Union's Charter of Fundamental Rights Two Years Later', 3(3) (2011) *Perspectives of Federalism* 40.

[39] On *Åkerberg Fransson* as symbolising the end of the possibility of dealing with fundamental rights solely based on domestic considerations see D. Sarmiento, 'Who's Afraid of the Charter? The Court of Justice, National Courts and the New Framework of Fundamental Rights Protection in Europe', 50 (2013) *CMLRev.* 1267, 1303.

[40] See on this possibility, briefly A. Rosas, 'When Is the EU Charter of Fundamental Rights Applicable at National Level?', 19(4) (2012) *Jurisprudencija/Jurisprudence* 1269, 1282 (rejecting it partly for practical (case load) reasons) (at 1285).

[41] V. Reding, 'Observations on the EU Charter of Fundamental Rights and the future of the European Union', Speech/12/403 held at the XXV Congress of FIDE (Tallin, 31 May 2012), at http://europa.eu/rapid/press-release_SPEECH-12-403_en.pdf, 11; C. Closa, D. Kochenov and J. H. H. Weiler, 'Reinforcing Rule of Law Oversight in the European Union', EUI Working Papers No. 2014/25, RSCAS, 12, 17; N. Chronowski, 'Enhancing the Scope of the Charter of Fundamental Rights?', 1 (2014) *JURA* 13–21. For the *ultra vires* argument see J. Kühling, 'Fundamental Rights', in A. von Bogdandy and J. Bast (eds.), *Principles of European Constitutional Law*, 2nd edn (Oxford: Hart Publishing, 2009), pp. 479, 500–501.

change is a cumbersome and slow process,[42] and treaty changes which lead to politicians losing some of their discretionary powers are especially difficult. A reinterpretation of existing treaty provisions is more realistic in such cases,[43] and in addition to the pragmatic reasons offered above, I have also tried to sketch out a doctrinal justification for this step.[44]

(c) Efficiency

The above solution could be objected on the basis of its efficiency from two opposing directions. The first objection concerns the fear that if fundamental rights protection is left in the hands of Member State courts, then this might not be an efficient way to protect fundamental rights, as local courts can lack the necessary training or may simply be corrupt.[45] While this is a justifiable concern, it applies to the whole edifice of preliminary referencing, which is generally considered as being one of the key mechanisms for ensuring the success of the ECJ and of EU law in general.[46] The second objection is related to concerns that the ECJ would not be able to cope with the increased workload which would likely result if a wider application of Article 51(1) CFR were accepted.[47] Again, this is a legitimate concern, but it is a general and ongoing issue and it would definitely be mistaken to reject fundamental rights cases *because* the ECJ is overloaded with other cases. Case-overload is not a legal argument.

(d) The Nature of the Conflict Situation

When the EU takes action, it is commonly viewed as reinforcing the idea that there is a large number of conflicts between EU and Member State

---

[42] C. Closa, *The Politics of Ratification of EU Treaties* (London: Routledge, 2013).

[43] A. Jakab, 'Full Parliamentarisation of the EU without Changing the Treaties. Why We Should Aim for It and How Easily It Can be Achieved', Jean Monnet Working Papers No. 2012/3; A. Jakab, 'Why the Debate between Kumm and Armstrong Is about the Wrong Question', Verfassungsblog, 20 June 2014, at www.verfassungsblog.de/debate-kumm-armstrong-wrong-question.

[44] On the phenomenon of the ECJ stepping in to further integration if politicians are unable to reach an agreement, see J. H. H. Weiler, 'The Transformation of Europe', 100 (1991) *Yale Law Journal* 2403.

[45] Closa, Kochenov and Weiler, 'Reinforcing Rule of Law', 17, 21.

[46] For a classic account see K. Alter, 'The European Court's Political Power', 19 (1996) *West European Politics* 458–87.

[47] Rosas, 'When is the EU Charter of Fundamental Rights Applicable at National Level?', 1285; E. M. Frenzel, 'Die Charta der Grundrechte als Maßstab für Mitgliedstaatliches Handeln zwischen Effektivierung und Hyperintegration', 51 (2014) *Der Staat* 1, 26.

interests and values. In contrast to the majority of suggestions relating the solution of fundamental rights problems in Member States,[48] our suggestion is different as according to it the conflict will arise between a Member State government and a Member State court (the ECJ only becomes involved indirectly, via preliminary reference). It is much more difficult (although not impossible) to portray such situations as being a struggle against Brussels bureaucracy. Generally, the imposition of formal sanctions against a state from the outside in order to change its domestic human rights policies is to a large extent inefficient and tends merely to reinforce the siege mentality within the country and only hurt those social groups which the sanctions are supposed to support.[49] As recently acknowledged by Łazowski, there is a strong contrast between the use of the Charter by the ECJ and by the European Commission: whereas the former has already referred to the Charter in 150 cases, the latter often uses the Charter in political rhetoric, but it is reluctant to do so in actual infringement proceedings.[50] We can only speculate about why the Commission is not eager to refer to the Charter. One explanation is simply risk avoidance: the Commission traditionally seems to prefer claims in which the chances of winning are very high, and there remain uncertainties (although less so after the *Fransson* case) about the right interpretation of Article 51(1) CFR. However, another explanation seems more convincing to me: if the Commission were to take a narrow interpretation of Article 51(1) CFR then it would be difficult for the ECJ to expand on it; but if the Commission were to attempt a wide (or activist) interpretation, then strong Member State resistance could be expected. So their strategy seems to be purposely not to get involved in the debate on the interpretation of Article 51(1) CFR and to hope for the best (or even to argue modestly for less, as in *Fransson*, where the Commission even argued that the Charter did not apply),[51] and rightly so: the value of the Charter can be fully realised only if the conflict is not between the Commission and

[48] See for example Jan-Werner Müller's proposal on a Copenhagen Commission: J.-W. Müller, 'Safeguarding Democracy inside the EU – Brussels and the Future of Liberal Order, 2012-2013', Transatlantic Academy Paper Series No. 3, at www.transatlanticacademy.org/sites/default/files/publications/Muller_SafeguardingDemocracy_Feb13_web.pdf. See also his chapter (Chapter 10) in this volume.

[49] See for an example of such a formal sanctions mechanism (systemic infringement procedure): K. L. Scheppele, 'Enforcing the Basic Principles of EU Law through Systemic Infringement Procedures' in this volume.

[50] A. Łazowski, 'Decoding the Legal Enigma: the Charter of Fundamental Rights of the European Union and Infringement Proceedings', 14 (2013) *ERA Forum* 573.

[51] *Ibid.*, 585–6.

the Member States, but rather between the Member State courts (and individuals) and the Member State governments.

(e) Competence Creep

An evident objection to the above is that in accordance with Article 6 TEU and Article 51(2) CFR, the Charter cannot be used to increase the competences of the EU.[52] However, if both Article 6 TEU and Article 51(2) CFR are interpreted in light of Article 2 TEU, then this restriction cannot affect the enforcement of the Charter by the courts. In addition, the principle of subsidiarity (also mentioned in Article 51 CFR) is only applicable with respect to legislative competence and therefore has no effect on judicial authority.[53] While this proposal could be described as a fresh step towards federalisation,[54] this is not the actual justification for but rather a side effect of (or a price that we should be willing to pay for) the above reinterpretation of Article 51(1) CFR.[55]

(f) Moral Authority

Our proposal does not mean that the ECJ would take over the role of the ECtHR. The two roles are and would remain quite different. First, the ECHR does apply not have direct applicability and supremacy in a large number of countries, so the domestic legal situation differs fundamentally. The ECtHR is thus in a weaker legal situation in most EU Member States. That said, the ECtHR is definitely stronger on one account: concerning

---

[52] On this phenomenon in general, but also specifically about the Charter, see for example S. Prechal, 'Competence Creep and General Principles of Law', 3 (2010) *Review of European Administrative Law* 5, 16–20.

[53] Groussot et al., 'The Scope of Application of Fundamental Rights', 23.

[54] For such worries based on the US experience see A. Knook, 'The Court, the Charter, and the Vertical Division of Powers in the European Union', 42 (2005) *CMLRev.* 367–98. For a comparative perspective, see M. Cappelletti, *The Judicial Process in Comparative Perspective* (Oxford: Clarendon, 1989), p. 395: 'there is hardly anything that has greater potential to foster integration than a common bill of rights, as the constitutional history of the United States has proved'. See also, on the centripetal force of any bill of rights, L. M. Díez-Picazo, 'Notes sur la nouvelle Charte des Droits fondamentaux de l'Union européenne', (2001) *Rivista italiana di diritto pubblico comunitario* 665–78.

[55] This new interpretation would give content to the otherwise currently legally useless opt-out protocol (Protocol No. 30 on the Application of the Charter of Fundamental Rights of the European Union to Poland and to the United Kingdom). For a view on the very limited current relevance of Protocol 30, see C. Barnard, 'The EU Charter of Fundamental Rights: Happy 10th Birthday?', 24 (2011) *EUSA Review* 5–10.

its moral authority. To secure the best result in the implementation of fundamental rights, the virtues of the two courts could be combined if the ECJ were to rely fully on ECtHR case law wherever possible.[56] In general, the EU should rely on the authority of the Council of Europe, including the Venice Commission, as otherwise economic or other sanctions would be regarded as part of a political game or as money-saving measures, especially if enforcement is in the hands of the Commission. It would also help the ECJ to counter potential objections relating to a juridical *coup d'Etat* by the ECJ and reduce the credibility of any abusive reference to the protection of national constitutional identities,[57] if it were to rely on the moral authority of the Council of Europe and especially of the ECtHR. The ECJ could give teeth to the ECtHR, as it would not only speed up enforcement but also ensure the efficiency of fundamental rights protection: EU enforcement mechanisms are not just stronger (and usually financially more burdensome), but the EU law-specific disapplication of national law by Member State courts could simply stop national measures from violating fundamental rights (as opposed to just buying them out, as in ECHR cases).

VI 'This Is Just Not the Law' – or the Nature of Leading Cases and the Values of European Integration

On the occasions I have presented the above argument, I have always been met with the simple objection that 'this is just not the law' from some colleagues.[58] I am entirely aware that my interpretative suggestion contradicts the mainstream view about what the current state of the law is. However, law is not a physical object which exists independently from us which we merely have to recognise. Law is what courts make of it.[59] Sooner or later the ECJ is going to receive a preliminary reference from a small rural court in one of the EU Member States (be it a large or a small Member State), and will thus be given the opportunity to decide, without

---

[56] See Arts. 52(3) and 53 CFR.   [57] Art. 4(2) TEU.

[58] For a *contra legem* objection explicitly against our suggestion see for example Closa, Kochenov and Weiler, 'Reinforcing Rule of Law', 21.

[59] See the constitutional law proverb: 'The Constitution is what the judges say it is': C. E. Hughes, *Speech at Elmira*, 3 May 1907, cited by B. Schwartz, *Constitutional Law* (New York: Macmillan, 1972), p. vii. For a similar view by R. Smend, 'Festvortrag zur Feier des zehnjährigen Bestehens des Bundesverfassungsgerichts am 26 Januar 1962', in *Das Bundesverfassungsgericht* (Karlsruhe: Müller, 1963), pp. 23, 24: 'The Basic Law Is Now Virtually Identical with Its Interpretation by the Federal Constitutional Court'.

exaggeration, one of the biggest leading cases of modern constitutionalism.[60] A European *Marbury* v. *Madison* is yet to come,[61] which will transform the Charter into a real Charter for all European citizens, into a Charter which guarantees their freedoms even when domestic channels fail. It is inevitable that the ECJ will have to confront this historical challenge, and it should not shy away from the task. Leading cases often seem impossible (or even doctrinally doubtful) at the time in which they are made, but if they comply with the general value system of a society at a given time (the *Zeitgeist*) and if they help the judiciary enhance these values, then they later seem obvious and unquestionable. At one point the direct effect of directives was considered by many to be a *contra legem* interpretation of the EEC Treaty, that is, until it became a permanent feature of the case law of the ECJ. If we wish to imbue Article 51 of the Charter with a meaning which does not deprive Union citizens of their fundamental rights, then the literal meaning of the provision should be seen as representing the minimum, and not the maximum, application of the Charter. Every society is held together by certain values, which are at least rhetorically unquestionable. In the Middle Ages, for instance, it was Christianity, and heretics faced serious consequences if they breached religious taboos. Since the end of the Second World War in Western Europe, and since the fall of communism across Europe, these integrating values have been the secular values of constitutionalism. The twentieth century in Europe can also be viewed as a period of experimentation and failure with what were considered as the time as being new secular taboo systems, such as nationalism or socialism. Today, democracy and the protection of fundamental rights (consider the aims of the Council of Europe) seem to be the only credible options left for organising society in Europe. Of course there are endless debates about what these concepts actually mean.[62] At the same time, there is a final institutionalised arbiter in Europe for these questions: the ECtHR. To put it differently, today's Vatican is in Strasbourg. There were and there will be heretical attempts to

---

[60] As a matter of fact, the ECJ has already been presented with the opportunity to do so, but unfortunately missed it. See Joined Cases C-488/12 to C-491/12 and C-526/12 *Nagy and others* ECLI:EU:C:2013:703. No doubt, however, new occasions will arise.

[61] We could also argue that *Van Gend en Loos* or *Costa* v. *ENEL* were already the *Marbury* v. *Madison* of European integration, so we just need *yet another* (and not 'the') *Marbury* v. *Madison*. This is a fair observation, but it does not change the actual argument we are making.

[62] See W. B. Gallie, 'Essentially Contested Concepts', 56 (1956) *Proceedings of the Aristotelian Society* 167.

question these values, but if we want to believe that European integration has a chance, then we have to stop these attempts before it is too late. If these values are allowed to be undermined in one EU Member State, then this will become possible in other Member States, and before you know it, the European edifice which is built on these values will fall apart. Through the use of creative reinterpretation, the European constitution in its current form already presents opportunities to stop any dangerous trends. The ECJ can use the moral authority of the ECtHR to enforce the values of European integration, and through the preliminary procedure it can turn all Member State courts into local agents who profess and enforce these values. Obviously, it is not sufficient for a court to simply refer to values when it makes a decision. A good lawyer always thinks at two levels: on the one hand, he or she tries to provide a doctrinal justification for the decision (see the doctrinal triggers above), but on the other hand, he or she must present a decision which is acceptable from a social and/or moral perspective (e.g. the values of European integration).[63] Both these general preconditions would be fulfilled by a brave judgment by the ECJ in the present situation.

VII   What the ECJ Should Do

The history of the ECJ is full of activist moves where decisions were made which were not obvious – to say the least – from the text of the Treaties.[64] How was the Court able to get away with this? What common features can be derived from these successful instances of competence expansions? (1) The arguments used in these cases were normally teleological arguments relying either on the core objective of European integration or on the objectives of specific rules or institutions. This is exactly the case in expansively interpreting Article 51(1) CFR in light of the above: the purpose is to protect fundamental rights as fundamental values according of Article 2 TEU. (2) Institutionally, it was generally the European Commission which first adopted a particular stance which was then followed by the ECJ.[65] In our case, this means that the Commission needs to explicitly state its aim to be to abolish the limits of Article 51(1) CFR. This has already actually happened: Viviane Reding, then the Commissioner responsible

---

[63]   On Magnaud, *le bon juge*, see A. Jakab, 'What Makes a Good Lawyer? Was Magnaud Indeed Such a Good Judge?' 62 (2007) *Zeitschrift für öffentliches Recht* 275.

[64]   See, for example, K. Alter, *Establishing the Supremacy of European Law: The Making of an International Rule of Law in Europe* (Oxford: Oxford University Press, 2001).

[65]   E. Stein, 'Lawyers, Judges, and the Making of a Transnational Constitution', 75 (1981) *American Journal of International Law* 1.

for justice, fundamental rights and citizenship, explicitly proposed this in her Tallinn speech.[66] (3) The third factor which makes expansions more likely is if political lawmaking appears to be inoperative.[67] This is also obviously the case: there is only the pretence of real action – for example in the form of the so-called Rule of Law mechanism[68] – but the necessary majority by the Member States is clearly absent. (4) A usual method for expanding judicial competences is to establish the competence but not to use it, or to use it in a way which does not lead to conflict with any government. This was famously done in *Marbury* v. *Madison*, but also in *Costa* v. *ENEL* in which 'the ECJ declared the supremacy of EC law' but 'found that the Italian law . . . did not violate EC law'.[69] The first step here should also probably be a *Costa* v. *ENEL* type of decision, establishing the full applicability of the Charter without establishing its actual violation. (5) The next step – after the establishment of the competence in a case where a violation is not established – is the establishment of a violation. For this second case, the more obvious a fundamental rights violation is and the more isolated the 'convicted' Member State, the more likely the judgment establishing the violation will be accepted by Member States.[70] We do not have to be pessimistic to predict that such cases can easily reach the ECJ in the near future. (6) Parallel to (4) and (5), in order to avoid becoming unnecessarily involved in domestic politics concerning questions which are far from obvious, the ECJ would also need to develop a margin of appreciation doctrine, similar to ECtHR's.[71] This would result in a situation where the ECJ would be able to intervene only in those cases

---

[66] Reding, 'Observations on the EU Charter of Fundamental Rights', but she wanted to achieve this via a formal Treaty amendment.

[67] Weiler, 'The Transformation of Europe'.

[68] 'A New EU Framework to Strengthen the Rule of Law,' Communication from the Commission to the European Parliament and the Council, Brussels, 19.3.2014, COM(2014) 158 final/2.

[69] K. Alter, 'Who Are the "Masters of the Treaties"? European Governments and the European Court of Justice', 52(1) (1998) *International Organization* 121, 131.

[70] See Groussot, Pech and Petursson, 'The Scope of Application of Fundamental Rights', 104: 'It must be remembered that the US Supreme Court's "legal coup" took place in rather unique historical circumstances – the persistent segregationist practices in Southern States – which required, in turn, a revolutionary expansion of the scope of the US Bill of Rights'. See also M. Cartabia, 'Article 51 – Field of Application', in W. B. T. Mock and G. Demuro (eds.), *Human Rights in Europe* (Durham, NC: Carolina Academic Press, 2010), pp. 315, 318–9 (on similarities between certain interpretation of Art. 51 CFR and the US constitutional law 'doctrine of incorporation').

[71] On the margin of appreciation doctrine as a special type of deference doctrine see A. Legg, *The Margin of Appreciation in International Human Rights Law* (Oxford: Oxford University Press, 2012), pp. 17–66.

where the common minimum level of fundamental rights protection was being violated. Concerning its deferential function it would be similar to the concept of 'systemic deficiency',[72] but the decision about this would remain with a judicial and not with a political body. To sum up, all the cards are in the hands of the ECJ.[73] European institutions do not seem to want to stop this move by the ECJ, and Member States have no means to do so. Member State coalitions against ECJ judgments and pictures about a judicial Armageddon are highly unrealistic. As Marcus Höreth put it:[74]

> non-compliance by Member States was not perceived as a threat by the European Justices but rather a welcome opportunity to develop their judicial regime even further. Member-State non-compliance generates legal actions, followed by new rulings; non-compliance with important new rulings again generates new litigation and new findings of non-compliance, and so on.

If the European integration process fails, then it will not be because of the stronger protection of fundamental rights. It will either be for purely economic reasons or it will be because of anti-constitutionalist and illiberal forces within some of the Member States.

With judicial statesmanship, patience for the right cases and a conscious strategy, the decisive move toward a community of fundamental rights can be achieved in the very near future.[75] To this end, the ECJ has to reassert

---

[72] See A. von Bogdandy, M. Ioannidis and C. Antpöhler, 'Reverse Solange and Systemic Deficiency', in A. Jakab and D. Kochenov (eds.), *The Enforcement of EU Law and Values: Ensuring Member States' Compliance* (Oxford: Oxford University Press, 2017, forthcoming).

[73] M. Höreth, 'Warum der EuGH nicht gestoppt werden sollte – und auch kaum gestoppt werden kann', in U. Haltern and A. Bergmann (eds.), *Der EuGH in der Kritik* (Tübingen: Mohr Siebeck 2012), p. 73. On the practical impossibility of the revision of ECJ rulings by Member States see M. Höreth, 'The Least Dangerous Branch?', in B. de Witte, E. Muir and M. Dawson (eds.), *Judicial Activism at the European Court of Justice* (Cheltenham: Edward Elgar 2013), pp. 32, 39–40.

[74] Höreth, 'The Least Dangerous Branch?', 43.

[75] Once achieved, some features of the ECJ judgments have to be re-thought. In particular, their cryptic and laconic style needs to become more discursive, and dissenting opinions may also need to be allowed in order to be more transparent and give more substantive reasons for decisions. For the former see G. de Búrca, 'After the EU Charter of Fundamental Rights: The Court of Justice as a Human Rights Adjudicator?', 20(2) (2013) *Maastricht Journal of European and Comparative Law* 168. The latter is not actually explicitly regulated anywhere, Art. 35 of the Statute of the Court provides only for the secrecy of deliberations, which does not exclude dissenting or parallel opinions. For a general anti-activist critique concerning the lack of transparency, including the lack of dissenting opinions, see

its responsibility in both enhancing European integration and promoting the values of the European Union. If we look for the Toynbeean response correct to the current historical challenge of dismantling the Rule of Law in Member States, then this seems to be the only viable and therefore the necessary one.

VIII   Conclusion

There is an obvious tension between the enforcement impotence of the EU on the one hand, and the moral and implied legal duty to enhance the Rule of Law within its territory on the other. This tension would not be disturbing if there were no currently emerging challenges within the EU which prominently illustrate this impotence. As treaty change does not seem viable, and the ongoing inaction is slowly eating up the moral and institutional capital of the EU, the solution (as it has been so many times in the history of Western constitutionalism) lies with the judiciary. The judiciary is the traditional guardian of the Rule of Law, which should not be conceived as blindly following the black letter of the law, but as an idea which prohibits the arbitrary use of government power. Under the current institutional circumstances, *only* the ECJ can realistically respond to this challenge by daring creatively to reinterpret Article 51(1), which would make the Charter also applicable in purely domestic cases.

H. Rasmussen, 'Plädoyer für ein Ende des judikativen Schweigens', in Haltern and Bergmann, *Der EuGH in der Kritik*, 113. Dissenting opinions are an important method of control restraining a court, see K. Kelemen, 'Dissenting Opinions in Constitutional Courts', 14 (2013) *German Law Journal* 1359.

10

Protecting the Rule of Law (and Democracy!) in the EU

The Idea of a Copenhagen Commission

JAN-WERNER MÜLLER*

I Introduction

Not long ago, the German social scientist Claus Offe observed that the European Union, as a 'historically unique supra-nation non-state' might, as a result of the horrors of European history, have developed a kind of special capacity.[1] Europe, he suggested, seemed to exhibit a unique ability for 'self-critical normative scrutiny', 'self-monitoring reflexivity' and 'auto-paternalism'.[2] In fact, he went so far as to claim that:

> propensities, temptations and just conventional habits of majorities to discriminate against minorities and of male-operated institutions against women, of civil servants to enrich themselves by taking bribes from clients or to embezzle public funds, of owners of large enterprises ('oligarchs') to control the conduct of public policy and courts of justice, of governments to interfere with the freedom of press of oppositional media or of religious elites to control legislation, of public authorities to neglect or mistreat refugees and asylum seekers or to deny the disadvantaged minimal poor relief and health services, of police forces to engage in brutal uses of violence – all these and many other kinds of violations, including military violence of armed groups or authoritarian regression of national

* Professor of Politics at Princeton University. This chapter elaborates and extensively draws on some previous work of mine on the idea of a Copenhagen Commission, in particular the Transatlantic Academy Working Paper 'Safeguarding Democracy inside the EU: Brussels and the Future of Liberal Order', as well as 'Defending Democracy Within the EU' (2013) 24(2) *Journal of Democracy*, 138; 'The EU as a Militant Democracy, or: Are there Limits to Constitutional Mutations within EU Member States?' (2014) *Revista de Estudios Políticos*, No. 165; and 'Should the EU Protect Democracy and the Rule of Law Inside Member States?' (2015) 21(2) ELJ, 141. I am grateful to C. Closa, D. Kochenov, M. Kumm and G. Nolte for commenting on drafts of the chapter.
[1] C. Offe, *Europe Entrapped* (Cambridge: Polity, 2015), p. 66.　　[2] *Ibid.*, 64.

regimes, are by no means categorically absent in EU-Europe; they are just considerably less likely to occur without being sanctioned, than they are virtually everywhere outside the EU.[3]

This rather long list, one might think, ultimately comes down to saying that the EU has special capacities in constructing and preserving democracy and the Rule of Law. The Union, Offe indeed concludes, is a 'normatively valuable asset of mutual monitoring, supervision, and control of its citizens and member states'.[4]

Or is it? What is by now routinely referred to as a 'Rule of Law crisis' in Europe casts some doubt, not so much on Offe's overall empirical assessment of the prevalence of the Rule of Law in Europe, but on the institutions that until recently had been assumed to serve as reliable supranational checks on dangerous 'propensities, temptations and just conventional habits'. While the Euro crisis has dominated headlines in the law five years or so, the Rule of Law crisis is arguably far more damaging for the political and moral core of the European project.[5] As we now know, the Eurozone was spectacularly misconceived, the Euro crisis has had horrendous consequences in lives damaged (and sometimes, literally, lost), it is also likely to have long-term effects on how whole generations think about the European Union: as a zero-sum game that pits nation against nation.[6] But nonetheless, the Euro crisis is mostly a matter of failed policies; it is not necessarily a sign of deep normative splits on the European continent. The Rule of Law crisis, on the other hand, is equated with a 'crisis of fundamental values' which all Europeans had been assumed to share (and to which EU Member States had committed themselves in Article 2 TEU). Politics within the Union, for all its defects and imperfections, was supposed to occur within shared liberal democratic parameters. Yet after what happened in Romania in summer 2012 and what has been unfolding in Hungary since 2010, this assumption can no longer be taken for granted.[7] Both countries experienced what I would

---

[3] *Ibid.*, 65.   [4] *Ibid.*

[5] But see also A. J. Menéndez, 'The Existential Crisis of the European Union', 14 (2013) *German Law Journal* 453.

[6] See C. Offe, *Europe Entrapped.*

[7] On Hungary, see the special section on Hungary's illiberal turn in the (2012) 23 *Journal of Democracy* and the collection edited by G. A. Tóth, *Constitution for a Disunited Nation: On Hungary's 2011 Fundamental Law* (Budapest: CEU Press, 2012); on Romania, see V. Tismaneanu, 'Democracy on the Brink: A Coup Attempt Fails in Romania' (2013) *World Affairs*, at www.worldaffairsjournal.org/article/democracy-brink-coup-attempt-fails-romania; V. I. Ganev, 'Post-Accession Hooliganism: Democratic Governance in Bulgaria

term attempts at 'constitutional capture'. By this I mean a scenario where one set of partisan actors tries to obtain control of the political system as a whole (as well as parts of the economy, the media and civil society), rendering subsequent changes in political control virtually impossible.[8] In Romania what was also described as a 'constitutional coup' eventually failed, but in Hungary capture has proceeded to a degree that would have seemed unimaginable in a more-or-less 'normal European democracy'. A country in which constitutional capture has succeeded might still have rule *by* law, but no longer Rule of Law, to paraphrase the distinction between *gubernaculum* and *jurisdictio* which Gianluigi Palombella develops in his contribution to this volume.[9] The likely consequences of such a state of affairs are wide-spread corruption and fundamental rights violations (which would ideally be addressed by the European Court of Human Rights and, within the EU institutional framework, monitored by the Fundamental Rights Agency). Note though that these are not necessary consequences, at least not in the short run. This point is not trivial, because framing a Rule of Law crisis with concepts which immediately point us to rights protection and building proper state capacity as remedies could result in missing important parts of the overall picture of political decay. Many well-meaning responses to developments in Hungary and Romania have been presented as essentially generous offers of assistance to 'legally underdeveloped countries' – instead of understanding the Rule of Law crisis as part of a larger political conflict.[10] They have also missed the fact that democracy itself might be at stake, and not just

and Romania after 2007', 27 (2013) *East European Politics and Societies and Cultures* 26; and V. Perju, 'The Romanian Double Executive and the 2012 Constitutional Crisis', 13(1) (2015) *I-CON* 246.

[8] We could further distinguish between formal and sociopolitical constitutional capture. The former results in an actual change of the essence of the codified constitutional order (in the most clear-cut case, by promulgating a new constitution, as happened in Hungary in 2012); the latter might leave the constitution largely intact but bring about a partisan capture of the state apparatus (including the judicial system), large parts of the media, and of course the economy. Contemporary Turkey might serve as a good example of the latter.

[9] For the distinction between the Rule of Law and rule by law and its importance for understanding the decline of a number of democratic regimes, see F. Fukuyama, 'Why Is Democracy Performing So Poorly?', 26 (2015) *Journal of Democracy* 11.

[10] M. Roth, 'Ein Grundwerte-Tüv für die EU', at http://miro.hessenspd.net/meldungen/32930/134299/Ein-Grundwerte-TUeV-fuer-die-EU.html. This is not to deny that in some contexts the problem really is lack of capacity. For evidence, see D. Anagnostou and A. Mungiu-Pippidi, 'Domestic Implementation of Human Rights Judgments in Europe: Legal Infrastructure and Government Effectiveness', 25(1) (2014) *EJIL* 205.

the quality of rights protection. After all, if media freedom is under threat, or the right to demonstrate significantly curtailed, or data protection no longer assured, it is far from obvious that even an election which is *not* rigged on the actual day of voting would be sufficient to demonstrate the existence of democracy.[11]

So far, the EU – but also individual European nation states (which, after all, are supposed to be committed to 'fundamental European values' irrespective of what is in the treaties) – have appeared weak in the face of the challenge of constitutional capture and dramatic deteriorations in the Rule of Law. As a result, a number of proposals have been put forward to strengthen the EU's 'mechanisms' for protecting fundamental values, and the Rule of Law in particular. In this chapter, I will rearticulate the plan to create what colloquially might be termed an 'EU democracy and Rule of Law watchdog' (something I tentatively call a 'Copenhagen Commission', alluding to the 'Copenhagen criteria' for accession to the Union). I want to use this occasion to answer the legitimate demand for more 'legal elaboration and detail', as far as the idea of such a new institution is concerned.[12] In particular, I would like to spell out how this watchdog is not only supposed to bark but also – if I may continue with the canine analogy – under certain circumstances to bite and at all times to sniff around wherever it likes.

I should make it clear that the arguments presented here operate in a kind of 'mid-range', as far as legal (and normative) discussions of the EU go. The proposal is not for immediate practical application (unless such a body were to be created by intergovernmental agreement, in the same way that many new institutions have been established as a result of the Euro crisis, absent treaty change).[13] In this regard, Armin von Bogdandy's 'reverse *Solange*' proposal and, in particular, Kim Lane Scheppele's

---

[11] Of course, we could wade into deeper theoretical waters here, in particular by drawing on Habermas's argument about how democracy and the Rule of Law have to be understood as 'co-original'. For reasons of space, this chapter will remain in rather shallow waters. See J. Habermas, *Between Facts and Norms: Contributions to a Discourse Theory of Law and Democracy*, trans. W. Rehg (Cambridge, MA.: MIT Press, 1996).

[12] D. Kochenov, 'On Policing Article 2 TEU Compliance – Reverse *Solange* and Systemic Infringements Analyzed', 33 (2014) *Polish Yearbook of International Law* 145.

[13] It is not inconceivable that, given political will, Article 352 TFEU could be used to create a Copenhagen Commission analogous to the Venice Commission – but it would not have any mandate for sanctioning, which I consider essential. On these options, see also the helpful report by L. Moxham and J. Stefanelli, 'Safeguarding the Rule of Law, Democracy and Fundamental Rights: A Monitoring Model for the European Union', Bingham Centre for the Rule of Law, 15 November 2013.

'systemic infringements' strategy have clear advantages: they could be implemented here and now.[14] While leaving aside the demand for immediate use, I also want to resist the notion that advances in democracy and Rule of Law protection lack credibility, or are possibly counterproductive, without the comprehensive reform of the Union as a whole to remedy its 'democracy deficit' and 'justice deficit'.[15] In other words, I would disagree with Dimitry Kochenov when he claims that 'the EU cannot possibly pretend that it is in the position of solving the Rule of Law crisis without a profound rethinking of how values are reflected at the supranational plane'.[16] For sure, I find such a 'profound rethinking' not just desirable, but urgent. But can we really tell citizens of countries experiencing constitutional capture that, alas, nothing can be done until we have completed the process of profoundly rethinking the place of values at the supranational level? First *le grand soir démocratique* and then we worry about our brothers and sisters in damaged or outright dysfunctional democracies?[17]

Nonetheless, there are some more specific objections to the idea of a Copenhagen Commission which I would like to address in the last part of this chapter. Some of them, it seems to me, are generated by the following (in my view legitimate) worry: even if such a 'watchdog' might be desirable in and of itself, critics could claim that it would strengthen the general vision of the EU as being predominantly an agglomeration of punitive rules and institutions which have largely displaced politics with some kind of policing – a vision which appears to be emerging mainly as a result of the Euro crisis. A European 'Political Union' in particular has to offer more than a neoliberal 'logic of discipline' and related mechanisms for punishment.[18] But as I shall suggest further below, more positive elements could be incorporated into the Copenhagen Commission – whereas a debate on which general ideals, if any, Europeans wish to pursue in the twenty-first century is clearly beyond the scope of this chapter.

---

[14] A. von Bogdandy et al., 'Reverse *Solange* – Protecting the Essence of Fundamental Rights against EU Member States', 49(2) (2012) *CMLRev.* 489; K. L. Scheppele, 'Enforcing the Basic Principles of EU Law through Systemic Infringement Procedures' in this volume.

[15] D. Kochenov, G. de Búrca, and A. Williams (eds.), *Europe's Justice Deficit?* (Oxford: Hart Publishing, 2015).

[16] Kochenov, 'On Policing', 149.

[17] A. Vauchez, *Démocratiser l'Europe* (Paris: Le Seuil, 2014), p. 9.

[18] A. Roberts, *The Logic of Discipline: Global Capitalism and the Architecture of Government* (New York: Oxford University Press, 2011).

II The Point of a Copenhagen Commission

Let us be as clear as possible about the problem. The main challenge, I would argue, is to locate (or rather create) what one might call an *agent of credible legal-political judgment* as to whether a country is systematically departing from what one might describe as the European Union's *normative acquis* – a task which is different both from narrowly assessing compliance with EU law and from ascertaining belief in values (whatever the latter might mean concretely anyway: a Committee on UnEuropean Beliefs and Activities in the European Parliament?). Technical-legal judgment of rule compliance in and of itself is insufficient, and philosophical consensus about values is simply not the issue (all governments continue officially to profess faith in democracy, the Rule of Law, etc.).[19] It is also not a matter of corruption, lack of state capacity, or fundamental rights violations – all of which can be very serious, of course, and compound or even be part of a perceived 'Rule of Law crisis', but might not in fact be immediately present as a result of constitutional capture.

We are dealing, then, with systemic, mostly constitutional challenges which will require some understanding of context, some sense of proportion, and not least, some meaningful capacity for comparison of what is actually occurring within different political systems. A simple checklist, as is so often used in the EU accession process ('Do the judiciary's offices have computers? Check!'), will not do;[20] somebody needs to see and understand the whole picture and also the particular *sequencing* of the creation – and possibly the dismantling – of a liberal-democratic system.[21] As Dimitry Kochenov has shown, we cannot simply take the Copenhagen criteria off the legal (or perhaps more accurately, normative) shelf and

---

[19] Luhmann offers an interesting argument in this context. In politics, he claims, values are generally only insinuated or evoked; their acceptance is simply presumed. On the other hand, given the need for trade-offs among values (i.e. value pluralism), 'values talk' inevitably introduces uncertainty into politics: to profess values is to accept the uncertainty of political outcomes. See N. Luhmann, *Die Politik der Gesellschaft*, published by André Kieserling (Frankfurt/Main: Suhrkamp, 2000), pp. 359–65. It is also worth mentioning in this context that any evocation of values necessarily brings in particular experiences (unlike talk of norms) – which automatically creates uncertainty about the particular interpretation of values, even if values are affirmed by all in the abstract. On this, see H. Joas, *Die Entstehung der Werte* (Frankfurt/Main: Suhrkamp, 1999).

[20] See also K. Nicolaïdis and R. Kleinfeld, 'Rethinking Europe's "Rule of Law" and Enlargement Agenda: The Fundamental Dilemma' Sigma Paper No. 49/2012; and A. Mungiu-Pippidi, 'EU Accession Is No "End of History"', 18(4) (2007) *Journal of Democracy* 8, 15.

[21] Many thanks to Renáta Uitz on this point.

pretend, on the basis of the experience with accession processes, that 'protection of liberal-democratic values' ultimately equals compliance with the *acquis*. After all, the criteria were never sufficiently defined and they were often inconsistently applied.[22]

An additional challenge is posed by the fact that authority in the EU remains highly diffuse and fragmented; there is not much by way of a consciousness of common European political space (let alone a shared public sphere where substantive arguments could be debated seriously across borders); it can be hard to get (let alone direct) something like common political attention. As of now, no legal or political actor is clearly charged with, so to speak, pushing a red button first in order to alarm others about a potential deterioration in democracy and the Rule of Law inside a Member State (unless the European Commission credibly persuade anyone that it now fulfils this function within the framework of the new Rule of Law mechanism which it presented in March 2014).[23]

How, then, to proceed? I believe that Article 7 TEU ought certainly to be left in place – as a political procedure possibly resulting in a kind of *normative quarantine* of a Member State, there is a lot to be said for it. But it should actually be extended. Situations can arise where democracy is not just slowly undermined or partially dismantled, but where the entire edifice of democratic institutions is blown up or comes crashing down, so to speak (think of a military coup). In such a case, the Union ought to have the option of expelling a Member State completely.[24] According to Article 50 TEU, states can of course decide to leave voluntarily, but there is no legal mechanism for actually removing a country from the Union. True, these all might seem remote scenarios. But especially those who insist on the symbolic value of something like Article 7 – by which they might actually mean something not just symbolic, namely its importance as a form of *deterrence* – ought to be sympathetic with including the option of complete removal.

---

[22] D. Kochenov, *EU Enlargement and the Failure of Conditionality* (Alphen aan den Rijn: Kluwer Law International, 2008).

[23] One problem here is that the Commission is likely to become ever more politicised – by design (think of the election of the Commission President) – and that such a politicisation would make it much less credible as a guardian of fundamental values.

[24] The details here would depend on a more comprehensive theory of EU constitutionalism. If we saw a kind of *pouvoir constituant mixte* at work in the EU today, we might feel compelled to argue that all other Europeans would have to agree on expulsion – a view I do not find entirely plausible. See H. Brunkhorst, *Das doppelte Gesicht Europas: Zwischen Kapitalismus und Demokratie* (Berlin: Suhrkamp, 2014).

This still does not answer the question of *who* a consistent and credible agent of political judgment could be, if Article 7 proves itself unusable, because Member States are too afraid that it could set off a chain-reaction of retaliations and ultimately lead to the disintegration of the EU. My proposal is to create an entirely new institution which would credibly act as a guardian of Europe's *acquis normatif*. I suggest a Copenhagen Commission (as a reminder of the Copenhagen criteria, flawed as they might have been), analogous to the Venice Commission – a body, in other words, with a mandate to offer comprehensive and consistent legal and political judgments.[25] However, where the Venice Commission offers opinions essentially as forms of advice and recommendations, the institution I envisage would pass judgment including in the sense of condemnations – and with such condemnations carrying with them a range of sanctions.[26]

III   Practical Aspects of a Copenhagen Commission

In what follows I shall lay out what I consider an optimal set-up, bearing in mind that there is clearly room here for the institutional imagination and for legitimate disagreement about the details. The hard constraints ought to be the following three, however: the Commission should be able to initiate investigations on its own; it should be able to draw on any materials it sees fit (from ECtHR case law to treaties, to accounts of individual national histories); it should be free to turn to whichever person or institution it thinks might contribute useful information and its determinations should be binding. All three notions will be elucidated further at the end of this section.

---

[25] I am indebted to Rui Tavares for discussions on this point. At first sight, it might seem most plausible that such a body should be legally constituted as an agency. The difficulty here is one that many political science studies of EU agencies have confirmed: agencies tend to be tightly controlled or even outright captured by Member States. This would be even more of a danger if a new body were to be established outside the existing treaties, by intergovernmental agreement. In theory, a mere advisory body or high-level working group within existing EU structures would also be a possibility, as long as the determinations of that body were actually binding for the European Commission. On the limits of what EU agencies can do, see D. Kelemen and A. Tarrant, 'The Politics of the Eurocracy: Designing EU Regulatory Agencies and Networks', 34(5) (2011) *West European Politics* 922.

[26] For a balanced assessment of the Venice Commission, see W. Hoffmann-Riehm, 'The Venice Commission of the Council of Europe – Standards and Impact', 25(2) (2014) *EJIL* 579.

Ideally, the new institution should be composed of legal experts (such as judges seconded from national systems, or retired judges or academics) as well as statesmen and stateswomen with a proven track record of political judgment.[27] Each Member State could nominate a candidate for the Commission, and the European Parliament would have to confirm them. While such a procedure would not attract the same attention that Supreme Court nominations generate in the United States, the hope is that truly unsuitable candidates would be caught in time and that relatively centrist candidates would emerge victorious. The experience with the Venice Commission suggests that most countries would comply with an informal norm that only serious contenders – and not advocates of the Member State's national interest – would be put forward. The experience from the Venice Commission also suggests that the Rule of Law and democracy can both be part of a mandate for an institution tasked with generating knowledge and advice. For the reasons mentioned at the outset – constitutional capture and other crises are not necessarily reducible to Rule of Law violations – democracy and the Rule of Law should both be legitimate areas for concern and, if necessary, investigations and sanctions.

The Copenhagen Commission should meet regularly and have a bureaucratic apparatus which allows it closely to investigate the situation in a particular Member State, if necessary (a word of caution, though, is in order here as well: experience suggests that a secretariat can also capture an institution as a whole).[28] There is no reason why the Commission could not work closely with the Fundamental Rights Agency or also draw on other sources of research on legal and political developments in the EU (even if in the initial set-up process, other institutions would no doubt try to protect what they regard as their 'normative turf', so to speak – witness the actions of the Council of Europe institutions in the run-up to the creation of the Fundamental Rights Agency, and think of the current debate about the accession of the EU to the European Convention on Human Rights).[29]

It is crucial that the Commission should be able to take the initiative in cases of possible threats to the EU's fundamental values. In other words, it

---

[27] We could imagine the 'three wise men' who ended up assessing Austria in 2000 as a kind of model – though clearly the analogy goes only so far. Arguably, at that point everyone involved had an incentive both to end the 'sanctions' and save face.

[28] Thanks to Georg Nolte on this point.

[29] It is an open question whether the institution should generate regular research itself, perhaps by subjecting countries to a kind of periodic review analogous to what the UN does.

should not be dependent on any other body, as far as triggering an investigation is concerned. I realise that this is a very controversial demand, perhaps even for those generally in favour of the idea of insulating certain institutions from electoral competition.[30] After all, as set out here, it could look like the Commission is entirely at liberty on the input side, and yet produces binding decisions as 'output' – something that could result in arbitrariness and a lack of accountability, or, in the technical language of political philosophy: domination. A reasonable alternative would be for the right to initiate investigations to rest with an institution clearly regarded as political – such as a parliament. The concern is that such a solution would give enable different parties to instrumentalise the Commission or, if the threshold for triggering an investigation were to be set very high, would bring us back to all the problems associated with Article 7. Nevertheless, I do see the point in a potential critique according to which an unconstrained Copenhagen Commission could look like a political police with a license freely to roam across Europe and arbitrarily suggest indicting governments, and the concern needs to be addressed.

First, investigations are not judgments, and every Member State ought to have at least three opportunities to put its case to the Commission: before an official investigation starts, during an investigation, and just before a report with specific recommendation as to sanctioning is released. Member States will always get a hearing – but so will any other actor who, in the eyes of the Commission, might offer important insights: legal experts, historians, civil society representatives, those who believe themselves to be victims of a fundamental rights violation but who have yet to have their day in (the Strasbourg) court, to name but a few examples. Needless to say, all Member States would be treated equally – unlike the European Commission or Member State governments, the Copenhagen Commission would not need the vote of a Member State 'going rogue' for its political and legal projects in other contexts (because it would not have any). There is little reason, then, not to approach all countries impartially.

True, the very language of 'investigations' and 'hearings' suggests that something sinister could be in the making: a kind of European McCarthyism. Even with a mandatory initial hearing before an investigation, a Member State government will argue that such public shaming on the occasion of a constitutional change which the government in question

---

[30] P. Pettit, 'Depoliticizing Democracy', 17(1) (2004) *Ratio Juris* 52.

feels is legitimate amounts to disrespect of a country's constitutional identity (perhaps even its entire national identity).[31] Recent statements of the European Council have put great stress on the need for 'respect' in the EU's dealings with Member States, they have also emphasised the need for ongoing 'dialogue'.[32] A Member State suspected of deviating from democracy and the Rule of Law will probably always claim that there has been insufficient respect – and insufficient dialogue.

Indeed, there is no doubt that such questions are sensitive or, to put it differently: political. But the EU cannot run a 'no political questions' doctrine if it wishes to take its own commitment to fundamental values seriously. In any event, the Union determines whether a country is democratic every time a state accedes to the EU. The real objection would be that only the European Council – in a peer-review process – can really settle such political questions, and that no other body has the legitimacy to do so. Such reasoning suggests that there should be ways to improve Article 7, but in practice there are no credible complements to Article 7 at all, because it is a political process for political questions. It is also the only institution which realises Offe's notion of 'auto-paternalism', in contrast to the paternalism which comes with being told by foreign experts how to write a proper constitution.

Again, there is something to this concern, but we have to bear in mind that a Copenhagen Commission would not be able to trigger the kinds of exclusions that Article 7 can (as said above, the Commission is not intended to be a substitute for Article 7). Rather, while a Copenhagen Commission could sanction a country, its actions would in the first instance amount to naming and shaming (as opposed to actual rights restrictions along the lines of Article 7 or the militant democracy found in domestic cases, where parties can be banned and rights to individual political participation restricted).

The Copenhagen Commission would make specific recommendations but leave as much room as possible for different routes to addressing particular problems. However, if its recommendations are not complied with in any meaningful sense, the Copenhagen Commission ought to have the power to issue a final determination that a Member State is violating

---

[31] See also E. Cloots, *National Identity in EU Law* (New York: Oxford University Press, 2015).

[32] See Council of the EU, press release no. 16936/14, 3362nd Council meeting, General Affairs, Brussels, 16 December 2014, pp. 20–21. For a trenchant critique, see D. Kochenov and L. Pech, 'Monitoring and Enforcement of the Rule of Law in the European Union: Rhetoric and Reality' 11 (2015) *EUConst* 512.

particular principles to which all Member States are committed under the TEU. It should issue a report which is as specific as possible about the remaining problems in a Member State and also explain how attempts, if any, to return the country to functioning democracy and Rule of Law have fallen short.

The European Commission – and here my proposal begins to overlap somewhat with Kim Lane Scheppele's contribution to this volume – should then be required to deduct funds for a country, depending on its ability to pay. This would be a different procedure than Article 260 TFEU, but the underlying idea to use penalty payments and lump sums to bring countries into compliance is similar (and the Commission might even use the formulas it currently employs to suggest the concrete amounts countries have to pay to the European Court of Justice).

It is crucial that there is no further decision-making step between the two Commissions, so to speak. Once Copenhagen has spoken, Brussels needs to act. Now, as critics have pointed out, it is probably a pious hope that financial sanctions will miraculously accomplish what public naming and shaming could not, and it is entirely possible that countries would buy themselves non-compliance simply by making the penalty payments more or less forever.[33] However, money might indeed talk for some countries, and while it might not for some others, even Article 7 may fail to change a Member State's mind where a change of mind would be brought about only by a regime change. Nonetheless, if we were to abandon the idea that sanctions of this kind can ever make sense, infringement proceedings, Article 260 TFEU and the modus operandi of the European Court of Human Rights would also have to be changed radically.

A last, but crucial, point concerns the question of who will guard the guardians. My suggestion here is that a Member State should be in a position to take the Copenhagen Commission to the European Court of Justice for violating the law (and, of course, also for acting *ultra vires*) – the law in question being what I presume would have to be a new Treaty (and the safeguards against abuse of power by the Copenhagen Commission contained therein). No doubt, a government which felt under severe attack, mobilising a nationalist backlash domestically, and which in any case had nothing to lose would probably always attempt this defence. Let us bear in mind, however, that these would in all likelihood still be

---

[33] B. Jack, 'Article 260(2) TFEU: An Effective Judicial Procedure for the Enforcement of Judgements?', 19(3) (2013) *ELJ* 404; and P. Wennerås, 'Sanctions against Member States under Article 260 TFEU: Alive, but Not Kicking?', 49(1) (2012) *CMLRev.* 145.

exceptional cases – the ECJ would not be flooded with cases alleging that a body of experts had victimised a Member State of the EU on a mere whim.

IV   ... and What about Something Positive...?

This famous, almost proverbial, line – 'und wo bleibt das Positive?' – is taken from a deeply pessimistic poem written by Erich Kästner in 1930.[34] Kästner was using the phrase ironically: there was little positive to speak of in his time, and art, he claimed, should not be used as cheap emotional consolation for failed lives or life chances missed. But it is a legitimate question about a new European institution which, after all, is to be part of a project which put forward ideals, and not just punishments, sanctions, fines, etc.

So here is something positive. To begin with, the Copenhagen Commission could be of value to Member States seeking advice on intended constitutional changes (just as the Venice Commission is regularly consulted on such matters). In other words, in addition to being an *ex post facto* reviewer of constitutional changes, it could be an *ex ante* advisor on legal projects. Secondly, the Commission could assist what Andreas Voßkuhle, the president of the German Constitutional Court, has called, using a virtually untranslatable phrase, a European *Verfassungsgerichtsverbund*: a venture in multilevel cooperation among Europe's constitutional courts.[35] It could facilitate the exchange of information, promote a deeper understanding of different constitutional traditions and help maintain dialogue among Europe's courts, parliaments and civil societies – and, not least, live up to an expectation that is codified in EU law: the *promotion* (as opposed to just the observance) of the Unions' fundamental values. As Christophe Hillion points out in his chapter in this volume, Article 3(1) TEU and Article 13(1) are particularly relevant for thinking of the protection and the promotion of EU values together.

For sure, in the past rather too much normative weight has been put on ideas such as the Open Method of Coordination or 'Charter Strategies' for fundamental rights. 'Best practices' is a term beloved of bureaucrats, and it is not always evident that mutual learning amounts to much beyond professions in what the Germans call *Sonntagsreden*. Nevertheless, an

---

[34] E. Kästner and S. List (eds.), *Das große Erich Kästner Buch* (Munich: Piper, 1975), p. 94.
[35] A. Voßkuhle, 'Multilevel Cooperation of the European Constitutional Courts: Der Europäische Verfassungsgerichtsverbund', 6(2) (2010) *EUConst* 175.

additional line of activity for the Copenhagen Commission would be increasing the visibility of the institution. This can sound like a mandate for self-promotion or even a power-grab. It would be perverse – but not unheard of – if the Commission set out to increase its power by seeking confrontation with Member States, or even if it tried to transform itself into something like a *de facto* European Constitutional Court. The institution should be activated only if there is a serious, systematic problem in a Member State, as opposed to engaging in anything that could appear to be constitutional micromanagement. Its members should be aware that over-reaching could lead to its discrediting (and even the sanctioning of the sanctioners). This of course creates the danger that many problematic goings on in EU Member States which fall short of constitutional capture would go unchallenged by the Copenhagen Commission: governments under scrutiny for dubious behaviour will conclude that their constitutional conduct is at least 'good enough' – which could result in the overall lowering of normative and legal standards across Europe.[36] However, this danger is somewhat mitigated by the fact that other actors would remain in play, so to speak: the ECtHR, the Commission as guardian of the treaties and others will remain free to criticise these problems, while explaining at the same time why they are not a case for the Copenhagen Commission.

V   Rock-Throwing Postponed?

This chapter is not concerned with questions of political feasibility (for one thing, it seems certain that the current offenders would not agree to treaty change). However, it will address a number of principled concerns that could be put forward about the proposal. One is that the institution is built ad hoc and too fixated on Hungary – as with generals always fighting their last battle, the Copenhagen Commission would forever be looking for another instance of constitutional capture as we have witnessed over the past five years or so. As Jan Komárek has argued, when Europe finds that it cannot solve a problem, it invents a new institution instead, but even if the institution turns out to solve the first problem, it might fail at the next one.[37]

---

[36] Thanks to Alan Patten for this point.
[37] J. Komárek, 'The EU Is More than a Constraint on Populist Democracy', VerfBlog, 25 March 2013, at www.verfassungsblog.de/the-eu-is-more-than-a-constraint-on-populist-democracy/.

Moreover, we could also object that the EU would simply be duplicating existing institutions. Have the Venice Commission and the European Court of Human Rights not done relatively well in addressing the situation created by the Hungarian government, for instance? Are my own frequent references to the Venice Commission not proof that the EU should just opt for more use of the real thing, rather than trying to create something which could end up as a pale copy? My response is that, first, the EU has reached a depth and density of integration that has no parallel in the Council of Europe. EU law is also much more specific in areas such as data protection, which arguably the Council and the Venice Commission could not really comment on. More important still, the EU relies on mutual trust and mutual recognition in a way that the Council of Europe does not – and hence, *prima facie*, more supervision from an EU-specific institution is justified. Second, it is worth mentioning that the Council of Europe is an even more fragmented political space (with no shared public sphere at all). Third, the Council also contains members who would probably have had a hard time meeting even the fuzziest or most consciously relaxed Copenhagen criteria. This fact does not impugn the work of the ECtHR or the Venice Commission, but the problem of double standards – charges of hypocrisy abound in virtually any discussion of democracy-protecting interventions by supranational institutions – would be exacerbated even further.

Finally, the European Court of Human Rights can only properly address individual rights violations, whereas the Copenhagen Commission should take a more holistic view; the Venice Commission cannot be proactive, whereas the Copenhagen Commission could routinely monitor the situation in Member States and raise an alarm without having to be prompted. It would thus also build up an institutional memory which would make it easier to prevent double standards both in assessing an individual country over time and in comparing different countries.[38] In sum, without wanting in any way to fault the Venice Commission, I wish to suggest that ultimately, there is no good principled argument for the Union permanently to 'contract out' core normative concerns.

For certain, there might be a *pragmatic* worry among some Member States that the EU is likely to deepen its own crisis of legitimacy if it were to pass judgment not just on budgetary numbers (and to sanction financial offenders), but also on liberal democracy (and to sanction political offenders). To deflect the blame, some Member State governments might

[38] Thanks to Kim Lane Scheppele for this point.

think that the Union should delegate the unpopular work to the Council of Europe – just as some of the blame for austerity could be laid at the doors of the IMF once the troika had been formed. But if we are to be serious about sanctions – and we ought to be – then it would still ultimately have to be the EU which does the sanctioning. So one might as well accept the responsibility for forming judgments (and not just for implementing them), since after all, there are also enough EU citizens who placed their trust in the Union precisely as a strong guardian of the liberal democratic order (as opposed to the Council of Europe which can hardly be said to have any 'normative power' at all).

That leaves two important normative concerns: first, the idea that what is distinctive (and valuable) about the EU is, in the end, *pluralism*: tolerance instead of homogenisation; mutual openness and respectful peer review, not a centralised institution which defines and defends democracy and the Rule of Law, thereby destroying the precious heterarchy of norms and institutions which has emerged in the Union.[39] We ought to have a longer argument about pluralism, which after all is not a first-order value such as liberty and equality, but which to gain any normative traction has to be justified by reference to another value or broader political principle: cultural diversity perhaps, or democratic autonomy, or the beneficial moral-psychological effects of living with differences.[40] For my present purposes it suffices to say that the EU has always been about *pluralism within common political parameters*. After all, the accession process itself did not aim at something like maximising difference, but was explicitly and officially intended to ensure sameness in certain regards (democracy, Rule of Law, state capacity, etc.) Moreover, for as long as it has been taking in new members, the EU has been in the business of making definitive judgments on whether a country really is a liberal democracy (even if the Copenhagen criteria might have given a false sense of certainty about these judgments), and more broadly, judgments on where the limits of pluralism are to be located. In that sense, mandating a distinct and highly visible body with keeping an eye on whether everyone is remaining a liberal democracy does not in any sense constitute a fundamental break with the EU's principles and practices.

[39] D. Halberstam, 'Constitutional Heterarchy: The Centrality of Conflict in the European Union and the United States', in J. L. Dunoff and J. P. Trachtman (eds.), *Ruling the World? Constitutionalism, International Law, and Global Governance* (New York: Cambridge University Press, 2009), p. 326.

[40] See also T. Isiksel, 'Global Legal Pluralism as Fact and Norm' (2013) 2(2) *Global Constitutionalism*, 160.

The second worry is that if the supposedly technocratic 'new constitutionalism' is partly to blame for 'backsliding' (as Paul Blokker has forcefully argued), then some form of 'democracy and Rule of Law oversight' from on high must surely just add to the problem.[41] Is it not further evidence of the hubris of the 'managerial mindset' which has characterised European elites and the institutions they have created over the past decades?[42] If constitutionalism never becomes part of a lived political experience in newer Member States in particular but is instead created and enforced by distant bodies of experts, then will more paternalistic 'guardianship' by Brussels not reinforce the lesson that constitutionalism is something that a particular 'we' does not do autonomously and is incapable of internalising, etc.? My – perhaps too flippant – answer is this: nothing prevents one from starting a European Citizens' Initiative to express concern about democracy and the Rule of Law in a Member State (and also from searching for allies within the national 'we' in question); nothing prevents a transnational European civil society from what governments will always condemn as 'meddling in internal affairs'. The alleged 'technocracy' of the Copenhagen Commission and 'grassroot initiatives' are not mutually exclusive; it makes little sense here to play popular democracy off against 'liberal technocracy'.

On this note, I also wish to stress that democracy protection in the EU is not analogous to the 'authoritarian liberalism' which some critics have seen emerge as a result of the Euro crisis.[43] Certainly, it might appear that both are punitive approaches which result in disciplining national democracies and which effectively limit the diversity of expressions of the popular will across Europe; both can look like projects to safeguard from popular democracy the economy and the Rule of Law, respectively; both seem to rely on an ideal image of a thoroughly depoliticised Europe or a politics-proof (or post-political) *Rechtsstaat* policed by economic experts and judges. Put less polemically: both are ultimately about dealing with externalities, whether normative or economic, through new assurance and enforcement mechanisms across national borders.

---

[41] P. Blokker, *New Democracies in Crisis? A Comparative Constitutional Study of the Czech Republic, Hungary, Poland, Romania, and Slovakia* (New York: Routledge, 2013).

[42] M. Koskenniemi, 'Constitutionalism as Mindset: Reflections on Kantian Themes about International Law and Globalization', 8(1) (2007) *Theoretical Inquiries in Law* 9. The distinction between managerial and Kantian mindsets has been creatively developed by H. Brunkhorst, *Das doppelte Gesicht Europas*.

[43] M. Wilkinson, 'The Spectre of Authoritarian Liberalism: Reflections on the Constitutional Crisis of the European Union', 14(5) (2013) *German Law Journal* 527.

Yet such a simple equation is ultimately implausible for two reasons: first, uniform austerity policies and the surveillance of national budgets by the European Commission – as well as economic prescriptions that are not even logical (not all countries can become 'more competitive' at the same time) – these are all about making Member States converge on one highly specific economic model, right down to specific national debt numbers (with no real justification in the dismal science – even mainstream economists simply do not agree on such numbers). This kind of specificity is absent from proposals for a Copenhagen Commission to ensure the protection of democracy and the Rule of Law. Having such specificity would amount to an insistence, for instance, that every country must have a particular kind of constitutional court. But nobody is proposing such constitutional micromanagement or an undue narrowing of 'pluralist constitutionalism';[44] democracy and Rule of Law protection is about guarding boundaries to pluralism, not about reducing, let alone abolishing pluralism.[45]

None of the foregoing quite eliminates the danger that an EU institution could end up throwing rocks from within a glass house, to pick up on a metaphor from Joseph Weiler's critical response to proposals for 'Rule of Law protection schemes'.[46] As said above, the creation of the Copenhagen Commission should not detract from addressing the Union's serious political problems, but neither should the existence of the latter prevent the former. It would be too simple to argue that the Union would stand exclusively for the 'Rule of Law', while the 'rogue states' can speak in the name of the people and claim democracy for themselves. According to such a rather Schmittian picture, the EU tries to safeguard liberalism; national governments, in contrast, assert democracy. But that picture is misleading. This claim could be made without having to argue that democracy and the Rule of Law are somehow identical or always fit together seamlessly, or necessarily require each other. As hinted at the

---

[44] M. Dani, 'The "Partisan Constitution" and the Corrosion of European Constitutional Culture', LEQS Paper No. 68/2013.

[45] A broader argument would have to address the question of whether 'Political Union' as currently envisaged by at least some European elites would amount to an illegitimate reduction in constitutional pluralism. I am sympathetic to this argument, but it would not be sufficient to claim that democracy protection is automatically hypocritical. See also A. Somek, 'What Is Political Union?', 14 (2013) *German Law Journal* 561.

[46] J. H. H. Weiler, 'Living in a Glass House: Europe, Democracy and the Rule of Law', in C. Closa, D. Kochenov and J. H. H. Weiler, 'Reinforcing Rule of Law Oversight in the European Union' EUI Working Paper No. 2014/25, RSCAS, 25. See also Weiler's Epilogue in this volume. See also Weiler's Epilogue in this volume.

beginning of this chapter, a political system with regular elections but with clear limits on media freedom, election campaigning and autonomous activity by civil society is not on the road to becoming something like an 'illiberal democracy'; it is on the road to not being a democracy at all. Unless we wanted to say that having elections is *all* that's required to call a country a democracy, we should emphasise that limits on media freedom, for instance, is not only a Rule of Law problem or a matter of fundamental rights violations, but a threat to democracy itself. Leaving the 'd word' – democracy – to proto-authoritarian governments is what we might call an unforced semantic-normative error.

VI   By Way of a Conclusion: Some Final Concerns

A sceptic of this proposal might say that if it were transposed to a domestic context, the whole idea would look rather peculiar: persistent political misbehaviour being punished by fines. It is like telling a neo-Nazi that if he persists in acting like a racist, his unemployment benefit will be cut. Would the truly ideologically committed care? Probably not. Would those who are in it for the money somehow care? Probably not, because the schemes they have concocted make them much more than what they might lose with fines. So what is the point?

First, it is the fact that someone would actually be watching. This might deter at least some potential offenders in the face of what Offe called 'propensities' and 'temptations'. Second, dialogue might actually result in reasonable outcomes: not everyone is a deeply committed ideologue or indifferent to what the rest of Europe might think – and the rest of Europe will be *made to think*, if the Copenhagen Commission is sufficiently prominent and manages to generate enough attention in specific cases. Finally, other options, such as Article 7 and systemic infringement proceedings, will remain on the table. A whole group of Member States could go against the opinion of the Copenhagen Commission – but they would have to justify publicly why. Could this create real rifts within the Union? Possibly. But taking fundamental values seriously by arguing about them could also lead to a deeper shared understanding of what, if anything, we actually mean by them.

11

From Copenhagen to Venice

KAARLO TUORI*

I The Copenhagen Dilemma

The EU suffers from what has fittingly been called the *Copenhagen dilemma*. The EU has relatively efficient means to impose constitutional reforms aiming at establishing a democratic *Rechtsstaat* in candidate countries and countries aspiring to association agreements. The EU has been the only European actor which has had at least some success in pushing forward reforms in some of the most problem-ridden non-Member States in Central and Eastern Europe, though experience has shown in, for instance, Ukraine and Bosnia and Herzegovina, that even the EU's influence has its limits. However, the Copenhagen dilemma arises from the fact that the EU seems to run out of instruments when the democratic *Rechtsstaat* is jeopardised in states which have already successfully acceded. Hungary and Romania are the two examples most often invoked.

In Copenhagen in June 1993, the European Council included in the accession criteria 'stability of institutions guaranteeing democracy, the rule of law, human rights and respect for and protection of minorities'.[1] Subsequently, these criteria were incorporated in the Treaty. Democracy, human rights and the Rule of Law are invoked in the Preamble to the Treaty on European Union (TEU), and included in Article 2 in the values on which the Union is founded. In turn, Article 49 TEU refers to respect for and commitment to promoting these values as a prerequisite for accession. Moreover, the TEU establishes a specific procedure to be followed if these values are threatened in a Member State, a procedure which, as Wojciech

---

* Professor, University of Helsinki; Member of the Venice Commission for Democracy through Law of the Council of Europe.
[1] Copenhagen European Council (21–22 June 1993), Presidency Conclusions.

Sadurski has shown, was largely designed with the Eastern enlargement in mind.[2]

At the first stage of the procedure set out in Article 7 TEU:

> on a reasoned proposal by one third of the Member States, by the European Parliament or by the European Commission, the Council, acting by a majority of four fifths of its members after obtaining the consent of the European Parliament, may determine that there is a clear risk of a serious breach by a Member State of the values referred to in Article 2.[3]

The second step involves the European Council, which:

> acting by unanimity on a proposal by one third of the Member States or by the Commission and after obtaining the consent of the European Parliament, may determine the existence of a serious and persistent breach by a Member State of the values referred to in Article 2, after inviting the Member State in question to submit its observations.[4]

At the third stage, the issue returns to the Council:

> Where a determination under paragraph 2 has been made, the Council, acting by a qualified majority, may decide to suspend certain of the rights deriving from the application of the Treaties to the Member State in question, including the voting rights of the representative of the government of that Member State in the Council.[5]

The procedure thus involves all the major EU institutions and requires either unanimity or a qualified majority in the Council of Ministers and the European Council. The obstacle to be overcome is the protection by European parties of Member State governments headed by their party affiliates. All in all, the threshold for application is high, which justifies the denomination 'nuclear option', employed by representatives of the former European Commission. During the recent events in Hungary and Romania, recourse to Article 7 TEU was never seriously on the agenda.

The procedure under Article 7 TEU provides a political device to safeguard Member State respect for the foundational values of the EU. The *cul-de-sac* encountered on the political road has led the academic discourse to seek succour in legal remedies: in expansion of EU fundamental rights review or in the infringement procedure under Articles 258–

---

[2] W. Sadurski, 'Adding Bite to a Bark: The Story of Article 7, EU Enlargement, and Jörg Haider', 16 (2010) *CJEL* 385.
[3] Art. 7 TEU.   [4] Art. 7 TEU.   [5] Art. 7 TEU.

260 TFEU. Reverse *Solange* would extend EU fundamental rights review of Member State action beyond the scope of EU law to internal issues, while horizontal *Solange* would charge Member States with monitoring each other's fundamental right records. In turn, systemic infringement action would facilitate a comprehensive assessment by the Commission and the ECJ of Member State policies threatening the core values of the Union: that is, the Copenhagen criteria. In the following I shall first discuss the doctrinal shortcomings of proposals taking the legal road. I shall also express doubts as to their functionality: that is, their ability to respond to such constitutional problems as have arisen in say Hungary and Romania.

In the final sections of this chapter, I turn to initiatives to complement the 'nuclear option' of Article 7 TEU with less dramatic and more dialogical political instruments, such as the EU Framework to strengthen the Rule of Law and a monitoring body of experts – a Copenhagen Commission – to monitor Member State observance of the Copenhagen criteria, which are now included in Article 2 TEU. My normative argument will be for Venice. During its twenty-five years of existence, the Venice Commission of the Council Europe has gained expertise, experience and authority in dialogical constitutional assessment and benchmarking. It has also proved to possess the necessary independence. A new Copenhagen Commission would mean institutional duplication, without any guarantees that the new body would really contribute to the strengthening of constitutionalism in Europe.[6] In addition to institutional issues, I also briefly comment on the standards to be used in constitutional monitoring and consulting. With regard to the institutional solution, my conclusion is that there are no relevant differences between EU and Venice Commission standards.

II   Expanding EU Fundamental Rights Review

Proposals to solve the Copenhagen dilemma through fundamental rights review boil down to expanding EU review to cover rights violations in internal Member State actions: that is, outside the scope of EU law. However, the proposals seem to fall on intractable doctrinal obstacles. These have their background in the sensitive balance which manages the pluralism in EU and Member State constitutionalism.

---

[6] The reader should be aware of the fact that the author has been a member of the Venice Commission since 1998.

In their *reverse Solange* initiative, Armin von Bogdandy and his co-authors[7] advocate attaching EU fundamental rights to European citizenship, which would enable judicial protection of the values enumerated in Article 2 TEU. The authors argue that Member States are expected to respect the foundational values in all their activities, although, as the authors concede, the values are not justiciable as such. Through the link forged between the foundational values enshrined in Article 2 TEU, EU fundamental rights and European citizenship, EU fundamental rights review would be brought to cover all Member State activity, that is including purely internal activity. Judicial protection, tapping the vigilance of individuals, would complement the political mechanism set out in Article 7 TEU.

Reverse *Solange* hinges on two crucial argumentative moves which should be vindicated: first, a redefinition of EU fundamental rights as rights of European citizens and secondly, attachment of fundamental rights *qua* citizenship rights to the values enshrined in Article 2 TEU. As regards the first move, von Bogdandy et al. build on recent citizenship jurisprudence, especially *Ruiz Zambrano*. Here the Court ruled that Article 20 TFEU on European citizenship:

> is to be interpreted as meaning that it precludes a Member State from refusing a third country national upon whom his minor children, who are European Union citizens, are dependent, a right of residence in the Member State of residence and nationality of those children, and from refusing to grant a work permit to that third country national, in so far as such decisions deprive those children of *the genuine enjoyment of the substance of the rights attaching to the status of European Union citizen* (emphasis added).[8]

von Bogdandy et al. draw quite far-reaching generalising conclusions from *Ruiz Zambrano*. First, *Ruiz Zambrano* is alleged to show that European citizenship can be invoked in a Member State in a purely internal situation with no cross-border elements. Second, 'the substance of the rights attaching to the status of European Union citizen'[9] is claimed to refer to EU fundamental rights in general, so that *Ruiz Zambrano* confirms their character as citizenship rights.

---

[7] A. von Bogdandy et al., 'Reverse Solange – Protecting the Essence of Fundamental Rights against EU Member States' (2012) 49 *CMLRev.* 489. The article has aroused wide discussion. As an overview see D. Kochenov, 'On Policing Article 2 TEU Compliance – Reverse Solange and Systemic Infringements Analyzed', 33(2014) *Polish Yearbook of International Law* 145.

[8] Case C-34/09 *Ruiz Zambrano* ECLI:EU:C:2010:560, summary.   [9] *Ibid.*, para. 45.

The first conclusion concerning the relevance of EU citizenship in purely internal situations may already need specification. However, what is more pertinent now is to problematise the link between citizenship and fundamental rights, allegedly established by *Ruiz Zambrano*. Articles 20–23 TFEU contain explicit provisions on the rights deriving from the status of European Union citizens, and the EU Charter of Fundamental Rights (CFR) includes a specific Chapter on Citizens' rights (Title V). As is well known, the ECJ has derived auxiliary social rights from explicitly stipulated citizenship rights, in particular rights to mobility and residence. But there is no case law evidence pointing to a constitutional connection between citizenship and EU fundamental rights in general. Nothing in *Ruiz Zambrano* intimates that 'rights attaching to the status of European Union citizen'[10] would cover EU fundamental rights as a whole and not only rights explicitly derived from the European citizenship in Articles 20–23 TFEU and Title V CFR, complemented by auxiliary social rights. von Bogdandy et al. are correct in pointing out the affinity of citizenship and fundamental rights in constitutional theory and history, but this does not suffice to establish a connection between the two in EU 'surface-level' constitutional law. Significantly enough, in its case law subsequent to *Ruiz Zambrano*, the ECJ has refrained from extending 'the rights attaching to the status of European Union citizen'[11] to EU fundamental rights in general.[12]

To define European citizenship in terms of fundamental rights and to claim jurisdiction for the Union in purely internal fundamental rights violations would involve a huge leap in the ECJ's incrementally constructed citizenship jurisprudence.[13] It also requires surmounting doctrinal hurdles so high that its chances of actual emergence are very low. The horizontal provisions in Article 51 CFR which define the Charter's

---

[10] *Ibid.* [11] *Ibid.*

[12] In *McCarthy* (C-434/09 ECLI:EU:C:2011:277) and *Dereci* (C-434/09 ECLI:EU:C:2011:734) the Court explicitly invoked the *Ruiz Zambrano* formula but refrained from invoking Art. 7 CFR, although both cases raised the issue of respect for family life. Cf. C. Raucea in 'Fundamental Rights: The Missing Pieces of European Citizenship?', 14(10) (2013) *German Law Journal* 2021. It is true though, that the list of citizenship rights in Art. 20(2) TFEU is open-ended and that reference is made to rights provided elsewhere in the Treaties. In future this could offer a basis for an expansive reading of citizenship rights.

[13] Calls for such a leap by academic commentators and even some advocates general are, however, not new. For an overview see D. Kochenov and R. Plender, 'EU Citizenship: From an Incipient Form to an Incipient Substance? The Discovery of the Treaty Text', 37 (2012) *ELRev.* 369.

scope of applicability are not directly pertinent to constructions which try to find their 'institutional support' elsewhere in the Treaties; indeed, escaping these limitations forms a central backdrop to reorientation of the search for solid doctrinal ground for the Union's general fundamental rights competence. However, the principle of conferral, explicitly set out in Article 5(2) TEU, is certainly relevant, as is the general concern of many EU Member States at steps being taken in a federal direction through the ECJ's fundamental rights jurisprudence. In the hybrid European constitutional space, doctrinal considerations within EU law, however convincing they might be, are not enough to ground such a significant constitutional change as an extension of Union fundamental rights jurisdiction to autonomous Member State activity. Such a divisive move by the ECJ would have to first gain acceptance by other significant participants in the European constitutional discourse, in particular national constitutional or supreme courts and the European Court of Human Rights (ECtHR). The German Constitutional Court, therefore, as the most important national interlocutor of the ECJ, has been quick to react to what it has considered threatening signs of the ECJ expanding its fundamental rights jurisdiction and to issue a reminder of the potential use of its *ultra vires* review.[14]

It is equally unlikely that the ECJ would adopt the proposal simply to set aside the restrictions on EU fundamental rights review laid down in Article 51(1) CFR and confirmed in post-Lisbon ECJ jurisprudence.[15] Article 51(1) sets out that the Charter only applies to Member States when they 'are implementing Union law'. According to the ECJ, 'implementing Union law' should be assigned a meaning equivalent to 'acting in the scope of EU law' in pre-Lisbon case law on fundamental rights principles. Though *Åkerberg-Fransson*[16] adopted a rather wide interpretation of the scope of EU law – which provoked a rapid reaction by the German Constitutional Court[17] – it is highly improbable that the ECJ would extend the reach of EU fundamental rights review to purely domestic issues. This

---

[14] The most important recent ruling is *Honeywell*, which was a reaction to the ECJ's ruling in *Mangold*. BVerfG, 2 BvR 2661/106, 6 July 2010; Case C-144/04 *Mangold* ECLI:EU:C:2005:709 [2005] ECR I-9981.

[15] See the contribution by A. Jakab in this volume.

[16] Case C-617/10 *Åklagaren* v. *Åkerberg Fransson* ECLI:EU:C:213:280.

[17] BVerfG, 1 BvR 1215/07, 24 April 2013. See the German court's Press release No. 31/2013 of 24 April 2013. See also the editorial comment '*Ultra Vires* – Has the *Bundesverfassungsgericht* Shown Its Teeth?', 50(4) (2013) *CMLRev.* 925.

would require wholly disregarding the explicit limitation in Article 51(1) CFR, further buttressed by referral to the principle of conferred powers in Article 51(2) CFR: 'The Charter does not extend the field of application of Union law beyond the powers of the Union or establish any new power or task for the Union, or modify powers and tasks as defined in the Treaties'.[18]

Differing from reversed *Solange*, horizontal *Solange* would entrust general fundamental rights review, extending to internal Member State action, to the courts of other Member States. If reverse *Solange* is intended to influence future case law, horizontal *Solange* is claimed already to have been confirmed by the ECJ. Iris Canor[19] grounds this claim on the ECJ ruling in *N.S.*[20] The ruling addresses the situation where a Member State must decide whether it should consider an application for asylum which does not fall within its responsibility under the Dublin II Regulation[21] or whether to hand the application – and the applicant – over to the state responsible. According to the Court, the Common European Asylum System is premised on the assumption that participating States observe fundamental rights and that the Member States can have confidence in each other in this regard.[22] However, the assumption is rebuttable. The system 'may, in practice, experience major operational problems in a given Member State, meaning that there is a substantial risk that asylum seekers may, when transferred to that Member State, be treated in a manner incompatible with their fundamental rights'.[23] Nonetheless, a mere violation of a fundamental right by the Member State responsible is enough to prevent the transfer of an asylum seeker. Only:

> if there are substantial grounds for believing that there are systemic flaws in the asylum procedure and reception conditions for asylum applicants in the Member State responsible, resulting in inhuman or degrading treatment, within the meaning of Article 4 of the Charter, of asylum seekers transferred to the territory of that Member State, the transfer would be incompatible with that provision.[24]

---

[18] Art. 51(2) CFR, Charter of Fundamental Rights of the European Union OJ 2000 No. L364.
[19] I. Canor, 'My Brother's Keeper? Horizontal Solange: "An Ever Closer Distrust among the Peoples of Europe"', 50(2) (2013) *CMLRev.* 383.
[20] Joined Cases C-411/10 and C-493/10 *N.S. and Others* ECLI:EU:C:2011:865.
[21] Council Regulation No. 343/2003 establishing the criteria and mechanisms for determining the Member State responsible for examining an asylum application lodged in one of the Member States by a third-country national 2003 OJ No. L50/1.
[22] *N.S. and Others*, para. 78.   [23] *Ibid.*, paras 80–81.   [24] *Ibid.*, para. 86.

If such grounds exist, EU fundamental rights law obliges a Member State not to transfer the asylum seeker.

Therefore, according to *N.S.*, EU fundamental rights law imposes on Member States, including their courts, an obligation to monitor compliance with that law in other Member States. However, the basic, though rebuttable, assumption guiding Member State action is that other Member States comply with the relevant fundamental rights, hence the term 'horizontal *Solange*'. It is important to note that EU law is the applicable law with regard to both the Member State considering the transfer of an asylum seeker and the Member State responsible. We are dealing with the application and observance of EU fundamental rights law in two Member States and not the horizontal relationship between national fundamental rights laws. The term 'horizontal *Solange*' is justified in the sense that the authorities of one Member State are monitoring the fundamental rights record of another Member State. But these authorities are actually exercising 'vertical' EU fundamental rights review.

Can a general doctrine of horizontal *Solange* and the Member States' general obligation to watch over each other's observance of EU fundamental rights be derived from *N.S.*? Canor answers in the affirmative. In her argument, two steps in particular would require 'institutional support' of *N.S.* or other ECJ case law. First, 'systemic violation of core European fundamental rights' in a Member State would oblige other Member States to suspend cooperation with that Member State. It remains unclear what kind of cooperation this obligation would cover. Canor's focus is on the obligation of Member States under certain conditions to refuse the cooperation stipulated by secondary legislation EU (Regulation 343/2003 in *N.S.*) – but she does not spell out the exact reach of horizontal *Solange*. Would the obligation preclude other Member States from applying the EU law principle of mutual recognition, which in some fields is acknowledged in political and in others in judicial legislation? It is difficult to find backing in *N.S.* for a general *Solange* doctrine applicable to Member State cooperation beyond the specific obligation under Regulation 343/2003 to require a Member State to use discretion either to decide an asylum application itself or transfer the applicant to the Member State responsible.

The other controversial argumentative step leads from EU law related to autonomous Member State action. *N.S.* concerned Member State action and cooperation in a fundamental rights sensitive field regulated by EU law. Not only was the decision-making of the Member State where the asylum seeker was present located within the scope of EU law, but so were the actions or omissions of the responsible Member State which rebutted the presumption of compliance with fundamental rights: at issue were systematic flaws in asylum procedure and the reception of asylum seekers, leading to inhuman or degrading treatment. It is a long road from this to the conclusion that Member States have an obligation to monitor each other's general fundamental rights records, regardless of whether the alleged flaws are related to EU law or EU-mandated cooperation.

Opinion 2/13 of the ECJ on the draft agreement providing for EU accession to the European Convention on Human Rights (ECHR), which has occasioned quite a stir among academic commentators,[25] is not particularly encouraging of horizontal *Solange*. In *N.S.* and related jurisprudence, including the recent Opinion 2/13, the Court laid an emphasis on the principle of mutual confidence (trust) and underlined the exceptional nature of 'horizontal' fundamental rights review. According to the Court, 'that principle requires, particularly with regard to the area of freedom, security and justice, each of those States, save in exceptional circumstances, to consider all the other Member States to be complying with EU law and particularly with the fundamental rights recognised by EU law'.[26] The principle of mutual confidence was one of the grounds for the Court's rejection of the draft agreement:

> In so far as the ECHR would, in requiring the EU and the Member States to be considered Contracting Parties not only in their relations with Contracting Parties which are not Member States of the EU but also in their relations with each other, including where such relations are governed by EU law, require a Member State to check that another Member State has observed fundamental rights, even though EU law imposes an obligation of mutual trust between those Member States, accession is liable to upset the underlying balance of the EU and undermine the autonomy of EU law.[27]

Even if the ECJ had accepted the expansion of EU fundamental rights review, the question remains whether such a review would suffice to prevent or remedy Member State violations of the Copenhagen criteria. Whatever the doctrinal merits and demerits of the proposals discussed above, it is evident that an extension of fundamental rights review would not significantly remedy the EU's ability to react to threats to its foundational values. Judicial control is of a fragmented character, and

---

[25] See for example the comments published at www.verfassungsblog.de/en/.
[26] Opinion 2/13 *EU Accession to the ECHR* (No. 2) ECLI:EU:C:2014:2454, para. 191.
[27] *Ibid.*, para. 194.

recent events in Hungary and Romania, for instance, could not have been addressed solely as individual or even systemic fundamental rights violations. Undoubtedly, the problems possess a fundamental rights dimension, this has been proved by the ECtHR ruling in *Baka* v. *Hungary* and the ECJ ruling in *Commission* v. *Hungary*.[28] In the former case concerning the dismissal of the former President of the Hungarian Supreme Court, the ECtHR found a violation of Article 6(1) ECHR (as no domestic process was available to contest removal from office through constitutional reform) – and Article 10 ECHR (as the removal was due to the applicant's criticism of the government). In the latter case, the ECJ found that dropping the retirement age of judges to sixty-two amounted to age discrimination and was in breach of the EU Employment Equality Directive (2000/78).

These are important rulings and express European concern at the situations in Hungary. They may have had repercussions in both the Hungarian (national) and European (transnational) public sphere, transcending the issues' immediate context. However, they nonetheless merely address individual aspects of much wider constitutional and political developments.

III   Systemic Infringement Action

In the case concerning the forced early retirement of Hungarian judges, the European Commission had recourse to the infringement procedure under Articles 258–260 TFEU. Another infringement case addressed the dismissal of the Hungarian data protection officer through reorganisation of the data protection authority. The Commission considered this a violation of the 'complete independence' required for the data protection officer by the EU Data Protection Directive and the ECJ agreed.[29] The two cases were successful in the sense that the ECJ subscribed to the Commission's claim, and Hungary was found guilty of an infringement. However, the rulings did not change much on the ground. The judges who had been forced to retire were not reinstated, and the data protection officer did not recover his position. However, even if the effects of lowering the retirement age or dismissal of the data protection officer had been annulled, that would not have significantly altered the overall

---

[28] ECt.HR *Baka* v. *Hungary* (App. No. 20261/12); Case C-286/12, *Commission* v. *Hungary* ECLI:EU:C:2012:687.

[29] C-288/12 *Commission* v. *Hungary*.

constitutional picture. The issues tackled are certainly not negligible, but still merely catch a rather narrow segment of the whole.

To increase the effectiveness of the procedure, Kim Lane Scheppele has proposed introducing a systemic infringement action, which would allow the Commission to 'bundle together a set of infringing practices of an offending Member State'.[30] A systemic infringement action would be backed by invoking a more general principle, either the principle of sincere cooperation (Article 4(3) TEU) or one of the principles enumerated in Article 2 TEU. If the Court found a breach of such a general principle, it could buttress the Member State's obligation to redress the situation not only by imposing fines, as is provided for in Article 260 TFEU, but also by cancelling the payment of EU funds. In Scheppele's view the systemic infringement procedure would not require Treaty change, and even the new sanctions mechanism could be established through secondary legislation.[31]

Scheppele's proposal deserves careful reflection, although it too is afflicted by doctrinal problems. Nothing prevents the Commission from collecting several alleged infringements into one action, and such bundling would probably add to its resonance as regards both the state concerned and national and European civil society. But what might be questionable is reference to a broader principle, such as the principle of sincere cooperation or principles derived from Article 2 TEU. The principle of sincere cooperation, of course, always looms in the background of infringement actions, whether bundled together or not. But what might be problematic is elevating it to an independent principle constitutionally justifying a particular sanction regime, such as suspension of payments of EU funds as sanctions for infringements unrelated to the purpose of the payments and complementing the sanctions explicitly provided for by Article 260 TFEU. Moreover, it is more than doubtful that the generic values enshrined in Article 2 TEU could give rise to justiciable Member State obligations, the breach of which could lead to an infringement action by the Commission. As the Commission states in its Communication on the new EU Rule of Law framework, 'infringement procedures can be launched by the Commission only where these concerns constitute, at the same time, a breach of a specific provision of EU law'.[32]

---

[30] For the latest iteration of this proposal, see K.L. Scheppele, 'Enforcing the Basic Principles of EU Law through Systemic Infringement Procedures', in this volume.

[31] *Ibid.*

[32] European Commission, Communication from the Commission to the European Parliament and the Council, 'A New EU Framework to Strengthen the Rule of Law', Brussels, 11

IV   The EU Framework to Strengthen the Rule of Law

The EU Framework for strengthening the Rule of Law, introduced by the Commission in March 2014, targets situations where legal measures such as the infringement procedure are not available and where the threshold for applying the 'nuclear option' under Article 7 TEU continues to be unsatisfied. The Framework was a reaction to the Tavares Report of the European Parliament of June 2013, which was highly critical of developments in Hungary under the Orbán government, and the letter sent to President Barroso by the foreign ministers of Germany, Denmark, the Netherlands and Finland in Spring 2013, calling for 'a new and more effective mechanism to safeguard fundamental values in Member States'.[33] The purpose of the Framework is 'to enable the Commission to find a solution with the Member State concerned in order to prevent the emergence of a systemic threat to the rule of law in that Member State that could develop into a "clear risk of a serious breach", within the meaning of Article 7 TEU'.[34] The Framework is supposed to be activated when 'the authorities of a Member State are taking measures or are tolerating situations which are likely to systematically and adversely affect the integrity, stability or the proper functioning of the institutions and the safeguard mechanisms established at national level to secure the rule of law'.[35]

The Framework sets out a three-stage process where a solution is sought through a dialogue with the Member State concerned.[36] The first stage consists of the Commission's preliminary assessment of the situation. If the Commission concludes that a systemic threat to the Rule of Law might exist, it sends a 'Rule of Law opinion' to the Member State, which then has the opportunity to respond. In a second stage the Commission may issue a 'Rule of Law recommendation' if it finds objective evidence of a systemic threat and that the authorities of that Member State are not taking appropriate action to redress. The Commission publishes both the sending of the recommendation and its main content. In a third stage, the Commission monitors the Member State addressed's follow-up activity. If no satisfactory remedy is provided, the Commission will

---

March 2014 COM(2014) 158 final. For critical academic discussion see D. Kochenov, 'On Policing Article 2 TEU Compliance'.

[33] European Parliament resolution of 3 July 2013 on the situation of fundamental rights: standards and practices in Hungary (2012/2130(INI)).

[34] European Commission, 'A New EU Framework to Strengthen the Rule of Law'.

[35] *Ibid.*

[36] See the detailed explanation in C. Closa, 'Reinforcing EU Monitoring of the Rule of Law: Normative Arguments, Institutional Proposals and the Procedural Limitations' in this volume.

consider activating the procedure set out in Article 7 TEU. The Commission thus conceives of the new mechanism as a pre-stage for antedating and if possible pre-empting recourse to Article 7. This explains the claim that the Framework is based on existing Commission competences under the Treaties. Establishing an EU framework for monitoring Member State compliance with foundational Union values – the Copenhagen criteria – raises both institutional and substantive issues. I will start from the institutional questions.

V Venice or Copenhagen?

Does the EU need a new consultative expert body, modelled after the Venice Commission, to assist in monitoring Member State respect for the foundational values now enshrined in Article 2 TEU? In his eloquent style, Jan-Werner Müller has advocated a Copenhagen Commission,[37] and the idea was picked up by the European Parliament's Tavares Report on Hungary. However, the Commission Framework advocated does not include institutional novelties, such as a Copenhagen Commission of experts. Instead, the Commission Communication invokes cooperation with the Venice Commission. The Communication adopts a broader European perspective and states that the Framework is also 'meant to contribute to reaching the objectives of the Council of Europe, including on the basis of the expertise of the European Commission for Democracy through Law [the Venice Commission]'.[38] The Commission stresses that within the Framework it 'will, as a rule and in appropriate cases, seek the advice of the Council of Europe and/or its Venice Commission, and will coordinate its analysis with them in all cases where the matter is also under their consideration and analysis'.[39]

Let us first consider the credentials of the Venice Commission. The Venice Commission was established in 1990 at the initiative of the renowned Italian constitutionalist Antonio La Pergola, who remained President of the Commission until his passing in 2007. Although the Commission functions under the auspices of the Council of Europe, it has never been part of the Council's regular organisation, based as it was on partial agreement, with not all Council of Europe Members joining (the United Kingdom only joined in 1999). With Russia joining in 2003,

[37] See J.-W. Müller, 'Protecting the Rule of Law (and Democracy!) in the EU: The Idea of a Copenhagen Commission' in this volume.
[38] European Commission, 'A New EU Framework to Strengthen the Rule of Law'.
[39] *Ibid.*

all Council of Europe Member States now participate. In 2003 the partial agreement was turned into an enlarged one, which enabled non-European states also to accede. Indeed, eleven non-European countries have since seized this opportunity. The Commission works in plenary sessions held four times a year in Venice, sub-commissions – such as those for Human Rights, the Rule of Law, the Judiciary and Democratic institutions – and *ad hoc* working parties composed of rapporteurs appointed for a particular issue. Furthermore, preparatory and coordinating work falls to the Secretariat, with its seat not in Venice, but in Strasbourg.

Venice Commission members are supposed to be internationally renowned experts in constitutional and institutional law. The majority of its members are judges from constitutional and supreme courts or university professors. However, membership is open to political scientists too, and indeed some members, such as one of the editors of the present volume, have made an important contribution to the work of the Commission. Members are appointed by the respective governments for a renewable mandate of four years but are supposed to work totally independently from their governments. Venice as the meeting place has guaranteed a high rate of participation, but understandably, the activity of members varies. However, perhaps twenty to twenty-five members are regularly available for rapporteur tasks and site visits. The issues the Commission considers fall into two main groups: country-specific opinions and general studies. The Commission never issues a country-specific opinion on its own initiative but always requires a request. This request can come for a constitutional authority of the country itself or a body of the Council of Europe, such as the Parliamentary Assembly or one of its Committees – usually the Committee for Human Rights and Legal Affairs – the Secretary General and even the Committee of Ministers. The ECtHR does not request *amicus curiae* opinions from the Commission but does, and actually increasingly so, refer to Commission opinions. Other international or transnational organisations are also allowed to turn to the Commission for an opinion. The BiH Office of the High Representative used to be an important client for the Commission, and the EU is also free to request assistance. The OSCE-ODHIR has been an important partner, especially in electoral matters and issues concerning political human rights. The Commission has prepared several opinions and guidelines with the OSCE-ODHIR.

The great majority of the Commission's opinions deal with the post-socialist countries of Central and Eastern Europe. The Commission played an important role in the first wave of post-socialist constitutionalisation in 1990s, and the demand for its advice and support does not show signs of diminishing during subsequent rounds of constitutional reform. In addition to assisting the countries concerned in carefully planned comprehensive reforms, the Commission has also come to play the role of a constitutional fire-brigade, which can also be called on when urgent constitutional issues arise. The Romanian incidents in Summer 2012 or the Crimean annexation and referendum are representative examples. Though clear emphasis in the opinions lies on Central and Eastern Europe, the Commission is at the disposal of all its Member States, that is even the so-called established democracies. The Commission has been asked to perform a comprehensive review of the functioning of the Finnish Constitution of 2000, it has addressed a constitutional *cul-de-sac* in Belgium and has adopted opinions on Luxembourg, Liechtenstein and Monaco as well.

The reception of Commission opinions in the countries concerned of course varies. If the opinion has been requested by the country itself, it is likely to be welcomed, but if the initiative has come from elsewhere, criticism is more likely to be in the offing. Beyond persuasion, the Venice Commission does not possess any specific means to secure compliance with its advice. However, the Commission always tries to establish contacts with not only the authorities but also with the opposition and if possible NGOs and other civil society representatives. The Commission favours a dialogical approach which also engages opposition political forces and civil society actors. Almost without exception, the rapporteurs conduct a site-visit in the country concerned.

As distinct from country-specific opinions, the Commission can undertake general studies not only at the requests of other institutions – which sometimes happens – but also on its own initiative. Over the last fifteen years, the Commission has produced several important studies, sometimes concluding in normative guidelines. The topics covered include the Guantanamo prisoners and CIA flights; kinship legislation; constitutional amendments; the independence of the judiciary and the prosecutorial services; democratic control of secret services; parliamentary immunity; and the political and legal responsibility of the executive. Through its country-specific opinions, of which compilations have also been prepared and published, and general studies and guidelines, the Venice Commission has made a significant contribution to European soft law. Indirectly, through the ECtHR's jurisprudence, it has even made its mark on hard human rights law.[40]

---

[40] For a general presentation of the Venice Commission see J. Jowell, 'The Venice Commission – Disseminating Democracy through Law' 24 (2001) *Public Law* 675; S. R. Dürr,

The prerequisites for the successful functioning of a body of constitutional consultation, such as the Venice Commission, include *expertise, experience, independence* and *authority*. Although the Commission members are expected to be internationally recognised experts, competence naturally varies. Yet the Commission has always included excellent jurists, from both legal academia and the judiciary. It also has a highly qualified and experienced secretariat, which assists the rapporteurs in preparing opinions and reports. The Commission has been able to gather exceptional experience in constitutional assessment and consultation. This experience is stored not only in Commission documents but also in institutional memory, borne by the long-time members of both the Commission and its secretariat. During its twenty-five years of existence, the Commission has issued more than 500 opinions on more than fifty countries and eighty studies. The Commission is not a judicial body, but its institutional and personal independence is still essential for its credibility. As a rule, its members have preserved their independence from instructions or other governmental influence, but it should not come as a surprise that in twenty-five years, sporadic exceptions have occurred. However, these have not affected the general picture.

Authority is a consequence of expertise, experience and independence. No institution can gain authority by the mere fact of its establishment: authority must be earned. The other bodies of the Council of Europe, primarily the Parliamentary Assembly and its Committees, rely in their country-specific assessments on Commission opinions, where they exist. Other international organisations, such as the OSCE-ODIHR, the Office of the High Representative in Bosnia and Herzegovina and even the EU, have also benefited from cooperation with the Venice Commission. However, as regards some of the new democracies, a certain change of attitude has perhaps become noticeable since accession to the EU: there is a Venice Commission and in broader terms Council of Europe analogy to the Copenhagen dilemma. Eagerness to comply with Venice Commission

'The Venice Commission', in T. Kleinsorge (ed.), *The Council of Europe* (Alphen aan den Rijn: Kluwer Law International, 2010); J. Wouters, *International Encylopaedia of International Laws: Intergovernmental Organizations* (Alphen aan den Rijn: Wolters Kluwer, 2010), p. 151; G. Buquicchio and S. Granata-Menghini, 'The Venice Commission Twenty Years on: Challenge Met but Challenges Ahead' in M. van Roosmalen et al. (eds.), *Fundamental Rights and Principles – Liber amicorum Pieter van Dijk* (Cambridge/Antwerp/Portland: Intersentia, 2013), p. 241; W. Hoffmann-Riem, 'The Venice Commission of the Council of Europe – Standards and Impact', 25(2) (2014) *The EJIL* 579. See also the information presented on the Venice Commission Web site, where also the opinions and studies are published at www.venice.coe.int.

recommendations can diminish after EU membership is achieved. It is hard to avoid noticing a certain instrumentality in the attitude towards the CoE on the part of at least some of the new democracies: the CoE is a stepping-stone to the EU, and once the final objective has been achieved, the CoE matters less.

The wisdom of establishing a new advisory body, parallel to the Venice Commission, is questionable. The rationality of organisational duplication should always be doubted. Furthermore, as argued above, it takes time for such a body to obtain the necessary expertise and experience and to prove its independence: that is, to acquire the credentials needed for authority and successful operation. The Venice Commission has already passed this test. Moreover, cooperation between the European Commission and the Venice Commission is already a reality and has shown positive results, not only in pushing forward constitutional reforms in countries still in the ante-chamber of the EU but also in monitoring respect for fundamental rights, the Rule of Law and democracy in EU Member States. Therefore, to take the perhaps most conspicuous example, the Venice Commission has issued several opinions on Hungary,[41] and these opinions have largely formed the basis for assessments within the European Commission. A representative of the European Commission regularly attends plenary sessions of the Venice Commission, and the European Commission legal service and the Venice Commission secretariat have already an established tradition of cooperation.

The Venice Commission is also completely capable of assisting the EU within the new Framework. There are no formal obstacles to supporting the Framework, either: the Statute of the Venice Commission permits the Union to request opinions. A possible objection to reliance on Venice could be that the Commission includes CoE countries with dubious records in human rights, democracy or the Rule of Law. That may be true, but it would be difficult to prove that this would have affected the opinion or reports of the Commission. Accepting the relevance of the membership argument would also make references to ECtHR case law in EU primary law and ECJ jurisprudence questionable: judges appointed from 'suspect' states sit in the ECtHR, too. Finally, resort to the Venice Commission could be queried on the grounds that the Commission does not possess the resources for field studies. Indeed, this is the case, but here the EU Fundamental Rights Agency, strengthened in line with the

---

[41] The most important and comprehensive being the Opinion on the new Constitution of Hungary CDL-AD(2011)016.

recommendations of the Tavares report, could remedy this lack as it would – again in line with the Tavares report – have to, to complement a novel Copenhagen Commission as well.

VI   The Problem of Standards

The specification of standards is an intricate issue in all European monitoring related to the foundational values enshrined in Article 2 TEU. According to its very designation, as well as to the Commission Communication, the Framework has been prepared for Rule of Law purposes. The Communication contains a list of central Rule of Law principles, based on ECtHR and ECJ jurisprudence and Council of Europe soft law. The principles include:

> 'legality, which implies a transparent, accountable, democratic and plural-istic process for enacting laws; legal certainty; prohibition of arbitrariness of the executive powers; independent and impartial courts; effective judi-cial review including respect for fundamental rights; and equality before the law.[42]

The clear implication is that monitoring under the Framework would focus on these principles. Above, I have argued that constitutional issues in, say, Hungary and Romania cannot be squeezed into individual fundamental rights violations. Rule of Law principles possess a wider scope and catch more of the current Hungarian problem, for instance. The Commission Communication argues that the Rule of Law is of particular importance within the EU. It considers the Rule of Law a prerequisite for the protection of all fundamental values listed in Article 2 TEU and for upholding all the rights and obligations deriving from the Treaties and from international law. Furthermore, the Commission alludes to the requirements of the Area of Freedom, Security and Justice, especially to the principle of mutual recognition and the underlying principle of confidence, which make Rule of Law failures in one Member State a concern for all others. We could add to the Commission's reasoning that respect for the Rule of Law by Member States is a prerequisite for the functioning of the EU not only as an area of freedom, security and justice but also as a single market: that is to accomplish the original and still crucial policy objective of European integration. This too explains why respect for the

---

[42] European Commission, 'A New EU Framework to Strengthen the Rule of Law'.

Rule of Law in a particular Member State is a legitimate concern for other Member States and the Union as a whole.

But if the worrisome constitutional developments in some Member States, notably in Hungary, cannot be addressed as individual fundamental rights violations, neither would a Rule of Law approach, focusing on criteria such as those listed in the Commission Communication, cover the whole breadth of the issue. Of the three generic values (or bundles of principles) of fundamental rights, the Rule of Law and democracy, the gravest threat has arguably beset democracy. In line with the Rule of Law (or fundamental rights), the state of democracy in a Member State is also a legitimate concern for other Member States, as well as the Union as a whole. As Fritz Scharpf, among others, has emphasised, the EU receives its democratic legitimacy mainly through a two-stage mechanism: that is through Member State democratic processes.[43] This is a major reason why the EU – or other Member States – cannot remain indifferent in the face of developments threatening democracy in individual Member States: at stake is not merely the democratic legitimacy in the country concerned but also in the EU as a whole.

Democracy belongs to the Copenhagen criteria, now explicitly confirmed in Article 2 TEU. As generic values, human rights, the Rule of Law and democracy require operationalisation, elaboration into more specific standards before they can offer guidance in constitutional design or assessment. The ECHR and the case law of the ECtHR, along with the CFR and ECJ's jurisprudence all define minimum standards for human rights. These are complemented by European soft law, to which the Venice Commission, for instance, has made important contributions, sometimes in cooperation with the OSCE-ODHIR. In addition to ECHR and CFR provisions, and ECtHR and ECJ case law, important Rule of Law aspects are covered by soft law documents related, for instance, to the independence of the judiciary and the prosecutorial service. The Venice Commission has produced an even more comprehensive Rule of Law checklist, alluded to in the Commission Communication.[44]

Of the three generic foundational values, democracy appears to be the most difficult to operationalise for the purposes of constitutional design and assessment. Human rights, democracy and the Rule of Law are interrelated, and standards specifying human rights and Rule of Law

---

[43] See for example F. W. Scharpf, *Reflections on Multilevel Legitimacy* (Cologne: Max Planck Institute for the Study of Societies, 2007).

[44] Venice Commission, Report on the Rule of Law. CDL-AD(2011)003rev-e.

requirements offer assistance in operationalising democracy as well. Accordingly, Article 3 of Protocol 1 ECHR enshrines the right to 'free elections at reasonable intervals by secret ballot, under conditions which will ensure the free expression of the opinion of the people in the choice of the legislature'.[45] This implies that the democratic legitimacy of the legislature obtained through free elections also belongs to the key standards of democracy. Furthermore, the ECHR guarantees political rights – freedom of assembly, association and the press – which aim to establish the public autonomy of citizens. They imply a conception of democracy where civil society, a free public sphere and public debate of common issues, occupy a central place: a conception of democracy which in recent debate has come to be termed deliberative democracy.

However, the requirements of a popularly elected legislature and fundamental political rights carving out a constitutionally defined place for civil society, the public sphere and public debate do not yet specify the political regime which constitutional design should opt for in order to secure and enhance democracy. Various types of political regime which fulfil the minimum formal constitutional criteria can be conducive to democracy. In effect, the Venice Commission has repeatedly stated that choice of political regime from the three principal alternatives of presidential, parliamentary and semi-presidential models is a political decision falling to the country in question: no strict European standards limit this choice. A controversial issue, located at the interface of all three foundational values, consists of constitutional justice. The Venice Commission, for instance, has been a staunch defender of constitutional courts in the new democracies of Central and Eastern Europe. However, can supervising majoritarian political democracy by a counter-majoritarian judicial body be elevated to a generally valid European standard, or is it only a necessary or at least advisable constitutional safeguard in a post-totalitarian country where the cultural and sociological prerequisites for a democratic *Rechtsstaat* are only slowly emerging? If this is how we view the issue, we are in the midst of a discussion on double standards. To my mind, such a discussion cannot be avoided, for the simple reason that the standards applicable to countries with a more robust political culture and a more developed and alert civil society may – legitimately – display differences from the standards applicable to countries with a less robust political culture and a less developed and alert civil society. This is a sensitive issue

---

[45] Art. 3, Protocol 1 ECHR.

within both the EU and the Council of Europe. Yet pretending it does not exist and does not help resolve it.

Are the standards relied on by the Venice Commission applicable to EU monitoring or do they have a specific Council of Europe tinge? The core values of the Council of Europe correspond to those enshrined in Article 2 TEU: human rights, democracy and the Rule of Law. In its opinions, the Commission employs what it calls European standards. Within the field of fundamental rights and the Rule of Law, ECtHR jurisprudence provides the baseline, but merely a baseline; the Venice Commission can set the criteria higher than the ECtHR. This has, for instance, been the case with regard to the prohibition of political parties. On the other hand, in its decisions, the ECtHR may cite Venice Commission opinions, thus, as it were, transforming Venice Commission soft law into hard law: here we can discern an upward spiral.[46] In addition to Strasbourg jurisprudence, the Venice Commission may also refer to the EU Charter, and Council of Europe soft law also constitutes an important normative source, which the Commission for its part enriches through its recommendations and guidelines. Furthermore, the Commission often uses comparative material from which to distil what might be called 'best European practice', which can then be used as additional justification for transcending the baseline defined by Strasbourg (or Luxembourg) jurisprudence.[47]

It is hard to see any relevant differences between the CoE and EU principles operationalising the common generic values of human rights, democracy and the Rule of Law. The Venice Commission does not apply strictly defined CoE standards but more broadly understood European standards, to which EU rules and ECJ case law also contribute. Moreover, in defining the Rule of Law principles underlying the new Framework, for instance, the European Commission expressly refers to CoE soft law, including the Venice Commission Report on the Rule of Law.

VII Conclusion

The new EU Rule of Law Framework has not yet been tested in practice. It was introduced by the outgoing Commission in the final phase of its mandate, and at the time of writing, no practical experience has yet been

---

[46] Since 2002, the ECtHR has cited the Commission in more than 50 cases.

[47] For an analysis of the standards used by the Venice Commission see Hoffmann-Riem, 'The Venice Commission of the Council of Europe: Standards and Impact' (also discusses the interplay between the Venice Commission and the ECtHR).

gathered.[48] However, there is no reason to deny *ex ante* its potential under an active and committed Commissioner to complement the available legal means of fundamental rights review and the infringement procedure, and to provide a more dialogically oriented political process than the cumbersome political mechanism under Article 7 TEU. The public and dialogical character of the process could also boost the political and legal culture, and civil society activism in the country under monitoring; indeed, promoting the cultural and sociological prerequisites of a democratic *Rechtsstaat* should be a major objective of the process. However, the effectiveness of the three-stage process depends on many largely unpredictable factors, such as the willingness of the Commission and especially of the Commissioner concerned to resort to the Framework in the first place; success in mobilising European and national public opinion, media and civil society; as well as in the responsiveness and cooperativeness of the Member State government.

In the last resort, the fate of democracy and of the other foundational values of the EU and the CoE is decided within the Member States themselves. But external monitoring, whether by EU or CoE institutions, could support or even launch cultural and social developments and alert national and European civil society and the public to what is occurring. Although monitoring target states, governments and constitutions, the final objectives transcend institutional and normative structures and reach out to society at large. External monitoring is a sensitive enterprise, which can also yield negative results: nationalist reactions, even backlashes. This further enhances the significance of consultative bodies which enjoy confidence and authority among both institutional and non-institutional actors, and at both national and the European level.

---

[48] See C. Closa, 'Reinforcing EU Monitoring of the Rule of Law: Normative Arguments, Institutional Proposals and the Procedural Limitations' in this volume.

PART III

Identifying Deeper Problems

12

EU Democratic Oversight and Domestic Deviation from the Rule of Law

Sociological Reflections

PAUL BLOKKER[*]

I Introduction

The troublesome Hungarian, Polish, and possibly Romanian, developments regarding democracy, constitutionalism and the Rule of Law call for the attention of the European Union and its Member States, in particular regarding violations of the principles of Article 2 TEU. Various proposals for monitoring mechanisms or even new institutions of oversight have been put forward, including a Copenhagen Commission and a systemic infringement procedure.[1] The core problem faced by the European Union regarding the democratic nature of its Member States seems to be one of 'safeguarding of the core values on which the Union has been established'.[2] If reasonable justifications for why the EU should engage in safeguarding those values can be found, then the Union cannot but avoid to scrutinise the structural efficacy of potential instruments and mechanisms for addressing this issue.[3] The larger part of the debate on this matter – which erupted with particular vigour with the Hungarian constitutional 'coup' and subsequently the Romanian and Polish constitutional and Rule of Law crisis – identifies a generally *legalistic* approach to the problem and endorses distinctive *legal* remedies, some of which need reform of the Treaties.

---

[*] University of Trento and Charles University, Prague.
[1] See, for example, the chapters by J.-W. Müller, 'Protecting the Rule of Law (and Democracy!) in the EU: The Idea of a Copenhagen Commission' and K. L. Scheppele, 'Enforcing the Basic Principles of EU Law through Systemic Infringement Procedures', in this volume.
[2] C. Closa, D. Kochenov, and J. H. H. Weiler, 'Reinforcing Rule of Law Oversight in the European Union' EUI Working Papers No. 2014/25, RSCAS, 3.
[3] *Ibid.*

My argument here will interrogate the purely formalistic and legal-istic approach, and for that matter, will be less 'policy-applied' and 'problem-solving', but rather a suggestion for a more comprehensive anal-ysis, grounded in sociological and political reflections. My approach will be a sociology of constitutional democracy and the Rule of Law, and I will ask whether current considerations and the solutions on offer sufficiently consider the distinctive dimensions of the functioning of constitutional democracy. Such dimensions are crucial for the actual 'safeguarding of the core values' of the EU but are in my view unlikely to be satisfied through a one-sided legalistic and formal-procedural approach.

The problems raised by the constitutional *coup d'État* in Hungary and the constitutional crises in Romania and Poland are at least twofold, the first having to do with issues of constitutionalism and the Rule of Law, the second with the actual operation of the liberal, democratic state. Regard-ing constitutionalism and the Rule of Law, I will argue that the problem-atic issues are not confined to the abandonment or violation of distinctive constitutional or legal procedures (such as with the troublesome manner in which the four-fifths rule regarding legitimate constitutional change was annulled in the Hungarian context, or the problematic tinkering with the referendum law in Romania) or to the arbitrary, partisan or par-ticularist use of political power. For the short-term correction of such matters, a legalistic approach might be largely sufficient. More impor-tantly, constitutionalism and the Rule of Law as such lack a firm social and politico-cultural entrenchment in civil and political society, as well as lacking support in empowered and critical democratic counter-forces. The democratisation of political and constitutional cultures and the fos-tering of capabilities oriented towards the common good are notoriously difficult to capture and understand,[4] but are unlikely to be constructed by mere legal instruments alone.

Regarding the status of the liberal, democratic state in a number of EU Member States, a key set of problems relates to self-interested, partisan and corrupted forms of politics, detached from ideas of the common good and largely alienated from wider society. Reflections of this include the predominance of *constitutional instrumentalism* as well as *legal resent-ment*. Constitutional instrumentalism entails the downgrading of com-prehensive constitutional reform to an instance of doing politics as usual, often serving narrow majoritarian or partisan objectives rather than the common good, or worse, abusing constitutional reform for illiberal or

---

[4] M. Krygier, 'The Rule of Law: Legality, Teleology, Sociology', in G. Palombella and N. Walker (eds.), *Relocating the Rule of Law* (Oxford: Hart Publishing, 2009), p. 45.

non-democratic purposes.[5] Legal resentment consists of a political reaction against liberal and legal constitutionalism.[6] The concept of legal resentment has affinity with notions of 'nonliberal constitutionalism',[7] 'illiberal constitutionalism',[8] 'abusive constitutionalism'[9] and 'counter constitutionalism',[10] in that it indicates a sceptical or critical relationship to legal formalism, the Rule of Law and liberal democracy, and proposes a different understanding of constitutional law. While liberal constitutionalism promotes a universally valid and formalistic programme for the separation of powers, the Rule of Law (rather than the rule of men) and the neutrality of the state, illiberal forms of constitutionalism question the universality of such notions, prioritise particularist and historical values related to a distinctive political community and on this basis justify political interference in legal matters. Liberal constitutionalism is put to the test in a variety of ways. As also captured by Landau's notion of 'abusive constitutionalism', legal resentment can enhance and justify the instrumental use or abuse of instruments of constitutional amendment to structurally favour or enhance the interests and power of particular groupings (such as in Orbán's Hungary and Ponta's Romania; Landau also mentions Egypt, Colombia and Venezuela). Legal resentment equally takes the form of questioning a decontextualised, universalistic understanding of constitutional and legal orders, and the proposition of the defence and recuperation of national legal-constitutional traditions instead (described by Scheppele in the case of Hungary as 'counter-constitutionalism').

In order to reinvigorate domestic democratic politics in deviant democracies, and to address tendencies such as constitutional instrumentalism and legal resentment, a purely legalistic set of instruments is in my view insufficient. Democracy in Europe is under general strain due

[5] D. Landau 'Abusive Constitutionalism', 47 (2013) *UC Davis Law Review* 190.

[6] P. Blokker, *New Democracies in Crisis? A Comparative Constitutional Study of the Czech Republic, Hungary, Poland, Romania and Slovakia* (London/New York: Routledge, 2013).

[7] G. Walker, 'The Idea of Nonliberal Constitutionalism', in I. Shapiro and W. Kymlicka (eds.), *Ethnicity and Group Rights* (New York: New York University Press, 1997). According to Walker, in 'postcommunist lands as elsewhere, there is sometimes less than full enthusiasm for the liberal, individual rights-oriented approach to constitutions' (p. 154).

[8] L.-A. Thio 'Constitutionalism in Illiberal Polities', in M. Rosenfeld and A. Sajó (eds.), *The Oxford Handbook of Comparative Constitutional Law* (Oxford: Oxford University Press, 2012), p. 133; M. Rosenfeld, 'Is Global Constitutionalism Meaningful or Desirable?', 25(1) (2014) *EJIL* 177.

[9] Landau, 'Abusive Constitutionalism'.

[10] K. L. Scheppele 'Counter-constitutions: Narrating the Nation in Post-Soviet Hungary', paper presented at George Washington University, Washington DC, 2 April 2004.

to an increasing gap between wider society and political elites. Such a gap is exacerbated by the financial and economic crisis, as indicated by diminishing public support for the European integration project in recent years[11] and the European-wide support for populist parties and movements.[12] The increasing public distance from and distrust towards institutions of liberal, representative democracy[13] importantly relates to the emergence of illiberalism and legal resentment in societies such as Hungary and Romania.[14] Populist movements frequently propose to close the society-elite gap by means of the direct representation of a homogeneous, ethno-national majority, to the detriment of various minorities as well as political pluralism in general. For example, in Orbán's project of 'national unification' in Hungary, the political project involves the defence of the Hungarian majority and the public announcement of the abandonment of liberal-democratic practices in favour of a nationalist approach.[15]

To counter illiberal tendencies and the populist threat to democracy, and to potentially diminish their causes, it is clearly important to safeguard legal institutions. Countering populism and illiberalism definitively needs to include the heightened protection of rights (for instance, regarding the freedom of expression or the freedom of conscience) and the strengthening of democratic procedures. But I suggest that it also needs a variety of a different kind of 'safeguards', including more society-based and informal ones.

In this chapter, I will first discuss what I see as the prevalence of a formalistic-technocratic view in the EU promotion of the Rule of Law and constitutionalism. I will relate three *problématiques* to this formalistic view: a *problématique* of formal and informal dimensions of the

---

[11] See the results of the Eurobarometer survey, December 2014, at http://ec.europa.eu/public_opinion/archives/eb/eb82/eb82_first_en.pdf. Admittedly, the last quarter of 2014 has seen some improvement in public support for the EU.

[12] Y. Mounk, 'Pitchfork Politics: The Populist Threat to Liberal Democracy' (September/October, 2014) *Foreign Affairs*.

[13] The Eurobarometer survey of Spring 2013 found that circa fifty percent of the EU population is 'dissatisfied with the way in which democracy works in their country', at http://ec.europa.eu/public_opinion/archives/eb/eb79/eb79_publ_en.pdf.

[14] According to the Eurobarometer survey of Spring 2013, the percentages of people who expressed satisfaction with how democracy works in their country were 31 and 18 percent in Hungary and Romania, respectively.

[15] G. Halmai, 'Illiberal Democracy and Beyond in Hungary', Verfassungsblog, 28 August 2014, at www.verfassungsblog.de/en/illiberal-democracy-beyond-hungary-2/#.VMDQ2-ZdrMs.

law; a *problématique* of universalist and particularist perceptions of the law and a *problématique* of representative and alternative dimensions of constitutional democracy. In the second part I will briefly discuss the domestic problems of the Hungarian case, particularly in light of the three *problématiques*. In conclusion, I argue that three areas need greater attention in the debate on democratic oversight: the sociological legitimacy of the constitutional framework and political and social commitment to the Rule of Law and constitutional democracy, existing constitutional and legal traditions, and the societal role in democratic oversight and checks and balances through empowerment of local societal actors.

II Promotion of Democracy and a 'Thin'Rule of Law

The legalistic approach now offered as a solution for systematic deviation from the EU's core values is a variation on a familiar theme.[16] In various relevant EU policy areas (e.g. Enlargement policy and the European Neighbourhood Policy) and also in the more general understanding of Article 2 TEU, the concept of the Rule of Law adhered to is largely a 'thin' one.[17] A 'thin' conception tends to understand the Rule of Law in largely formalistic terms and prioritises legal institutions and procedures. The emphasis is on a system of Rule of Law in which the arbitrary nature of the 'rule of a person or persons' and ad hoc decisions are avoided.[18] In general, the formalistic view of the law proposes to avoid the use of arbitrary power and/or forms of domination, to stabilise social relations by making such relations predictable, and to protect individual autonomy from being interfered with by 'malicious and unpredictable interferences by public authorities and others'.[19]

---

[16] Cf. K. Nicolaïdis and R. Kleinfeld, 'Rethinking Europe's "Rule of Law" and Enlargement Agenda: The Fundamental Dilemma', 49 (2012) *SIGMA Papers*; A. von Bogdandy and M. Ioannidis, 'Systemic Deficiency in the Rule of Law: What It Is, What Has Been Done, What Can Be Done', 51 (2014) *CMLRev.*

[17] See for the notion of a 'thin' understanding of the rule of law, for instance, B. Tamanaha, 'The History and Elements of the Rule of Law' (2012) *Singapore Journal of Legal Studies* 232, 233–6. In Tamanaha's view, a 'thin' understanding of the rule of law refers to the fact that this concept of the Rule of Law does not include notions of democracy and human rights, but focuses strictly on citizens and institutions abiding to and bound by the law. I will use the adjectives 'thin, formal', and 'formalistic' regarding the Rule of Law in an interchangeable fashion.

[18] R. Bellamy, 'The Rule of Law and the Rule of Persons', 4(4) (2001) *Critical Review of International Social and Political Philosophy* 221.

[19] *Ibid.*, 225.

The formalistic idea is that, by means of adherence to an instrumental rationality and the support of robust formal, legal institutions, it is possible to tame political power and to channel its exercise in transparent and predictable directions. There is an important emphasis on the output legitimacy and the effectiveness of the law. This formalistic or 'anatomical' approach perceives the Rule of Law as strictly related to 'particular sets of legal arrangements'[20] or 'legal and institutional checklists'.[21] Such checklists highlight formalistic institutional set-ups which are supposedly easy candidates for legal transfer but wider social and political conditions, preconditions and implications remain largely unexamined. In such a narrow view of the Rule of Law, the Rule of Law is almost fully equated with the law itself, rather than with the law as a 'social fact'. Indeed the social function of the law – its 'social role as the default mechanism to solve social and political conflicts'[22] – is downplayed in favour of narrow, technocratic formalism based on supposedly universal standards.

A formal view seems corroborated in the EU's promotion of the Rule of Law in for instance the Eastern Enlargement Policy, where it was largely a technical view of the Rule of Law which prevailed, grounded in an instrumental legitimacy of outcomes, while substantive aspects such as democratic rule and social justice were largely sidelined.[23] As argued by Bogdan Iancu, discussing conditionality in the Romanian case,

> The Commission was and continues to be interested in the measurable constitutional problem areas of judicial reform and the fight against corruption. These objective matters, broken down into the four benchmarks of the Cooperation and Verification Mechanism (CVM), can be sub-itemized into a number of concrete, clear tasks. Guidelines can be advanced, deadlines can be set, overall progress can be monitored, and results can be periodically assessed.[24]

In my view, such a technical-instrumental view of the Rule of Law tends to be equally upfront in the current debate on democratic oversight and prevention of democratic backsliding, and the correction of states which

---

[20] Krygier, 'The Rule of Law', 46.
[21] Nicolaïdis and Kleinfeld, 'Rethinking Europe's "Rule of Law" and Enlargement Agenda', 6.
[22] Ibid., 8.
[23] J. Přibáň, 'From "Which Rule of Law?" to "The Rule of Which Law?": Post-Communist Experiences of European Legal Integration', 1(2) (2009) Hague Journal on the Rule of Law 337; B. Iancu, 'Post-Accession Constitutionalism with a Human Face: Judicial Reform and Lustration in Romania', 6(1) (2010) ECLRev.; Cf. Blokker, New Democracies in Crisis?
[24] Ibid., Iancu, 30.

persistently challenge EU values. In for instance Kim Lane Scheppele's proposal for a 'systemic infringement action',[25] the emphasis is on the 'simple extension of an existing mechanism', which would bundle a 'group of individual infringement actions together under the banner of Article 2'.[26] This extended mechanism would provide more effective powers to the European Commission and the CJEU. Furthermore, the emphasis is on a somehow *indirect* mechanism which reacts to the violation of allegedly universal EU objectives and core values, rather than addressing the structural dimensions of domestic democratic backsliding and the distinctive democratic problems in a Member State head on. It is the technical violation of EU law, rather than substantive issues with non-democratic domestic practices, which seems the predominant concern. The assumption is that 'systemic compliance' resulting from a systemic infringement action could be limited to the compliance of domestic institutions with formal EU law, rather than also requiring important sociopolitical structural and cultural changes.

From a sociological point of view, there are at least three *problématiques* raised by a 'thin' understanding of the Rule of Law and a one-sided insistence on a technocratic-legalistic 'solution' to national democratic deviation and systemic threats to the Rule of Law. The first *problématique* – regarding the *formal* and *informal dimensions of law* – is that of the insufficiency or incompleteness of a view which merely considers formal legal institutions (e.g. the formal independence of the judiciary) and the technical transfer of rules and norms. While legal institutions supporting the Rule of Law are a *conditio sine qua non*, this does not mean such institutions are in themselves sufficient guarantees for the Rule of Law to actually operate in a satisfactory manner. In the words of Martin Krygier, 'legal institutional features' 'always need *supporting circumstances*, social and political structures and cultural supports, which are not always available and are difficult to engineer'.[27] Such supporting circumstances include not least a general, diffused legal (and constitutional) culture, or in other words, prevailing, shared cultural value orientations *vis-à-vis* the Rule of Law (and constitutionalism) in a given society. Legal cultures offer insight into the level of compliance with the law, the social legitimacy of the law, and levels of impersonal trust in given societies.[28] As argued by Krygier, it

---

[25] See Chapter 5 in this volume.   [26] *Ibid.*

[27] Krygier, 'The Rule of Law: Legality, Teleology, Sociology', 52 (emphasis added).

[28] D. Nelken, 'Using the Concept of Legal Culture', 29 (2004) *Australian Journal of Legal Philosophy* 1.

is possible to imagine a society in which all the formal institutions of the Rule of Law exist, but in which the law does not rule after all.[29] In order for the law to rule, it has to *count* or *matter* in a given society, in the exercise of social power, and the Rule of Law has to be effective. The law has to count as a 'constraint on and an *ingredient* in the exercise of power and as a source of social guidance, both for the officials who exercise power as well as for the subjects of such power'.[30] Krygier outlines four indicators (two negative, and two positive) of what it means for the law to count in a society. A first indicator is the general obedience by citizens and officials to the law, and their expectation of fellow citizens or fellow officials to show the same. A second indicator is the extent and substance of such obedience. We could roughly distinguish here between obedience merely informed by fear of legal sanctions, on the one hand, and the consideration of the law as legitimate, on the other. In the latter case, we would expect a much more solid social and political embedment of the law.[31] A third indicator is the extent to which the law counts among the people who politically, socially, economically or religiously count, that is, those 'people or institutions which wield effective power'.[32] A fourth indicator regards not the mere obedience to the law but its actual use and how it is used. In other words, the extent to which politics operates through or by the law, as well as under the law, and the extent to which we can speak of 'legality' (laws understood as public guidelines and facilities) rather than of 'legal instrumentalism' (law as one instrument among others, used when convenient).[33] In social terms, it is important that the law is an 'institution of the everyday lifeworld itself, available to citizens as a resource and protection in their relations with the state and with each other'.[34]

The formal–informal *problématique* indicates that EU attempts to safeguard democracy in Member States would need to include attention to the political and sociological legitimacy of both the Rule of Law and the constitutional framework. Sociological legitimacy is understood here as

---

[29] M. Krygier 'Transitional Questions about the Rule of Law: Why, What, and How?', 28(1) (2001) *East Central Europe* 1.

[30] *Ibid.*, 12–3.

[31] In this regard, it can be argued that in the case of EU sanctions, as proposed for instance by Scheppele (*inter alia* in her contribution to this volume), a likely result would be a heightened 'fear' of sanctions on the part of non-complying states, but not necessarily an increase in the perception of *legitimacy* of EU norms and principles.

[32] Krygier, 'Transitional Questions about the Rule of Law', 15.

[33] *Ibid.*, 15–6.   [34] *Ibid.*, 16.

a 'matter of justifications of rule empirically available, one that the citizens, groups, and administrative staffs are likely to find valid, under the given historical circumstances'. Attention needs to be paid to the prevailing norms in society and views of legitimacy as held by relevant actors.[35] A key related issue is whether it is institutions (the 'hardware') which produce 'supporting conditions' (the 'software') for the Rule of Law or whether it is the availability of supporting conditions which makes the set-up and functioning of institutions possible in the first place.[36] I cannot provide a definitive answer to this complex problem here, but it seems clear that a mere transfer of the formal institutions of the Rule of Law to an otherwise indifferent or even hostile (e.g. post-authoritarian) context is very likely not to produce positive results.[37] From a legal-sociological perspective, it seems a *conditio sine qua non* that local social and political actors, who value the Rule of Law as a principle differently, have ways of engaging in ('investing in') the actual design and setup of (political, legal and constitutional) institutions (this point will be further elaborated in the context of the third *problématique*). This would not only have the advantage that the Rule of Law would be created in a way that reflects local mores and needs but also that it contributes to a political learning *process* in which a variety of actors engage with the production, implementation and use of the law.

A second, related *problématique* – regarding a tension between *universalistic* and *particularist* understandings of the law – inquires into a universalistic perception of the Rule of Law and the related identification of a universally valid template of 'best practices' or checklist of institutions and norms, and understands the Rule of Law as always (historically and semantically) situated. A universalistic understanding tends to ignore local, particularistic dimensions of law, which unavoidably influence and shape the day-to-day operation of the law in distinct societies. An important issue which emerges in this problem field is that of 'legal transplant' and the tension or irritation between an abstract norm, rule or institution, and the local interpretation, functioning and sociopolitical implications of the law. This dimension is obviously of particular relevance in the new EU Member States which have been

---

[35] A. Arato 'Regime Change, Revolution and Legitimacy in Hungary', in G. A. Tóth (ed.), *Constitution for a Disunited Nation: On Hungary's 2011 Fundamental Law* (New York/Budapest: Central European University Press, 2011), p. 40.

[36] I thank the editors for bringing this point up.

[37] G. Frankenberg (ed.), *Order from Transfer. Comparative Constitutional Design and Legal Culture* (Cheltenham and Northampton: Edward Elgar, 2013).

engaging in a massive legal transplantation process through the accession and are still dealing with significant legal and political legacies. The
existing legal and constitutional cultures – in terms of the systems of legal
meaning-giving or perceptions of the Rule of Law and constitutionalism –
at the receiving end are important factors in the transplantation process.
The tension between the abstract nature of a universally articulated rule
and the application of such a rule in a distinctive context plays a role here,
as well as prevalent legal understandings and perceptions of the law. This
problématique indicates that an effective form of EU democratic oversight
needs to include a historical and cultural-contextual sensibility, and due
attention for 'living' legal and constitutional understandings and narratives. This means that EU democratic oversight would need to take into
account:

1. Distinctive local problems with the Rule of Law and democracy
   (e.g. issues of transitional justice or lustration, or complex problems of political community-building in the wake of authoritarian
   experiences);[38]
2. Relevant legal-constitutional legacies, which inform for instance the
   behaviour and operation of legal personnel or compromise the idea of
   the independence of judicial institutions[39] and
3. The possibility of a 'subversive reception' of external legal transplants,
   which could fundamentally alter the meaning of a received abstract
   norm.

A third *problématique* – regarding the *representative* and *alternative dimensions of democracy* – is that of the social and political (formal *and* informal)
institutions lying beyond the formal building blocks of representative, liberal democracy. Of particular relevance here are different forms of civil
society organisation. The third *problématique* overlaps with the first (the
formal–informal dimensions of the law) in that it concerns the societal
dimensions of the Rule of Law. However, while the first *problématique*
emphasises the general importance of sociocultural entrenchment of the
law, here the emphasis is on active civil society engagement with the
law and its critical monitoring capacity *vis-à-vis* formal institutions. I

---

[38] J. Přibáň, *Legal Symbolism: On Law, Time and European Identity* (Aldershot: Ashgate,
   2007); Iancu, 'Post-Accession Constitutionalism with a Human Face'.
[39] M. Guţan, 'The Challenges of the Romanian Constitutional Tradition. I. Between Ideological Transplant and Institutional Metamorphoses', 25 (2013) *Giornale di Storia Costituzionale* 223; G. Skapska, *From 'Civil Society' to 'Europe': A Sociological Study on Constitutionalism After Communism* (Leiden: Brill, 2011).

take inspiration here from the work of Pierre Rosanvallon, who describes a 'decentering' of democratic systems and emphasises the importance of tendencies towards diffraction and pluralism in contemporary democratic systems which relate to novel answers and practices regarding democratic political interaction. The belief that the issue at hand is 'protecting liberal democracy' in the debate on democratic oversight and the Rule of Law in the EU[40] contrasts importantly with Rosanvallon's suggestion that '[n]o one believes any longer that democracy can be reduced to a system of competitive elections culminating in majority rule'.[41]

Rosanvallon proposes a 'mixed regime', which involves a plurality of powers of oversight and includes multiple layers and agents. A European dimension of democratic oversight would be adding to the mix of a mixed domestic regime but would in itself probably not be sufficient.[42] At the domestic level, parliamentary oversight would need additional forms of oversight, such as independent institutions of oversight, but also societal ones, including those of public opinion and the media (including the new media), a critical role for opposition parties, social movements and citizen organisations, and ad hoc democratic institutions.[43] While the EU can act as an external provider of incentives and/or sanctions, it is difficult to perceive how a vital and sustainable democratic Rule of Law state could do without the deeper knowledge, social embedment and engagement of local political and social actors. This *problématique* hints at the idea that an effective form of EU democratic oversight would need to stimulate the empowerment of not only formal-political and legal actors but also of a variety of civil society forces as well as the media.[44]

Let us now turn to a brief analysis of the case that most prominently triggered the debate on EU democratic oversight – Hungary[45] – with due attention to the three *problématiques* mentioned above.

---

[40] J.-W. Müller, 'Defending Democracy within the EU', 24(2) (2013) *Journal of Democracy* 138.

[41] P. Rosanvallon, *Democratic Legitimacy: Impartiality, Reflexivity, Proximity* (Princeton, New Jersey: Princeton University Press, 2011), p. 219.

[42] Compare Nicolaïdis and Kleinfeld, 'Rethinking Europe's "Rule of Law" and Enlargement Agenda', 48.

[43] P. Rosanvallon, *Counter-democracy: Politics in an Age of Distrust* (Cambridge: Cambridge University Press, 2008), p. 301.

[44] Cf. Nicolaïdis and Kleinfeld, 'Rethinking Europe's "Rule of Law" and Enlargement Agenda', 49.

[45] For a discussion of the case of Romania, see Blokker, *New Democracies in Crisis?*. See also P. Blokker 'Constitution-Making in Romania: From Reiterative Crises to Constitutional Moment?', 3(2) (2013) *Romanian Journal of Comparative Law* 187.

III The Hungarian Case

It was not least the rapid and largely non-participatory and majority-driven drafting of a new constitution by the centre-right *Fidesz* government that has triggered the current debate on democratic oversight and backsliding in the EU. The new constitution, drafted and adopted in 2010–11, entails a shift away from the Hungarian attachment to a 'secular state based on a pluralist society', grounded in European traditions, as has been evident in the constitutionalisation process since 1989. It has led to the institutionalisation of a new constitutional order which has its foundations in sovereignist, 'historical and religious considerations'.[46] In 'many respects it does not comply with standards of democratic constitutionalism and the basic principles set forth in Article 2 of the Treaty on the European Union', as observed by a number of critical Hungarian legal scholars as well as by the Council of Europe's Venice Commission.[47]

The illiberal developments in Hungary have been analysed and condemned widely, but relatively less sustained attention has been paid to how the context emerged in which a 'constitutional *coup d'État*' could become reality in the first place. My argument is that the backlash against liberal constitutionalism, pluralist democracy and the Rule of Law – culminating in the *Fidesz* constitutional project – needs to be situated in the distinctive transformational path that Hungary has followed since 1989. This path needs specific attention because in the early transition years it was based on the opposite rationale of the current political project: an elite narrative which strongly emphasised liberal, representative democracy, the Rule of Law, European constitutionalism and technocratic governance. Hungary was long considered a frontrunner in the Eastern Central European region, with the most successful record in adopting a form of legal or 'new constitutionalism', including an enormously strong Constitutional Court, an elite endorsement of a Europeanist constitutional culture and powerful forms of rights protection.[48]

---

[46] K. Kovács and G. A. Tóth, 'Hungary's Constitutional Transformation', 7(2) (2011) *ECLRev.* 183, 198.

[47] A. Arato, G. Halmai and J. Kis, 'Opinion on the Fundamental Law of Hungary' (June 2011), at http://lapa.princeton.edu/hosteddocs/amicus-to-vc-english-final.pdf, 3.

[48] A. Örkény and K. L. Scheppele, 'Rules of Law: The Complexity of Legality in Hungary', in M. Krygier and A. Czarnota (eds.) *The Rule of Law in Post-Communist Societies* (Aldershot: Ashgate, 1999). Cf. Blokker, *New Democracies in Crisis?*

In the light of current developments, a key question becomes: how did the most successful liberal constitutional regime in the region turn into its opposite almost overnight? My argument is that, in part, the unentrenched, elitist nature of the legal-constitutionalist-cum-rule-of-law state and the lack of widespread support for the liberal-constitutional framework[49] facilitated strong counter-reactions. From the Roundtable Talks of 1989 onwards, the project of constitutional democracy was one driven by technocratic elites, who promoted a programme of 'Westernization, free speech, freedom of the press, human rights, checks and balances, Rule of Law with strong guardian institutions like the constitutional court and the ombudsman'. As András Bozóki argues, '[i]t was a very sophisticated set of institutions – but without the *spirit* of democracy' and the '*participatory aspect* of democracy was missing.'[50] Various observers have noted the lack of a robust, positive consensus on a constitutional framework in the early 1990s.[51] Some observers have criticised the 1989 arrangement for merely constituting 'formal constitutionalism', devoid of shared values and principles which could have invoked an integrative constitutional dimension.[52] When the – anyhow limited – elitist liberal consensus started waning in the late 1990s, a counter-reaction had room to emerge, mobilised by a transformed *Fidesz* party which manipulated nationalist and populist sentiments amongst the losers in the transformation.[53] *Fidesz* mobilised parts of the population by

---

[49] G. A. Tóth, 'Macht statt Recht. Deformation des Verfassungssystems in Ungarn' (2013) *Eurozine*, at www.eurozine.com/articles/2013-06-05-totha-de.html; G. Lengyel and G. Ilonszki, 'Simulated Democracy and Pseudo-Transformational Leadership in Hungary' 37 (2012) *Historical Social Research/Historische Sozialforschung* 107, 110.

[50] A. Bozóki, 'Hungary's U-turn', at www.johnfeffer.com/hungarys-u-turn (emphasis added).

[51] J. Kis, 'Introduction: From the 1989 Constitution to the 2011 Fundamental Law', in G. A. Tóth (ed.), *Constitution for a Disunited Nation: On Hungary's 2011 Fundamental Law* (New York/Budapest: Central European University Press, 2011), p. 1. G. Halmai, *Perspectives of Global Constitutionalism* (Utrecht: Eleven International Publishing, 2014); Tóth, 'Macht statt Recht'. A public opinion poll held in April 2011 found that only eleven percent of the Hungarian population thought the 1989 Constitution was 'good as it is'. Thirty percent thought a new constitution was needed. See http://hvg.hu/itthon/201115_megoszto_alkotmany.

[52] Hörcher, mentioned in: Halmai, *Perspectives of Global Constitutionalism*, p. 213.

[53] Support for *Fidesz* appears to come predominantly from the rural, socially conservative, religiously oriented, nationalist and anti-communist parts of Hungarian society, G. Tóka and S. Popa 'Hungary', in S. Berglund et al. (eds.), *The Handbook of Political Change in Eastern Europe*, 3rd edn (Cheltenham: Edgar Elgar, 2013), p. 291.

identifying liberalism and the Rule of Law increasingly with a Western import, foreign interests and upper class ideas.[54]

In terms of the formal and informal dimensions of the law, the Hungarian path in the early transition years prioritised a formalistic approach to the institutionalisation of constitutional democracy, with a certain disregard for supportive political and sociocultural institutions (including limited attention being paid to the symbolic and integrative aspects of the Constitution).[55] The Hungarian constitutional transformation was unique in that it did not involve a major legal rupture with the preceding communist Act XX of 1949, but was rather a case of legal continuity. The intensive amendments which started with the Roundtable Talks produced a *novel* modern constitution that 'met all the standards a modern, democratic constitution is expected to meet', based on 'binding norms', and protected by extensive judicial review powers of the Constitutional Court.[56] It is undeniable that the formal-legal setup of the post-communist system closely followed a well-established European template. But while the constitutional agreement of the Roundtable Talks produced a new constellation of formal-legal institutions, the informal, political and cultural support for the legal-rational make-up of the Hungarian democratic state proved much less forthcoming. The political forces which unreservedly defended a liberal-democratic conception of constitutionalism were only few even in the early 1990s (in practice restricted to the *Alliance of Free Democrats* and *Fidesz*). Then, throughout the 1990s, it was the Constitutional Court which took up the role of 'consolidating force', while the 'political class became progressively estranged from the constitution'.[57] A 'low degree of respect for the constitutional provisions in force'[58] translated into a more general constitutional instrumentalism, which involves disobedience on strategic grounds as well as a heightened willingness to change the rules of the game (as becomes *inter alia* apparent in the large number of amendments made: twenty-three until the 1989 Constitution was replaced by the Fundamental Law).

Turning to the tension between universalistic and particularistic views of the law, the lack of a widespread legal-rational engagement with the

---

[54] Indeed, *Fidesz* has on various occasions portrayed liberal democracy as a foreign import. In a speech given in August 2014, Orbán portrayed civil pro-democracy organisations as 'political activists attempting to promote foreign interests' (cited in Halmai, *Perspectives of Global Constitutionalism*).

[55] Cf. Tóth, 'Macht statt Recht'; Halmai, *Perspectives of Global Constitutionalism*.

[56] Kis, 'Introduction: From the 1989 Constitution to the 2011 Fundamental Law'.

[57] *Ibid.*, 10–11.   [58] *Ibid.*, 9.

1989 Constitution signals the absence of a strong universalistic, liberal-democratic tradition as well as of a widespread consensus on the constitutional order in post-1989 Hungary. Instead, various political actors articulate the constitutional views of a 'primacy of politics' and majoritarianism or partisanship, and tend to question a universalistic attachment to rights and democratic principles in favour of a contextualised view. On the centre-right of the Hungarian political spectrum, a historically relevant illiberal tradition can be identified (not least related to the interwar period).[59] This tradition has lent significant support to the emergence of the counter-constitutionalism which informs the current project and has helped to cast the economic and political crisis of the mid-/late 2000s as an outcome of the weaknesses of the post-1989 legal constitution.

The culmination of this illiberalism came with *Fidesz* winning an absolute majority in the 2010 elections, which allowed it to start its constitutional counter-project. This project involves clear dimensions of what I have labelled 'legal resentment' above.[60] The thrust of much of the counter-constitutional process is against the democratic-constitutional order which has emerged since 1989, as the leaders 'sensed a fundamental (and in the short term irremediable) disillusionment with the liberal democratic system across all segments of the Hungarian political community and think they have a long-term solution that will appeal to the masses'.[61] Resentment is being justified by reference to a different idea of constitutionalism, the unwritten 'historical constitution'.[62] The conservative thrust in the *Fidesz* project can be related to 'communitarian' as well as 'illiberal' views of constitutionalism.[63] What identifies such forms of constitutionalism is the perception of a 'common enemy' in

---

[59] Orbán's project is now openly about 'illiberal democracy' (G. Halmai, 'Illiberal Democracy and Beyond in Hungary'). Various observers have noted the *Fidesz* invocation of the interwar period in its 'national unification' project. As Bozóki argues, *Fidesz* 'feeds nostalgia for the period between 1920 and 1944, characterised by Admiral Miklós Horthy's nationalist and revanchist policies' (A. Bozóki 'Occupy the State: The Orbán Regime in Hungary', 19(3) (2011) *Journal of Contemporary Central and Eastern Europe* 649, 656). For the illiberal character of counter-constitutionalism and the historical constitution, see Scheppele 'Counter-constitutions'.

[60] See also Blokker, *New Democracies in Crisis?*

[61] K. Szombati, 'The Betrayed Republic: Hungary's New Constitution and the "System of National Cooperation"' (2011) *Heinrich Böll Stiftung*, at www.cz.boell.org/web/52-972.html.

[62] Scheppele, 'Counter-constitutions'.

[63] Cf. Thio, 'Constitutionalism in Illiberal Polities'.

liberal constitutionalism, and a critique of both the 'meta-liberal value of normative individualism' and its understanding of the 'neutral state'. In contrast, illiberal constitutionalism emphasises community interests and the active promotion of a particular vision of communal life.[64] If liberal or legal constitutionalism emphasises a 'court-centric rights-based consti-tutionalism', legal resentment invokes a contrasting vision of individuals embedded in and owing allegiance to a given community, and endorses an understanding of constitutionalism as a means to protect a distinct community, its ethos and its traditions.[65] A communitarian view under-stands the individual as a 'socially embedded' self and the community as highly important in forming the individual.[66] In this view, courts play a 'secondary rather than counterbalancing role' in that a political view of constitutionalism is regarded as corresponding best to a community preservation project.[67] What emerges as a problem for EU democratic oversight is those tensions which stem from the perception that the Rule of Law has been imposed from the outside, undermining local traditions and identities.

Turning to the counter-democracy dimension and the range of existing forms of democratic oversight and civic engagement, the Hungarian case reveals the availability of only a limited range of such forms before the emergence of the counter-constitutional project, and a clear deteriora-tion afterwards. This modest set of options for public engagement and counter-democratic scrutiny has made widespread resistance against the *Fidesz* project more difficult. Here I will explore only one dimension of counter-democratic activity, namely, in the routes to societal engage-ment with constitution-making, constitutional rules and reform. I tend to

---

[64] In the Hungarian Fundamental Law, the emphasis on the Hungarian nation and its cultural legacy is more than evident in the elaborate preamble, which starts with 'We, Members of the Hungarian Nation', as well as in such articles as Article D (protection of Hungarians living abroad) or Article L on marriage ('the family as the basis of the nation's survival'), Fundamental Law 2011. The Fundamental Law further makes the enjoying of rights conditional on satisfying duties, Kis, 'Introduction: From the 1989 Constitution to the 2011 Fundamental Law', 1. In religious terms, the Fundamental Law has been identified as an 'Ode to Christianity and a Reluctance to Separate Church and State'; R. Uitz 'Freedom of Religion and Churches: Archeology in a Constitution-making Assembly', in G. A. Tóth (ed.), *Constitution for a Disunited Nation: On Hungary's 2011 Fundamental Law* (New York/Budapest: Central European University Press, 2011), pp. 197–236.

[65] Thio, 'Constitutionalism in Illiberal Polities', 135–6.

[66] *Ibid.*, 142.   [67] *Ibid.*, 143.

concur with Andrew Arato's analysis that the 1989 Constitution suffered from a lack of empirical or sociological legitimacy.[68] This is particularly the result of the fact that the Roundtable Talks could not claim democratic legitimacy, that important amendments consisted of agreements between only a few political parties rather than being grounded in consensual politics involving the entire political spectrum (in particular the pact between the *Alliance of Free Democrats* and the *Hungarian Democratic Forum* in the early 1990s), and finally, because of the explicitly interim status of the amended constitution. Here I argue that this problem can be taken even further, in that not only did an actual consensus-based final text (which could have resulted in a new constitution supported by a wide range of political forces and approved of by citizens through a confirmatory referendum) fail to emerge, but the role of extra-parliamentary forces in the incremental constitutional amendment process was also limited.[69] The revision process indicates a form of restricted pluralism or parliamentary monism (both before and after 2012), where societal forces are unable to initiate constitutional revision.[70] The constitutional text did not detail the relevant institutions, but the Constitutional Court confirmed the parliamentarism of the Hungarian system in the early 1990s by confirming that only parliament has the right to an initiative for revision.[71]

If the 1989 Constitution ultimately failed to provide opportunities for social input, the 2011 Fundamental Law rather exacerbated than ameliorated this shortcoming. The need for consensual constitution-making enshrined in the four-fifths rule on the adoption of a new constitution[72] – which imposed collaboration between government and opposition – was eliminated by the *Fidesz* government by means of an amendment. The actual constitution-writing process was carried out extremely opaquely by people from the *Fidesz* party who are even now not fully identifiable,

---

[68] A. Arato, *Civil society, Constitution, and Legitimacy* (Lanham, Maryland: Rowman & Littlefield, 2000), p. 40.

[69] Admittedly, one unique institution with potential constitutional implications was that of the *actio popularis*, which allowed individuals and non-governmental organisations and advocacy groups to petition the Constitutional Court directly. This institution was discontinued in the Fundamental Law.

[70] Arato, *Civil Society, Constitution, and Legitimacy*, speaks of the 'Monopoly of a Purely Parliamentary Revision Rule', 153.

[71] 2/1993 [I.22]; Arato, *Civil Society, Constitution, and Legitimacy*, 153–4.

[72] Art. 24(5) of the 1989 Constitution, introduced in 1995.

and rushed through Parliament in March and April 2011.[73] At an earlier stage in 2010, a public consultation process had been started, in which the views of the public, NGOs and opposition parties were solicited, but this process did not involve any direct engagement on draft proposals, nor were its results taken into account in the actual drafting in March 2011.

What becomes clear from this brief discussion of alternative democratic forms in terms of civic and social engagement with Hungarian constitutionalism, is that until the Fundamental Law, few consolidated forms of societal engagement and involvement with constitutionalism developed, and that constitution-making and amendment were largely elite matters. No institutional vehicles (such as constitutional deliberative fora), nor a vibrant societal culture of constitutional 'surveillance' or 'constitutional patriotism' developed in the twenty years of political and constitutional transformation.

IV   Conclusion

This chapter makes a case for a more comprehensive legal and extra-legal, sociological approach to the problem of deviating democracies or 'systemic deficiencies in the Rule of Law' within the EU.[74] I argue for the need for consideration of 'supporting circumstances' in terms of the 'social and political structures and cultural supports'[75] for institutions of the Rule of Law and constitutionalism. In my view, current proposals, including a 'systemic infringement action' and a 'Reverse Solange' mechanism, have too narrow a focus and one-sidedly engage with the legal-formalistic, technical-instrumental side of the Rule of Law and constitutionalism, most tangibly expressed in the proposal for various legal mechanisms and legal and institutional checklists, without engaging in issues of democratic socialisation, value diffusion and reflection, and civic and political engagement and learning. While I realise that widening the relevant field of inquiry regarding the Rule of Law and constitutionalism tends to muddle and complicate the view and brings us further away from clear-cut solutions and modes of interference, this is in a way exactly the intention.

---

[73] K. L. Scheppele, 'Constitutional Coups and Judicial Review: How Transnational Institutions Can Strengthen Peak Courts at Times of Crisis (With Special Reference to Hungary)', 23 (2014) *Transnational Law & Contemporary Problems* 51.

[74] von Bogdandy and Ioannidis, 'Systemic Deficiency in the Rule of Law'.

[75] Krygier, 'The Rule of Law: Legality, Teleology, Sociology', 52.

In my brief discussion of the case of Hungary, I have proposed widening the analysis by focusing on three *problématiques*: of formal and informal dimensions of the law; of universalist and particularist perceptions of the law and of representative and alternative dimensions of constitutional democracy. In terms of the formal and informal dimensions of the law, it is clear that the Hungarian case displays a lack of *sociological legitimacy* of constitutional democracy as well as a lack of the political classes' commitment to constitutionalism and the Rule of Law. Instead, a high degree of *constitutional and legal instrumentalism* is evident, made evident not least in the propensity to engage in comprehensive constitutional reform. In universalistic versus particularistic terms, it is clear that commitment to the Rule of Law and liberal constitutionalism does not widely extend beyond a rather narrow political and legal elite, while both have been frequently apprehended through a particularist lens – emphasising local traditions – and have been widely instrumentalised. The lack of entrenchment of constitutional democracy can be related to a weakly diffused liberal-democratic tradition and the availability of relatively well-established traditions of illiberalism and a related 'legal resentment'. Finally, counter-democratic routes and practices, understood here as important forms of societal counterbalancing and extra-institutional democratic oversight, remain relatively underdeveloped in the Hungarian case.[76]

Returning to the issue of EU democratic oversight and its potential as an antidote for deviant Member States practices, I propose that three areas need more in-depth engagement in both conceptual and practical terms. These areas are related to what Thomas Carothers has indicated as 'type three reforms' in terms of 'changes in the values and attitudes of those in power',[77] but also of citizens and civil society organisations, I would add. In EU democratic oversight, it is important to consider the following dimensions:

1. Regarding the *sociological legitimacy of* and *commitment to the Rule of Law*, how the law and the constitution matter in distinctive cases, by what means, and for whom, needs to be considered and analysed.[78] While proposals for EU democratic oversight predominantly focus

[76] Similar conclusions could be made about Romania.

[77] T. Carothers 'The Rule of Law Revival', 77(2) (1998) *Foreign Affairs* 95.

[78] As suggested by Nicolaïdis and Kleinfeld, 'Rethinking Europe's "Rule of Law" and Enlargement Agenda', 50–3, one could develop new methodologies for sociological surveying and the assessment of civic, political and administrative attitudes. A further area of interest

on persuading and correcting governments, it is crucial that the civic awareness of legality, constitutionality and rights is raised. Without significant civic engagement, it is difficult to see how durable social and political attachment to the law and 'constitutional patriotism' could emerge. As one example, the sociological legitimacy of constitutional frameworks is likely to be importantly enhanced by the allowance for consequential public constitutional debate *ex ante* in constitutional revision processes, and the use of constitutional referenda on constitutional revision *ex post*. In general, EU democratic oversight would do well to recommend governments to pursue open, transparent and inclusive legal and constitutional reform processes.

2. Regarding an *interpretative approach* towards the Rule of Law, it is crucial to identify, map and assess distinctive local contextual issues concerning the Rule of Law and democracy. These could include problematic or incomplete forms of social and political integration around constitutions, problematic legal-constitutional legacies and/or the local 'translation' of legal transplants.[79] In the case of the New Member States, such problems should at least be partially understood as parts of complex processes of post-communist transformation. A crucial issue is the incomplete *Vergangenheitsbewältigung* or confrontation with the past in various societies (for instance, regarding the contestation of the nature of the regime change, as in Hungary, or the problematic way past injustice has been dealt with, as in the case of public access to the *Securitate* archives in Romania).[80]

3. Regarding *societal democratic oversight* and *civic empowerment*, enablement, political engagement and participation by a variety of actors needs greater emphasis in democratic oversight. This points to the need for support for and empowerment of distinctive actors, such as local actors, civil society groups and an independent media.[81] Of importance here is the extent to which citizens are able to monitor and publicise the behaviour of political elites, to mobilise resistance to policies and political projects, and to use institutional channels and

---

could be the promotion of an intra-European dialogue on higher educational curricula regarding the Rule of Law and forms of legitimacy.

[79] It would be crucial to promote the creation of European-wide networks of scholars and professionals, in which national specificities and problems with the Rule of Law can be assessed and debated.

[80] Iancu, 'Post-Accession Constitutionalism with a Human Face'.

[81] Support for intra-European civil society networks and pro-democracy organisations is relevant here.

legal instruments to counter such policies and projects. Particularly in cases in which democratic deviancy is the result of an explicit political programme (and the abuse of a dominant position) by an incumbent government, the socialisation and empowerment of societal counter-forces is of great significance. As mentioned above, a crucial area in this respect is the encouragement of civic participation in constitutional reform.

13

Why Improve EU Oversight of Rule of Law?

The Two-Headed Problem of Defending Liberal Democracy and Fighting Corruption

MILADA ANNA VACHUDOVA[*]

I Introduction

While the focus of this book is on how the EU should monitor and foster the Rule of Law in EU Member States, the purpose of this chapter is to explain when and how the Rule of Law became a centrepiece of EU conditionality in the pre-accession process, and what lessons from this process could help create enduring and effective instruments for the EU to help combat corruption in EU Member States. I argue that EU efforts to safeguard the Rule of Law in all of its Member States should focus equally on defending liberal democratic institutions and on preventing widespread, high-level corruption that can lead to state capture.[1] Concerns about the EU's inability to sanction anti-democratic behaviour have been heightened by the Fidesz party's rule in Hungary, which has severely attacked democratic institutions and used corrupt practices to capture the state and the economy.[2] However, high-level corruption and

---

[*] University of North Carolina at Chapel Hill, Department of Political Science.

[1] On the roads to state capture in the post-communist world see: J. Hellman, 'Winners Take All: The Politics of Partial Reform in Post-Communist Transitions', 50(1) (1998) *World Politics* 203; J. Kornai and S. Rose-Ackerman, *Building a Trustworthy State in Post-Socialist Societies* (New York: Palgrave, 2004); V. I. Ganev, *Preying on the State: The Transformation of Bulgaria after 1989* (Ithaca: Cornell University Press, 2007). J. Gould, *The Politics of Privatization: Wealth and Power in Postcommunist Europe* (Boulder, CO: Lynne Rienner Press, 2011); D. Dolenec, *Democratic Institutions and Authoritarian Rule in Southeast Europe* (Colchester: ECPR Press, 2013); A. Kleibrink, *Political Elites and Decentralisation Reforms in Post-Socialist Balkans: Regional Patronage Networks in Serbia and Croatia* (Basingstoke: Palgrave Macmillan, 2015).

[2] On the anti-democratic developments in Hungary, see the chapter by K. L. Scheppele, 'Enforcing the Basic Principles of EU Law through Systemic Infringement Procedures', in this volume.

state capture can come more stealthily – without such a grand nationalist project and without such overt tampering with existing democratic institutions.

The effects of corruption are significant. Over time, unchecked high-level corruption and state capture erode the Rule of Law and other aspects of liberal democracy.[3] Political elites violate the legal limits of their power to steal money and gain power, flaunting the Rule of Law and corrupting executive and judicial institutions.[4] More broadly, the work of state officials and institutions is corrupted: the state acts for private gain instead of the public good. Civil society groups are often oppressed or co-opted by powerful networks. The citizenry loses trust in state institutions and becomes cynical about politics, withdrawing from democratic participation.[5] Corruption also impoverishes society by reducing economic growth, increasing income inequality, undermining entrepreneurship and, of course, stealing money which could have been used by the state for investments in areas such as education and infrastructure which in turn help grow the economy.[6]

Thus far, however, the governments of certain EU Member States have strongly resisted giving EU institutions substantial tools to protect democratic institutions or combat corruption. EU institutions defend market rules and economic freedoms much more strongly than the Rule of Law or democracy.[7] The main reason is that high levels of corruption are also found in some of the EU's old Member States. The divide on corruption is not between the West and the East, or between the old and the new. Across corruption indexes and over time, old EU members

---

[3] On the Rule of Law and state capture, see also J.-W. Müller, 'Protecting the Rule of Law (and Democracy!) in the EU: The Idea of a Copenhagen Commission' and P. Blokker, 'EU Democratic Oversight and Domestic Deviation from the Rule of Law: Sociological Reflections' in this volume.

[4] On the difference between state capture and lower level forms of corruption, see R. Karklins, *The System Made Me Do It: Corruption in Post-Communist Societies* (Armonk, New York: M.E. Sharpe, 2005); and S. Rose-Ackerman, *Corruption and Government: Causes, Consequences, and Reform* (Cambridge: Cambridge University Press, 1996).

[5] On the relationship between corruption and democratic participation, see B. Ceka, 'The Perils of Political Competition: Explaining Participation and Trust in Political Parties in Eastern Europe', 46 (12) (2003) *Comparative Political Studies* 1610.

[6] S. Gupta, H. Davoodi and R. Alonso-Terme, 'Does Corruption Affect Income, Inequality and Poverty?', 3(1) (2002) *Economics of Governance* 23.

[7] On how the EU's integration strategies may undermine democratic governance, see L. Bruszt, 'Regional Normalization and National Deviations: EU Integration and the Backsliding of Democracy in Europe's Eastern Periphery' (May 2015), unpublished paper on file with the author.

Greece and Italy are ranked as just as corrupt as the two most corrupt post-communist EU members, Romania and Bulgaria. Spain, meanwhile, was perceived as more corrupt than Poland in the 2014 corruption rankings of Transparency International.[8] For decades already, Greece and Italy, often joined by Spain and even France, have preferred to keep the struggle against corruption out of the hands of EU institutions.[9] As I discuss below and in other work, this has crippled the ability to combat corruption in the EU's post-communist candidates by using EU leverage as part of the pre-accession process.[10] This was sorely needed because corruption has been a severe problem in many post-communist EU candidates. The end of the communist system created a political and economic vacuum – and spectacular opportunities for elites to steal from the state. Those in power could write rules to benefit themselves. Even when adequate rules were written, actors could rely on political connections, dysfunctional state institutions and corrupt judiciaries to perpetuate corrupt practices and prevent prosecution.[11]

The rest of this chapter is divided into five parts. The first part explores the conditionality of the EU's pre-accession process – and how EU leverage has helped foster democratic institutions and regimes in post-communist Europe after 1989. The second part sets out the limits of EU leverage, which turn out to include the design of institutions critical to strong Rule of Law protection and to combating corruption. The third part looks at the Cooperation and Verification Mechanism, an innovative tool of EU leverage created to deal with severe Rule of Law and corruption problems in Romania and Bulgaria on the eve of their accession in 2007. The fourth part argues that EU leverage continues to have a positive impact on the Western Balkan candidates, in part because of a new strategy for increasing conditionality in the design of institutions which safeguard the Rule of Law and prosecute the fight against corruption. The fifth part reflects on how the EU might move forward in creating incentives for all Member States to safeguard the Rule of Law.

---

[8] The Transparency International Corruption Perception Index for 2014 can be found at www.transparency.org/cpi2014/results. See also the Worldwide Governance Indicators (WGI) project of the World Bank directed by D. Kaufmann, A. Kraay and M. Mastruzzi at http://info.worldbank.org/governance/wgi/index.aspx#home.

[9] Personal interviews, European Council and European Commission, 1998, 2001, 2004.

[10] M. A. Vachudova, 'Corruption and Compliance in the EU's Post-Communist Members and Candidates', 47(1) (2009) *JCMS* 43.

[11] J. Kornai and S. Rose-Ackerman, *Building a Trustworthy State in Post-Socialist Societies* (New York: Palgrave Macmillan, 2004).

II   The Leverage of the European Union

EU enlargement has been a remarkable tool for fostering domestic change which has included strengthening the Rule of Law and improving democratic institutions. Indeed, I have argued that enlargement has been the most successful democracy promotion policy ever implemented by an external actor.[12] It is worth stressing, however, that the bar for the EU here is very low: scholars have generally found that external actors have had little success in fostering democratisation from the outside.[13] The EU, moreover, has not acted alone, and its influence has more or less been limited to credible future EU members. When it comes to the mechanics of EU leverage, for twenty years now the basic equation underpinning the enlargement decision has not changed: the substantial benefits of joining the EU and the costs of being excluded create incentives for post-communist governments to satisfy the EU's comparatively high entry requirements. Membership brings economic benefits and also a very agreeable geopolitical change in fortunes through the protection of EU rules, a new status *vis-à-vis* neighbouring states and a voice in EU institutions.[14] These benefits continue to be substantial despite the financial crisis and the loss of confidence which have plagued European integration since 2008.[15] In comparison, other international organisations and other kinds of external actors still have, individually, much less to offer – and have asked for much less in return.[16] For all of the benefits of membership, however, joining the EU does not mean overcoming longstanding economic backwardness for most post-communist regions and states.[17]

---

[12] M. A. Vachudova, *Europe Undivided: Democracy, Leverage and Integration after Communism* (Oxford: Oxford University Press, 2005).

[13] Among many, G. O'Donnell and P. Schmitter, *Transitions from Authoritarian Rule* (Baltimore: Johns Hopkins University Press, 1986); and V. Bunce, 'The Political Economy of Postsocialism', 58 (4) (1999) *Slavic Review* 756.

[14] M. A. Vachudova, *Europe Undivided*; F. Schimmelfennig and U. Sedelmeier, 'Governance by Conditionality: EU Rule Transfer to the Candidate Countries of Central and Eastern Europe', 11 (2004) *JEPP* 661.

[15] M. A. Vachudova, 'EU Leverage and National Interests in the Balkans: The Puzzles of Enlargement Ten Years On', 52(1) (2014) *JCMS* 122.

[16] On the utility for democratising states to join certain kinds of international organisations, see E. Mansfield and J. Pevehouse, 'Democratization and the Varieties of International Organizations', 52(3) (2008) *Journal of Conflict Resolution* 269.

[17] R. Epstein, 'Overcoming "Economic Backwardness" in the European Union', 52(1) (2014) *JCMS* 17. See also R. Epstein and W. Jacoby, 'Eastern Enlargement Ten Years On: Transcending the East–West Divide?', 52(1) (2014) *JCMS* 1.

What kinds of domestic changes can EU leverage really help bring about, and what are the causal mechanisms which translate EU policies into consequential domestic change? In its most basic form, the EU enlargement process helps lay bare the agency of elites and the weakness of institutions. Scholars have shown how the EU's pre-accession process has shaped policymaking in specific policy areas where the EU's *acquis* is extensive and well enforced.[18] Here, the key causal mechanisms include government officials responding directly to conditionality, and domestic actors using the EU process to further their *acquis*-compatible policy goals. EU leverage is, however, very weak in areas where the EU does not have a well-developed *acquis* – and, as we discuss below, this is precisely the case when it comes to tools purpose-built to combat corruption.[19]

Over time, the ways EU leverage translates into domestic change in areas where the *acquis* is strong can be fascinating and complicated: Conor O'Dwyer shows, for example, that in the area of LGBT rights, it was the mobilisation of hostile groups in response to the EU's demands that sparked the mobilisation and organisation of groups which have been able to push domestically not just for legislative changes but also for changes in social attitudes.[20]

More broadly, EU leverage can help determine regime type by pushing states eligible to become candidates from one trajectory of political change to another. While in some cases EU leverage reinforces an existing liberal democratic trajectory, in other cases it has been critical in helping to move a state away from illiberal or authoritarian rule.[21] Here, the causal mechanisms centre around political parties: over time even formerly authoritarian political parties adopt an EU-compatible agenda

---

[18] R. Epstein, *In Pursuit of Liberalism: the Power and Limits of International Institutions in Postcommunist Europe* (Baltimore: The Johns Hopkins Press, 2008); H. Grabbe, *The EU's Transformative Power: Europeanization through Conditionality in Central and Eastern Europe* (New York: Palgrave Macmillan, 2006); W. Jacoby, *The Enlargement of the European Union and NATO: Ordering from the Menu in Central Europe* (Cambridge: Cambridge University Press, 2004); J. G. Kelley, *Ethnic Politics in Europe: The Power of Norms and Incentives* (Princeton, NJ: Princeton University Press, 2004).

[19] D. Kochenov, *EU Enlargement and the Failure of Conditionality: Pre-accession Conditionality in the Fields of Democracy and the Rule of Law* (Alphen aan den Rijn: Kluwer Law International, 2008).

[20] C. O'Dwyer, 'Does the EU Help or Hinder Gay-Rights Movements in Postcommunist Europe? The Case of Poland', 28(4) (2012) *East European Politics and Societies* 332.

[21] M. A. Vachudova, *Europe Undivided*. See also D. Cameron, 'Post-Communist Democracy: The Impact of the European Union', 23(3) (2007) *Post-Soviet Affairs* 185.

in order to stay in the political game, because competing political parties, interest groups, local civil society groups and even voters coalesce around the goal of joining the EU.[22] The case of Macedonia provides a stark counterpoint. Since Greece used its veto to make any progress in the EU's pre-accession process impossible for Macedonia, the political parties have used nationalism to justify corruption and state capture on a massive scale, obviously moving far from an EU-compatible governing agenda.[23]

What has changed dramatically over the last decade is how scholars and other observers debate the merits of the EU's enlargement process for the quality of democracy and the functioning of EU institutions in new and prospective members. For years, many observers argued that the EU was too heavy handed and too dictatorial in imposing its rules and institutions on post-communist members, thereby undermining fledgling democratic institutions and processes. This concern has been almost entirely eclipsed by criticism that the EU was not stringent, explicit and consistent enough in its demands – and not vigilant enough in its enforcement. This criticism is fuelled by frustration at the assault on liberal democracy in today's Hungary, and by the problems with corruption and the Rule of Law in Bulgaria and Romania. While Hungary's assault on liberal democracy stems from an exceptional set of circumstances, the problems with corruption and the Rule of Law are more universal and perhaps more urgent. Other recent graduates of the EU's pre-accession process such as the Czech Republic and Slovakia are also playgrounds for elites who prey on the state, and reform may be even more challenging in the Western Balkan candidates where war, sanctions and isolation have warped more profoundly the rebuilding of the state after communism.[24]

---

[22] M. A. Vachudova, 'Tempered by the EU? Political Parties and Party Systems before and after Accession', 15(6) (2008) *JEPP* 861; M. A. Vachudova, 'The Puzzles of Enlargement'.

[23] On state capture by the government of Gruevski government culminating in a national crisis in 2015, see B. Ceka, 'The Tug of War in Macedonia' *Foreign Affairs*, 3 June 2015, at www.foreignaffairs.com/articles/macedonia/2015-06-03/tug-war-macedonia; F. Bieber and A. Vangeli, 'Macedonia's Gruevski does not Deserve any more Chances', European Leadership Network, 22 June 2015, at www.europeanleadershipnetwork .org/macedonias-gruevski-does-not-deserve-any-more-chances_2868.html. See also E. Fouéré, 'The Worsening Crisis in Macedonia: Waiting for EU Leadership', Center for European Policy Studies, 13 April 2015, at www.ceps.eu/publications/ worsening-crisis-macedonia-waiting-eu-leadership. For an overview of the Greek veto of Macedonia's negotiations on EU accession, see 'Macedonia's Dispute with Greece', European Stability Initiative, at www.esiweb.org/index.php?lang=en&id=562.

[24] D. Dolenec, *Democratic Institutions and Authoritarian Rule in Southeast Europe*.

In this area, it is fair to say that too many scholars have mirrored the behaviour of politicians: it is easier for politicians to blame the EU for what frustrates their voters than to offer them a necessarily complicated picture of real causes and possible remedies. Similarly, when faced with stalled or shoddy reform in a prospective or new EU member, it is easier for scholars to point to the shortcomings of EU policy than to untangle the complicated domestic factors which have allowed contented power holders to perpetuate the status quo. It is ultimately domestic actors who respond to EU incentives – or not – as they make choices about the pace and quality of reform. Given the complexity, breadth and relative uniformity of the EU's accession requirements, the great variation in outcomes even across the EU's ten new post-communist members underscores that many details of domestic reform have largely been determined by domestic factors.

III   The Limits of EU Leverage

This brings us back to the question of the nature and durability of domestic changes which occur in response to EU leverage.[25] The answer is probably best tackled through the counterfactual: how much worse would things look if the country had been denied the prospects of EU membership? Even Romania and Bulgaria, the mal-performers of EU enlargement, have made progress in some areas.[26] Ten years on, there is not a single country on the EU's borders with an association agreement but without the prospects of membership which can be described as a stable liberal democracy with a well-functioning market economy. And while the recent illiberal behaviour of governments has caused concern, there is no question that EU membership has had a restraining influence on

---

[25] For thoughtful discussion, T. Haughton, 'Half Full but also Half Empty: Conditionality, Compliance and the Quality of Democracy in Central and Eastern Europe', 5(2) (2008) *Political Studies Review* 233; and A. Dimitrova, 'The New Member States of the EU in the Aftermath of Enlargement: Do New European Rules Remain Empty Shells?', 17(1) (2010) *JEPP* 137.

[26] P. Levitz and G. Pop-Eleches, 'Why no Backsliding? The European Union's Impact on Democracy and Governance before and after Accession', 43(4) (2010) *Comparative Political Studies* 457; U. Sedelmeier, 'Europeanisation after Accession: Leaders, Laggards, and Lock-In', 35(1) (2012) *West European Politics* 20; A. Spendzharova and M. A. Vachudova, 'Catching up? Consolidating Liberal Democracy after EU Accession', 35(1) (2012) *West European Politics* 39; V. Ganev, 'Post-Accession Hooliganism: Democratic Governance in Bulgaria and Romania after 2007', 27(1) (2013) *East European Politics & Societies* 26.

them.[27] Nevertheless, the egregious ways with which the government of Viktor Orbán has dismantled liberal democracy in Hungary have revealed how little the EU can do to rein in or reverse policies which erode the quality of democracy.[28] Indeed, the EU and IMF policies which forced austerity on Hungary helped Orbán to win such great power in several important ways; subsequently, neither EU nor IMF policies could restrain him.[29] And in the case of the behaviour of the Hungarian government today, there is relatively little evidence that the EU's social environment has restrained Fidesz's takeover of the Hungarian state and polity. This has in turn raised the questions of whether and how the EU should bolster its ability to materially punish democratic backsliding among existing Member States.[30]

As I highlighted in the introduction, it is important to identify and address two different if overlapping problems among EU members. The first is the Hungary problem: the ruling Fidesz party is dismantling the 'liberal' in a liberal democracy.[31] It has used its parliamentary supermajority to concentrate power in the hands of party members, chiefly by passing legislation and constitutional amendments but also by violating norms related to the participation of rival political party members and independent individuals in the running of public institutions.[32] The second is the endemic corruption problem: rent-seeking elites taking advantage of weak Rule of Law and a weak state to capture state institutions and funnel public money to private bank accounts.[33] Some of this corruption

---

[27] G. Pop-Eleches, 'Learning from Mistakes: Romanian Democracy and the Hungarian Precedent', Newsletter of the European Politics and Society Section of the American Political Science Association, Winter 2013; J. Wittenberg, 'Back to the Future? Revolution of the Right in Hungary', *East European Politics and Societies* (2016, forthcoming); U. Sedelemeier, 'Anchoring Democracy from above? The European Union's Measures against Democratic Backsliding in Hungary and Romania after Accession', 52(1) (2014) *JCMS* 105.

[28] K. L. Scheppele, 'The Rule of Law and the Frankenstate: Why Governance Checklists Do Not Work', 26(4) (2013) *Governance* 559.

[29] J. Johnson and A. Barnes, 'Financial Nationalism and Its International Enablers: The Hungarian Experience', 22(3) (2015) *Review of International Political Economy* 535.

[30] C. Closa, D. Kochenov and J. H. H. Weiler, 'Reinforcing Rule of Law Oversight in the European Union', EUI Working Paper No. 2014/25, RSCAS.

[31] Viktor Orbán's Hungary: 'An Illiberal Democracy', *The Hungarian Spectator*, 26 July 2014, at http://hungarianspectrum.wordpress.com/2014/07/26/viktor-orbans-hungary-an-illiberal-democracy/.

[32] See K. L. Scheppele, 'Enforcing the Basic Principles of EU Law' and also P. Blokker, 'EU Democratic Oversight and Domestic Deviation from the Rule of Law'.

[33] J. Gould, 'Out of the Blue? Democracy and Privatization in Post-Communist Europe' 1(3) (2004) *Comparative European Politics* 277.

is certainly organised by and around political parties – but it needs no constitutional majority to go forward, and in some areas it is agnostic about which political parties are in power.

A good example of how economic elites can capture state institutions quietly is the Czech Republic. Without any grand nationalist narrative or any dramatic constitutional tampering, the Czech government seems to have been captured almost entirely. The constitutional shenanigans of the Czech president Miloš Zeman in 2013 raised alarm bells about the spread of 'the Hungary problem': this was really nothing compared to the endemic corruption over the last twenty years which the police and judiciary have barely touched – and which appears now to be accelerating. This corruption, in turn, has pushed voters towards new, populist and anti-establishment parties that promise much but deliver little.[34]

The capture of the Czech state by oligarchic economic interests has deepened as the country's second richest oligarch, Andrej Babiš, has gained substantial political power. Until the October 2013 elections, the relatively strong media and civil society in the Czech Republic had staved off 'state capture' – what political scientists call the capture of the state to serve the narrow political and economic interests of a small elite.[35] The October 2013 elections amounted to a 'political earthquake' for the Czech party system as the new ANO party managed an electoral breakthrough, receiving 18.65% of the vote (and 47 seats) at the expense of established right and left-wing parties. After a strong showing in the Senate and local elections in the Czech Republic in October 2014, one commentator observed 'Babiš undoubtedly represents a grave danger due to the concentration of political, economic and media power which has no precedent in the democratic stages of our history'.[36]

ANO stands for *Akce nespokojených občanu*, or Movement of Dissatisfied Citizens. It was founded in 2011 by the billionaire Andrej Babiš, the second-richest man in the Czech Republic[37] and the sole owner of the

---

[34] S. Hanley and A. Sikk, 'Economy, Corruption or Floating Voters? Explaining the Breakthroughs of Anti-establishment Reform Parties in Eastern Europe' 22 (2016) *Party Politics* 522.

[35] A. Innes, 'The Political Economy of State Capture in Central Europe', 52(1) (2014) *JCMS* 88.

[36] J. Leschtina, 'Bědovat nad Babišem uz nestačí', *Respekt*, 17 October 2014, at http://respekt .ihned.cz/externi-hlasy/c1-62960970-bedovat-nad-babisem-uz-nestaci.

[37] Forbes estimates Babiš's net worth at USD 2.4 billion and ranks him the 779th richest person in the world. See www.forbes.com/profile/andrej-babis/.

company Agrofert Holding, a large food and chemicals conglomerate.[38] Agrofert is valued at nearly EUR 2 billion. In January 2014 ANO became a coalition partner in the new Czech government, and Babiš became Deputy Prime Minister and the Minister of Finance.[39] The scale of Babiš's economic and political power is enormous, especially in the context of a country as small as the Czech Republic.[40] One metric is the 'Global Billionaires Political Power Index' published in September 2014, which ranks Babiš as the fifth most politically powerful billionaire in the world.[41] Babiš stands out in the top twenty on that list: he is the only billionaire who is a member of government in a democratic country. But what has landed Babiš so high on this list is that he has used his wealth to dominate the Czech polity. This has included hugely increasing his influence over the supervisory boards of many state-owned companies, replacing many government officials in ANO-controlled ministries with people with very close connections to *Agrofert*, using his media empire to exert pressure on his rivals and even on his coalition partners – all the while deflecting criticism about the colossal conflicts of interest stemming from his ownership of *Agrofert* and also about the close associations which he, as well as many of his closest associates, had with the Czechoslovak communist secret police before 1989.[42] For their part, the opposition is weak – and the Czech president has revealed himself as a strong ally of Babiš, even siding with him in disputes among the three coalition parties.[43]

Babiš emerged from political obscurity to run such a successful election campaign by accusing the established political parties of incompetence and corruption, and promising that he would run the state 'efficiently'

---

[38] For background on Babiš and the rise of Agrofert, see J. Spurný, 'The Richest Czech Keeps his Secret', *Respekt in English*, 13 May 2002, at http://respekt.ihned.cz/respekt-in-english/c1-36325060-the-richest-czech-keeps-a-secret.

[39] This government is a coalition between the Czech Social Democratic Party (ČSSD), the Christian and Democratic Union – Czechoslovak People's Party (KDU-ČSL), and ANO. The Prime Minister is ČSSD leader Bohuslav Sobotka.

[40] 'Babiš bez Bureše: Hvezda české politiky si vyzehlila minulost, k duveryhdnosti ale bude potreba víc', *Respekt*, 28 June 2014.

[41] This Index has been created by Darrell West for his forthcoming Brookings Institution Press book *Billionaires: Reflections on the Upper Crust*. The book explores 'the political uses of great wealth'. For more information, see: www.brookings.edu/research/interactives/2014/billionaires-global-political-power-index.

[42] 'Kvetnovy žebríček popularity politiku', *STEM – Stredisko empirickych vyzkumu*, 6 June 2014, at www.stem.cz/clanek/2957.

[43] J. Candole, 'Keeping an Eye on Andrej', *Aktualne.cz*, 15 January 2014, at http://blog.aktualne.cz/~ikr~/blogy/james-de-candole.php?itemid=22046.

thanks to his experience as a successful businessman.[44] ANO campaigned almost exclusively on this 'clean hands' platform, pledging to fight vigorously against corruption and tax evasion. As highly respected Czech journalist Adam Drda points out in *The European Voice*, 'The Czech Republic is now a paradox: a society disgusted with corruption has given huge power to a man whose business interests amount to the biggest conflict of interest in the country's post-1989 history'.[45] So far the EU has done nothing to check Babiš's power: indeed, there has likely been nothing that it could do given the tools at hand.

IV   The Cooperation and Verification Mechanism (CVM)

The Cooperation and Verification Mechanism (CVM) was an attempt to create tools which *would* extend some of the EU's leverage in the pre-accession process to the post-accession period for two new members – Romania and Bulgaria. Unlike the Czech Republic or any other EU Member State, Romania and Bulgaria were identified by EU leaders as having unacceptably high levels of corruption at the time of accession.[46] The CVM consists mainly of monitoring and reporting on whether governments and state institutions have complied with benchmarks in the areas of judicial reform, the fight against corruption and, for Bulgaria, the fight against organised crime. Some scholars have rightly argued that the CVM, having only very weak enforcement mechanisms, has been unequal to these monumental tasks.[47] Others, however, have shown that the CVM did have some effect: specific legislative and institutional reforms were clearly pushed through in response to the CVM reports, especially when progress was tied either, early on, to the provision of EU funds or, more

---

[44] V. Havlík, 'The Economic Crisis in the Shadow of Political Crisis: The Rise of Party Populism in the Czech Republic', in H. Kriesi and T. S. Pappas (eds.), *European Populism in the Shadow of the Great Recession* (Colchester: ECPR Press, 2015), p. 199.

[45] A. Drda, 'Andrej Babiš – Czech oligarch: Profile of the Czech Republic's Finance Minister and Deputy Prime Minister', *The European Voice*, 19 September 2014, at www.europeanvoice.com/article/andrej-babis-czech-oligarch/.

[46] For tables showing how perceptions of corruption compare across EU Member States, see Vachudova, 'Corruption and Compliance in the EU's Post-Communist Members and Candidates'.

[47] E. Gateva, 'Post-Accession Conditionality – Translating Benchmarks into Political Pressure?', 29(4) (2013) *East European Politics* 420; and V. Ganev, 'Post-Accession Hooliganism: Democratic Governance in Bulgaria and Romania after 2007', 27(1) (2013) *East European Politics and Societies* 26.

recently, to entry into Schengen by Germany and some other EU Member States.

Constitutional tampering to concentrate power in Hungary post EU accession can be described as 'backsliding' in the quality of democracy. But it is worth pointing out that this is not the case for corruption. The EU's new post-communist members did not slide backwards; they joined the EU with a weak judiciary and very high levels of corruption in place. Several current Member States consistently blocked attempts by the European Commission to highlight corruption and even problems with the judiciary in the Regular Reports, and to demand institutional changes to address them. The logic for states such as Italy, Greece and even France was that they did not want corruption to become part of the EU's purview.[48] It was only when the corruption problems in Bulgaria and Romania hit their national media during the growing financial crisis that some EU governments could be persuaded to address the problem.

By 2006, things had changed dramatically as EU governments recognised the extent of the corruption problem in Bulgaria and Romania. The Commission reported that only feeble attempts had been made by either government to fight corruption, crack down on organised crime and strengthen the judiciary. It asked for immediate action, especially on institutional reform. Bulgaria and Romania were held back from concluding negotiations in 2002 and joining the EU in 2004 with the eight other post-communist states due to concerns that their institutions and economies were unprepared to implement the EU's *acquis*. A key component of this concern was widespread corruption and the lack of transparency and professionalism of state institutions, especially the judiciary. When Bulgaria and Romania did become members of the EU in 2007, their membership came with an unprecedented condition: an ongoing Cooperation and Verification Mechanism (CVM) that the Commission would use to monitor whether they lived up to their outstanding commitments in satisfying the requirements of EU membership.[49]

The CVM is a tool to maintain the reform momentum in the two countries and prevent reversal of the Rule of Law reforms enacted during

---

[48] Personal interview, officials of the European Commission and the European Council, 2003, 2005.

[49] See European Commission, 'Commission Decision of 13 December 2006 establishing a mechanism for cooperation and verification of progress in Romania to address specific benchmarks in the areas of judicial reform and the fight against corruption', C(2006) 6570 final; and its Bulgarian counterpart. Both are available at http://ec.europa.eu/cvm/index_en.htm.

the EU accession negotiations. Every six months, the Council issues a CVM report for Bulgaria and Romania, evaluating progress on the established benchmarks and flagging the most pressing issues which should be addressed before the next report.[50] These monitoring reports have been praised for being very detailed and for following the evolution of specific administrative reforms, judicial cases and political developments.[51] As such, they have played an important role in gathering and disseminating information about the state of reform in both countries. The main reports have been published in July and the so-called interim 'technical' reports or updates have come in February.

The CVM had the most traction on Bulgarian and Romanian governments when ruling political parties saw a positive report as being directly tied to their electoral chances. Unlike in Hungary, EU institutions are highly trusted by the citizens of Bulgaria and Romania – far more than their own institutions – and this can give the EU considerable traction. However, the CVM was reminiscent of the pre-accession process for all ten of the post-communist new members in areas such as the reform of the public administration and the judiciary: it seemed as if the EU did not believe in its own mechanism. The number of officials working on it was so small and, more importantly, the sanctions attached to misbehaviour were very limited from the start.

In an article evaluating the CVM, Aneta Spendzharova and I concluded that it has been a controversial and modest but nevertheless successful instance of innovation by the EU as it has extended the EU's active leverage into the post-accession period.[52] The Romanian and Bulgarian governments have both responded to specific demands in the CVM reports, strongly suggesting that in the absence of the CVM there would have been less reform. The detailed monitoring and assessment in the CVM reports, coupled with political pressure and concrete sanctions, can deliver substantial results.[53] Given the huge problems besetting the Rule of Law, judicial quality and the fight against corruption in the Western Balkans states, the EU would do well to set up a CVM structure for each

---

[50] The reports are available at http://ec.europa.eu/cvm/.
[51] U. Sedelmeier, C. Lacatus and A. Dimitrova, 'The Power of Monitoring without Enforcement? The European Union's "Cooperation and Verification Mechanism" and Anti-corruption Policy in Romania and Bulgaria', unpublished paper.
[52] Spendzharova and Vachudova, 'Catching up?'.
[53] For more on Romania's Rule of Law reforms, M. Hein, 'The Fight against Government Corruption in Romania: Irreversible Results or Sisyphean Challenge?', 67(5) (2015) Europe-Asia Studies 747.

acceding state. This could always be dismantled rapidly if it were found to be unneeded. Some have observed a significant deterioration in the comportment of public officials in the areas of accountability, transparency and combating corruption after their country joined the EU. A CVM structure would help deter backsliding.

EU pressure can be powerful when it is twinned with domestic incentives related to winning elections and holding power. Civil society groups play an essential role in highlighting corruption and the need for judicial reform. The EU needs to rethink the civil society funding which is funnelled through government institutions, since this undermines the readiness of civil society groups to highlight corruption. EU leverage tied to the CVM process is more also effective in motivating governments if the EU threatens to withhold something that voters really want. The decision by some EU members in late 2010 and 2011 to block Romania's and Bulgaria's Schengen entry as a sanction for not meeting CVM benchmarks, did help trigger reform in both countries, since Schengen membership is valued by citizens.[54]

V   What about the Western Balkans?

Meanwhile, the EU enlargement process continues in the Western Balkans. Some Western Balkan candidates and proto-candidates are responding to the incentives of EU membership in much the same way as their post-communist predecessors in the membership queue did. As predicted, in some cases, political parties have fundamentally changed their agendas to make them EU-compatible, and governments have implemented dramatic policy changes to move forward in the pre-accession process.[55] The underlying dynamic of the EU enlargement process remains asymmetric interdependence: the candidate states stand to gain more from joining the EU than existing members do.[56] It is therefore in their national interest to comply with extensive entry requirements in order to secure membership through a lengthy and uncompromising process – and one which arguably imposes more conditions on the Western Balkan candidates than on previous candidates, and which interferes more extensively in areas related

---

[54] Spendzharova and Vachudova, 'Catching up?'.
[55] Vachudova, 'The Puzzles of Enlargement'.
[56] A. Moravcsik and M. A. Vachudova, 'National Interests, State Power, and EU Enlargement', 17(1) (2003) *East European Politics and Societies* 42.

to national sovereignty and identity, where its legitimacy and efficacy is being strained.[57]

State capture has been greatest in post-communist states where a narrow group of elites initially governed with little political competition from other political forces, and with little effective scrutiny from the media and civic groups. All of the Western Balkan states fit this bill. Authoritarian rule gave ruling elites absolute power in Croatia, Serbia and Montenegro from 1990 to 2000, and war and sanctions intensified the grip of organised crime on the economy. In the three constituent nations of Bosnia the same nationalist parties have controlled the different parts of the state since 1990 and continue to control much of the country's economic activity for the benefit of the few at the expense of the many. There has been greater political competition in Macedonia and Albania, but in conditions of extremely weak administrative capacity and little or no willingness to combat corruption. Throughout the region, elites protect old clientalistic networks and the rewards of a partially reformed economy: they benefit from relationships with organised crime but are also intimidated and pressured into protecting them from prosecution.[58]

Croatia has nevertheless made important strides – and now Montenegro and Serbia may follow suit.[59] EU leverage on these candidates is impressive if you evaluate it from the perspective of the difficulty of the issues it has forced governments to confront. And the confrontation continues: in response to the more significant domestic problems of the Western Balkan candidates and the shortcomings of the EU's newest members, the EU has made some important changes to its pre-accession process. Territorial issues, for example, must be resolved early in the process. Once negotiations begin, they begin with Chapters 23 and 24, the most difficult chapters, which cover the Rule of Law and the fight against organised crime and corruption. These chapters remain open for the duration of the negotiations, with interim and closing benchmarks being set by the European Commission to keep each candidate making steady progress.

As EU leverage zeroes in on building independent institutions and fighting corruption, it does pose a greater threat to the wealth and power

---

[57] G. Noutcheva, *European Foreign Policy and the Challenges of Balkan Accession: Conditionality, Legitimacy and Compliance* (London: Routledge, 2012).

[58] Personal interviews, government officials in Belgrade, Sarajevo and Skopje, 2005, 2008, 2012.

[59] F. Bieber 'Building Impossible States? State-Building Strategies and EU Membership in the Western Balkans', 63(10) (2011) *Europe-Asia Studies* 1783.

of entrenched rent-seeking elites than before. As Croatia's membership path and the sentencing of its former pro-European Prime Minister on corruption charges illustrates, what is good for the country as a whole is not necessarily good for corrupt ruling elites, and it remains to be seen how many can be unseated by political competition in concert with EU leverage. Conditionality is credible only because the EU is willing to stop the process when a government does not make progress on crucial domestic reforms. For this reason, the enlargement process must some-times come to a standstill for some candidates – and this is not necessarily a sign that it is being poorly managed. That said, in certain areas the EU is grappling with problems of expertise, legitimacy and consistency, which have, for example, helped to undermine the incentives for reform in Bosnia and Macedonia.[60]

The EU has immense leverage, but can it use it effectively? The 'new approach' that started with Croatia's accession negotiations and includes the new Chapter 23 seems to have incorporated fundamental rights, the Rule of Law, and the performance of the judiciary more effectively in the pre-accession process. Everything is supposed to be done before accession. However, having a CVM in effect now with Croatia would be enormously helpful – not least to domestic groups pushing for continued reform of the Croatian state. The CVM has an advantage over infringement proceedings: the biannual reports which monitor progress towards the CVM benchmarks describe not just where governments are coming up short but also where they are doing well – and what their next steps should be. This makes them much more usable for domestic non-governmental organisations and even opposition parties pushing for reform.

VI A Rule of Law Agenda for All EU Member States

One of the most significant consequences of Romania and Bulgaria join-ing the EU is that it has helped put combating corruption on the EU agenda. In June 2011 the European Commission launched a new ini-tiative, the EU Anti-Corruption Report. The report is accompanied by country analyses of each EU Member State and contains country-specific recommendations. The thrust of this initiative consists of soft law (i.e. non-binding) measures such as identifying trends and best practice in the

---

[60] On problems with expertise, legitimacy and consistency, see Noutcheva, *European For-eign Policy and the Challenges of Balkan Accession*. See also Vachudova, 'The Puzzles of Enlargement'; and Bieber, 'State-Building Strategies'.

struggle against corruption, and improving information exchange among the Member States. Yet countries will also face scrutiny in the individual reports and will be obliged to take action in response to the Commission's recommendations. The biannual EU Anti-Corruption Report follows up on the Stockholm Programme, 'An open and secure Europe serving and protecting the citizen', adopted by the European Council in 2009.

This brings us to a more fundamental and theoretical question of how any new EU-level mechanisms would affect domestic politics in the offending state. The liberal democracy and the corruption problem exist for a common reason: political accountability stemming from strong domestic political competition has not dissuaded or punished the perpetrators. In theory, ruling political parties which engineer the erosion of liberal democracy or which preside over and benefit from corruption ought to be exposed by their rivals and thrown out by the voters. But Fidesz has remained quite popular in Hungary. EU admonishments of the Fidesz government were unlikely to have any effect since they were not costly domestically. Meanwhile, in Bulgaria high levels of protest against the government and high levels of trust in the EU have not helped dislodge state capture so far. In Romania greater indifference to corruption and low levels of protest make state capture seem even more intractable, but reformers in key institutions have made some progress. Polarisation and collusion exist side-by-side in both countries, making it hard for any high-quality party to succeed.

The challenge is to identify the specific mechanisms which translate international influence into change: change in the behaviour of domestic elites, and change in broader domestic outcomes. For sanctions to be effective they would have to resonate with the agenda of at least some powerful domestic groups and have strongly negative electoral consequences for the ruling political parties. Studies in the rationalist camp generally argue that mechanisms based on material interests and rewards explain the lion's share of policy change, owing to international influence.[61] Studies in the constructivist camp argue that other, cognitive mechanisms based on the power of the normative social environment socially must *also* be taken into account to understand fully the timing and content of externally driven domestic change.[62] But what we generally hear and see is that

---

[61] Among many, Vachudova, *Europe Undivided*; Kelley, *Ethnic Politics in Europe*; and Schimmelfennig and Sedelemeir, 'Governance by Conditionality'.

[62] Among many, Epstein, *In Pursuit of Liberalism*; and Grabbe, *The EU's Transformative Power*.

European leaders rarely apply that kind of normative pressure in informal gatherings, or indeed in more formal structures such as the European party groupings.

VII   Conclusions about Deepening EU Rule of Law Oversight

I have argued in this chapter that when it comes to safeguarding democracy and the Rule of Law, it is important to identify and address two distinct if overlapping problems among EU members. On the one hand, there is the problem of dismantling liberal democracy, as perpetrated in recent years by Hungary's Viktor Orbán. Using extreme nationalism, chauvinism and xenophobia, he has justified a full-blown attack on Hungary's liberal democratic institutions and hugely restricted the independence of Hungary's media, civic groups and private enterprises. In other words, he has used nationalism to justify concentrating political and economic power in the hands of his party, Fidesz. However, as Sean Hanley argues, it would be wrong to see ruling elites in other post-communist EU Member States as paler or earlier-stage versions of Orbán.[63] In many ways, 'Hungary is the great exception'.[64] Yet many of these countries suffer from the more subtle problem of high-level corruption: rent-seeking elites taking advantage of weak Rule of Law and weak state capacity to capture state institutions and funnel public money to private bank accounts. Some of this corruption is certainly organised by and around political parties – but it needs no ideology, no virulent nationalism and no constitutional majority to go forward, and in some areas it is agnostic about which political parties are in power. The concentration of economic and political power in the hands of one of the Czech Republic's oligarchs, Andrej Babiš, exemplifies this problem, but so does corruption and control of important parts of the political process for economic gain by oligarchs in Italy, Greece, Bulgaria and Romania.

This opens up very important questions for future academic research. One is to what extent post-communist countries are more susceptible to erosion of liberal democracy and state capture – and why. Another is whether the 'hollowing out' of democracies observed by Peter Mair

---

[63] Amongst the EU candidate states, Macedonia's Nikola Gruevski comes closest to following in Orbán's footsteps, using nationalism to concentrate and massively abuse power.

[64] S. Hanley, 'East European Democracy: Sliding Back or Hollowed Out?', 21 July 2015, at https://drseansdiary.wordpress.com/2015/07/21/east-european-democracy-sliding-back-or-hollowed-out/.

in old and new EU Member States is creating a permissive environment for state capture and authoritarian rule. Mair described the 'hollowing out' of democracy as the diminishing engagement of citizens in politics, including voting and identifying with a political party, and decreasing connections between parties and civic groups.[65] In a recent essay, Bela Greskovits explores to what extent 'hollowing out' and democratic backsliding go hand-in-hand – and found substantial variation across the post-communist EU members, raising many questions about how these two problems fit together.[66]

What does stand out is that democracy in the post-communist EU members has, on balance, been resilient despite the financial crisis. Articles which herald the collapse of democracy in these countries exaggerate hugely. However, the concentration of power and the weak commitment of some elites to liberal democratic principles signals the need for EU institutions to create more robust tools for protecting liberal democracy. At the same time, as Laszlo Bruszt argues, they need to work to create strategies for economic growth in less developed EU members in the East and the South to create more beneficiaries of European integration and greater political capital to legitimise more robust political tools.[67]

The track record of EU Member States in handling the Rule of Law and combating corruption in the context of the EU enlargement process helps reveal the potential and the limitations of the EU in these areas. It makes clear that any new oversight mechanism should be as insulated as possible from states which have a history of opposing the use of EU leverage within the pre-accession process in combating corruption and reforming state institutions. As a rule, the Commission has wanted to be more proactive in these areas, and its efforts have been watered down consistently by certain Member States. Informal social relations among Europe's leaders also seem to have the opposite effect: instead of shaming miscreants into better behaviour, they help them make friends who are ready to protect them from any formal proceedings. It also makes clear the importance of making any new mechanisms a part of the EU. It would not be effective for the EU to outsource its democracy and Rule of Law assessments to

---

[65] P. Mair, 'Ruling the Void? Hollowing out of Western Democracy', 42 (1996) *New Left Review* 25; B. Greskovits, 'The Hollowing and Backsliding of Democracy in East Central Europe', 6(1) (2015) *Global Policy* 28.

[66] B. Greskovits, 'The Hollowing and Backsliding of Democracy in East Central Europe', 6(S1) (2015) *Global Policy* 28.

[67] L. Bruszt, 'Regional Normalization and National Deviations: EU Integration and the Backsliding of Democracy in Europe's Eastern Periphery', 6(S1) (2015) *Global Policy* 38.

the Council of Europe. Its members include states run by authoritarian regimes. To give one example, its relationship with Azerbaijan makes the idea that it has the legitimacy to trigger any real sanctions against an EU Member State experiencing an erosion of democracy laughable.

Twenty years of conditionality within the EU's pre-accession process have also shown us that strong sanctions work most of the time: governments change their policies or, in time, sanctions help get them voted out of office. They have also taught us that monitoring which includes positive and negative assessments can help pro-reform domestic groups keep up the pressure for reform. This suggests that a mechanism similar to the existing CVM should be in place for all EU members, but with clear sanctions related to the flow of EU funding. It also suggests that Kim Lane Scheppele's proposal for a systemic infringement action to allow for a holistic picture in the most severe cases makes sense.[68] Together, these mechanisms would put the problem in the hands of the Commission and the Court of Justice. It may also be helpful if the Court of Justice could leverage the EU Charter for Fundamental Rights into new competences, as András Jakab proposes,[69] but it is hard to see how the broad institutional problems of a country sliding toward authoritarianism could be addressed through challenging individual fundamental rights violations alone.

[68] Scheppele, 'Enforcing the Basic Principles of EU Law'.
[69] A. Jakab, 'The EU Charter of Fundamental Rights as the Most Promising Way of Enforcing the Rule of Law against EU Member States' in this volume.

14

The Missing EU Rule of Law?

DIMITRY KOCHENOV*

I Introduction

This chapter discusses the claim that the European Union (EU) suffers as a result of misrepresenting legality at the EU level, selling it to friendly observers under the label of the Rule of Law, while compelling reasons exist to distinguish the two.[1] To do so, Gianluigi Palombella's vision of the Rule of Law as an institutional ideal is employed, implying that the law – *gubernaculum* – should always be controlled by other law – *jurisdictio* – lying outwith the sovereign's reach.[2] Unable to boast any *jurisdictio* expressly intended as the legal aspect of positive law (rather than the mere existence of a simple judicial guarantee)[3] beyond the internal market logic programmed into the Treaties by the *Herren der Verträge*,[4]

* Visiting Professor and Martin and Kathleen Crane Fellow in Law and Public Affairs, Woodrow Wilson School, Princeton University (2015–2016); Professor of EU Constitutional Law, University of Groningen; Visiting Professor, College of Europe (Natolin). I would like to thank numerous colleagues who helped with this chapter through engagement and advice, especially Marija Bartl, Carlos Closa, Jan-Werner Müller, Laurent Pech, Suryapratim Roy and Kim Lane Scheppele. My special thanks go to Gianluigi Palombella, whose writings provided the chief inspiration for my thinking about the essence of the Rule of Law. This argument exists in two emanations. A second, enlarged, version of the argument presented in this chapter appeared in the *Yearbook of European Law* (2015).
[1] G. Palombella, 'The Rule of Law as an Institutional Ideal', in L. Morlino and G. Palombella (eds.), *Rule of Law and Democracy: Inquiries into Internal and External Issues* (Leiden: Brill, 2010), p. 3.
[2] For an analysis of this perspective, see, G. Palombella, *È possibile una legalità globale?* (Bologna: Il Mulino, 2012); Palombella, 'The Rule of Law as an Institutional Ideal'; G. Palombella, 'The Rule of Law and its Core', in G. Palombella and N. Walker (eds.), *Relocating the Rule of Law* (Oxford: Hart, 2009), p. 17. See also his chapter (Chapter 2) in this volume.
[3] Palombella, 'The Rule of Law as an Institutional Ideal'.
[4] O. Gerstenberg, 'The Question of Standards for the EU: From "Democratic Deficit" to "Justice Deficit"?', in D. Kochenov, G. de Búrca and A. Williams (eds.), *Europe's Justice Deficit* (Oxford: Hart, 2015); N. Nic Shuibhne, 'The Resilience of EU Market Citizenship', 47 (2010) *CMLRev.* 1597.

the EU emerges as a somewhat rudimentary legal system, with no strong legal guarantees of legal non-domination extending beyond the Treaty text.[5] Its core – akin to the Prussian constitution – is pure *gubernaculum*: its law is not controlled by Law.[6] The Court of Justice of the EU (ECJ) has taken upon itself to ensure that the Rule of Law, most counter-intuitively, is turned into one of the tools to guarantee the autonomy of EU law, shielding it from contestation. The Rule of Law is thus not the EU's 'institutional ideal'.[7]

This chapter's findings should necessarily be qualified by the wise words of Martin Krygier: 'whatever one might propose as the *echt* meaning of the rule of law is precisely that: a proposal'.[8] Consequently, although this chapter aspires to paint a convincing picture, it obviously cannot pre-empt alternative approaches to the concept of the Rule of Law in the EU. Taking Gianluigi Palombella's insights as a starting point, as well as assuming that the 'Rule of Law' has a meaning,[9] this chapter presents the EU as conflating the Rule of Law with formal legality 'conveyed by the formality of pre-defined rules'.[10] This is the trap into which many *Rechtsstaat*-faithful states have fallen, including, let us not forget, Hungary, which is rightly criticised in this volume.[11] Ironically, an argument could be made that the EU as such is barely different from Hungary, as far as adherence to the Rule of Law is concerned.

Worse still, the EU appears to be keen to take active steps to defend its impoverished vision of legality against any external or internal Socratic contestation, which would be indispensable in a mature constitutional system.[12] In this context it is no surprise that the core of its values – the Rule of Law included – is ephemeral and unenforceable even (and

---

[5] A. Williams, 'Taking Values Seriously: Towards a Philosophy of EU Law', 29 (2009) *Oxford Journal of Legal Studies* 549.

[6] Palombella, *Legalità globale?*, Chapter 1.

[7] Palombella, 'The Rule of Law as an Institutional Ideal'.

[8] M. Krygier, 'Inside the Rule of Law', 3 (2014) *Rivista di filosofia del diritto* 77, 78.

[9] But see J. N. Shklar, 'Political Theory and the Rule of Law', in A. C. Hutcheson and P. Monahan (eds.), *The Rule of Law: Ideal and Ideology* (Toronto: Carswell, 1987), p. 1 (arguing that 'the phrase "Rule of Law" has become meaningless').

[10] G. Palombella, 'Law's Ideals and Law's Global Connections. Some Concluding Notes', 3 (2014) *Rivista di filosofia del diritto* 123, 124. For a broader vision of legality see for example, L. Favoreu, 'Constitutionnalité et légalité', 3 (1997) *Cahiers du Conseil Constitutionnel*.

[11] See in particular Paul Blokker's contribution in this volume, p. 249 (and the literature cited therein); M. Bánkuti, G. Halmai and K. L. Scheppele, 'Hungary's Illiberal Turn: Disabling the Constitution', 23 (2012) *The Journal of Democracy* 138.

[12] M. Kumm, 'The Idea of Socratic Contestation and the Right to Justification: The Point of Rights-Based Proportionality Review', 4 (2010) *Law and Ethics of Human Rights* 142.

particularly) against itself, which explains the highly atypical role played by the values of *inter alia* Article 2 TEU in the context of the EU *acquis*. The EU's Rule of Law mythology, where the Treaties have been hailed as 'the constitutional charter of a Community based on the rule of law'[13] might well be weaker than we are accustomed to assume, leaning heavily on the borrowed clay feet of internal market ideology[14] and the prohibition on the Member States – in line with the duty of loyalty – to question each others' performance, thus barring the facts from the ideal picture.[15] In this context, any keen observer of the Rule of Law *malaises* in the EU should start with the Union itself, not merely with the Member States, when approaching the questions related to the effects of Article 2 TEU. To be absolutely clear, this is not to downplay the problems existing at the national level, but rather to attempt to provide a fuller picture of the extent of the tasks we are facing. It is thus plausible that the enforceability of the EU's values against the Member States is not the only, possibly even not the core problem we should be discussing.

For the purposes of this analysis, our understanding of the Union is necessarily holistic, following Sabino Cassese's account of the interpenetration logic of global law:[16] the EU's problems in the field of the Rule of Law observable at the supranational level are thus intrinsically connected to the Member States', 'national-level' issues. Consequently, dealing *only* with Hungary – or any other Member State – or *only* with the EU is bound to be insufficient. This chapter articulates the distinction between the two levels of the law in the section which follows, outlining two categories of outstanding issues pertaining to the Rule of Law in the EU: design problems related to the EU's understanding of the Rule of Law conflated with legality, and the functionality problem related to the issues of enforcement of the Rule of Law as an Article 2 TEU value at the national level (II.). This is done only to proceed to look at both in greater detail later in this chapter, as it investigates whether the Rule of Law functions as an institutional ideal in the European legal context, attempting to locate the

---

[13] Opinion 1/91 *EEA I* ECLI:EU:C:1991:490.

[14] M. Bartl, 'Internal Market Rationality, Private Law and the Direction of the Union: Resuscitating the Market as the Object of the Political' 21 (2015) *European Law Journal* 572.

[15] For example Opinion 2/13 *ECHR II* ECLI:EU:C:2014:2454, para. 192; Cases C-411 & 493/10 *N.S. and Others* ECLI:EU:C:2011:865, paras 78–80. Analyzed below part IV(c).

[16] S. Cassese, '"Una furiosa espansione della legge?" Spazio giuridico globale e rule of law', 3 (2014) *Rivista di filosofia del diritto* 109. But see, F. C. Mayer, 'Multilevel Constitutional Jurisdiction', in A. von Bogdandy and J. Bast (eds.), *Principles of European Constitutional Law*, 2nd edn (Oxford/Munich: Hart/CH Beck, 2010), p. 400.

necessary *gubernaculum–jurisdictio* duality within the fabric of EU law. While the *gubernaculum* – the *acquis* – is easy to see, several candidates for *jurisdictio* are considered, from human rights to the internal market, only to conclude that the main priority of the EU – in emphasising autonomy and the crucial role of the internal market – comes dangerously close to *undermining* the indispensable duality of law lying at the core of the concept of the Rule of Law employed in the context of this work (III.). Turning to the enforcement problems, the picture becomes potentially even more worrisome: being uninformed by the institutional ideal of the Rule of Law, the Union naturally cannot enforce the Rule of Law in the Member States. Moreover, the context of conflation of the Rule of Law and legality generates a highly problematic environment where the EU, merely by enforcing EU law and the highly peculiar vision of the world it espouses, can seriously undermine the Rule of Law in the Member States. One reason for this is the legal deactivation of what is referred to as 'reality checks' in this chapter: the Member States are expected to function on the basis of presumptions about each other, discouraged to subject such presumptions to critical scrutiny even in contexts when non-compliance is obvious and the Union cannot do anything about it. Such a situation is far from atypical, given the severity of the values' enforcement problems amply documented throughout this volume. The autonomy of the EU legal order thus takes precedence, in law, over any values and principles the Member States might espouse – Rule of Law included. Knowing this presents the discourse related to the need to increase the Union's enforcement capacity in an unfamiliar light: moves in this direction are revealed to be potentially dangerous, capable of undermining the Rule of Law in the Member States (IV).

Although this chapter thus comes to a conclusion similar to the one articulated by Joseph Weiler in his contribution to this volume,[17] the reasoning is very different. In the context of scrutinising the EU Rule of Law as an institutional ideal, democracy is not the crucial consideration.[18] The worries which Weiler masterfully outlines at the level of democratic politics are also present, this contribution argues, within the realm of Rule of Law as such, while the latter is not necessarily political. Crucially,

---

[17] See J. H. H. Weiler's Epilogue in this volume, 313.

[18] I thus side with Gianluigi Palombella's critique of Joseph Weiler's arguments, presented in Chapter 2 in this volume, p. 51. For a general analysis of the interrelations between the two concepts, see for example L. Morlino and G. Palombella (eds.), *Rule of Law and Democracy: Inquiries into Internal and External Issues* (Leiden: Brill, 2010).

presenting the current Rule of Law-related problems which the Union addresses as *enforcement* problems – taken as a given in the main bulk of policy analyses and scholarly literature, including the majority of the contributions in this volume[19] – most likely falls short of achieving its aims, as articulated by scholars and EU institutions,[20] that is, finding effective solutions to the on-going Rule of Law crisis in the Union.

II   Two Problems to Solve Not One: Design and Operation to Be Considered

From Lord Mackenzie Stuart[21] to *Les Verts*, which characterises the Treaties as 'a constitutional charter based on the Rule of Law',[22] what we have been hearing about the Rule of Law in the EU really amounts to compliance with the law.[23] This is an established understanding of legality.[24] Legality is not enough to ensure that the EU behaves like – and is – a true rule of law-based constitutional system, which is characterised here as the *design problem*. Should one submit that equating the Rule of Law and legality does not undermine the constitutional system, then, as Gianluigi Palombella rightly argues in Chapter 2 in this volume, our thinking 'shifts the issue from the Rule of Law to the respect for the laws of a legal system'.[25] Yet 'the Rule of Law cannot mean just the self-referentiality of a legal order'.[26] Consequently, the absolute majority of the scholarly proposals which concern turning Article 2 TEU into a

---

[19] For notable exceptions, see the contributions by Gianluigi Palombella and Joseph Weiler in this collection.

[20] For an overview, see C. Closa, D. Kochenov, J. H. H. Weiler, 'Reinforcing Rule of Law Oversight in the European Union', EUI Working Papers No. 2014/25, RSCAS.

[21] Lord Mackenzie Stuart, *The European Communities and the Rule of Law* (London: Stevens and Sons, 1977). See also G. Bebr, *Rule of Law within the European Communities* (Brussels: Institut d'Etudes Européennes de l'Université Libre de Bruxelles, 1965).

[22] Case 294/83 *Parti Ecologiste 'Les Verts'* v. *Parliament* ECLI:EU:C:1986:166, para. 23. See also Opinion 1/91 *EEA Agreement*.

[23] Also, U. Everling, 'The European Union as a Federal Association of States and Citizens', 701; and M. Zuleeg, 'The Advantages of the European Constitution', in A. von Bogdandy and J. Bast (eds.), *Principles of European Constitutional Law*, 2nd edn (Oxford/Munich: Hart/CH Beck, 2010), pp. 772–9, 763.

[24] For example the contributions in L. F. M. Besselink, F. Pennings and S. Prechal (eds.), *The Eclipse of Legality in the European Union* (Alphen aan de Rijn: Kluwer, 2010).

[25] See Chapter 2 in this volume, p. 39.

[26] *Ibid*. Compare with Krygier: 'To try to capture this elusive phenomenon by focusing on characteristics of laws and legal institutions is, I believe, to start in the wrong place and move in the wrong direction', M. Krygier, 'The Rule of Law. An Abuser's Guide', in A. Sajó (ed.), *The Dark Side of Fundamental Rights* (Utrecht: Eleven, 2006), p. 129.

binding and effective provision to address these issues, fall short of going to the deeper and most problematic core of the problem we are trying to address.[27] This ultimately concerns the EU's constitutional nature, rather than its mere operation and/or inability to push the Member States towards behaving in a particular way. Scholars thus mostly address the *operational problem*, consisting in the EU's inability to articulate the substance of Article 2 TEU values consistently, to promote them internally and externally and to ensure that all the Member States are rallied behind the values they themselves agreed to rely upon when establishing the EU. By only addressing the operational challenges – that is merely correcting how the EU operates as a proclaimed Rule of Law-bound Union – it is impossible to tackle the outstanding issues of the Union's design and vice-versa. Action is required at both levels. Regrettably, the EU institutions – including the European Commission[28] and the Council[29] – when offering their own visions of what is to be done,[30] are also guided by such mere enforcement thinking, thus focusing on the operational facet of a dual-faceted problem. It is submitted that trying to enforce away EU's age-old deficiencies – focus on enforcement, while pretending that design is not at issue – is not a reliable strategy capable of ensuring that the Rule of Law problems in the EU are resolved.

III   The Design Problem: There Is No Rule of Law in the EU

Values are *not* EU's founding ideas, or – to paraphrase Joseph Weiler – not in EU's DNA,[31] which is the first key deficiency this chapter aims to bring to light: many a proclamation to the contrary notwithstanding, democracy and the Rule of law are and have always been left seemingly

---

[27] For important exceptions, see Chapter 2 and the Epilogue in this volume by Gianluigi Palombella and J. H. H. Weiler respectively.

[28] European Commission, 'A New EU Framework to Strengthen the Rule of Law', Strasbourg, 11 March 2014, COM(2014) 158 final.

[29] Conclusions of the Council of the European Union and the Member States meeting within the Council on ensuring respect for the Rule of Law. General Affairs Council meeting Brussels, 16 December 2014 Doc. 16862/14 COR 1, at: www.consilium.europa.eu/uedocs/cms_Data/docs/pressdata/EN/genaff/146323.pdf. See also P. Oliver and J. Stefanelli, 'Strengthening the Rule of Law in the EU: The Council's Inaction' 54 (2016) *JCMS*.

[30] For a detailed analysis and criticism, see Chapter 1 in this volume; and D. Kochenov and L. Pech, 'Monitoring and Enforcement of the Rule of Law in the EU: Rhetoric and Reality' 11 (2015) *EUConst* 512.

[31] J. H. H. Weiler, 'The Schuman Declaration as a Manifesto of Political Messianism', in J. Dickson and P. Eleftheriadis (eds.), *Philosophical Foundations of European Union Law* (Oxford: Oxford University Press, 2012).

entirely to the Member States to care about. While it is immaterial how this came about – it might even reflect the wishes of the Member States either now or sometime back – this is a serious design flaw which destabilises the EU's constitutional system. To see the extent to which this design flaw is capable of affecting the EU negatively, it is worth putting the process of the EU's legal evolution in the context of the meaning of the Rule of Law.

(a)   What Is the Rule of Law?

The Rule of Law is a classic example of an essentially contested concept:[32] the EU is seemingly as hopeless at defining what it means as its Member States and the broad academic doctrine.[33] The debate is constantly ongoing.[34] It is clear, however, what the Rule of Law is not. It is not democracy, the protection of human rights or similar wonderful things, each of them definitely boasting its own sound claim to existence as a notion independent from the Rule of Law.[35] And it is not mere legality, which is adherence to the law.[36] Once the Rule of Law and legality are distinguished, the basic meaning of the Rule of Law comes down to the

---

[32] For a brilliant outline of the history of contestation, see, J. Waldron, 'Is the Rule of Law an Essentially Contested Concept (in Florida)?', 21 (2002) *Law and Philosophy* 127.

[33] For a multi-disciplinary overview see for example G. K. Hadfield and B. R. Weingast, 'Microfoundations of the Rule of Law', 17 (2014) *Annual Review of Political Science* 21; as well as the literature cited in Laurent Pech, 'The Rule of Law as a Constitutional Principle of the European Union', Jean Monnet Working Paper No. 04/09, NYU Law School. See also L. Pech, 'Promoting the Rule of Law Abroad', in D. Kochenov and F. Amtenbrink (eds.), *The European Union's Shaping of the International Legal Order* (Cambridge: Cambridge University Press, 2013), p. 108 on the 'holistic understanding' of the Rule of Law. For a special 'Eastern-European' perspective, which is particularly important in the context of the on-going developments in the EU, see J. Přibáň, 'From "Which Rule of Law?" to "The Rule of Which Law?": Post-Communist Experiences of European Legal Integration', 1 (2009) *Hague Journal on the Rule of Law* 337.

[34] Most recently see, L. Morlino and G. Palombella (eds.), *Rule of Law and Democracy* (Boston: Brill, 2010); G. Palombella and N. Walker (eds.), *Relocating the Rule of Law* (Oxford: Hart, 2009).

[35] One should not forget the wise words of Joseph Raz: 'We have no need to be converted into the rule of law just in order to believe . . . that good should triumph': J. Raz, 'The Rule of Law and its Virtue', in J. Raz, *The Authority of Law: Essays on Law and Morality* (Oxford: Clarendon, 1979), p. 210.

[36] Even in Soviet legal theory, which was profoundly sceptical of the very existence of the Rule of Law, the principle of 'socialist legality' which *de facto* replaced this notion was richer than simple adherence to the law: O. S. Ioffe and M. D. Shargorodsky, *Voprosy teorii prava* (Moscow: Juridicheskaja literatura, 1961), pp. 267–310.

idea of the subordination of the law to another kind of law, which is not up to the sovereign to change at will.[37] This idea, traceable back to mediæval England,[38] is described with recourse to two key notions, to reflect the fundamental duality of the law's fabric, indispensable for the operation of the Rule of Law as a principle of law:[39] *jurisdictio* – the other law, untouchable for the day-to-day rules running the legal system and removed from the ambit of purview of the sovereign – and *gubernaculum*, which is the general rule-making power.[40] As Krygier put it in his commentary on Palombella's theory, 'the king was subject to the law that he had not made, indeed that made him king. For the king – for anyone – to ignore or override that law was to violate the rule of law'.[41]

Unlike despotic or totalitarian regimes, where the ruler is free to do anything he pleases; or problematic EU Member States, such as Hungary, where the constitution is a political tool – as also recognised by the Venice Commission; or pre-constitutional democracies, which equate the law with legislation,[42] the majority of constitutional democracies in the world today recognise the distinction between *jurisdictio* and *gubernaculum*, thus achieving a sound approximation of Palombella's Rule of Law as an institutional ideal, in terms of maintaining and fostering the constant tension between these two facets of the law. The authority should be itself bound by clear legal norms which are outside of its control. Indeed, this is the key feature of post-war constitutionalism. The *jurisdictio–gubernaculum* distinction, lying at the core of what the Rule of Law is about, can be policed either by courts, or even by the structure of the constitution itself. The ideology of human rights is of huge significance in this context.[43] Furthermore, the existence of international

---

[37] See Chapter 2 by Palombella in this volume, p. 36.

[38] J. P. Reid, *Rule of Law: The Jurisprudence of Liberty in the Seventeenth and the Eighteenth Centuries* (DeKalb: Northern Illinois University Press, 2004).

[39] Palombella, *Legalità globale?*

[40] For a detailed exposé, see Chapter 2 in this volume. See also G. Palombella, 'The Rule of Law and Its Core', in G. Palombella and N. Walker (eds.), *Relocating the Rule of Law* (Oxford: Hart, 2009), pp. 17, 30, emphasising that this duality should not be disturbed by democratic outcomes and ethical choices.

[41] M. Krygier, 'Inside the Rule of Law', 3 (2014) *Rivista di filosofia del diritto* 77, 84.

[42] In a pre-constitutional state, the *Rechtsstaat* shapes a reality, in the words of Gianfranco Poggi, where 'there is a relation of near-identity between the state and its law': G. Poggi, *The Development of the Modern State: A Sociological Introduction* (Stanford: Stanford University Press, 1978), p. 238 (as cited in Krygier 'Inside the Rule of Law', 84).

[43] G. Frankenberg, 'Human Rights and the Belief in a Just World', 12 (2013) *I-CON* 35.

law[44] and, of course, supranational legal orders,[45] definitely contributes to the policing of the said duality,[46] to ensure that one law does not impinge on the other: this is precisely why the EU should be praised as a promoter of liberal constitutionalism.[47]

Contemporary constitutionalism implies additional restraints through law: restraints which are, crucially, not simply democratic or political.[48] Such restraints make violation of the *gubernaculum–juristictio* border difficult, preventing the sovereign (the 'King', the 'Parliament' or 'the people') from collapsing the duality of law,[49] thereby unquestionably contributing to the legitimacy of the legal systems.[50] This fundamental starting point to the meaning of the Rule of Law, which is brilliantly explained by Gianluigi Palombella in Chapter 2 in this volume, supplies the crucial lens for the assessment of the on-going Rule of Law crisis of the EU, which this collection embarks on exploring.[51]

(b)   Does Rule of Law Exist at the EU Level?

Observing EU's supranational law, a legitimate question which arises is whether the EU *itself* – as an autonomous supranational legal order – has

---

[44] R. Dworkin, 'A New Philosophy of International Law', 41 (2013) *Philosophy and Public Affairs* 2.

[45] For an argument that numerous Central and Eastern European States were actually motivated by the desire for external legal checks on their laws – a *jurisdictio* – when joining the CoE, see W. Sadurski, *Constitutionalism and the Enlargement of Europe* (Oxford: Oxford University Press, 2012).

[46] Palombella, *Legalita globale?*, Chapter 2.

[47] W. Kymlicka, 'Liberal Nationalism and Cosmopolitan Justice', in S. Benhabib, *Another Cosmopolitanism* (Oxford: Oxford University Press, 2006), p. 134.

[48] Naturally, this is not to say that we should do away with the political restraints. Indeed the virtually complete depoliticisation of the law has been one of the key criticisms of the EU legal order: J. Přibáň, 'The Evolving Idea of Political Justice in the EU: From Substantive Deficits to the Systemic Contingency of European Society', in D. Kochenov, G. de Búrca and A. Williams (eds.), *Europe's Justice Deficit?* (Oxford: Hart, 2015), p. 193 and M. A. Wilkinson, 'Politicising Europe's Justice Deficit: Some Preliminaries', in D. Kochenov, G. de Búrca and A. Williams (eds.), *Europe's Justice Deficit?* (Oxford: Hart, 2015), p. 111. For a clear discussion of the relationship between constitutionalism and the Rule of Law, see, M. Krygier, 'Tempering Power: Realist-idealism, Constitutionalism, and the Rule of Law', in M. Adams et al. (eds.), *Constitutionalism and the Rule of Law: Bridging Idealism and Realism* (Cambridge: Cambridge University Press, 2016).

[49] It is difficult, of course, to speak about 'law' when the basic requirements of the Rule of Law are not attained: Palombella, *Legalità globale?*

[50] Dworkin, 'A New Philosophy of International Law', esp., 17.

[51] See the Introduction to this volume, p. 1.

heeded the indispensable requirement of the duality of the law in the sense of the necessary components outlined above. Having no problem with finding its *gubernaculum* (the law made in compliance with the principle of legality in accordance with all procedural requirements, which is the body of the *acquis* in the EU context)[52] – the question is: where is EU's *jurisdictio* (i.e. the law to check the *acquis* against)?

To offer an answer we need to analyse the elements of EU law which could supply *jurisdictio* in the context of the supranational legal order. In the context of such an analysis, the *jurisdictio* internal to that order, derived from the values mentioned in Article 2 TEU or the internal market, should necessarily be considered alongside the possible articulation of *jurisdictio* which, although external to the supranational legal order, would nevertheless be able to inform it in line with Dworkin's thinking. For instance, we should not forget that it is the key task of the ECHR, among other international institutions, to keep European legal orders in check. However, any holistic vision of the essence of the EU's law notwithstanding, the ultimate checks of its supranational law are 'from below', that is, from the level of the Member States, and cannot be presented as viable *jurisdictio* guarantees. The sub-sections which follow address these elements individually, proceeding in reverse order: thus starting off with the 'external sphere' as a possible supplier of *jurisdictio* (since this is the key role that the ECHR plays in all the European constitutional systems except for Belarus), to move to the scrutiny of the possible sources of EU's *jurisdictio* internal to the EU's supranational legal order.

That the EU does not boast a vibrant political life, resulting in conditions where there is natural protection against 'the forces of political absolutism [. . . able to] unbalance the constitution in favour of the political',[53] does not offer any relief – contrary to what Neil Walker claims[54] – since, once again, *gubernaculum* is not necessarily political.[55] Indeed, Palombella's model of the Rule of Law as an institutional ideal is

---

[52] It is necessary to note that not all the body of the *acquis* meets the basic requirements of legality. The Luxembourg Compromise, which is unquestionably part of the *acquis*, is an *ad hoc* arbitrary compromise arrived at by ignoring all the Treaty procedures.

[53] N. Walker, 'Law's Global (Re)Connection', 3 (2014) *Rivista di filosofia del diritto* 99, 103.

[54] *Ibid.*

[55] On the problems of the political legitimation of global law, see, for example, Cassese, 'Una furiosa espansione della legge?'. On the dangers of deploying the rhetoric of just objectives of the *acquis* to suppress politics, see, for example A. J. Menéndez, 'Whose Justice? Which Europe?' in D. Kochenov, G. de Búrca and A. Williams (eds.), *Europe's Justice Deficit?* (Oxford: Hart, 2015), p. 137.

particularly attractive, since it focuses, specifically, on taming law with law: 'it amounts to preventing one dominant source of law and its unconstrained whim, from absorbing all the available normativity'.[56] In fact, the EU would be a superb example of a legal order where an all-encompassing non-political *gubernaculum* is as problematic as 'political absolutism' is in Walker's terms: the EU makes its law, (mis)representing the underlying pre-set rationale as apolitical, which has proven to be a reliable tool for switching off politics.[57] Its alleged political incapacity is thus precisely the source of its absolutism.

(c)   Human Rights

At the external level, the EU seems to be virtually the only legal system in Europe which fiercely objects to any outside scrutiny, finding pride in its autopoietic nature. Outside scrutiny 'from below', has remained only an albeit productive threat,[58] and the ECJ has expressly prohibited – now twice[59] – outside scrutiny from above, all in the name of 'autonomy'. In essence, in the EU's particular case, autonomy means that the EU tends to tolerate no constraints on its ability to rule. The defence of its *gubernaculum* – its *acquis* – from the internal or external contestation is clearly elevated to its main priority. '[W]hen implementing EU law, the Member States may, under EU law, be required *to presume* that fundamental rights have been observed by the other Member States, so that [...] they *may not check* whether that other Member State has actually, in a specific case, observed the fundamental rights guaranteed by the EU'.[60] Where the Rule of Law is *not* enforced in the Member States of the EU via the

---

[56] G. Palombella, 'The Pincipled, and Winding, Road to Al-Dulimi. Interpreting the Inter-preters', 1 (2014) *Questions of International Law* 17, 18. Similarly, see D. Georgiev, 'Politics of Rule of Law: Deconstruction and Legitimacy in International Law', 4 (1993) *European Journal of International Law* 1, 4.

[57] M. A. Wilkinson, 'Politicising Europe's Justice Deficit: Some Preliminaries', in D. Kochenov, G. de Búrca and A. Williams (eds.), *Europe's Justice Deficit?* (Oxford: Hart, 2015), p. 111; A. J. Menéndez, 'Whose Justice? Which Europe?'.

[58] BVerfGE 37, 271 (*Solange I*). For an analysis of the whole story see F. C. Mayer, 'Multilevel Constitutional Jurisdiction', in A. von Bogdandy and J. Bast (eds.), *Principles of European Constitutional Law*, 2nd edn (Oxford/Munich: Hart/CH Beck, 2010), pp. 400, 410–20; J. H. H. Weiler and N. J. S. Lockhart, '"Taking Rights Seriously" Seriously' (I and II), 32 (1995) *Common Market Law Review* 51, 579.

[59] Opinion 2/94 *ECHR I* ECLI:EU:C:1996:140; Opinion 2/13 *ECHR II* ECLI:EU:C:2014: 2454.

[60] Opinion 2/13 *ECHR II*, para. 192 (emphasis added).

supranational legal order – the subject of all the contributions to this volume – the Member States themselves are not free to consider each others' deficiencies in the arena of values, particularly the Rule of Law. Officially, this is about ruling within the EU's own sphere of competences. However, given that the latter is highly blurred[61] and is unlikely – as in any other federal system[62] – to be defined with static clarity, what we are dealing with is a recurrent claim to power unchecked externally on the strength of an 'autonomy' argument. This is precisely the reason to be suspicious and to want more Socratic contestation.

The EU, acting chiefly through its Court, seems to be immune to irony: it *does* consider itself better than the Member States' constitutional systems,[63] which apparently need the European Court of Human Rights *on top* of their machinery of internal legal constraints to police their respective *jurisdictio–gubernaculum* divide, constraints which the EU seemingly does not have.[64] Although it has its procedures and legality can be observed, what is missing is precisely what Palombella characterises as 'a limitation of *law* (-production), through law'.[65] This reality results from a most problematic approach adopted by the Union: in addition to an inexplicable immodesty (which is not illegal, *per se*, of course), the Union suffers from a fundamental misrepresentation of the key function of the European system of human rights protection, which is *to ensure*

---

[61] Which fact can negatively affect the operation of the law: D. Kochenov 'Citizenship without Respect', Jean Monnet Working Paper No. 08/10, NYU School of Law.

[62] O. Beaud, *Théorie de la fédération* (Paris: Presses Universitaires de France, 2007); R. Schütze, *From Dual to Cooperative Federalism* (Oxford: Oxford University Press, 2009).

[63] See Joseph Weiler's enlightening criticism of a very positive presentation of the latest case law: J. H. H. Weiler, 'Epilogue: Judging Europe's Judges – Apology and Critique', in M. Adams et al. (eds.), *Judging Europe's Judges* (Oxford: Hart, 2013), p. 235. See also Koen Lenaerts in the same volume, emphasising the coherence of the Court: K. Lenaerts, 'The Court's Outer and Inner Selves: Exploring the External and Internal Legitimacy of the European Court of Justice', in M. Adams et al. (eds.), *Judging Europe's Judges* (Oxford: Hart, 2013), p. 13.

[64] Here we need to distinguish between the constraints related to the policing of the competences border – a federal animal – and the Rule of Law constraints *within* the EU's sphere of competences. While the former might be said to be present – albeit weak – the latter is less pronounced still. On the ECJ's self-censorship in policing the federal competences border, see, for example N. Nic Shuibhne, 'EU Citizenship as Federal Citizenship: What Are the Implications for the Citizen?', in D. Kochenov (ed.), *EU Citizenship and Federalism: The Role of Rights* (Cambridge: Cambridge University Press, 2017). On the problematic outcomes of such modesty when not informed by any thought of going beyond the protection of the *acquis*, see D. Kochenov, 'Citizenship without Respect'.

[65] G. Palombella, 'Law's Ideals and Law's Global Connections. Some Concluding Notes', 3 (2014) *Rivista di filosofia del diritto* 123, 124.

that no legal system in Europe feels itself autonomous *from human rights concerns.* This issue is reviewed in detail below.[66]

(d)   The Internal Market

Boasting *jurisdictio* – the awareness of the law placed outwith the reach of the sovereign – is not necessarily dependent on external checks, of course: we can note plenty of jurisdictions – either democratic, such as Australia – or not – such as mediaeval England – which can (or could) boast of adherence to the Rule of Law without significant external checks. Most obviously, the majority of Western European states are definitely rooted in the Rule of Law.[67] The constant policing of the *jurisdictio–gubernaculum* boundary is crucial, as is the presence of an identifiable body of law which is not open to the sovereign to change at will. It is premature speak of the Rule of Law if no such law and boundary exist[68] – this is when the alarm bells start ringing. As it stands today, the EU, just like Prussia in its day, cannot boast of any *jurisdictio* besides perhaps the principles of the Internal Market. Indeed, if *jurisdictio* is taken to mean the DNA of the polity placed out of reach for the sovereign, then the EU has only one candidate to occupy this place. However, how much of a Rule of Law are we talking about – in the modern constitutional sense – if the internal market rules are granted the role of a *jurisdictio* in an autopoietic system, which is also a self-proclaimed constitutional order ('who cares what it "really" is?'[69])? The engagement of EU law, the dispensation of its protections and the rights it grants, are usually connected to internal market thinking. The internal market as *the* founding value is protected with true ferocity. Moreover, the EU has been very effective in mobilising the discourse of knowledge and expertise,[70] or of bright unchallengeable

---

[66] See Part IV(c) below.

[67] Sadurski made a fundamentally important point about the different function which the Council of Europe system came to play in Western and in Eastern Europe: in the former is corrects the outliers, while in the latter, it is called upon to ensure the survival of (even if rudimentary) democracy and the Rule of Law. In other words: while the UK is perfectly conceivable as a Rule of Law state adhering to human rights outwith the CoE, Albania is probably not. W. Sadurski, *Constitutionalism and Enlargement of Europe* (Oxford: Oxford University Press, 2012).

[68] Palombella, *Legalità globale?*

[69] J. H. H. Weiler and U. R. Haltern, 'The Autonomy of the Community Legal Order – Through the Looking Glass', 37 (1996) *Harvard International Law Journal* 411, 422.

[70] Bartl, 'Internal Market Rationality'. See also Suryapratim Roy on the instrumental deployment of the justice discourse in the EU to justify any outcome: S. Roy, 'Justice as Europe's Signifier', in D. Kochenov, G. de Búrca and A. Williams (eds.), *Europe's Justice Deficit?* (Oxford: Hart, 2015), p. 79.

goals,[71] to decapacitate claims of political (and also legal) contestation of its law[72] – the emergence of *jurisdictio* from within is as difficult as the blocked external scrutiny.

Even if we assume for a moment that a constitutional system can evolve around the internal market serving as a crucial element of its essential Rule of Law core,[73] the question remains open whether the internal market has actually ever played such a role in the EU. The brevity of a single chapter in a book does not allow for a detailed investigation, but the answer, most likely, will be 'no'. Not because it would obviously be an affront (given the generally accepted sets of values in any European society) to measure rights and protections against the ultimate rationale of the market, but because the internal market rules simply do not play such an elevated role. They are what they are: part of the *gubernaculum*, playing a role in guaranteeing EU legality, but falling short at the same time of establishing a viable *jurisdictio–gubernaculum* border.

(e) EU Values

It is true that the EU also has Article 2 TEU.[74] However, since the time of the Copenhagen Criteria from which it largely originates,[75] it has never – probably ironically – been law in the sense of forming part of the body of the ordinary EU *acquis*.[76] Unsurprisingly, given that the *acquis* on values – unsurprisingly – largely does not exist, the EU is powerless to define their content.[77] Consequently, the case law of the ECJ seems to be pointing towards Article 2 TEU not having acquired any self-standing value.[78]

---

[71] G. Davies, 'Social Legitimacy and Purposive Power: The End, the Means and the Consent of the People', in D. Kochenov, G. de Búrca and A. Williams (eds.), *Europe's Justice Deficit?* (Oxford: Hart, 2015), p. 259.

[72] A. J. Menéndez, 'Whose Justice? Which Europe?'.

[73] For very well reasoned doubts about this see Nic Shuibhne, 'The Resilience of EU Market Citizenship'; D. Kochenov, 'On Tiles and Pillars: EU Citizenship as a Federal Denominator', in D. Kochenov (ed.), *EU Citizenship and Federalism: The Role of Rights* (Cambridge: Cambridge University Press, 2017).

[74] For a wonderful analysis embedding Art. 2 TEU in the context of other provisions of EU primary law, see Chapter 3 by Christophe Hillion in this volume, p. 59.

[75] For a legal-historical presentation see, D. Kochenov, *EU Enlargement and the Failure of Conditionality* (Alphen aan de Rijn: Kluwer, 2008), Chapters 1 and 2.

[76] The key reason for this, of course, is in the competence limitations imposed by *Herren der Verträge* on the Union; yet the cause does not change the result: Art. 2 TEU and its predecessors are no ordinary part of the EU's *gubernaculum*.

[77] Since this would clearly amount to a claim of *Kompetenz Kompetenz* and a radical redrawing of the competence boundary in the delicate system of EU federalism.

[78] Look, for instance, at the recent cases involving Hungary: the EU fights against the anti-constitutional movement in the Member State by attempting to tackle deep-rooted Art. 2

Technical explanations for that are readily available: respect of the limited nature of EU's powers. The EU turns its own rhetorical weakness into a tool for escaping the Rule of Law checks on its system of formal legality.

From the perspective of approaching the Rule of Law as a balance in the duality of two types of law within the constitutional system – *jurisdictio* and *gubernaculum*, as opposed to conflating the meaning of the EU Rule of Law with legality – the EU thus emerges as a legal system that cannot boast the Rule of Law. In this context the 'Rule of Law' in Article 2 TEU cannot have any meaning beyond a requirement to observe basic legal procedures and, possibly, a set of other well-known elements of legality.[79] In a system with rhetorical adherence to legality through considerations of autonomy – which largely pre-empts reality checks – and without the Rule of Law, generating injustice is not viewed as a problem,[80] and the legitimacy of the law as such thereby naturally remains undermined, while outstanding issues are interpreted away either as non-existent or falling to some other legal order – either national[81] or ECtHR[82] – to resolve. The 'autonomous legal order'[83] confidently emerges as a formally coherent system directly bound by nothing beyond the day-to-day rules of its own creation and operation. The Treaty text is its limit, with no greater aspiration in sight beyond being shielded from outside influence. Joseph Weiler's take on its nature, which dates back to the nineties, is thus still profoundly correct today – it is a market standing alone without a mantle of ideals[84] – all the recent values-inspired commotion notwithstanding. Checks on the *substance* of the law, which aim to ensure that the law is limited

---

TEU problems using ordinary *acquis* elements, abundantly failing as a result. Never mind that it wins its cases: Hungary, having lost for petty *acquis* grounds, is nowhere nearer an improvement in its adherence to Art. 2 TEU values.

[79] J. Raz, 'The Rule of Law and its Virtue', in J. Raz, *The Authority of Law: Essays on Law and Morality* (Oxford: Clarendon, 1979), p. 210; R. Fallon, '"Rule of Law" as a Concept in Constitutional Discourse', 97 (1997) *Columbia Law Review* 1.

[80] D. Kochenov and A. Williams, 'Europe's Justice Deficit Introduced', in D. Kochenov, G. de Búrca and A. Williams (eds.), *Europe's Justice Deficit?* (Oxford: Hart, 2015), p. 1; S. Douglas-Scott, 'Justice, Injustice and the Rule of Law in the EU', in D. Kochenov, G. de Búrca and A. Williams (eds.), *Europe's Justice Deficit?* (Oxford: Hart, 2015), p. 51.

[81] For example, Case C-135/08 *Janko Rottmann* v. *Freistaat Bayern* ECLI:EU:C:2010:104.

[82] For example Case C-434/09 *Shirley McCarthy* v. *Secretary of State for the Home Department* ECLI:EU:C:2011:277; Case C-256/11 *Murat Dereci and Others* v. *Bundesministerium für Inneres* ECLI:EU:C:2011:734.

[83] Case C-6/64 *Flaminio Costa* v. *ENEL* ECLI:EU:C:1964:66.

[84] J. H. H. Weiler, 'Bread and Circus: The State of the European Union', 4 (1998) *Columbia Journal of European Law* 223, 231.

by Law do not exist, thus impairing the Rule of Law as an institutional ideal.

IV The Functionality Problem: Rule of Law Is Unenforceable in the EU

The EU not only suffers from its inability to approach the *jurisdictio* question and thus supply a legitimate answer to what it stands for beyond the market – or to come up with a procedure to provide such an answer by itself. It also lacks any ability (and possibly the will, too, its constant state of constitutional crisis notwithstanding) to enforce the values it mentions in Article 2 EU in legal terms. The limitations of both Article 7 TEU and of the standard enforcement procedures in this context are clear as day.[85] For many decades the Union has been consistently denying the very possibility that any Article 2 problems could ever arise, presenting itself as solely working within the paradigm of the internal market, which seems largely to deny any serious treatment of the majority of the values and principles listed in Article 2 EU. Only in the context of the preparation for its Eastern enlargement was the situation any different, where by fascinating paradox the EU *de facto* ended up seemingly enforcing its foundational values through the pre-accession conditionality policy, with virtually no other capacity to do so elsewhere and with highly questionable results. The arguable failure of conditionality in the fields of democracy and the rule of law, which I analysed elsewhere,[86] now stands overwhelmingly proven by the Hungarian and Polish developments. In goes without saying that an optimist would point out plentiful successes, yet the whole point of solid enforcement is the capacity to be efficient in dealing with the extremes. These do not arise every day.

(a) Non-Existent Enforcement Machinery

Immediately moving beyond Article 7 EU, the ineffectiveness of which has been brilliantly explained by Wojciech Sadurski,[87] ordinary enforcement mechanisms designed to ensure that EU law works in the Member States

---

[85] For a restatement, see for example D. Kochenov, 'On Policing Article 2 TEU Compliance', 33 (2014) *Polish Yearbook of International Law* 145.

[86] Kochenov, *EU Enlargement and the Failure of Conditionality*.

[87] W. Sadurski, 'Adding Bite to a Bark: The Story of Article 7, EU Enlargement, and Jörg Haider', 16 (2010) *Columbia Journal of European Law* 385. For a more optimistic reading also see the chapter by Bojan Bugarič in this volume, p. 82.

are always at our disposal. In the context of chronically non-compliant states, where, as in Hungary, non-compliance is *ideological* and cannot be explained by reference to the lack of capacity, 'simple' corruption and outright sloppiness, Article 260 TFEU becomes the *crux* of the whole story, as simple restatements of the breach under Article 258 TFEU will presumably not be enough.[88] However, the clear difference between the enforcement of *acquis* implementation (the law) and the enforcement of values is omnipresent in this context.[89] As has been demonstrated above, this is not entirely surprising, as EU's *jurisdictio* does not exist, strictly speaking.

It is thus also unsurprising that the Rule of Law in Article 2 TEU is unclear and unenforceable in practice. By and large – and here we return to the EU's deficiencies at the level of legality – values do not inform the day-to-day functioning of EU law, neither internally[90] nor externally.[91] Indeed, unless we take the Commission's views for granted, the EU's steering of countless issues directly related to the values at hand is more problematic than not.[92] The EU's very self-definition is not about human rights, the Rule of Law – especially as an institutional ideal – or democracy: EU law functions differently: there is a whole other set of principles which actually matter and are held dear, from loyalty, supremacy and direct effect, to a rather dogmatic vision of legality, which the ECJ and other institutions refer to as the Rule of Law.

---

[88] On the main deficiencies of the system, see most importantly, B. Jack, 'Article 260(2) TFEU: An Effective Judicial Procedure for the Enforcement of Judgments?', 19 (2013) *European Law Journal* 420; P. Wennerås, 'Sanctions against Member States under Art. 260 TFEU: Alive, but not Kicking?', 49 (2012) *CMLRev.* 145.

[89] In its own pre-Article 7 mechanism, the Commission draws a clear distinction between what can be done under ordinary infringement procedures and what is to be channeled via Article 7. This distinction is fundamental, as it refers to the boundaries of the scope of EU law, with values, ironically, presumed to be lying outwith such scope.

[90] J. H. H. Weiler, 'Europa: "Nous coalisons des Etats nous n'unissons pas des hommes"', in M. Cartabia and A. Simoncini (eds.), *La sostenibilità della democrazia nel XXI secolo* (Bologna: Il Mulino, 2009), p. 51; A. Williams, *The Ethos of Europe* (Cambridge: Cambridge University Press, 2010).

[91] See for example M. Cremona, 'Values in EU Foreign Policy', in M. Evans and P. Koutrakos (eds.), *Beyond the Established Legal Orders: Policy Interconnections between the EU and the Rest of the World* (Oxford: Hart, 2011), p. 275.

[92] The crucial argument along these lines has been made, most powerfully, by Andrew Williams: A. Williams, 'Taking Values Seriously: Towards a Philosophy of EU Law', 29 (2009) *OJLS* 549. See also J. H. H. Weiler's unpublished paper 'On the Distinction between Values and Virtues in the Process of European Integration'.

(b)   Mutual Recognition vs. the Rule of Law

It will be insufficient, as explained above, to introduce change by boosting enforcement. By misrepresenting the Rule of Law through the combination of legality and 'autonomy' while at the same time revealing a lack of interest to clearly substantiate the elements lying at the heart of the values of Article 2 TEU, the EU not only fails to continue on the path of perfecting its Prussia-like pre-constitutional nature. It also threatens to contaminate the Member States with its own wilful neglect of *jurisdictio*, by imposing the same impoverished vision of the law on them through supremacy and direct effect.

Indeed, talking about enforcing the values seriously amounts to nothing less than conceding that the presumption that all the Member States form a level playing field in terms of the Rule of Law does not always hold true – something the ECtHR has already clearly hinted at in, *inter alia*, *M.S.S.* v. *Belgium and Greece*.[93] Acknowledging this, alongside the EU's obvious powerlessness as far as values are concerned, is a potentially explosive combination in a Union *built on Member State equality and the principle of mutual recognition*.[94] In a situation where the core values are not respected by Hungary, for instance, we are not dealing with a Member State revolting for one reason or another against a binding norm forming part of the EU's *gubernaculum*: the *acquis*. At the level of values, we are dealing with a *Member State of distinct principles*, causing the Belarusianisation of the EU from the inside.[95] It is clear that EU's claim to enforcement and legality therewith is flawed if *jurisdictio* is not developed. Enforcement in the name of a formal hierarchy established by a system closed to the key idea of the Rule of Law is dangerous and potentially harmful for the Member States, as the only possible *jurisdictio* is the internal market, enforced with

---

[93]   *M.S.S.* v. *Belgium and Greece* [2011] Application No. 30696/09. This view has been reconfirmed in *Tarakhel* v. *Switzerland* Application No. 29217/12, dealing with the same issue and restating that the ECJ's 'systemic' standard articulated in *N.S. and others* (C-411/11 ECLI:EU:C:2011:865) and restated in *Abdullahi* v. *Bundesasylamt* (C-294/12 ECLI:EU:C:2013:813) sits uneasily with the idea of full protection of the Convention rights. For the purposes of the argument here suffices it to say that what we are concerned with is not the particular standards, which the Member States of the Dublin II system should or should not follow, but, indeed, 'the *raison d'être* of the European Union', as the ECJ put it in *N.S.* (para. 83) and whether this *raison d'être* requires the Union to disregard Art. 2 TEU, as the Court – no doubt wrongly – implies.

[94]   M. Poiares Maduro, 'So Close Yet So Far: The Paradoxes of Mutual Recognition', 14 (2007) *Journal of European Public Policy* 814.

[95]   U. Belavusau, 'Case C-286/12 *Commission* v. *Hungary*', 50 (2013) *CMLRev.* 1145.

the teeth of supremacy and direct effect. The EU's claims that it ensures legality in the context of the enforcement of its law are, in fact, potentially problematic in the light of the above.

While recognising this an obvious problem from the perspective of the EU, we should pay particular attention to how the Union, through its Court, reacts when it is reminded that its legal system is built on a clearly illusory presumption that the Member States will always be 'good enough' in terms of the substance of their rules, making them worthy of mutual recognition and always willing play along. Lacking a *jurisdictio* – given that the internal market fails to qualify for the role and Article 2 TEU is not up to the task and external checks are not allowed by the ECJ – allowing the Union to police its vision of legality could be a very dangerous move indeed, negatively affecting the very core of the Member States' constitutionalism and making the effective protection of human rights barely possible. Not only is it unlikely to solve Hungary's problems, the EU could undermine established democracies, reducing trust in the EU even further.

(c)   Pre-Empting Reality Checks

The Union is built on the presumption of the Member States' adherence to the basic values of Article 2 TEU, while being unable to police and enforce these values and thus being entirely incapable of dealing with the emerging problems. Not only is there no Rule of Law in sight, but the Court prefers to insist on an exclusive reliance on EU law without looking beyond its presumptions about what the Member States are or are not like, even in the face of an abundantly clear disruption of the foundational assumptions behind mutual trust signalled by the ECtHR. In not considering what is actually behind the presumption of loyalty, the same rhetorical tool is constantly deployed by the ECJ: the need to protect the 'autonomy of EU law'.[96] For the sake of 'autonomy', the appeals to a reality beyond the one presumed by the EU's *acquis* are pre-empted.

Indeed, as is well known, EU 'legal structure is based on the fundamental premise that each Member State shares with all the other Member States, and recognises that they share with it, a set of common values on which the EU is founded, as stated in Article 2 TEU. That premise implies and justifies the existence of mutual trust between the Member States that

---

[96] Cases C-411 and 493/10 *NS and Others* ECLI:EU:C:2011:865.

those values will be recognised and, therefore, that the law of the EU that implements them will be respected'.[97] Moreover, 'The autonomy enjoyed by EU law in relation to the laws of the Member States and in relation to international law requires that the interpretation of those fundamental rights be ensured within the framework of the structure and objectives of the EU'.[98] This is the constitutional framework of the functioning of fundamental rights in the context of the EU legal order, according to the Court.[99] In this framework the fundamental assumptions are set in stone, and the reality of flagrant non-compliance, *en par* with the idea of the Rule of Law – which must necessarily be rooted in *reality*, not *proclamations about reality* – is accorded but auxiliary value.

The culmination of this thinking is summed up by the Court in para. 192 of its Opinion 2/13 on accession to the ECHR: '[W]hen implementing EU law, the Member States may, under EU law, be *required to presume* that fundamental rights have been observed by the other Member States, so that not only may they not demand a higher level of national protection of fundamental rights from another Member State that that provided by EU law, but, save in exceptional cases, they may not check whether that other Member State has actually, in a specific case, observed the fundamental rights guaranteed by the EU'.[100] The fundamental rights, to remind the reader, which are 'interpret[ed] [...] within the framework of the structure and objectives of the EU'[101] – that is, unlike in the ECHR context, or the constitutional context of the Member States, compliance with fundamental rights is not an end in itself but is approached as a tool within the body of the *acquis* clearly endowed with an instrumental value: this is where the internal market pretends to wear a *jurisdictio* hat. Any idea of checking each others' compliance with fundamental rights by the Member States is thus regarded by the Court as contradicting EU law *per se*,[102] notwithstanding the fact that this law, as has been demonstrated above, is incapable of enforcing Article 2 TEU values. The Rule of Law is thus pre-empted along with the checks against a reality behind the assumptions on which the EU's *gubernaculum* rests. The dangers of such a misapprehension of the Rule of Law are clear as day: while the Member States are prohibited by the EU from considering the real picture in the

---

[97] Opinion 2/13 *ECHR II* ECLI:EU:C:2014:2454, para. 168.   [98] *Ibid.*, para. 170.

[99] *Ibid.* para. 177.   [100] *Ibid.*, para. 192 (emphasis added).   [101] *Ibid.*, para. 170.

[102] Joined Cases C-411/10 and 493/10 *N.S. and Others* v. *Secretary of State for the Home Department* EU:C:2011:865, paras 78–80. Case C-399/11 *Stefano Melloni* v. *Ministerio Fiscal* EU:C:2013:107, paras 37 and 63. See also Opinion 2/13 *ECHR II*, paras 193 and 195.

context of the application of EU law, the EU is as such incapable of solving Article 2 TEU problems in the Member States.

Turning to human rights, in one example it is not difficult to find ECJ decisions which are inhumane in their consequences for the parties and which also potentially contradict the ECHR case law. *Mohamed M'Bodj v. Belgium* is a case in point: the ECJ left the Member States no margin of discretion,[103] requiring them to remove seriously ill third-country nationals to countries where they will definitely meet premature death without adequate healthcare provision as serious illness has 'no connection with the rationale of international protection'.[104] Of course not, if interpreted in the light of the goals of the internal market and ever closer Union. Such a treatment of human rights provoked righteous outrage from Strasbourg.[105]

The current state of play in the EU within the triad of reality, human rights and the Rule of Law is thus quite deficient: reality is turned into a presumption; human rights are included among the tools of the internal market alongside primacy and direct effect; and the Rule of Law is equated with loyalty: an obligation on the Member States not to question this shaky construct, thus acting 'in accordance with the law'. Opinion 2/13 is a most typical example of what the EU's 'Rule of Law' is about. It is difficult in this context to disagree with Eleanor Sharpston and Daniel Sarmiento's view that 'in the balance between individual rights and primacy, the Court in Opinion 2/13 has fairly clearly sided with the latter. The losers under Opinion 2/13 are not the Member States of the signatory States of the Council of Europe, but the individual citizens of the European Union'.[106] The Opinion is no new law, however – it is just a summary by the Court of what the EU is about. This summary has a lot to say about the ECJ's understanding of the Rule of Law: the idea of *jurisdictio* checking on the *gubernaculum* is *not* tolerated. Quite the contrary, the ECJ presumes that in contrast with the very essence of the idea of the Rule of Law as an institutional ideal, EU Rule of Law means that *gubernaculum* – the

---

[103] In interpreting Art. 3 Council Directive 2004/83/EC of 29 April 2004 on minimum standards for the qualification and status of third country nationals or stateless persons as refugees or as persons who otherwise need international protection and the content of the protection granted, OJ 2004 No. L304/12, 30 September 2004.

[104] C-542/13 *Mohamad M'Bodj* v. *Belgium* ECLI:EU:C:2014:2452, para. 44.

[105] See the dissenting opinion of Judge Pinto de Albuquerque in the ECtHR case *S.J.* v. *Belgium* [2015] Application No. 70055/10, paras 3, 4.

[106] E. Sharpston and D. Sarmiento, 'European Citizenship and Its New Union: Time to Move on?', in D. Kochenov (ed.), *EU Citizenship and Federalism: The Role of Rights* (Cambridge: Cambridge University Press, 2017).

acquis – should *not* be checked either against the law or even against reality itself.

It is puzzling but not surprising to see that in the face of the need to ensure autonomy, the Court is ready to dismiss reality itself as virtually irrelevant in the context of the operation of the law. Enjoying the plenitude of power is more important for the Union than effectively dealing with such power's harmful effects. The EU thus behaves as a pre-constitutional state: replacing the Rule of Law with legality removes any questioning of the blind spots of the system from within, and the ECtHR is out of the picture too. The EU cannot boast of any Rule of Law as a functioning legal principle.

V Conclusion

The EU is not in fact that special in having no *jurisdictio–gubernaculum* divide. Other polities have been quite successful without it: the pre-constitutional law-based states of the eighteenth century usually emerge as examples. As in the EU today, their democracies were highly atypical from our contemporary standpoint: moreover, their understanding of the Rule of Law was *identical* to the contemporary EU-level one, it seems. The Rule of Law for them consisted in not deviating from laws made in accordance with all the required legal procedures. This is exactly the sort of orthodoxy that true Rule of Law was designed to combat: a constant control of law through Law, as Palombella repeatedly and rightly emphasises, is indispensable for a system to be based on the Rule of Law. The place of *jurisdictio* in the EU is largely vacant, beyond the idea of the internal market, but the internal market cannot possibly fulfil a task so ambitious: to become a critical legal measure within the EU's *acquis*. In Philip Allott's diagnosis, there was a 'cold modernist void, a spiritual absence at the heart of the European integration project'.[107] Worse still, the ECJ seems to be doing its best to present the idea of autonomy of EU law in this light, making any kind of contestation of the *acquis* based on considerations external to it – however important – excessively difficult, if not impossible. As this chapter has demonstrated, even turning to reality itself is unwelcome, should such a turn challenge the assumptions lying at the heart of the *acquis*. The Rule of Law is perversely interpreted as a tool to deactivate potential contestation – precisely the contrary to what a

---

[107] P. Allott, 'The European Community is not the True European Community', 100 (1991) *Yale Law Journal* 2485, 2499.

classical understanding of it would imply. It is thus the absent *jurisdictio–gubernaculum* balance and *not* the enforcement legal shortcomings that should occupy commentators the most: the EU's Rule of Law mythology requires strict academic scrutiny, which it has not been receiving so far. The void is not inconsequential. As Gráinne de Búrca rightly notes, in many observers' eyes the EU creates 'patent injustice'.[108]

---

[108] G. de Búrca, 'Conclusion', in D. Kochenov, G. de Búrca and A. Williams (eds.), *Europe's Justice Deficit?* (Oxford: Hart, 2015), p. 458.

Epilogue: Living in a Glass House

Europe, Democracy and the Rule of Law

J. H. H. WEILER*

I

Here is a little puzzle: Cast your mind back to the second Barroso Commission. It was the period of the unfolding of the Hungarian situation, the French expulsion of 'clandestine' Roma in France – which was the subject of a terse and even inflamed exchange between an EU Commissioner and the French Presidency, and more generally an anti-migrant mood sweeping the continent, the results of which were felt in the results of the EP elections in May 2014.

The view developed, notably within the Commission, that the Union could not remain indifferent to egregious Member State violations of Union values, and that as both a moral and legal imperative, a more robust apparatus and policy should be put in place not simply to ensure compliance with European legal requirements but to guard the deeper fabric of European values. A draft document on the Rule of Law began making the rounds.

Legally speaking this was a fraught issue where the desire to 'do good' on the substance ran up against the value of containing appetite for jurisdictional and competence expansion of the Union in general and the Commission in particular.[1] In fact, once the dust settled on the Roma issue, the Commission had to climb down, some might say ignominiously, from its initial expansive legal claims, it being the French who had actually applied the Rule of Law, at least.

---

* President, European University Institute, Florence.
[1] See the excellent and challenging comment of J. Cornides, 'The European Union: Rule of Law or Rule of Judges?' (2013) *EJIL Analysis* (blog) at www.ejiltalk.org/the-european-union-rule-of-law-or-rule-of-judges/.

313

Issues of constitutional legality apart, the overall approach and intentions of the Commission were mostly[2] noble: the Union cannot and should not remain indifferent to states' violation of its core values. The puzzle concerns the framing of this issue as one concerning the Rule of Law, and not, for example, as one of the nature and content of European Democracy. Why frame the objections to attitudes and practices which offend in their content the sense of decency of those objecting and cut against what many may think are core values of the European construct in the language of the Rule of Law?

The answer in my view can be read from between the lines of the much-vaunted Communication of the Commission to the European Parliament and the Council of March 2014 conveying a New EU Framework to Strengthen the Rule of Law.[3] It is a well-known document discussed extensively elsewhere in this volume.[4] I want to suggest the following consideration as the interpretative meta-key of the decision to frame the issue as one of the Rule of Law: The aggression against the core values is often done in the name of national democracy and as an expression of popular will as represented by voter preference in national elections. It might have appeared more delicate to frame the issue as one of democracy when the attitudes and actions which were the subject of concern emanated from democratic processes. Orbán might be many things, but Dictator[5] he is not: he gives perfect expression to the wishes of a majority of Hungarian citizens and for many of whom he is even considered moderate. Hence, the Rule of Law – implicitly understood in its thick substantive and not thin procedural sense – was raised as a kind of check on democratic majoritarian decisions.

But in fact, adopting this approach (rather than a direct appeal to substantive values) sowed the seeds of its own self-destruction. For the appeal to the Rule of Law calls obvious attention to the rules-of-law of how the Union may or may not deal with the issue. Much less public

---

[2] Commissioners are politicians, and considerations of popularity are part-and-parcel of the job description. It comes with the territory and is not as such objectionable. Likewise, the Commission is a political body, and considerations of its legitimacy are similarly part of the territory and not as such objectionable.

[3] European Commission, Communication from the Commission to the European Parliament and the Council, A new EU Framework to strengthen the Rule of Law, Brussels, 11 March 2014 COM(2014) 158 final.

[4] See C. Closa, 'Reinforcing EU Monitoring of the Rule of Law: Normative Arguments, Institutional Proposals and the Procedural Limitations' in this volume.

[5] See 'Juncker to Hungarian PM Orbán: "Hello, Dictator!"', at www.euronews.com/2015/05/22/juncker-to-hungarian-pm-orban-hello-dictator/.

attention was given to the political response to the Commission *demarche* which can be found in the *Conclusions of the Council* of 14 December 2014 on the same subject.[6] They are worth citing *in extensu*:

WELCOMING the note of the Presidency on 'Ensuring Respect for the Rule of Law' [16862/14 COR 1];

EMPHASISING that the European Union and its Institutions are committed to promoting EU values, including respect for the rule of law as laid down in the Treaties;

UNDERLINING that the rule of law is one of the key values on which the Union is founded;

EMPHASISING the role of the Council in promoting a culture of respect for the rule of law within the European Union;

THE COUNCIL OF THE EUROPEAN UNION AND THE MEMBER STATES MEETING WITHIN THE COUNCIL,

1. commit themselves to establishing a dialogue among all Member States within the Council to promote and safeguard the rule of law in the framework of the Treaties;
2. underline that this dialogue will be based on the principles of objectivity, non-discrimination and equal treatment of all Member States;
3. agree that this dialogue will be conducted on a non-partisan and evidence-based approach;
4. emphasise that such an approach will be without prejudice to the principle of conferred competences, as well as the respect of national identities of Member States inherent in their fundamental political and constitutional structures, inclusive of regional and local self-government, and their essential State functions, including ensuring the territorial integrity of the State, maintaining law and order and safeguarding national security, and should be brought forward in light of the principle of sincere cooperation.
5. agree that this dialogue will be developed in a way which is complementary with other EU Institutions and International Organisations, avoiding duplication and taking into account existing instruments and expertise in this area; 1 16862/14 COR 1 2/2
6. agree that this dialogue will take place once a year in the Council, in its General Affairs configuration, and be prepared by the COREPER (Presidency), following an inclusive approach. The Council will consider, as needed, to launch debates on thematic subject matters. The

---

[6] Press Release of the Council, 16 December 2014, PRESSE 652 PR CO 74.

Presidency will ensure the full respect of the principles mentioned above (paragraphs 2, 3, 4 and 5) throughout the organisation of the dialogue;

7. will evaluate, by the end of 2016, the experience acquired on the basis of this dialogue.

These Conclusions cannot, in my view, be read as anything less than an embarrassing climb down, with on the one hand a mealy-mouthed commitment from the 'Let's Talk' and 'Will be studied further' stable, and on the other hand, a series of guarantees towards the never-identified 'usual suspects.'

This 'kiss of death' was not, in my view, driven by any less concern for the substantive issues underlying the original Commission Communication on the part of most Member States. It was driven, instead, from an implicit acknowledgement (misguided perhaps, in the eyes of some) of the rules-of-law and the constitutional limits they imposes on the Union in dealing with the underlying issues.

Recital 1 of the Conclusions spells out the action to be taken: dialogue – a molehill from a mountain. Dialogue with whom, for what reason and with what underlying concern are only to be guessed at.

Recitals 2–5, supposedly the heart of the matter, are a series of conditions and restrictions under which the Dialogue is to take place: the grandiose Rule of Law imploding under the mundane rules-of-law – an 'in real time' spectacular exemplar of deconstruction.

II

What I want to do in this brief epilogue is not to undermine the Commission initiative, the spirit of which I have much sympathy with but, following earlier work on this issue,[7] try and explain why this separation between Rule of Law and Democracy is untenable, and to suggest that the high moral ground from which it emanates is far more precarious and has some pretty slippery slopes. So first, perhaps, a rapid primer on the relationship among the Rule of Law, democracy and human rights.

---

[7] See for example J. H. H. Weiler, 'Deciphering the Political and Legal DNA of European Integration. An Exploratory Essay', in J. Dickson and P. Eleftheriadis (eds.), *Philosophical Foundation of European Union Law* (Oxford: Oxford University Press, 2012), p. 137; See also J. H. H. Weiler, 'Demokracja bez narodu: kryzys europejskości', 3(16) (2013) *Nowa Europa, Przegląd – Natoliński* 25.

The horrors of the Second World War but also of the six years leading to it within Germany provoked a contemporary conceptual reconsideration of the ideal of the Rule of Law. We can take as an example the degradation and dispossession of the Jews within Germany in the first eight years of the regime prior to their deportation and mass murder. There were of course violent and lawless episodes such as Kristallnacht in 1938, which saw the burning and looting of most synagogues and in which the government was complicit by commission (incitement and encouragement) and omission (failure to prosecute the perpetrators). But what is striking is the exceptional nature of this episode. For the most part, degradation and dispossession were orderly, systematic, following a legal and hence lawful path. The exclusion of Jews from public life was effected by the infamous Nuremberg *Law* of 1935, which contained elaborate legal definitions and mechanisms. The disposal of Jewish property followed a similar path of legality. Similar legal structures, including courts and judicial procedures, were put in place to enforce even the most invidious features of the regime. Enemies, real and imagined, were not hunted down by clandestine death squads or simply 'disappeared'. They were arrested, tried and then, often 'lawfully', executed.

The quiet chilling horror of legalised and bureaucratised discrimination, humiliation and death is captured in a marvellous book, *One Life*, by Tom Lampert[8] – a minor masterpiece with serene documentary tone of which has veritable Sebald qualities – which presents a number of episodes captured through extrapolation from official files and the strength of which is the very absence of blood and gore. In effect the process was achieved through, and with full respect for, the 'Rule of Law'.

Another such example is the striking film, *Conspiracy*[9] with an all-star cast led by the hugely versatile Kenneth Branagh, which in equally serene and bureaucratic tone reconstructs the non-drama of the Wansee Conference, in which the Final Solution was adopted. It is a 'must see' for anyone interested in that by now banal but still most apt expression – the banality of evil. It is indispensable in understanding the post-Second World War metamorphosis of the Rule of Law.

It is this reality which, already in the context of the Nuremberg Trials, provoked a conceptual reassessment. Since the Rule of Law was considered as one of the assets of liberal democracies, one could not grace German

[8] T. Lampert, *One Life* (Boston: Houghton Mifflin Harcourt, 2004).
[9] http://www.imdb.com/title/tt0266425/.

practice in those years with that appellation. Put differently, one had to move away from a formalist, entirely positivist (even Kelsenian) notion of the Rule of Law and replace it with one which had substantive and not merely procedural content.

The reconceptualisation of the Rule of Law contained two principal elements: folded into the concept as an ontological condition was an insistence on democratic legitimation as the source of authority and authorship of the legal rules and procedures – essential components in an understanding of the Rule of Law. Democracy, understood as majoritarianism, is only as good or as vile as those composing the majority. Thus, the second ontological condition for the reconceptualised rule of law has been an insistence on fundamental individual rights, protected, again and again and again, at the state, regional and international levels. Human rights were to become not simply a set of guarantees to protect against the tyranny of the majority, but the defining feature of the political culture of the West, the common denominator of so-called Western Liberal democracies.

If one asks, say, a European politician to define the foundational values of Europe, the trinity of democracy, human rights and the Rule of Law will almost instantly be trotted out. But in fact, and that is my contention, these concepts are not distinct. Democracy and human rights, especially human rights, are part of the ontology of the Rule of Law. A legal regime not validated in democratic practices and not respecting human rights would not qualify as a manifestation of the Rule of Law. The focus of this reflection will be on the democratic component of the Rule of Law within the European Union.

One can start such a critical examination by going to the foundation of the Union's Rule of Law edifice in *Van Gend en Loos* itself. Direct effect of Union law, which is an essential part of its Rule of Law, is not only a legal proposition. It is also a proxy for governance. The fact that the writ of Union law runs through the land, indeed is the law of the land, is a hallmark of governance, whereby the Union's legislative and administrative branches do not need the intermediary of the Member States, as is the default position in general public international law, to reach individuals both as objects and subjects of the law. And herein lies the challenge.

Van Gend en Loos itself is the fountainhead. In arguing for the concept of a new legal order, the Court reasoned in the following two famous passages as follows:

The conclusion to be drawn from this is that the Community constitutes a new legal order of international law for the benefit of which the states have limited their sovereign rights, albeit within limited fields, and the subjects of which comprise not only Member States but also their nationals. Independently of the legislation of Member States, Community law therefore not only imposes obligations on individuals but is also intended to confer upon them rights which become part of their legal heritage. These rights arise not only where they are expressly granted by the Treaty, but also by reason of obligations which the Treaty imposes in a clearly defined way upon individuals as well as upon the Member States and upon the institutions of the Community.

This view is confirmed by the preamble to the Treaty which refers not only to governments but to peoples. It is also confirmed more specifically by the establishment of institutions endowed with sovereign rights, the exercise of which affects Member States and also their citizens. *Furthermore, it must be noted that the nationals of the states brought together in the Community are called upon to cooperate in the functioning of this Community through the intermediary of the European Parliament and the Economic and Social Committee.*[10]

The problem is that this 'cooperation' was extremely weak. It was, in truth, a serious 'dumbing down' of democracy and its meaning by the European Court. At the time, the European Parliament only had the right to offer its opinion – when asked, and it was often not asked. Even in areas where it was meant to be asked, it was well known that the Commission and Council would stitch up their deals ahead of such advice, which thus became *pro-forma*.

Accordingly, can that level of democratic representation and accountability, viewed through the lenses of normative political theory, truly justify the immense power of direct governance which the combined doctrines of direct effect and then supremacy placed in the hands of the Community institutions? Surely posing the question is to give the answer.

You might think that since those early days the European Parliament has become a very different body, hugely increased in powers and a veritable co-legislator with the Council. You would be right. But the widely shared assumption that the democracy problems of the Union would simply be solved by increasing the powers of the European Parliament is simply misconceived. There remains a persistent, chronic, troubling democratic deficit which cannot be talked away.

---

[10] Case 26/62 *NV Algemene Transport- en Expeditie Onderneming van Gend & Loos* v. *Netherlands Inland Revenue Administration* ECLI:EU:C:1963:1 [1963] ECR 1 (emphasis added).

In essence it is the inability of the Union to develop structures and processes which adequately replicate or, 'translate,'[11] at the Union level even the imperfect habits of governmental control, parliamentary accountability and administrative responsibility which are practiced with different modalities in the various Member States. Make no mistake: it is perfectly well understood that the Union is not a state. But it is in the business of governance and it has taken over extensive areas previously in the hands of the Member States. In some critical areas, such as the interface of the Union with the international trading system, the competences of the Union are exclusive. In others they are dominant. Democracy is not about states. Democracy is about the exercise of public power – and the Union exercises a huge amount of public power.

We live by the credo that any exercise of public power has to be legitimated democratically and it is exactly here that the problems loom. In essence, the two primordial features of any functioning democracy are missing – the grand principles of accountability and representation.[12] As regards accountability,[13] even the basic condition of representative democracy that at election time the citizens 'can throw the scoundrels out'[14] – that is, replace the government – does not operate in Europe.[15] The form of European governance,[16] governance without government, is and will remain for a considerable time – perhaps forever – that there is no 'Government' to throw out. Dismissing the Commission by Parliament

[11] N. Walker, 'Postnational Constitutionalism and the Problem of Translation', in J. H. H. Weiler and M. Wind (eds.), *European Constitutionalism beyond the State* (Cambridge: Cambridge University Press, 2003), p. 27.

[12] A. Przeworski, S. C. Stokes and B. Manin (eds.), *Democracy, Accountability, and Representation* (Cambridge: Cambridge University Press, 1999); P. C. Schmitter and K. T. Lynn, 'What Democracy Is . . . and Is Not', 2(3) (1991) *Journal of Democracy* 76.

[13] On the concept of accountability, see D. Curtin, *Executive Power of the European Union: Law, Practices and the Living Constitution* (Oxford: Oxford University Press, 2009), Ch. 9. See also C. Harlow, *Accountability in the European Union* (Oxford: Oxford University Press, 2002); A. Arnull and D. Wincott (eds.), *Accountability and legitimacy in the European Union* (Oxford: Oxford University Press, 2002).

[14] I. Shapiro, *Democracy's Place* (Ithaca: Cornell University Press, 1996), p. 96; J. H. H. Weiler, 'To be a European Citizen: Eros and Civilization', in J. H. H. Weiler, *The Constitution of Europe: 'Do the New Clothes Have an Emperor?' and Other Essays on European Integration* (Cambridge: Cambridge University Press, 1999), pp. 324, 329.

[15] R. Dehousse, 'Constitutional Reform in the European Community: Are There Alternatives to the Majority Avenue?, in J. Hayward (ed.), *The Crisis of Representation in Europe* (London: Frank Cass, 1995), pp. 118, 123.

[16] P. Allott, 'European Governance and the Re-Branding of Democracy', 27 (2002) *ELRev.* 60.

(or approving the appointment of the Commission President)[17] is not quite the same, not even remotely so. The *Spitzenkandidaten* exercise,[18] an important breakthrough and a step in the right direction, does not change this reality.

Startlingly, but not surprisingly, the political accountability of Europe is also remarkably weak. There have been some spectacular political failures of European governance. The embarrassing Copenhagen climate fiasco;[19] the weak (at best) realisation of the much-touted Lisbon Agenda (aka Lisbon Strategy or Lisbon Process),[20] the very story of the defunct 'Constitution'[21] to mention but three. It is hard to point in these instances to any measure of political accountability, of someone paying a political price, as would be the case in national politics. In fact, it is difficult to point to a single instance of accountability for political failure as distinct from personal accountability for misconduct in the annals of European integration. This is not, decidedly not, a story of corruption or malfeasance.[22] My argument is that this failure is rooted in the very structure of European governance. It is not designed for political accountability.

In a similar vein, it is impossible to link in any meaningful way that the results of elections to the European Parliament relate to the performance of the Political Groups within the preceding parliamentary session, in the way that is part of the mainstay of political accountability within the Member States.[23] Structurally, dissatisfaction with 'Europe' when it exists

---

[17] Arts. 17(7) and 17(8) TEU.

[18] For a detailed description and thoughtful analysis see J. Priestley and N. P. García, *The Making of a European President* (Basingstoke: Palgrave Macmillan, 2015).

[19] See European Parliament, Resolution of 10 February 2010 on the outcome of the Copenhagen Conference on Climate Change (COP 15) OJ 2010, Electronic 341-06/25 especially at 26, points 5, 6.

[20] I. Begg, 'Is there a Convincing Rationale for the Lisbon Strategy', 46(2) (2008) *JCMS* 427; European Commission, 'Facing the Challenge: The Lisbon Strategy for Growth and Employment', Report from the High Level Group chaired by W. Kok (Luxembourg: Office for Official Publications of the European Communities, 2004).

[21] Treaty establishing a Constitution for Europe OJ 2010 No. C310/1 (European Constitution). See I. Ward, 'Bill and the Fall of the Constitutional Treaty', 13(3) (2007) *European Public Law* 461; Editorial Comments, 'What Should Replace The Constitutional Treaty?', 44(3) (2007) *CMLRev.* 561.

[22] On this aspect, see V. Mehde, 'Responsibility and Accountability in the European Commission', 40(2) (2003) *CMLRev.* 423.

[23] J. Priestley, 'European Political Parties: The Missing Link' in R. Matarazzo (ed.), *Democracy in the EU after the Lisbon Treaty* (Rome: Edizioni Nuova Cultura, 2011), p. 15; F. R. Bastos, 'Des "partis politiques au niveau européen"? Etat des lieux à la veille des élections européennes de juin 2009', 71 (2009) *Notre Europe, Etudes and Recherches.*

has no channel to affect, at the European level, the agents of European governance.

Likewise, at the most primitive level of democracy, there is simply no moment in the civic calendar of Europe where the citizen can influence directly, or in a meaningful way even indirectly, the outcome of any policy decision facing the Community and Union in the way that citizens can when choosing between parties which offer sharply distinct programmes at the national level. The political colour of the European Parliament, as an expression of voter preference, only very weakly translates into the legislative and administrative output of the Union.[24]

The Political Deficit, to use the felicitous phrase of Renaud Dehousse[25] is at the core of the democratic deficit. The Commission, in its self-awareness linked to its very ontology, cannot be 'partisan' in a right-left sense, neither can the Council, by virtue of the haphazard political nature of its composition. Democracy normally needs to have some meaningful mechanism for the expression of voter preference predicated on choice among options, typically informed by stronger or weaker ideological orientation.[26] That is an indispensable component of politics. Democracy without Politics is an oxymoron.[27] And yet that is not only Europe, but it is a feature of Europe – the 'non-partisan' nature of the Commission – which is celebrated. The stock phrase found in endless student text books and the like, that the Supranational Commission vindicates the European Interest, whereas the intergovernmental Council is a clearing house for Member State interests, is at best naïve. Does the 'European Interest' not necessarily involve political and ideological choices, at times explicit, but always implicit?

Thus the two most primordial norms of democracy, the principle of accountability and the principle of representation, are compromised in the very structure and process of the Union. This is not merely a theoretical construct. It is, in my view, validated in the practice of direct elections

---

[24] V. Bogdanor, 'Legitimacy, Accountability and Democracy in the European Union' (2007) A Federal Trust Report, 7, 8, at http://fedtrust.co.uk/wp-content/uploads/2014/12/FedT_LAD.pdf; A. Føllesdal and S. Hix, 'Why There is a Democratic Deficit in the EU: A Response to Majone and Moravcsik', 44(3) (2006) *JCMS* 533.

[25] R. Dehousse, 'Constitutional Reform in the European Community', 124. See also, J.-M. Ferry and P. Thibaud, *Discussion sur l'Europe* (Paris: Calmann-Lévy, 1992).

[26] A. Føllesdal and S. Hix, 'Why There is a Democratic Deficit in the EU', 545.

[27] On EU's 'policy without politics', see V. A. Schmidt, *Democracy in Europe: The EU and National Polities* (Oxford: Oxford University Press, 2006), p. 157.

to the European Parliament. One of the most famous political puzzles of European politics has been the relationship between the powers given to the European Parliament and voter turnout in direct elections. It would have been, and for sometime was, a commonsense hypothesis that the relatively low turnout (when compared to national electoral results within the Member States) in direct elections to the European Parliament were linked to its absence of powers. Why bother voting if the body for which you are voting lacks any political clout.

As mentioned above, that cannot be said of today's Parliament. It is far from perfect (but which national parliament is perfect? What does perfection even mean in this context?), but it cannot credibly be argued that the European Parliament, in so many areas a co-legislator with the Council, lacks political clout. And yet, as has been endlessly observed, this has not translated linearly into voter turnout. The much-touted slogan invented by the European Parliament itself for the May 2014 elections was React, Act, Impact! There was the added excitement of the *Spitzenkandidaten*. The results are well known: fewer than ever reacted and acted – it was the lowest turnout in the history of direct elections – although impact there was in the selection of the President of the Commission!

The inextricability of the Rule of Law from the democratic travails of the Union is easily stated even if usually uncomfortably discussed. The late Federico Mancini in his *Europe: The Case for Statehood* forcefully articulated the democratic malaise of Europe.[28] There were many, myself included, who shied away from Mancini's remedy, a European State and shied away from his contention that this remedy was the only one available.[29] But few quibbled with his trenchant and often caustic denunciation of the democratic deficiencies of European governance.

Turning then to the nexus between democracy and the Rule of Law, imagine yourself, say, as a Judge of the European Court of Justice charged with enforcing the Union writ within the Member States. What would I do if you felt, as Mancini did, that the European Community suffered from this deep democratic deficit which he described so unflinchingly and which according to him could only be cured by a European State? Would you want to give effect to the Community's undemocratic laws – adopted in his words by 'numberless, faceless and unaccountable

---

[28] G. F. Mancini, 'Europe: The Case for Statehood', 4(1) (1998) *ELJ* 29.
[29] J. H. H. Weiler, 'Europe: The Case Against the Case for Statehood', 4(1) (1998) *ELJ* 43.

committees of senior national experts'[30] and rubber-stamped by the Council – supreme over the very constitutional values of the Member States? Whatever the hermeneutic legitimacy of supremacy and direct effect, the interaction of these principles with the non-democratic decision-making process was at the time Mancini wrote and is today, not without some delicate normative issues. He may have been wrong about the rubber-stamping in some contentious cases, but he is probably right as regards the run-of-the-mill legislation.

Seen from the perspective of the individual citizen, in effect, if not in design, giving direct effect in the context of European governance objectifies the individual or re-objectifies him or her. In the Member States with imperfect but functional democracies the individual is 'the' political subject. In the European Union with its defective democratic machinery where the individual has far less control over norm creation, the Rule of Law has the paradoxical effect of objectifying him or her – an object of laws over which he or she has no effective democratic control.

To put it somewhat bluntly, from the perspective I just outlined it might be thought that the Rule of Law underpins, supports and legitimates a highly problematic decisional process. Substantively then, the much-vaunted Community rights which serve almost invariably the economic interests of individuals were 'bought' at least in some measure at the expense of democratic legitimation.

Procedurally we find a similar story. One secret of the Rule of Law in the legal order of the European Union rests in the genius of the preliminary reference procedure. The compliance pull of law in liberal Western democracies does not rest on the gun and coercion. It rests on a political culture which internalises, especially in public authorities, obedience to the law rather than to expediency. Not a perfect, but one good measure of the Rule of Law is the extent to which public authorities in a country obey the decisions, even uncomfortable, of their own courts.

It is by this very measure that international regimes are so often found wanting, and why we cannot quite in the same way speak about the Rule of International Law. All too frequently, when a State is faced with a discomfiting international norm or decision of an international tribunal, it finds ways to evade them. Statistically, as we know, the preliminary reference in more than eighty percent of cases is a device for the judicial review of Member State compliance with their obligations under the

---

[30] G. F. Mancini, 'Europe: The Case for Statehood', 40 (footnotes omitted).

Treaties.[31] However, it is precisely in this context that we can see the dark side of this moon. The situation implicit in the preliminary reference always posits an individual vindicating a personal, private interest against the national public good. That is why it works, that is part of its genius, but that in a way just expands the tension between democratic processes and the Rule of Law to the entire judicial branch.

There is a second dimension to the issue of democracy which has a more subtle though no less powerful nexus to the issue of the Rule of Law. It is an issue which comes and goes in academic and intellectual writing.[32] But in the current political constellation of increased Euroscepticism and the travails of the Greek Debt saga has suddenly emerged again with force. In conceptual terms, demos, of a unique or multiple nature,[33] is understood as providing a normative foundation for the claims of obedience to majoritarian decision-making in a democracy – hence the nexus to the Rule of Law. A majority, in this view, enjoys a claim to impose its will on a minority only within the context of a demos commonly shared in the polity. Democracy by the People, means just that: a people – however understood. Put differently, the root *demos* in the word democracy is not a lexical construct but part of the normative ontology of how we understand democracy. Even if the various structural deficiencies of European democracy as described above were corrected, the absence of a common understanding of demos would still rob it of the moral authority for a claim to obedience to the Rule of Law. I will leave to the reader to decide whether we can speak today of a European demos with sufficient 'thickness' to carry the normative weight of the claim for democratic obedience – the Rule of Law.

---

[31] R. Lecourt, 'Quel eut été le droit communautaire sans les arrêts de 1963 et 1964', in J. Boulouis, *L'Europe et le droit: Mélanges en hommage à Jean Boulouis* (Paris: Dalloz, 1991), p. 349; H. G. Schemers et al. (eds.), *Article 177 EEC: Experiences and Problems* (Amsterdam: North-Holland, 1987); M. Broberg and N. Fenger, *Preliminary References to the European Court of Justice* (Oxford: Oxford University Press, 2010); T. de La Mare and C. Donnelly, 'Preliminary Rulings and EU Legal Integration', in P. Craig and G. de Búrca (eds.) *The Evolution of EU Law*, 2nd edn (Oxford: Oxford University Press, 2011).

[32] See for example K. A. Nicolaïdis, 'The New Constitution as European Demoi-cracy?', 7(1) (2004) *Critical Review of International Social and Political Philosophy*. See also J. H. H. Weiler, 'European Union: Democracy without a Demos?' (1996) *Sussex Papers in International Relations* No. 1.

[33] For an exploration of multiple *demoi* as a basis of understanding European democracy, see for example, J. H. H. Weiler, 'To Be a European Citizen: Eros and Civilization', 4(4) (1997) *JEPP* 495, and more recently and innovatively K. A. Nicolaïdis, 'The New Constitution as European Demoi-cracy?'.

The moral is not for the Union to shy away from taking robust action, within its competences and jurisdictional limits, to quell gross violations of the Rule of Law in and by some of its Member States. But it should simultaneously hurry up and put its own democratic house in order lest it be reminded again that those living in glass houses should be careful when throwing stones.

INDEX

Ingram Content Group UK Ltd.
Milton Keynes UK
UKHW020643200723
425471UK00029B/581